Tommaso U. A. Sperotto
Axel Honneth and the Movement of Recognition

Deutsche Zeitschrift
für Philosophie Sonderbände
46

Tommaso U. A. Sperotto

Axel Honneth and the Movement of Recognition

—

Structure of the Self and Second Nature

DE GRUYTER

This book is based on a doctoral dissertation discussed on May 17, 2021. The research was conducted in a joint project between the University of Palermo and University of Potsdam, under the supervision of Professor Francesca Di Lorenzo and Professor Hans-Peter Krüger.

ISBN 978-3-11-153449-7
e-ISBN (PDF) 978-3-11-077212-8
e-ISBN (EPUB) 978-3-11-077214-2
ISSN 1617-3325

Library of Congress Control Number: 2022933403

Bibliographic information published by the Deutsche Nationalbibliothek
The Deutsche Nationalbibliothek lists this publication in the Deutsche Nationalbibliografie; detailed bibliographic data are available on the Internet at http://dnb.dnb.de.

© 2024 Walter de Gruyter GmbH, Berlin/Boston
This volume is text- and page-identical with the hardback published in 2022.

www.degruyter.com

*Sagt, wo findet sich die Gerechtigkeit,
welche Liebe mit sehenden Augen ist?*
                              Friedrich Nietzsche

Contents

Introduction —— 1

Chapter 1
A Negative Approach to Normativity —— 13
1.1 Social Pathologies as Kindler of Critique: Three Different Programmatic Views —— 15
1.2 Vulnerability and the Normative Experience of Injustice —— 27
1.3 Some Preliminary Issues: Psychologization, Culturalization, and Teleology —— 33

Chapter 2
A Post-Metaphysical Moral Grammar: *The Struggle for Recognition* —— 36
2.1 Honneth's Hegel: An Intersubjective Social Ontology —— 37
2.2 'I' and 'me': Mead's Concept of Practical Identity —— 50
2.3 Disrespect as Misrecognition and Conflict —— 60
2.4 A Formal Conception of Ethical Life: An Anthropological Justification —— 69
2.4.1 Love and Self-Confidence —— 76
2.4.2 Respect and Self-Respect —— 82
2.4.3 Esteem and Self-Esteem —— 85
2.5 Some Open Issues: Recognition, Subject-Formation, and Social Ontology —— 87

Chapter 3
***Reification* and the Antecedence of Recognition** —— 90
3.1 Some Premises: Visibility, Authenticity, and Mimesis —— 92
3.2 Reification as Forgetfulness of Recognition —— 98
3.3 The Priority of Recognition —— 107
3.3.1 Recognition as Apperception of Human Features —— 112
3.3.2 A Triangular Relationship with the World —— 114
3.3.3 Self-Recognition as Inner Proximity —— 115
3.4 Some Open Issues: Ontology or Normativity, Recognition or Identification —— 117

Chapter 4
***Freedom's Right* and the 'Historical Turn'** —— 121
4.1 Ethical Life as Place of and for Freedom —— 123
4.1.1 Justice as Non-Discursive Justification —— 127
4.1.2 Overlapping and Noncoincidence of Ethical Spheres and Practices —— 132

4.2	Surplus of Validity: from Interaction to Principles —— 135
4.2.1	The Unavoidability of Moral Experiences —— 139
4.2.2	Between Norms and Facts —— 143
4.2.3	Justification, Validity, and Progress —— 149
4.3	Being with Oneself in the Other: Social Freedom in Modern Societies —— 153
4.3.1	Normative Reconstruction as Critical Method —— 155
4.3.1.1	Three Modes of Freedom —— 161
4.3.2	The Spheres of Social Freedom —— 171
4.3.2.1	Personal Relationships —— 173
4.3.2.2	The Market (Society) —— 178
4.3.2.3	Democratic Public and Constitutional Democracy —— 186
4.3.3	Some Open Issues: Immanent Critique, Recognition, and the Third —— 196

Chapter 5
Recognition: from Affirmation to Mutual Authorization —— 204

5.1	"Grounding Recognition": Response, Actualization, and Progress —— 205
5.2	"Recognition as Ideology": Is there a Way Out? —— 214
5.3	*Recognition:* from Affirmation to Authorization —— 220
5.3.1	One Word, Different Concepts —— 221
5.3.2	An Attempt at Harmonization —— 234
5.4	Some Open Issues: A Spatial Account of Recognition —— 246
5.5	Sediments of Reconstruction —— 249

Chapter 6
Recognition between Actuality and Potentiality —— 256

6.1	Interpersonal Recognition: Four Different Ideas —— 257
6.2	What is Recognition? —— 270
6.3	A Detrascendentalized Account: Limitation and We-Structures —— 276
6.4	A Demanding Concept: Sketches for a Generative Account —— 282
6.5	Back to Hegel: Recognition and Forgiveness —— 284
6.5.1	Guilt as Finitude and Being-For-Others —— 287
6.5.2	Confession and Forgiveness, Acknowledgment, and Mutual Recognition —— 292
6.6	Conclusion: Generativity as Critical Criterion —— 299

Bibliography —— 309
   Works by Axel Honneth —— 309
   Other works —— 311

Index of Subjects —— 324

Index of Names —— 329

Introduction

In recent decades, the term 'recognition' has become increasingly relevant not only in philosophical debates, but also—and perhaps especially—as a political and sociological concept. In our times of globalization and pluralism, the demand for recognition becomes ever more widespread and relevant. Or perhaps what is increasing is the impression of being misrecognized or not recognized, the feeling of not existing in the eyes and voices of others. With the dialectic proper to socio-political claims, recognition presents itself both as a need of social actors and as a theoretical concept. Thus, the concept stems from acknowledged needs, and theory (at any level), by giving these needs a voice, interpreting them, contributes to making them explicit and hence to grounding new claims. It is therefore no coincidence that the amplification of theoretical debates and the intensification of demands for recognition by social actors go hand in hand. However, this is not without possible ambivalences.

Hence, recognition of *what?* Even remaining within the philosophical-political realm, the answer to this question seems to be extremely complex. A first hermeneutic step is certainly provided by Charles Taylor's intuition, by which the recognition of 'equality' is distinguished from the recognition of 'difference.' The first form of recognition would essentially concern the granting of equal rights, according to a certain universalism proper to liberal societies and the related conception of individual rights. The "what" of recognition would thus be the equal status of every individual, and the "how" of recognition would be the social-juridical instantiations of such equality. The recognition of difference, instead, would go beyond such a generalized fairness, to the extent that it would capture and frame more particularistic aspirations of individuals, groups, and minorities that strive for seeing their peculiar identities affirmed. In this case, even though the how is almost the same, the what seems closely related with the concept of 'identity,' which cannot be assumed as equal for every individual. Clearly, equality and difference—especially in their respective relationship with identity—are not to be sharply disjointed. In the name of equality with the other, one can demand recognition of one's own particularity. But particularity itself—one's own identity—can also be at the basis of requests and struggles for equal rights, autonomies, and powers. Thus, the issue of recognition—of difference *and* equality—has emerged as a pivotal concern in debates and conflicts over civil rights not only in the demands made by the most diverse minorities, but also in demands for greater political autonomy and in independence movements, in nationalist reactions to globalization, and in conflicts to preserve an identity perceived as at risk, both in post-colonial contexts and those regarding migratory flows. In other words, the term recognition has assumed a leading role in the contemporary socio-political landscape as a conceptual catalyst for identities within pluralistic contexts. Given the breadth and dissimilarity of the issues at stake, it follows that this concept can hardly be framed or rendered as one-sidedly characterizing *one* political conception, movement, or even party. The impression is that the demand for being recognized concerns every range of the spectrum.

It follows from this that such a polysemy of the what and the how of recognizing (and being recognized) cannot be restricted to the political sphere in the strict sense. And in fact, the term is used in different practical, linguistic, applicative, educational, scientific, and academic contexts. Facing such a variety of approaches and inquiries, philosophy must stop and think in order to deepen the understanding of the concept of recognition. Is there any underlying element capable of reconciling the meanings involved in a minority's political demands for recognition, facial recognition applications, the recognition given to an artist by the critics, or the recognition that the ruins discovered correspond to the ancient city sought after in the excavations? How can the same term be used in such different cases as recognizing an old acquaintance on the street, recognizing that I was wrong, recognizing a melody in a waiting room, recognizing a sovereign state, or recognizing the validity of an appeal to the court? With these examples—there are many others available, from daily life or philosophical reflection—we are shifting from questions concerning the what and how *of* recognizing to the question "what *is* recognition?"

What *is* recognition, then? The above examples primarily indicate the receiving, perceiving, or knowing a physiognomy of an identity. But they also oscillate toward a more attributive dimension, which can be articulated through political measures, the reactions of critics, or the validation of the appeal. We are faced with a polarity, the one between reception and attribution, which lurks in how we speak the word recognition. Recognizing is not simply the passive acceptance of an always-already given, nor can it be considered as an actively unbalanced attribution, understood as a creative act. On the one hand, re-cognition is not mere cognition but cannot be disjointed from the apperceptive movement of grasping something as *the* something it is. On the other hand, recognition is not a straightforward attribution, but it cannot be disjointed from the affirming and confirming movement of giving recognition. This hybrid nature of recognizing, which oscillates between knowing and acting, is blurred even more by the fact that the term entails different implications of meaning in the different languages in which the philosophical debate about it is conducted. To recognize and to acknowledge, *erkennen* and *anerkennen*, and *reconnaître* bring with them numerous nuances, often leading to incomprehension and misunderstandings that frequently remain undetected. Above all, and in addition to identity and the reception-attribution polarity, conceptual disagreements become manifest regarding two other conceptual plexuses that are closely linked to recognition. These are the intersubjective character of recognition and the distinction between the so-called positive and negative theories of recognition.

Regarding the issue of intersubjectivity, we can outline two principal insights by drawing from John Searle, on the one hand, and Fichte and Hegel, on the other. A first idea of recognition echoes the Searlean formula of collective intentionality, which acts as a constitutive rule for institutional realities: X counts as Y in C.[1] Searle's well-known example is that of the piece of paper (X) that counts as a five dollar bill (Y) in the context of economic transactions (C). As we will see especially in chapter 5, this formula is translated in terms of recognition as follows: X is taken/treated *as* Y in C, whereby C is the context or sphere of recognition, and Y the status or significant traits granted or endowed to the recognizee. For example, a human being (X) is taken/treated—namely, recognized—as legal person (Y) in the context of a contract or a process (C). What is noteworthy at this point is that X can be basically anything: a person, a law, an animal, a rock, a situation, etc. A dog (X) is treated as my pet (Y) at home, by the neighbors, or by anyone thanks to the collar plate (C). Or a stone (X) is taken as a keystone (Y) by the Roman architect at the aqueduct site (C). Regardless of what X actually is, what matters is a certain "harmony" between the mode by which X is regarded and the as Y, so that the treatment can be considered as a form of acting accordingly with respect to X's features: taking a dog as a keystone would certainly not fall under the idea of recognition we encounter in everyday language. This first insight, therefore, does not prevent our thinking of recognition as being outside of intersubjective relations. And clearly, such a definition of recognizing leaves the reception-attribution binomial undecided, oscillating between conceiving it as "giving what is due" or as constituting capabilities or powers, so it leaves open whether we are supposed to understand recognition according to a more epistemological or a more normative matrix—both issues become blurred concerning individual rights and statuses.

The other insight about intersubjectivity adopts a different approach, not simply by stressing the interpersonal character of recognition, but rather a certain kind of it, namely, reciprocity or mutuality. Or better: mutuality, considered inherent to recognition, is understood as requiring both relational poles to be recognizers—either at a logical level, or at an explicit, reflexive level shared by the participants. Fichte, for example, describes the relationship of recognition as emerging from and instantiating in A's summon (*Aufforderung*) toward B, and in the latter's responding. This presupposes that A has already recognized B as a free being (since you do not invite a chair to act or to assume a stance) and that B, by responding, understands A's exhortation as flowing from a free being, in a game of mutual conditioning. The interaction between human beings would necessarily be inhabited by the reciprocity of recognizing each other as persons endowed with freedom. But on a second level, this can concern the most everyday case for which we feel affirmed and recognized, only when the compliment addressed to us comes from a person whom, in turn, we esteem or at least consider a competent judge. In being considered, our consideration of the considerer is constantly at stake. In this case, mutual conditioning leads recognition practices in a more receptive and normative framework. However, the epistemological matrix seems difficult to erase, because in order to "invite" B,

---

[1] See John R. Searle 1995, p. 43.

I must already have "seen" that *B* is a human person. And moreover, some room for discussion opens as one notices that recognition itself does not represent, especially for Hegel, a simple "addition" to the participants' being free, but the actual condition for and existence of freedom. Almost paradoxically, in order to be recognized as a free person, I have to already inhabit the space-for-freedom constituted by reciprocal recognition. In order to act autonomously, we must have mutually attributed each other (or "seen" in each other) the status of responsible actors. In this sense, the attributive/constitutive dimension of recognition also cannot be ruled out. But a further problem of this second insight concerns how this mutuality should be understood. This discloses, in addition to the logical-structural dimension of reciprocity, the *moral* problem of recognition relationships on multiple levels. While the equality of participants and the symmetry of their reciprocal consideration seem to guarantee a solid moral standard, the concept of recognition is often appreciated as capable of decentering and unbalancing modern atomism and contractual views on sociality and morality, which revolve around symmetrical obligations and statuses. Conversely, we cannot say that the factors that allow us to distinguish recognition relationships from domination and subordination lie in imbalance per se – because imbalance can consist in or lead to deep asymmetries between me and the other. Also in this case, therefore, recognition is conceptualized in hybrid forms, halfway between symmetry and unbalance, between freedom's becoming shared and (in-)voluntary subjection.

Basically, it is with respect to these dilemmas that, in recent years, secondary literature has identified and distinguished negative and positive theories of recognition.[2] On the one hand, in fact, disparate authors such as Jean-Jacques Rousseau, Louis Althusser, and Judith Butler consider recognition relationships as the main way an individual's subordination to society is instantiated and reproduced. As is well known, according to Rousseau, the entry into society coincides with being grafted onto with non-authentic forms of desire (*amour propre*) that bind the individual, in herself free, to other's gaze and to the urge for approval. Thus, always watching oneself from a second-person perspective, the access to one's own selfhood becomes blurred, if not compromised. According to Althusser, mutual recognition exemplified in reciprocal interpellation represents the way in which the social order that towers above the subjects is daily confirmed, crystallized, and reproduced. The reciprocal confirmation of being subjects—namely, subjected to the social order—is in fact carried out according to modes and expressions not decided by the participants, but proposed and imposed by the context they live in. The same might be said about the object of the confirming gestures, namely, the social roles with their related tasks, faculties, powers, that subjects can biographically pursue, but cannot autonomously outline.[3] Butler also adopts and stresses this ambiguity and ambivalence of

---

2 See e.g. Rahel Jaeggi 2006; and Georg W. Bertram and Robin Celikates 2015.
3 See Louis Althusser 2014.

the term 'subject.' In a nutshell, Butler's question concerns voluntary (more or less conscious) subjection and the ways subjects become attached to the modes of their own subordination. Given the evident vulnerability and interpersonal dependence that characterize the human lifeform, relationships of recognition thus represent a constitutive form of power, which—almost behind the participants' backs—favors the assumption of roles, the transmission of ethical-cultural patterns, and the internalization of norms, leveraging on the need for acceptance and inclusion and, as it were, delivering the individual into the arms of heteronomy by granting her subjectivity.[4]

On the other hand, the positive theories of recognition—which basically include various re-elaborations of Hegel's thought—move in an almost opposite direction. That is, they look positively at the fact that recognition represents a vital human need and they thus ground the possibilities of developing an undamaged practical identity and the actualization of freedom on certain relational forms. Therefore, both an empirical and a normative dimension would be outlined. On the one hand, the concept of recognition would make it possible to take the intersubjective constitution of selfhood seriously and, on the other hand, it would provide evaluative criteria for judging and criticizing the intersubjective-institutional concretions within which we find ourselves living. Clearly, these positive theories also entail various facets and provide different theoretical options. For instance, while recognition can be read in more deontological-normative terms, as, for example, by Robert Brandom and Robert Pippin,[5] Andreas Wildt argues that it would represent an alternative to the "legalistic" forms of Kantian morality.[6] Ludwig Siep, by placing the principles of recognition at the center of practical philosophy, draws an evaluative framework for institutions from the norms of reciprocity;[7] Heikki Ikäheimo emphasizes that recognition represents a fundamental element of humanization, of inclusion in personhood;[8] Paul Ricoeur emphasizes that, besides being a fundamental element by the formation of the "capable person," the experience of mutuality coincides with those states of peace connected with giving and good receiving.[9]

From these brief arguments, it is already possible to grasp how varied the theoretical panorama on the concept of recognition is. It ranges over multiple disciplines, from philosophy to research on artificial intelligence; it concerns the macro-level of theories of society and justice, and the micro-level of individuation and of personal relationships; the concept veers either toward a cognitive act or toward an ethical-normative practice. Furthermore, we have already noticed some issues and problematic binomials that will accompany us throughout the course of this work. What is the

---

[4] See Judith Butler 1997; and Amy Allen 2006.
[5] See Robert B. Brandom 2007, pp. 25–51; Robert B. Pippin 2008.
[6] See Andreas Wildt 1982.
[7] See Ludwig Siep 1979.
[8] See Ikäheimo 2009, pp. 31–45.
[9] See Paul Ricoeur 2005.

connection between recognition and identity? Does the former simply attest the latter, constitute it, or contribute to its formation? Or does it fluidify the individual? And, in any of these cases, is the act of recognition to be understood as the passive reception of other's features, or as attributing new ones? Can one speak of recognition even when there is no interactional mutuality and, if not, why? What relationship, if any, do mutuality and reciprocity, symmetry and asymmetry entertain with each other? And, finally, should the evident connection between recognition and individual's social integration be understood as a form of (ideological) power that conforms and flattens the person to a given context, or as the possibility of breaking down the walls of atomism, providing the individual with (motivational and contextual) elements to effectively *exercise* her autonomy?

In this theoretical quagmire, there seem to be two alternatives for research to gain more clarity on the concept of recognition. It is possible to make a comparative work, entering the debate by comparing the alternatives proposed by different authors or paradigms. Or—and this is the choice made for our inquiry—one might attempt to deepen the perspective of a single thinker. Our focus will be on Axel Honneth. The reasons for dealing with a single author and for choosing Honneth specifically are closely related.

First, Honneth is certainly the philosopher who has contributed most, both in Europe and America, to reviving the contemporary debate on the concept of recognition. While Siep and Wildt (along with others) catalyzed German academic attention on the concept back in the 1980s and Charles Taylor has shaped the North American debate on recognition within the opposition between liberalism and communitarianism since 1992, Honneth has been able to develop a multi-faceted recognition paradigm, a prism through which the concept itself has been able to gain autonomy from unilateral approaches, thus revealing its richness and polysemy. This is closely linked to Honneth's methodological and theoretical approach, which, in a nutshell, can be defined as socio-philosophical, critical, and normative. Honneth's approach is socio-philosophical primarily because it pays specific attention to the social facticity in its expressions and concretions. Moving from a more action-theoretical approach to a more institutions-related one, Honneth's thinking deals with different dimensions and philosophical domains without being locked into them exclusively. It should therefore come as no surprise that anthropology plays a fundamental role, as does sociological inquiry in the strict sense, or that literary works and novels—even autobiographical documentations, in his first publications—are taken as authoritative access points to society's opacities. Nor should it surprise us that Honneth joins the philosophical-political debates on justice, on the priority either of the right or of the good, on the relationship and tensions between the personal and public spheres, or those between the market and democratic institutions. It is no coincidence that he refers to social psychology, psychoanalysis, and developmental psychology both from a phylogenetic and ontogenetic perspective, or that working conditions in the global market and the role of public education find their place in his investigations. Honneth's thought is composite, meaning that it can hardly be reduced to a single concept—that of recognition—even though he is of the view that recognition can provide an interpretative key to decipher the complexity of contemporary societies. However, Honneth's approach is not only socio-philosophical, but also critical. Continuing the tradition of the Frankfurt School, he is not only interested in describing the social phenomenon, the *is* of society, but aims to detect, unveil, and expose an almost unfathomable *ought* immanent to society, to be found among its frustrations, wounds, fractures, pathologies, injustices. Through an attempt of identification with social actors, with the participants involved in recognition relationships and institutional spheres, Honneth's intention is to question and criticize those social concretions that are (more or less explicitly) perceived as harmful or unjustified by the actors themselves to the extent that they cannot find recognition in them. In this sense—it seems apt to emphasize it—even if his paradigm would certainly fall within the positive theories of recognition, such positivity is given in the social facticity always in backlight, hindered, more yearned for than merely present. This issue can only be adequately grasped by hinting to the normative dimension that characterizes Honneth's approach. In fact, Honneth anchors the possibilities of critical theory on the dialectical relationship between the normative principles underlying social integration and their disregard, negation, and subtraction in intersubjective institutional contexts. This relationship is dialectical for three main reasons. First, the "good," normative forms of (inter-)acting become evident in their own failure, that is, when mutual expectations, demands, or obligations are denied. This implies that the definition of a good life and the related norms of recognition are primarily under the responsibility of the social actors involved with the practices they perform, and that theory cannot anticipate this elaboration in its entirety, but only outline its contours. Being a *social* critical philosophy, social development steers theory, not the other way around—also considering the Left-Hegelian matrix that characterizes Honneth's work.[10] The relationship is therefore dialectical, first, to the extent that normative principles would emerge in their immanence to social reality only through their negation, and this negation is not seen as definitive, but as constructive. In a word, experiencing injustice raises a certain awareness about hitherto unthematized (and even blurred, incomplete, provisional) ideas of justice. But, second, this relationship is dialectical also because this dynamic is not unilateral. In fact, in order to be disregarded, actors' normative expectations must be based on and shaped by principles already present and operative in some way and at some degree. Experiencing injustice presupposes evaluative criteria already embedded in our social life. And, finally, it is dialectical because Honneth is convinced that this conflicting polarity of norms and facts represents the trigger of social conflicts aimed at reformulating of the latter to better realize the former, which in turn can be refined as their factual instantiations change. Injustice and jus-

---

[10] I will discuss this issue above all in chapter 4.

tice, being immanent to social reality, are changeable, historical, and dependent on their actualizations—that is, dialectical.

While such a theoretical and methodological complexity is the first reason why the focus on Honneth seems well-founded, the second reason is more closely related to his paradigm of recognition. Indeed, Honneth grants to recognition the pivotal role of embedding the conditions for undamaged practical identity and freedom's realization—according to his Hegelian approach, he considers autonomy "actualized" if and when capable of not excluding otherness from its premises and motives, and during its unfolding process. But this generic definition does not take into account *how* this is supposed to happen. The dialectical relationship between the principles of recognition and social reality is in fact portrayed as dynamic underlying both social integration and the processes of differentiation typical of modern and contemporary societies. Thus, Honneth differentiates three modes of recognition—love, respect, and esteem—which (dialectically) outline and are outlined by related spheres of recognition, which coincide with, underlie, and emerge from institutionalized forms of intimate-personal relationships, juridical relationships, and relationships in cooperative contexts (spanning from the workplace to the democratic public sphere).[11] Although Honneth himself defines his approach as a moral-theoretical monism hinging on recognition, it is internally differentiated and complex. Furthermore, even if Honneth's aim is to propose a strictly interpersonal, mutual, and normative concept of recognition, the threefold differentiation betrays the diversity inherent to the concept and the difficulty of reaching a unitary definition of it. For these three modes of interaction (love, respect, and esteem) present themselves in very different guises and respond to different norms and logics of action—which are hardly inscribable in pure normative and symmetrical terms in the first place. Therefore, Honneth's paradigm oscillates between a non-unilateral approach and the risk of reducing very different practices to a single hypernym. But it is precisely these possible ambivalences that make the confrontation with Honneth's theory particularly interesting, since between the lines, through the clash with criticisms and the encounter with other paradigms of recognition, possibilities of different conceptualizations, formulations, and insights disclose themselves. But Honneth's paradigm of recognition is differentiated not only because of the internal conceptual distinctions between three forms of recognizing/being recognized. Rather, it is differentiated also because it undergoes internal evolutions that are too often left aside by critics. Indeed, defining *the* idea of

---

11 My ambiguity in expressing what could be superficially defined as cause-effect links between forms of recognition, relationships of recognition, and spheres of recognition is deliberate. In fact, Honneth himself often leaves a trace of ambiguity in the socio-ontological derivations of his thought as a consequence of his action-theoretical approach, first (*The Struggle for Recognition*), and of the focus on normative integration and legitimacy processes, then (*Freedom's Right*). Put in positive terms, this ambiguity is due to his Hegelian approach that imposes a certain impossibility to conceive a pure (a priori) beginning. The problem, that is, is not only hermeneutical, but pertains to the thing itself.

recognition in Honneth can appear an affordable undertaking—we have already sketched the two basilar outcomes of recognition (positive self-relation and shared freedom), from which their intersubjective causes could be induced. But being clear about the outcomes of recognition is not the same as being clear about *what* recognition *is*. Defining *the* idea of recognition in Honneth seems to come at the price of certain simplifications that do not take into account the different nuances and the different socio-theoretical roles that are assumed by the paradigm itself over time—one might venture to say that what will be dealt with in the following research are the *ideas* of recognition proposed by Honneth. Therefore, internal differentiations and evolutions of the concept represent a promising starting point for an investigation into the notion of recognition in general, since different facets of recognition in general have the chance to emerge.

The third reason why dealing with Honneth's thought seems particularly well-suited indirectly derives from the first two. In fact, although focusing on a single author may lead to a narrower view, Honneth's relevance in the contemporary landscape, his multi-faceted approach, and his internally differentiated concept of recognition, make the confrontation with this philosopher a unique springboard to enter the debate on recognition, something that other authors could not offer. Following the interdisciplinary approach that traditionally characterizes the Frankfurt School, Honneth ranges from psychoanalysis to theories of justice, from the investigation of social conflicts to a normative theory of institutionalization. His thought thus relates to traditions of thought, philosophical fields, methodologies, and objects of research that are in some cases extremely distant from each other, without dispersing in them the peculiar identity of his philosophical approach. In this way, Honneth's work can draw attention and criticisms (which will be addressed in detail in each case) at such a level that dealing with the former requires constant dialogue with the latter, which in turn provides the present research with an access point to the multiple voices involved in the contemporary debate on recognition, while not embracing a specifically comparative approach.

Given this brief overview on the difficulty of defining recognition, and having enumerated some preliminary reasons of interest in Honneth's thinking, what is left to this introduction is to sketch the structure of what follows.

The first task (chapter 1) is to frame the peculiarities of Honneth's approach and aims, which also helps to understand many of the differences with other paradigms of recognition. A first step in this direction becomes possible by entering into his thinking through the door of the negative, that is, by focusing on the issues of social pathologies and moral injuries. As mentioned earlier, Honneth's own attempt is to identify with damaged life, deriving from it the normative criteria that can enable social criticism. While the issue of moral injuries is directly linked to the possibilities of outlining an action-theoretical and normative account of social conflict that hinges on recognition (section 1.2), the matter of social pathologies appears in broader, more blurred terms. For now, it suffices to mention, at a general level, that they indicate the *mis*developments of social reality, dysfunctional phenomena in which the processes of integration and differentiation run into contradictions. An analysis of three writings that span a large part of Honneth's production—"Pathologies of the Social" (1994), "A Social Pathology of Reason" (2007), and "The Diseases of Society" (2013)—will make it possible to better outline the contours of this problem and to understand the decisive role played by the negative (section 1.1). The closing section deals with some criticisms levelled at the consequences of the accounts on social pathologies and moral injuries. Honneth is indeed criticized for psychologizing or culturalizing injustice, as well as of implying an excessively substantive idea of teleology (section 1.3). After starting with these meta-methodological issues, chapters 2–5 represent a critical reconstruction of Honneth's four main works, focusing on the concept of recognition.

The second chapter focuses on the first pillar of Honneth's paradigm of recognition: *The Struggle for Recognition*. Our inquiry starts with an analysis of Honneth's relationship with Hegel, who represents the main interlocutor of the work. Here we will stress the mediating role of Jürgen Habermas, Ludwig Siep, and Andreas Wildt by Honneth's framing his own theory (section 2.1). A similar task concerns the second section of the chapter, dealing with George Herbert Mead, who represents one of the greatest points of both proximity and distance with Habermas. Indeed, Mead plays a decisive role to the extent that his depiction of social integration and practical identity—understood as naturalization of Hegel—lays the foundations for Honneth's intersubjective anthropology, idea of progress, and moral account of social struggles (section 2.2). After again assigning a central position to the negative by deriving the positive forms of recognition from those of misrecognition (section 2.3), we will deal with the formal concept of ethical life and Honneth's quasi-phenomenological reconstruction of the recognitional spheres within which it is instantiated. Here, recognition is defined as a multi-polar intersubjective practice (love, respect, and esteem), instantiating in different interactive contexts (love-relations and friendships, legal relations, social and cooperative relations) and underlying three forms of undamaged practical identity (self-confidence, self-respect, and self-esteem) (section 2.4). Finally, as at the end of each chapter, I will raise some issues, giving voice to and relaunching the debate (section 2.5).

Honneth's Tanner Lectures of 2005 are published in the essay *Reification*, and the novelties brought with it to the concept of recognition represent the focus of the third chapter. But before dealing directly with this work, it seems useful to address three previous writings that disclose the path to it and mark certain discontinuities with *The Struggle for Recognition* (section 3.1). Discussing the concept of reification implies new determinations of recognition and—especially through the criticisms aimed at Honneth's approach—for deepening his critical perspective and approach (section 3.2). Subsequently, our attention shifts more explicitly to the concept of 'antecedent recognition' or 'emotional identification'—which constitutes the heart of the re-definition of the concept—as well as on its threefold declination: toward others, toward the world, and toward one's own self (section 3.3). Finally, we are going to pull the strings and deepen the discussion, above all by making explicit the two-level account of recognition that Honneth sketches in this work, as well as its implications (section 3.4).

The fourth chapter is certainly the most broad and wide-ranging. We will begin by focusing on *The Pathologies of Individual Freedom*, a text that Honneth draws from the Spinoza Lectures he held in 1999. In a theoretical context similar to that outlined in *The Struggle for Recognition* and "Pathologies of the Social," Honneth turns for the first time to Hegel's *Philosophy of Right*, taking his first steps in structuring a theory of justice in terms of social freedom. Here we pay due attention to how the Hegelian concept of 'right' (*Recht*) is interpreted, which plays a decisive role also for Honneth's later accounts of legitimation (section 4.1). We then analyze the exchange with Nancy Fraser contained in *Redistribution or Recognition?*, specifically by granting due attention to the concept of 'surplus of validity,' which effectively shows Honneth's gradually shifting from the justifying framework offered by formal anthropology to a historical-normative one, as well as the dialectical relation between principles of recognition, social reality, and its becoming (section 4.2). The last section turns to *Freedom's Right*, which can be considered as the second pillar of Honneth's theory. Our attention will be drawn again by recognition relations, whose specific characteristics seem at times generalized in the direction of a more neutral theory of intersubjectivity. In the course of this analysis, the two key concepts are certainly those of normative reconstruction and social freedom, which represent the aforementioned fulcrums of this second phase of Honneth's thought, which hinges on Hegel's *Philosophy of Right*. On the one hand, Honneth performs a reconstruction of western societies' recognition order and their institutionalized normativity. And, on the other hand, he depicts recognition in almost opposed terms as those of identity politics: the main contribution offered by recognitional relations is not so much the affirmation of already-formed identities, but rather the mutually disclosed realization of freedom via complementary involvement and obligations, that is, the possibility of being oneself with the other (section 4.3).

Our reconstruction ends with Honneth's last monograph: *Recognition: A Chapter in the History of European Ideas*. Here, Honneth further addresses the issue of recognition providing a more in-depth depiction. Indeed, these last considerations are rooted in a debate left open since 2002, when *Inquiry* published an issue focused on Honneth's concept of recognition. The first section will therefore focus on the issues that emerged there and by Honneth's response—"Grounding Recognition"—which was subsequently inserted as an afterword to *The Struggle for Recognition*; the exchange of 2002 revolves around defining what recognition is and how it is related to the personal features it addresses: it is the distinction between the attributive and receptive models mentioned above (section 5.1). The second section focuses on other open problems, in particular those presented by ideological recognition and power relations, dealt with in "Recognition as Ideology" (2004) and by many critics (section 5.2). The third section will focus on *Recognition*: here Honneth takes up precisely the problems opened in the two writings just mentioned, contextualizing them in a history of ideas that tries to posit the different meanings that recognition assumes in three traditions of European thought: French, English, and German—*reconnaissance*, recognition, and *Anerkennung*. Without dwelling too much on the many historical inquiries and comparisons carried out by Honneth, our aim here will be to distil the image of recognition that thereby emerges, namely, the idea of mutual authorization to normative co-authorship (section 5.3). We will then emphasize the last evolutions undergone by the concept of recognition and its problems (section 5.4), and finally, we will provide an overview on the reconstruction carried out in these first five chapters (section 5.5).

The reconstruction of Honneth's paradigm of recognition through the primary focus on four works—*The Struggle for Recognition*, *Reification*, *Freedom's Right*, and *Recognition*—guarantees an adequate understanding of the various tensions and possibilities that inhabit the contemporary debate on recognition, but also of the points and nodes left unsolved and in shadow. The first step is taken by recollecting four ideas of recognition put in place—critically or positively—by Honneth, and by explaining four major perplexities about his paradigm and the concept of recognition in general, especially with regard to the issue of identity (section 6.1). Next, we distinguish between three macro-meanings of recognition, which prove to be useful in throwing analytical clarity on the contemporary debate on recognition, too often conditioned by inexplicit positions. Distinguishing between re-cognition, acknowledgement, and mutual recognition, the aim is to spotlight a set of practical modes —linked together by a thin action-theoretical thread—that is complex and holistic, which hardly lends itself to unilateralizations (section 6.2). The following steps embrace Honneth's emphasis on detranscendentalization as Hegel's fundamental operation with respect to Kant and Fichte, strengthening the bond of recognition with our lifeform, thus acquiring elements to outline the specificity of interpersonal recognition (sections 6.3 and 6.4). The decisive focus of this chapter consists in analyzing the confession-forgiveness dialectic depicted by Hegel in the *Phenomenology of Spirit*. Through this analysis, it becomes possible to place the concept of mutual recognition in Hegel's broader action-theoretical account, which is articulated between the dialectical poles of expressive action and necessity of the finite. Thus, it will emerge that the normative core of mutual recognition concerns not so much identity as reconciliation (section 6.5). From these elements, we will sketch a concept of mutual recognition as generative movement, which stands in discontinuity with the crystallizing role to which the notion is often confined. I argue that, as a fluidifying We-form, mutual recognition can represent a peculiar and specific critical criterion aimed at identifying emancipatory and reformulating interests (section 6.6).

Chapter 1
A Negative Approach to Normativity

There is an issue to face before deepening our understanding of the dimensions the concept of recognition assumes in Honneth's work. Due to the polysemous constellation of theoretical levels at stake, certain unavoidable difficulties become apparent as one approaches Honneth's corpus. The term recognition is indeed an all-encompassing philosophical scope, through which Honneth approaches and manages many different fields. It allows and discloses, among others, a critical theory of society, an intersubjectivistic anthropology, a theory of justice and of freedom, and a certain social ontology.[1] And all these fields are also included, thanks to the concept of recognition, in a unitary depiction, that is, the so-called "moral-theoretical monism" continually at stake in Honneth's elaborations (Honneth 2003d, p. 157).

However, recognition is not merely a starting point or theoretical key useful for opening and unfolding Honneth's social philosophy. It also represents the conclusion of Honneth's efforts. The different fields Honneth engages are illuminated through the concept of recognition, which thus provides the lens useful to focus on social reality, but also on a justificatory and critical level. Because certain elements and structures of contemporary societies emerge as problematic, unjust, and pathologic only by virtue of their announced solution or reconciliation. For example, one could say that recognition represents the blueprint of a rational and real freedom—as it is described in *Freedom's Right*—while pathological forms of autonomy become apparent only through the idea of recognition and its historical concretions. Given this double-faced vest of recognition, one might legitimately worry that Honneth's thought revolves around a certain vicious circle.

The literature interpreting Honneth's approach is clearly divided, accentuating different aspects that are present in his works. On the one hand, questioning the relevance of his monism to social reality, depicting the latter as indescribable and unconceivable through the lens of a unique principle. Hence, recognition would result as a theoretical tool that makes critical theory overstep its real objects and goals, as incapable of accounting for the dynamics of power, domination, and the structures of material inequality within capitalism.[2] On the other hand, one could also claim that the monism should not be interpreted as exclusive, but as a theoretical threshold that can, and in fact does, encompass an "intertranslation between the very different approaches, methods, vocabulary, and focal problems" (Christopher F. Zurn 2015, p. 28).[3] Honneth does not demand that we interpret sociality in a monological-exclusive way, but rather in a monological-oriented one. Thanks to the concept

---
[1] For more on the social-ontological implications of a Frankfurt-informed social theory, see Italo Testa 2015.
[2] See, e.g. Danielle Petherbridge 2013, chs. 3 and 5; and Michael J. Thompson 2019a.
[3] See also Eleonora Piromalli 2012, p. 210.

of recognition, then, social criticism would be provided with a proper perspective, with a common denominator.

Finally, the status or structure of recognition is at issue, since it possesses diverse facets. If we accept that recognition represents a suitable tool for each theoretical and philosophical level hinted at above, then we must grant it a certain multipolarity: it is, therefore, an anthropological, a moral, an ethical, a political, and a critical concept. In fact, there is a clearly acknowledgeable tension between different dimensions in Honneth's work. However, Honneth almost always clearly labels recognition as a normative concept. Indeed, the formulation of a "formal conception of ethical life" rooted in specific practices of recognition represents the principal aim of his whole production (Honneth 1995c, p. 175). And, if one takes a closer look, the depiction of a undamaged personal integrity is always operating, although sometimes just as a shadow in the background. Expressions such as self-confidence, self-respect and self-esteem,[4] "inner aliveness" (Honneth 1999, p. 239), freedom from indeterminacy,[5] "expressionism" (Honneth 2008, p. 71), "self-appropriation" (Honneth 2009b, p. 128), "inner freedom," and "inward tolerance" (Honneth 2009c, pp. 160 and 164) all describe a normative account of personhood through recognitional gestures and relations. If the result of recognitional interactions is the formation of a normative account of personhood, then such recognition practices do result in normativity as well.

Approaching Honneth's thought, we face three problems. First, the paradigm of recognition's bi-dimensionality: it represents a key that discloses social critique and, simultaneously, its result. Second, the suitability of recognition as a theoretic-critical tool and the according dichotomy between those that interpret Honneth's monism radically and others who consider it a unifying horizon among a multiplicity of methodologies and approaches. Third, the multi-dimensionality of recognition itself, keeping in mind its clearly self-declared normative label.

Naturally, these questions are not easy to answer, and one could be at pains to find a conclusive explanation to any one of them. My claim is that to dissolve these Gordian knots, we must start from a meta-methodological question, that is, by questioning what constitutes an adequate approach to Honneth's thought. More precisely, we must focus on his own methodology. Thus, I argue that setting forth from Honneth's "methodological negativism" represents the most suitable approach to his paradigm of recognition (Jean-Philippe Deranty 2009, p. 355).[6] For, if Honneth's theory represents a critical theory of the social, it is crucial to interrogate it for its foremost perspective, its interpretative capacities, and its grip on social reality. In other words, what is the "grid of intelligibility" the theory implies and proposes?[7] By doing so, one engages an internal critique of Honneth's thought.

---

4 See Honneth 1995c, ch. 5.
5 See Honneth 2010.
6 See also Deranty 2004.
7 See Michel Foucault 2003, pp. 163–64.

1.1 Social Pathologies as Kindler of Critique: Three Different Programmatic Views

Put synthetically, we can derive three main advantages from this point of departure. First, one better comprehends one of the main traits of Honneth's kinship with the first generation of the Frankfurt School and his related concern in identifying an intramundane transcendence, that is, the emergence of emancipatory interests within social reality.[8] In other words, it becomes easier to grasp the "critical" dimension of his works. For one of the distinctive features of the Frankfurt School's critical theory is not the mere description or depiction of social dynamics, but its effort to identify with social suffering, "adopting the point of view of those who are practically interested in the transformation of society" (Emmanuel Renault 2010, p. 222). Second, the idea of recognition itself becomes clearer. In contrast with many perspectives, which might refer to the so-called identity politics, Honneth's paradigm is wider, and aimed at encompassing a spectrum of phenomena that emerge precisely due to his focus on the experience of damage.[9] Accordingly, the normative character of recognition becomes easier to acknowledge, whereby normativity is rooted in the epiphenomena that such a negative approach highlights. Finally, I argue that, with this approach, we can tackle and clarify the monism in its theoretical and critical dimension. Starting from the experience of the negative, recognition receives the character of a desideratum, both by the theory and by social actors themselves. That would be Honneth's claim. Insofar, the paradigm of recognition should be a—more or less adequate—highlighting of what actually structures the social demands and of how they could be better answered, not a predetermined simplification of the social complexity.

This methodological negativism instantiates Honneth's tendency to unfold his different analyses from the social suffering, which has two principal faces: social pathologies and experiences of injustice.

1.1 Social Pathologies as Kindler of Critique: Three Different Programmatic Views

It seems helpful here to sketch three Honnethian contributions that focus on social pathologies and that show different vectorialities and evolutions: "Pathologies of the Social," "A Social Pathology of Reason," and "The Diseases of Society." My claim here is that, by looking at these writings we can distinguish between three different phases, or directions, within Honneth's elaborations, with regard to how he interprets

---

[8] "It is perhaps not entirely wrong to speak here of 'quasi-transcendental interests' of the human race; and possibly it is even justified to talk at this point of an 'emancipatory' interest that aims at dismantling social asymmetries and exclusions" (Honneth 2003d, p. 174). See Deranty 2009, pp. 456–60
[9] It is noteworthy that Honneth's first work represents precisely an example of this effort, that is, the researched and as much as possible particular identification with the issues at stake in social reality. See Honneth 1979.

social pathologies and, correspondingly, how he conceives critique's apt engagement with those pathologies is quietly illuminating.

The first text we will look at is the early essay "Pathologies of the Social" (original German: 1994), where Honneth proposes a concise historical interpretation of social philosophy, which is expressed as a critical social philosophy. He notes how, from Rousseau onward, a number of thinkers engaged with social analysis have used formulations such as "alienation," "bifurcation," "reification," "massification," "social leveling" (Honneth 2007b, pp. 10 – 16), "demystification," "depersonalization," and "commercialization" (Honneth 2007b, p. 35). Although there are clear differences between the concepts (and the authors who elaborate them), all these terms express a shared theoretical and ethical drive that "is primarily concerned with determining and discussing processes of social development that can be viewed as misdevelopments (*Fehlentwicklungen*), disorders, or 'social pathologies'" (Honneth 2007b, p. 4).

Honneth's claim here is not so much the definition or the explication of the concept of social pathology. Rather, he scrutinizes the methodological possibilities of a philosophy able to determine it. Systematically, there are three main features of Honneth's argument to be emphasized. [10]

First, Honneth argues that social philosophy never appears "as a positive theory" (Honneth 2007b, p. 34). It does not deal with a substantial, detailed prefiguration or prescription of how the society *should* be or which norm-systems should guide ist reproduction. Rather, it gets involved with social reality, and more particularly with those aspects of it that do not simply appear unjust or unfair, but which reflect actual suffering, harm, and the deprivation of meaning. Thus, two claims are advanced. On the one side, the abovementioned concepts highlight phenomena that are meant to be social. They are not the mere consequence of an individual decision, fault, or error,[11] but represent a pervasive dysfunction that social partners ought to live in within their own context. On the other side, and consequently, these concepts rely "upon criteria of ethical nature" (Honneth 2007b, p. 4). Thus, given that the symptoms emerge in the individual condition and life-elaboration of an individual life, the ethical dimension shows itself in the "destruction of the conditions necessary for human flourishing" (Deranty 2009, p. 321). Hence, such pathologies would be social precisely because they hinder the ethical possibilities of individuals who live in a particular environment.

Therefore, the second point Honneth emphasizes is that the very possibility of becoming aware of these social diseases is based on normative, ethical criteria that announce (from reflex) a certain—albeit indeterminate—figure of healthiness:[12]

---

[10] For an extensive study Honneth's account of social pathologies, see R. C. Smith 2017, ch. 2.
[11] This idea is well explicated in the interpretation of Lukács's idea of reification. See Honneth 2008, pp. 25 – 26.
[12] "The concepts of 'diagnosis' and 'pathology,' both of which are closely tied to that about which social philosophy seeks to gain knowledge, stem from the realm of medicine. 'Diagnosis' is under-

the determination of social pathologies in social philosophy always proceeds with a view to the social conditions that promote the individual's self-realization. The fact that a whole spectrum of highly diverse standards of evaluation is nevertheless revealed as soon as these approaches are compared with one another is not related to differences in formal-ethical perspective, but to the respective foundational concept of personal self-realization (Honneth 2007b, p. 37).

Honneth's strong historical interpretation therefore goes in the following direction: in order to grasp pathology as such, certain ethical standards are required, which determine our judgments over the state of health. These criteria are ethical in the sense that they concern the social context and a certain perspective about the good, but formal because they concern the social conditions of an open-ended development, not a precise and predetermined vision of it. It is, moreover, interesting to notice that, despite the open character of such a formal ethics, oriented as it is toward a non-determined personal self-realization, this concept is considered sufficient to indicate those developmental outcomes that can be identified as harmful. The development is therefore open and formal, but its misdevelopments would be identifiable.

Turning back to Honneth's historical interpretation, the formal character of ethics is not simply apparent, but is rather the fruit of his interpretation. In the history of social philosophy there are two main substantial currents through which flesh was put on the bones of formal ethics:

> Starting with Rousseau and continuing through Hegel, Marx, Adorno, Plessner, and Arendt, social philosophy has always been characterized by anthropological or historical-philosophical figures of thought out of which ethical criteria for determining social pathologies have arisen so seamlessly that they could never have been recognized as such (Honneth 2007b, pp. 40–41).

But, for the decisive impact of Nietzschean perspectivism,[13] such substantive grounding statements illustrating an ideal social development that proceeds according to the original figure of human beings or a teleological vectoriality have been set aside. The methodological possibilities of social philosophy are then pushed to a crossroads: either they reduce themselves to a culturally restricted perspective—namely, a hermeneutical point of view—or they are somehow allowed to persist in observing the sociality from an ethical viewpoint that represents a universal standard, a theoretical and ethical threshold useful for identifying misdevelopments:

---

stood here as the precise detection and definition of an illness affecting the human organism. The clinical notion of 'health' serves as a standard for the evaluation of abnormal symptoms—a notion that is often, for the sake of simplicity, regarded as consisting in the body's ability to function. The concept of 'pathology' complements this concept of 'diagnosis': whereas 'pathology' originally indicated the theory of illnesses, it now mostly indicates an abnormal state of affairs. Pathology therefore represents precisely that organic aberration that is disclosed or defined in a diagnosis" (Honneth 2007b, p. 34).

[13] See Deranty 2009, p. 323.

> Social philosophy's current problem thus consists in the following question: if, in accordance with its theoretical aim, social philosophy is dependent upon universal criteria whose validity can no longer be indirectly proven by a presupposed anthropology, then its continued existence is wholly contingent upon whether a formal ethics can be justified or not (Honneth 2007b, p. 40).

In other words, how can social philosophy find or determine the ethical normal standard in light of which social suffering could be identified, thus indicating a path to healthiness? How is this healthiness to be conceived? How should such a formal ethics be justified? A proceduralization of ethics—as proposed by Habermas—would be, according to Honneth, unsuccessful, since the "interpretive authority" of social philosophy "would be passed on to those who, as members of a concrete society, would alone decide on what is to be considered 'pathological' about their social form of life" (Honneth 2007b, p. 41). The issue at stake is theory's immanence to the analyzed society. And here it becomes clear that some criticisms directed against Honneth's searching for universal ethical standards are either misdirected or coming from an external point of view,[14] since what is sought is not a universal a priori or even a mere deductive justification, as if the position sought was ahistorical.

Honneth is on the lookout for criteria that are certainly formal and, therefore, transcultural. But this means that he does not want to endorse culturally determined visions above the good or substantial social goals. Clearly, the shortcoming he sees in procedural ethics is that they lack grip. That is, they prescribe certain rules, but they do so besides and before social facticity. What Honneth is looking for is precisely the possibility of an immanent critique that, in order to articulate itself, cannot be totally enveloped in a particular historical and cultural context. That context must represent its material and its starting point, but the theory needs a certain distance to be able to move, to be able to illuminate, or even just to be able to say that something is wrong in the social situation. Even such a minimalist observation, from which the discussion over social pathologies takes its impetus, requires certain ethical criteria. In order for philosophy to avoid being condemned to aphasia, it needs standards that have at least some foundation and, therefore, some detachment from the immanence—that is, critical philosophy must not be completely assimilated in the observations to which they are applied.

Moreover, the formality of ethics Honneth seeks would also be able to accept the challenge posed by liberal pluralism. The procedural overlapping consensus systems have no say on the consequences: according to Honneth, they lack political engagement.[15] Honneth intends, by means of the prospective position gained by (and proper of) critical thinking, to identify where the appearance of health is already announced. The tasks of symptomatology, epidemiology, etiology, and, above all, of prognosis are to be accomplished by a critical philosophy embedded in those social

---

[14] See Fabian Freyenhagen 2015, pp. 133–34.
[15] See Honneth 2012a, pp. 35–55.

1.1 Social Pathologies as Kindler of Critique: Three Different Programmatic Views

ethical perspectives that, seen in the light of a generalizing attitude, can be considered as valid within the view of pluralism.[16]

Consequently, Honneth does not disregard the role that can be played by a "historically relativized justification of ethics," claiming that it allows us to conceive of social philosophy "as an instance of reflection" (Honeth 2007b, p. 42). Yet, historically situated—and where else, if not there?—critique requires adhering to a term of comparison, which, following Honneth, can be found only in the formulation and elaboration of a "weak, formal anthropology" (Honneth 2007b, p. 41).

Although Honneth is rather hermetic in this text, that is, he does not fully outline what features this merely formal anthropology should possess, we can already identify three of them that will accompany us throughout our investigation. More precisely, here the reasons behind the paradigm of recognition emerge. First, given the hermeneutical consequences of perspectivism, such a paradigm cannot find its justification in a philosophy of history which attributes the role of "bearer of historical progress" to certain groups (Deranty 2009, p. 323). Hence, since, according to Honneth's reading, the ethical justification has always been performed thanks to a historical or an anthropological ideal term of comparison, he opts for the latter. However, second, in order to avoid the patent difficulties that availing such a concept would involve, 'anthropology' is not meant to be a substantive definition of the human being, at least programmatically. Therefore, third, the formality of such anthropology is to be understood in a twofold meaning.

First, it concerns the individuation and discussion of social conditions: "This ethical background condition is formal in the sense that it only normatively emphasizes the social preconditions of human self-realization, and not the goals served by these conditions" (Honneth 2007b, p. 36). The ethical idea of a formal anthropology derives its characters only in acknowledging and posing the conditions of an undamaged human development, and is not therefore oriented to and does not stem from a substantive image of human nature or its goals. Although one can argue that in the idea of self-realization a certain substantial image of human nature and good is already present, Honneth believes that the absence of content that he gives to this tendency of individuals should screen his thinking from such charges. Focusing on social conditions and allowing the premises of the critique to be led by a (quasi-)phenomenological observation of social reality should be sufficient to guarantee the formality of the theory. But formality has another fundamental character: it also concerns *how* this anthropology shall be elaborated. Indeed, what is at stake in the proposals considered by Honneth—especially Habermas's proposals—is an analysis of the social practices of speech. Honneth wants to highlight social and human interactions and thereby to derive subjectivity from intersubjectivity: actors from acts. The formality consists of—and therefore also can be found in—the very structure of the self, which cannot be determined monologically, but only through

---

[16] Regarding the medical tasks of a critical theory before social pathologies, see Zurn 2011.

certain types of relations: 'self' is not to be intended as substance, but as pole of interaction in the first place. The proposal derived from Honneth's first confrontation with social pathologies is then a formal ethics based on a formal anthropology, namely, on an analysis of intersubjectivity.

Analyzing two further Honnethian writings—respectively, "A Social Pathology of Reason" and "The Diseases of Society"—we can obtain an insight into various themes that will be shown as decisive in the development of Honnethian thought.

In "A Social Pathology of Reason" (original German: 2007), Honneth engages the tradition of the Frankfurt School directly. In this case as well, his approach can be defined as negative, since the starting point, taken as the key to critique, is represented by the category of social pathology. But, after a closer look, Honneth's writing focuses on a binomial consisting of rational universal and, correspondingly, rational deficit. As Frayenhagen emphasizes,[17] three main features of this later essay could be sketched as follows: the idea of social rationality, capitalism as object of criticism, and the conjoined analysis of Freud's thought. Regarding the first point, Honneth claims that the pivotal concept of critical theory, which discloses its methodological possibilities as well, is that of the "rational universal," shared with or inherited from Hegel through Marx and the Left Hegelians. Always speaking from an ethical point of view, that is, considering the concept as concerning the conditions of individual self-realization, Honneth outlines two main features. First, society is seen as the rationality's complex field of concretion, where its forms take shape and reproduce themselves through practices. Second, and consequently, such rationality requires a social —namely, an intersubjective—dimension.

> The representatives of Critical Theory hold with Hegel the conviction that the self-actualization of the individual is only successful when it is interwoven in its aims—by means of generally accepted principles or ends—with the self-actualization of all the other members of society (Honneth 2009g, p. 26).

However, in his arguments aimed at distinguishing the Frankfurt School—and his own position—from liberalism and communitarianism,[18] Honneth deepens further useful concepts, namely, those of reciprocity and universality. On the one hand, given the aims of social analysis, critical theory cannot narrow its own horizon to an atomistically understood individual but must comprehend and embrace the cooperative and reciprocal dimension of social practices as the extents in which instances of rationality can find their better instantiation and realization. As Heikki Ikäheimo observes, the Frankfurt School would propose a kind of normative essentialism that characterized Hegel,[19] according to which social forms of interaction embody and realize human rationality in an ongoing process. On the other hand, social realizations

---

[17] See Freyenhagen 2015, pp. 134–35.
[18] See Honneth 2009g, pp. 27–29.
[19] See Heikki Ikäheimo 2011.

of rationality through historical forms have to be considered as a universal dynamic, that is, as something that could be rationally justified: thereby, despite the necessary cultural and historical specificity of any particular social form, certain rational standards would represent a sort of comparative guarantee.

Without giving too much ontological weight to Honneth's reading, it seems that rationality in some way pushes for its own realization. Keeping in mind that the matter is normative, it becomes clear why the boundaries between "description" and "prescription" are respectively "blurred" (Honneth 2009g, p. 29). One could say that this very blurring lies along the twofold dimension of rationality. This concept—understood normatively as expressing forms of social life that conduct along paths of self-realization—occupies the position both of the observer and of the observed. In this sense, a social pathology would be that (observed) form of rationality, that is, that social instantiation of it, which the rationality-as-observer identifies as frustrating its own claims. This hiatus between the observer and the observed, which should share the same—historically located, but justified—normative rationality, is precisely the key to comprehend what "pathology of reason" means: "The organizational form of social relations in capitalism prevents rational principles that, as far as our cognitive potential is concerned, are already at hand, from applying to practical life" (Honneth 2009g, p. 29). The fact that rationality is "already at hand" can be seen in its dimensions that were—and are—already unfolded in social formations through their historical development—at least in that rationality that is exercised by the observer. (Though not only in this way, as we shall see.) In this sense, the hermeneutical threshold, the theoretical perspective useful to the actualization of critique, as well as to the perception of its universalism, once again should not be considered as an ahistorical eye that judges history from outside. On the contrary, thanks precisely to the historical development of reason, some domains of society are endowed with those normative standards that allow the critique to be exercised, to make it an immanent critique. Moving to the second point of the essay, Honneth underscores that the Frankfurt School's tradition aims at criticizing the complex and pervasive social formations of capitalism. Indeed, the focus of critical theory points a finger not only at social injustice, but should also provide an apt "explanation of the processes that obscure that injustice" (Honneth 2009g, p. 30). In this sense, the rational *mis*developments shall be unveiled in two dimensions: a) the "objective" one, which focuses on the irrationality of social instantiations that hinder, through their mechanisms and consequences, a full-fledged path of self-realization; and b) the "subjective" one, which names the reasons behind individuals' detachment from their actual situation, preventing them from becoming aware of the state of things, which lies concealed.

At this point, we can raise a major question about the reliability of such a critique, for the theoretical perspective is supposed to be immanent to society and imputes dysfunctions that can be hidden from the eyes of those who experience them firsthand. How is it meant to disclose a rational and, correspondingly, universal level of comprehension, more than simply a voice in the crowd, confinable as merely a culturally punctual point of view? In other words, how are we allowed to understand that *this* immanent critique addresses and spotlights dynamics actually present in society?

Once again, the answer comes from the negative dimension of the critical attitude, explicated by Honneth's reference to the Freudian influence on the Frankfurt School. It is suffering from certain symptoms that shows a social condition as pervasively frustrating, whether its subjects find the situation inextricable or not:

> Critical Theory no doubt takes Freudian psychoanalysis as its methodological model for how it establishes a connection between defective rationality and individual suffering.... [T]he impetus to bring the category "suffering" into connection with the very pathologies of social rationality probably finds its origin in the Freudian idea that every neurotic illness arises from an impairment of the rational ego and must lead to individual cases of stress from suffering (Honneth 2009g, p. 38).

Keeping again the clinical simile that plays a decisive role in "Pathologies of the Social," Honneth upholds that suffering emerges as symptom when certain impairments or failures present themselves as identifiable epiphenomena of a social dysfunction. Although this nexus rests on a strong assumption, namely, that one can infer to social conditions an inability to disclose one's own self-realization, another Freudian insight appears fundamental in order to test the claims of critical theory:

> the stress from suffering presses toward a cure by means of exactly the same rational powers whose function the pathology impedes. An assumption about what in general is to count as a self-evident condition for admission into psychoanalytic treatment also accompanies this suggestion—namely, that the individual who subjectively suffers from a neurotic illness also wants to be free from that suffering (Honneth 2009g, pp. 39–40).

And it is precisely this push for healthiness that Honneth individuates as the keystone of the tradition of the Frankfurt School and of its possibility to survive.[20] The importance of the "emancipatory interest" can be clarified by referring to two main issues, different sides of the same coin, as it were. First, it would represent a sort of test that reflects the fallacy of certain forms of social interaction. Second—and to this extent—it would show the objectivity of critical analysis: without the aforementioned objective side of rationality, a reflexive awareness on the part of those involved in and touched by social pathologies could not take place. If, on the one hand, suffering shows the actual possibilities of a critique that adheres to social reality, the presence of an emancipatory interest shows, shows on the other hand, a vectoriality of social rationality: the latter, in some way, manifests itself in

---

[20] "Without a realistic concept of 'emancipatory interest' that puts at its center the idea of an indestructible core of rational responsiveness on the part of subjects, this critical project will have no future" (Honneth 2009g, pp. 41–42).

1.1 Social Pathologies as Kindler of Critique: Three Different Programmatic Views — 23

its own tendency to evolution. However, this cannot be presupposed by the critique, but only ascertained from it.

In the last text that we are going to consider here, "The Diseases of Society," Honneth faces the issues of social pathologies twenty years after the first time and formulates, according to Hirvonen, a thick conception of social pathologies.[21] The subtitle, "Approaching a Nearly Impossible Concept," already shows that Honneth once more wants to deal with the problem by starting from the elusiveness of the concept and consequently to elaborate a programmatic view for critical theory. To this point in his inquiries, Honneth has not comprehensively defined the concept of social pathology. Rather, he has defined the possibilities to be fathomed and grasped by deriving it from socially experienced suffering. This work also starts precisely by considering the affected subject: any question to be asked should concern first and foremost the "addressee" of the supposed diseases, since, as Zurn emphasizes,[22] an accepted epidemiology represents an irreplaceable step for such analysis, which starts from the emerging negative epiphenomena within social life. But, inasmuch as the very determination of the spectrum of pathologies does not represent a mere empirical datum or evidence,[23] the identification of society as pathogenic presupposes some hypotheses over the issue.

For this reason, Honneth decides to focus on Mitscherlich and Freud as significant examples for both their methodological approach and their conclusions. They try to explain the symptomatology inquiring "psychic constellations" and take into account the social environment—thus not splitting individual and societal (Honneth 2014a, p. 685). For both Freud and Mitscherlich, the deficiencies manifesting within a personal existence must be traced back to their interactions with and within their social context or, more precisely, to the personal process of social integration. In this sense, there are two particular issues that convince Honneth of the cogency of the arguments. On the one hand, both treat the diseases without narrowing them to the level of individual life-choice or responsibility: though they share the assumption, according to which there is actually "an intimate bond between such" social "pathologies and individual symptoms" (Honneth 2014a, p. 690), the sought solution implies an analysis of the environment, which lays the foundations for a structuralist diagnosis. Long story short, given the increase in cases without physical explanation, the causes of disease must reside in a dysfunctional coping with social demands, which would in turn lead to impairment or neurotic experiences.

However, and on the other hand, what seems rather convincing in the Freudian and Mitscherlichian depictions of such diseases is the assumption behind the nexus

---

21 See Onni Hirvonen 2018, pp. 9–14.
22 See Zurn 2011, pp. 362–66.
23 As Honneth shows, for all the three possible attributions of pathogenic causes (individuals, collective subjects and groups, and the society itself) there are several examples. See Honneth 2014a, pp. 684–85.

of individual symptomatology and social integration, namely, a certain perspective on how social reality should be conceived:

> They never endorsed the idea that social pathologies would present nothing but the generalized or extended psychic disorders of the members of society. On the contrary, both perceive society as an entity sui generis, whose potential functional disorders also have to be of another categorical kind than the illnesses that might strike singular persons during their lifetime. The "diseases" of society are to be understood as the causes of individuals' illnesses, but between these two terms stands an ontological difference prohibiting the use of one and the same psychological or psychoanalytical language in both cases (Honneth 2014a, p. 688).

Although this ontological vision—according to which the social cannot be obtained through a generalization of the individual—meets the initial and pivotal intuition in keeping with which social pathologies must be attributed to the social in its entirety, the limits of Mitscherlich's perspective (on which Honneth focuses most) represent the key through which Honneth outlines his own perspective. The shortcomings can be imputed to a missing critical potential and a concern with what could be called the ideological dimension of social pathologies.

The first flaw consists of a sort of medicalization of the matter, that is, in narrowing the analysis to the spectrum bound by taking only individual symptoms of impairment or nonfulfillment performances into account. Indeed, even if this is the most adequate starting point for Honneth, too—as shown in "Pathologies of the Social" and in "A Social Pathology of Reason"—relying exclusively on the subjectively perceived psychical encumbrances or imbalances could prevent one from acknowledging those pathologies, which "consist of behavioral patterns that cause no individual suffering and thus also do not necessarily constitute psychic disorders" (Honneth, 2014a, p. 690). In other words, there could also be no psychic or suffering emergence that help in spotting a pathology, since, as already mentioned, the individual capability of awareness regarding her own situation can be affected by a systemic hindering. In this sense, though the two references explicitly expressed by persons—psychical suffering and the emancipatory interest—represent the main circumstantial evidence of *mis*developments and of rationality's pressures to self-actualization, the position gained by the critique should also disclose phenomena that do not reach the observable surface.

The second shortcoming of Mitscherlich's position consists precisely in his structuralist approach. Focusing on the dynamics of internalization of environmental norms and values and attributing the causes of pathologies to difficulties in coping with the demands implied by such processes, Mitscherlich elaborates a model of social efficiency based on the balance between individual and social instances. That is, the social whole could harmoniously reproduce if two conditions are respected during the process of social integration:

> (a) the rules of behavior to be learned must not be so rigid and restrictive as to suffocate the characteristically human need for individuation; and (b) these rules must be constantly adapted

to an environment in steady flux due to being transformed by human innovative capacity in a manner that allows for motivated and competent adolescents. Openness for individual deviation and power to provide security in dealing with new technological or social challenges—flexibility as well as confidence-giving determinacy—these are the two not easily combined capacities that, according to Mitscherlich, prevailing norms and values need to have if social integration is to run smoothly (Honneth 2014a, p. 694).

Once the key to social reproduction has been identified in the accordance between these two factors, it becomes clear that pathologies arise when the values or norms leave either too much or too little space for individual experimentation and innovation. Neither in one case nor in the other would the person be truly free, either because she is totally surmounted by the presence of an intrusive alterity, or because she is exposed to it without any possible access, that is, without being provided, through culture and education, with the necessary means of biographical elaboration. However—and here lies Honneth's second criticism—Mitscherlich means for the correct measure between the contrasting instances to be definable "independently of any information about the normative self-understanding of the society in question" (Honneth 2014a, p. 696). In other words, the aim would be to test the social formation's reproduction rules and norms from the point of view of their efficiency, measuring their ability to provide the new social members with the appropriate conditions for implementing their self-realization. Representing what might seem to be the solution presented in "Pathologies of the Social"—the determination of formal social conditions for self-realization—Honneth claims that overseeing society's normative content is rather misleading: "To cut a long story short, determining the functional requirements of social life and, with it, getting to the bottom of what a potential systematic disorder might consist in, involves restricting oneself to the current self-understanding of a historical epoch" (Honneth 2014a, p. 697). Indeed, one could also say that already in Mitscherlich's perspective some historically situated values are at stake, insofar as such an importance of the individual possibility of freedom within the social context represents a modern and contemporary idea. Nonetheless, in Honneth's criticism lie two important hints. On the one hand, it confirms that over time he maintains a clear—if not increasing—importance that historical non-naïvity holds within the critique: while seeking a formal level capable of accommodating the challenge posed by pluralism, he proposes a critique *of* time, *from* time. On the other hand, keeping in mind the argument previously set forth against the position of Freud and Mitscherlich, one can say that a too formalist approach would not be able to adequately notice the ideological features of an apparently healthy society.

A third problem lies in the unidirectionality of this analysis of social pathologies, which in Honneth's eyes is too concentrated on the process of social integration and on the hitches that could occur by the internalization of social demands. Though the learning dynamics of mediation between the inner life and environmental constraint is certainly essential for the purposes of social reproduction, social life is constituted from and survives through other dimensions that cannot be faced through such a monological perspective.

Referring to the "traditional line of inquiry from Marx to Parsons," Honneth argues that there are three fundamental dimensions that constitute what a society is, what are its challenges, and its possibility to survive: "confrontation with external nature, social shaping of inner nature, and regulation of inter-human relations" (Honneth 2014a, p. 698). Hence, given the intuition according to which social criticism should perceive dysfunctions within a society itself, an adequate account of social pathologies should result from the consideration of these three dimensions. Neglecting their importance would narrow its own diagnostic gaze.

Honneth therefore makes a proposal that can do justice to the second fruitful premise of Freud and Mitscherlich, that is, that the analysis of society should move on its own level, not anthropomorphizing the social world through a generalization of human and individual illnesses. Taking this into account and aiming to properly consider the aforementioned dimensions of social life, Honneth argues that what must be considered in order to grasp social diseases is the "institutional arrangement" of a given society (Honneth 2014a, p. 699). The solution provided therefore aims to leave a mere subjectivist level by engaging in a more social-ontological inquiry, that is, the analysis of institutional reality. Honneth thereby does not neglect the importance of referring to individual experience, since this is the place where the chances to conceive the social pathology take their clues: in what "we experience as a restriction of freedom" (Honneth 2014a, p. 700).

If the discussion of what concerns the relation between subject and society cannot be unilateral, focusing on the latter implies that it must be regarded as a whole, namely, in its three essential cycles of reproduction: relation with nature, social integration, and interpersonal practices. More precisely, by not focusing on every single dimension, the critique has to turn its attention to their interplay and to their mutual adjustments:

> Here, on this higher level of the entanglement of diverse functional spheres, there might also occur disorders and frictions, namely, in cases where the respective institutional regulations contradict or even mutually disenable each other.... What such frictions and tensions have in common with individual illnesses is that they display a troubled relationship of a subject to its self, whether this subject is a person or a society. And in the case of societies, the restriction of freedom, which belongs to our concept of "disease," consists in these functional spheres' mutually preventing each other from successfully developing, as their specific institutional solutions get in each other's way (Honneth 2014a, p. 701).

By so doing, Honneth also closes this writing with a programmatic proposal, that is, with a necessary rehabilitation of an organic conception of society. This social-ontological move represents in his eyes the only chance to detect social pathologies:

> One can only eventually speak of "diseases of society" coherently and substantially enough if one represents the society as an organism in which the individual spheres or subsystems,

thought of as organs, are cooperating so harmoniously that we can work out an idea of its unhindered, "free" development (Honneth 2014a, p. 701).

Starting from the analysis of these three Honnethian writings, we have reached an overlook, a point of access to his thought. Indeed, these three respectively programmatic intentions show what could be called three distinct phases of his thought or—probably better—three different but always present dimensions or accents that reciprocally involve each other and take over, in subsequent periods, the balance of his productions. Put synthetically, in his reflections on social pathologies, Honneth takes the ascertainment of such dysfunctions and misdevelopments as an unfolding point of critique, as a reflection point in the presence of suffering. Depending on the various assumptions and focuses gradually employed by Honneth, he himself makes the following programmatic statements. The attainability of critique should rely on a) the formulation of a weak, minimal, and formal anthropology, as ethical and normative landmark; b) the faculty to identify an emancipatory interest, which would represent the objective pressures of rationality's tendency to self-realization within and through social concretions; c) an organic depiction and conception of social reality and of its inner interplays.

Here, the characteristic multipolarity of Honneth's paradigm already emerges, since, as Jean-Philipp Deranty makes clear, the anthropological and the normative levels overlap and follow one another in a framework of justification and critique.[24] One can add to this binomial a third element or dimension, that is, the social-ontological one that crops up in the last lines of "The Diseases of Society."

1.2 Vulnerability and the Normative Experience of Injustice

The other side of Honneth's methodological negativism concerns a bundle of phenomena that could be summarized by the concept of 'moral injury.' As Deranty explains, this theme helps Honneth to show the normative fabric social life is woven with "either in a historical sense, in the reconstruction of the normative core of modern society, or in a critical sense, when it comes to uncovering new applications of those principles" (Deranty 2009, p. 399). To deal with the subject—without already approaching *The Struggle for Recognition*—we will focus on two aspects of the issue: a) the identification of the demands of justice as a pre-theoretical fact capable of disclosing the critique; and b) the connection between the concept of human dignity and that of vulnerability. By so doing, we will add further elements to the concepts of emancipatory interest and self-realization, and introduce the dimension of conflict.

---

24 See Deranty 2009, p. 463.

In "The Social Dynamics of Disrespect," (original German: 1994) Honneth again engages the theoretical possibilities of critical thinking, taking Horkheimer's aim of developing a theory that could be conceived as self-reflection of the social itself as his point of departure. Briefly sketching a history of the Frankfurt School, Honneth describes its difficulties—due to its inability to escape positively from the Marxian setting—to connect to pre-theoretical phenomena, thus falling into a negative sociology. At this point, he embraces Habermas's communicative shift, because the linguistic rules of agreement can actually represent "a pre-theoretical sphere of emancipation through which critique can ground its normative standpoint within social reality" (Honneth 2007c, p. 68). In other words, linguistic consensus stands for that practical context addressed by the theory in order not to self-produce its own aims and conceptual frameworks: in verbal interactions, individuals meet and confront one another, bringing with themselves certain expectations, already sharing a horizon of meaning and the form of their communicative exchanges. The structure of these elements therefore represents an a priori, (quasi-)transcendental dimension embedded in practical life. According to Habermas, the task of the critical theory is to consider the replacement of this normative horizon, proper to the practical and plastic facticity of the lifeworld, with other practical logics and imperatives coming from rationalized systems—that is, the so-called 'colonization thesis.' Identifying such a dimension of communication—which is indeed practical and structural at the same time, that is, which belongs to the experience and shapes it—the theory would represent an instance of reflection capable of giving voice to the demands already at stake in social life, and of justifying a not-substantially conceived account of progress:

> In shifting Critical Theory from the production paradigm to the paradigm of communication, Habermas unveiled a social sphere that fulfills all the presuppositions included in the claim to intramundane transcendence. In communicative action, subjects encounter each other within the horizons of normative expectations whose disappointment becomes a constant source of moral demands that go beyond specifically established forms of domination (Honneth 2007c, p. 69).

Honneth embraces Habermas's communicative shift and shares the perspective from which the pre-theoretical sources of critical theory should be found within intersubjective interaction and those normative expectations that inhabit and shape it. Moreover, Honneth shares once again the idea that it is always by an interruption, a discrepancy, a negative that the fabric of normative expectations is revealed, a fabric that until then had been hidden behind the explicit. But, Honneth claims, approaching factual interactions, it becomes clear that the fundamental experience revealing such an underpinning structure and network cannot be represented by a failure of linguistic rules, but by the unfulfilled demands for identity. Living (and acting) persons "experience an impairment of what we can call their moral experiences, i.e., their 'moral point of view,' not as a restriction of intuitively mastered rules of language, but as a violation of identity claims acquired in socialization" (Honneth 2007c, 70).

Many "historical and sociological studies" show that the core of the moral experience embedded in such discrepancy-moments—namely, Honneth specifies, in the experience of the lower social classes and of protest movements—never appears as an explicitly formulated and coherent scheme of principles. Rather, the spark of protests is always "the experience of having their intuitive notions of justice violated" (Honneth 2007c, p. 71). Thus, Honneth is taking at the same time three significant steps, actualizing "the so-called 'negative phenomenology' of social life" (Hirvonen 2019, p. 5). First, he is pointing to conflict as the primary epiphenomenon in which individuals' motivations can be pinpointed. Second, Honneth identifies critical theory as moment of social self-reflection, as an element of society capable of unravelling such motives. Third, and given these first two points, such a theory must be able to identify with the non-positivity of expectations of justice, which arise when they are ignored or infringed upon, and which are only intuitively intertwined with positive moral content.

One could therefore say that Honneth, thanks to his attention to the negative, conceives of critical theory as responsible for giving voice to a certain type of suffering that reveals itself in the mesh of society and in the very individual experience of such suffering.[25] Here, with respect to the analysis of social pathologies, we can add a further determination of the critical field of inquiry: the normative criteria that were presuppositions for identifying the so-called misdevelopments are described as emerging in the intersubjective interaction and in "the human lifeform" (Hirvonen 2019, p. 6). As Honneth explains:

> this model asserts a close connection between the kinds of violation of the normative assumptions of social interaction and the moral experiences subjects have in their everyday communication. If those conditions are undermined by the fact that people are denied the recognition they deserve, they will generally react with moral feelings that accompany the experience of disrespect—shame, anger or indignation.... The feelings of injustice that accompany structural forms of disrespect represent a pre-theoretical fact, on the basis of which a critique of the relations of recognition can identify its own theoretical perspective in social reality (Honneth 2007c, p. 72.).

The veering from the Habermasian communicative shift toward a paradigm of recognition is therefore motivated by the persuasion that the experiences of injustice reveal a deeper normative level than that explicable through linguistic rules, a field

---

25 As Renault explains well, the experience of injustice represents the field or the moment where subjects themselves become aware of the normative ground that underpins their social interactions. See Renault 2004, pp. 28–61 and 117–27. Therefore, social criticism's reflexive character is considered here, contrary to what has been argued during the reflection on social pathologies, almost as a reproposition and a formalization of the experiences of the involved subjects, rather than as a diagnosis of symptoms that are to be considered even as virtually inaccessible on the part of lifeworld actors —because of their eventual unawareness with regard to the misdevelopments they are affected by.

that precedes the dialogical one and therefore coincides with the pre-theoretical anchorage the theory must refer to.

However, two issues have not yet been addressed at this stage. First, it is not yet clear why the intersubjective field already preferred by Habermas should actually represent the privileged starting point for critical theory. Second, we are yet to understand why, leaving aside linguistic normativity, one has to land on the concept of recognition. These two questions can be answered precisely, I argue, through the binomial of "human dignity" and "vulnerability."

In "Integrity and Disrespect,"[26] Honneth approaches, referring to Bloch, the concept of human dignity, endorsing that idea by which it can only be accessed through a negative path. The moral reactions to insults, humiliations, offences and contempt reflect the normative assumptions to which the subjects have supposedly always referred, shedding light on one content—that of dignity—which therefore receives its definition by subtraction. Honneth claims that, by taking as point of departure the "language of everyday life", where those affected by moral harm "describe themselves" as injured in their positive self-comprehension (Honneth 1992a, p. 188), one can obtain a certain image of human self-realization that lies on intersubjective conditions. In this way, the theory does not need to presuppose a more or less positive concept of dignity, which could be easily criticized as substantial or as culturally determined. Once again, Honneth enforces the reciprocal implication of the notions of health and suffering: not only does the presence of suffering denote a lack of healthiness, but also the means for health are determined in opposition to those for damage. For, if moral damage is first perceived as disrespect that hinders a certain positive self-relation—that is, damage to one's own dignity as a person—this would imply, according to Honneth, that the moral intuitions of the affected refer to a positive image of dignity constituted within relationships in which such an image is formed, informed, and affirmed:

> If in a concept of the dignity, the complete integrity of man is only to be approximated by determining what forms personal insult and disrespect take, then, conversely, it would hold that the constitution of human integrity is dependent on the experience of intersubjective recognition.... the integrity of human subjects, vulnerable as they are to injury through insult and disrespect, depends on their receiving approval and respect from others (Honneth 1992a, p. 188).

It then becomes clear why Honneth decides to keep the Habermasian intersubjective framework. Not only, in fact, does intersubjectivity represent the field where our normative expectations, in their disappointment or frustration, arise. If the self-notion or self-perception of one's own integrity depends on the gestures that another *can* address to her, intersubjectivity represents not only the threshold of manifestation of

---

[26] Honneth 1992a. This essay is a revised version of the inaugural lecture given by Honneth on June 28, 1990, for his first year of teaching in Frankfurt. It therefore evidently has a programmatic value, useful in framing his entire theoretical perspective.

such a normative concept of the person, but also its genealogical spring with regard to the moral demands on the addressee.

And that is why such a concept of the person embeds, derives from, and relies on a particular relevance accorded to the concept of vulnerability. Without anticipating too many aspects, one can already say, however, that this importance can be attributed to "the internal, conceptual, and empirical connection between *physical vulnerability and social dependence*"(J. M. Bernstein 2005, p. 314). If, from the experience of moral damage, the decisiveness of the intersubjective dimension to the constitution of the idea of human dignity is derived, then one could argue that the primary character of the person consists in her vulnerability—namely, in her being dependent on the approval of others, or more generally on the position that others assume toward her.

So, the introduction of the concept of recognition within the communicative shift has two main reasons. The first has to do with the aspiration of a theory that can be nearer to the experience of injustice as it appears. The second concerns the content of the demands of justice (which are directed—also indirectly—to the possibility of considering oneself as worthy) and their addressee: the other is the only one who can confirm such worthiness, which has been eventually wounded. For her social exposition, the person is vulnerable to moral damage and needs recognition from others, because her own self-consideration is clearly not self-posed.

Hence, the framework within which the paradigm of recognition receives its theoretical dimensions begins to emerge.

First, social suffering represents a decisive element in anchoring theory to the effectiveness of lifeworld. Also in this sense, the dimension of conflict emerges as epiphenomenon capable of unveiling an emancipatory interest that is experienced by the involved subjects thanks to their moral intuitions and triggered by such suffering. As insightfully stated by Renault, Honneth's social philosophy, due to its clinical approach, implies anthropological and social-ontological presuppositions,[27] for the very possibility of identifying an always already embedded normative network presupposes a reference to positive social conditions (institutional spheres), intersubjective practices (relations), and an image of human dignity (self-relations).

This brings us to the second point, namely, the programmatic possibilities of the paradigm of recognition, which has to be, so to speak, porous and open. Without underestimating the positive theoretical premises of Honneth's elaborations, it nonetheless clearly emerges that his very aims arise from the consideration of the normative

---

27 "[T]he idea of the normative presuppositions of social life implies that the argument belonging to philosophical anthropology (some institutions are essential for human life) is associated with an argument that is belonging to social ontology (some behaviors are essential to institutions). In brief, Honneth's model could be interpreted as a mixed program of social philosophy combining a weak understanding of the descriptive side (as philosophical anthropology and social ontology) and a strong understanding of the normative side (as normative presupposition of the social life)" (Renault 2010, p. 236).

implications that come into play through the experience of moral injury. If, for example, Habermas's communicative shift certainly represents an embraced positive presupposition that determines the field of inquiry, it is its inadequacy in accounting for social experiences that persuades Honneth to broaden it in recognitional terms. It is, hence, not inaccurate to say that the paradigm of recognition receives its inquiry-issues from the opacity of moral feelings. Already taking social suffering regarding one's own identity and integrity as a point of departure encompasses a multidimensional structure, where the boundaries between the sociological, psycho-sociological, anthropological, moral, and political levels become blurred and entangled because of the (desired) adherence to actual phenomena.[28]

Respectively, third, the opacity of moral intuitions and reactions to damage and the experience of injury itself concern polarities, where a pivotal role is played by the mutual implication of hurt and health. Honneth in fact describes every form of recognition as the counterpart of damage-experiences and must therefore show itself able to penetrate the different levels within the moral damage that are shown to be inextricable. Honneth perceives this as the main task of his thinking: the redefinition of morality,[29] of the concept of justice, and of the idea of autonomy within an ethical perspective. For in the perception of injustice, normative standards are always embedded, and in social conflict, moral issues concerning dignity are always pursued; the critical proposal cannot be reduced to the level of a better equal distribution. Thus, not only does the horizon of the recognition paradigm have to be porous, but it should shape a "formal conception of ethical life" (Honneth 1995c, p. 175). That is, its fields have to be, according to Honneth, included in a perception of the good— a moral content lived as such by the lifeworld-subjects—intertwined in social practices, but within which the theory assumes a structural approach, aiming to a certain formality and not to culturally punctual visions of the good. In this sense, Honneth wants to distinguish "any concrete instantiations" of socially posed goods and "the structurally universal features of any socially organized forms" and preconditions for undamaged personal integrity (Zurn 2000, p. 118).

---

[28] See Renault 2010, p. 222.
[29] Such philosophical position can be summarized through a passage from Habermas:
"I conceive of moral behavior as a constructive response to the dependencies rooted in the incompleteness of our organic makeup and in the persistent frailty (most felt in phases of childhood, illness, and old age) of our bodily existence. Normative regulation of interpersonal relations may be seen as a porous shell protecting a vulnerable body, and the person incorporated in this body, from the contingencies they are exposed to. Moral rules are fragile constructions protecting *both* the physis from bodily injuries and the person from inner and symbolic injuries." (Jürgen Habermas 2003, pp. 33–34)
At the same time, it is interesting to note that such an all-encompassing tendency of Honneth's concept of recognition does not embrace a reflection on the so-called identity politics, without ever directly engaging in a dialogue with Charles Taylor's thinking. See, e.g. Simon Thompson 2006; and Wendy Martineau, Nasar Meer, and Simon Thompson 2012.

To summarize, the closeness with suffering would allow and imply an intersubjective perception of normativity as well as a recognitional perspective on intersubjectivity. But, given such a perspective, some important issues must arise. As Fraser states it, critical theory should be able to determine "what really *merits* the title of injustice, as opposed to what is *merely* experienced as injustice" (Fraser 2003a, p. 205). In other words, Fraser is asking whether Honneth's point of departure is legit. And are its implications theoretically bearable?

1.3 Some Preliminary Issues: Psychologization, Culturalization, and Teleology

In what follows, I want to mention three of the main criticisms that are moved against Honneth's perspective by which the *experience* of moral suffering is the starting point of the critique. Rather than arguing for or against such criticisms, the intention is rather to leave the issues open, in order to then let Honneth's texts speak for themselves and go deeper into the issues. Such observations can therefore play a guiding role, that is, they can help to better frame Honneth's paradigm, because a minimal consideration of them can immediately exclude certain doubts and deepen the justifying claim of some positions.

The first criticism could be named 'psychologization of injustice.' In fact, taking as a starting point—both in the case of social pathologies and in that of moral injury —the suffering experienced by individuals and their consequent inability to develop a positive image of themselves could imply the reduction of normative matters into psychological terms. Similarly, the positive representation of what is damaged, that is, the intuition on which the images of human dignity and integrity hinge, would come to coincide with an idea of psychological health. In doing so, Honneth would end up embracing a specific substantial content of the good, failing to define a formal concept of ethical life.[30] But, above all, two further consequences seem to seriously limit the potential of critical theory. Since Honneth's theory has to refer to psychologically perceived suffering, it risks, on the one hand, not being able to give voice to the injustice for which there is no symptoms—think of the ideological processes and dynamics[31]—and, on the other hand, it is also unable to justify any identity demand that is accompanied by phenomena of social exclusion or disrespect. If, therefore, Honneth is absolutely aware of this second risk—that is, that of more or less explicitly justifying demands for recognition of violent or reactionary

---

[30] "Despite [Honneth's] claim that he does not endorse a particular conception of the good, it can hardly be denied that his notion of self-realization is closely associated not only with Aristotle's notion of human flourishing (the fulfilment of a person's capacities and desires) but more importantly to psychological well-being or health" (Renante D. Pilapil 2011, p. 87).

[31] See Rosie Worsdale 2017.

groups[32]—the paradigm of recognition must provide further normative standards that do not directly derive from its negative access.

A second charge aimed at Honneth, raised by Nancy Fraser and Michael J. Thompson, is that of the 'culturalization of injustice,' which would imply an idealistic turn in critical theory. Such criticisms possess two principal cores. On the one hand, they claim that, due to an approach centered on identity claims, Honneth proposes "a reductive culturalist view of distribution" and therefore overstep fundamental objective issues of (in)justice (Fraser 2003b, p. 34).[33] Conversely, Fraser proposes a two-dimensional concept of justice, where "classical" justice issues and identity issues would be given due weight. In this sense, given an aim of parity of participation for every adult citizen in the democratic sphere, objective and intersubjective conditions cannot be reduced to one another. The participants of a democratic context must be able to benefit from a fair material distribution and be protected from phenomena such as cultural or racial discrimination. Confusing identity demands with material conditions of equality would make critique "detached from a confrontation with the economic and structural organization of society" (Thompson 2018, p. 575). In other words, the priority of the intersubjective dimension—that is, of recognition—would lead to a misunderstanding of the ontological status of the social, which is not "constituted by intersubjective social practices," and rather "is distinct from that intersubjectivity and possesses causal powers separate from it as well" (Thompson 2018, p. 575). These two criticisms, taken together, effectively question decisive points of Honneth's theory, which, in order to respond, must justify its empirical claims, the onto- and phylogenetic capabilities of recognition and its social-ontological consequences. In other words, what is under discussion is precisely the diameter, the adequacy, and the comprehensiveness of Honneth's paradigm.

A third problematic point can be tied with Honneth's teleological setting. In fact, by describing social justice as the achievement of a good—even formally posed through the determination of its intersubjective conditions—Honneth does not employ a deontological justification, but rather a teleological one,[34] trying to derive "an 'ought' from an 'is'" (Zurn 2000, p. 119). If justice has to be somehow determined as counterweight to intersubjective hindrances to positive self-perception, then the theory itself relies upon a (not yet precisely outlined) strong assumption: the desire of individuals to achieve self-realization, and its collocation in the social normative demands of subjects. Therefore, two of the main challenges facing Honneth—besides having to maintain the formality of his ethical concept without losing the link with lifeworldly facticity—are: a) to justify the motility of human beings toward self-realization within an intersubjective context and outside a substantial conception of human nature; and b) to provide a post-metaphysical concept of progress,

---

32 See Honneth 2007c, pp. 77–78.
33 See also Lois McNay 2008b.
34 See Pilapil 2011, p. 87.

by which this can be thought of as directed to a goal without an assumed aim, but conceived only as a result of an unfolding process. In other words, progress should be distinguishable a posteriori and not delineable a priori.

Thanks to this introductory incursion into the negative methodology and phenomenological tendency of Honneth's social thought, we have clarified some directions, while some challenges have emerged. The paradigm of recognition will have to prove that it can respond adequately.

First, an intention to implement Habermas's communicative turn with a deeper focus on damaged life, derived from the first generation of the Frankfurt School and especially from Adorno, has clearly emerged. Second, although starting from the wounds to the identity, integrity, and dignity of individuals, Honneth's claim would be not to reduce the spectrum of recognition to identity politics, but to include a more structural dimension of life in society and of the formation of the person. Precisely for this reason, third, the normativity of recognition derives above all from the experience of suffering understood as a grid of intelligibility of expectations always at stake: those on the good, submerged into the plot of relationships. Thus, finally, Honneth's monism, which consists in the persuasion of identifying in recognition *the* key to a post-modern ethical theory, would be legitimized by the overlap of the different levels present in the experience of injustice, which must represent the point of anchorage and the theoretical foundation for a critical theory not locked in either an aphasic perspective or a relativistically reducible one.

Chapter 2
A Post-Metaphysical Moral Grammar: *The Struggle for Recognition*

The Struggle for Recognition is the first work in which Honneth defines his paradigm of recognition in all its dimensions, laying the foundations for the later evolutions of his thought. For this reason, the analysis of this work is more detailed, and it is necessary to face and question many of its aspects. In fact, Honneth's concept of recognition and its implications in the elaboration of a social theory are indivisible: to deeply understand the former it is necessary to consider the latter. Thus we have to address the motivations that lead to identifying recognition as the pivot of social normative theory, but also the background that brought Honneth to his own definition of recognition, with its theoretical purposes and justifications.

The present chapter opens with an analysis of the relationship between Honneth and Hegel, oriented above all to show that the first's reading of the latter is significantly mediated by Jürgen Habermas, Ludwig Siep, and Andreas Wildt: in this sense, Honneth's interpretation, decidedly original, explicitly nonexegetical, and totally oriented to the tasks perceived as relevant for the social theory, finds a place in the *Hegelforschung* of his time (section 2.1).

The second section focuses on the use Honneth makes of George Herbert Mead, which represents one of the greatest points of both proximity and distance with Habermas. The discussion is not about the three distinct spheres of recognition that Honneth details in this case, but about the theoretical centrality of the Meadian ideas of social integration and practical identity to the determination of a subjective figure intersubjectively conceived, for the idea of progress, and for the justification of a moral account of social struggles (section 2.2).

The next section returns to the negative methodology set out in the previous chapter, retracing the steps through which Honneth defines three forms of moral damage in terms of misrecognition. In fact, although they are explicitly derived from the positive forms of recognition, the focus on misrecognition gives us an insight into the normative character of recognition and its link with the concept of relation-to-self (section 2.3).

Section four will turn to the Honnethian paradigm of recognition, connecting the formal concept of ethical life and Honneth's quasi-phenomenological reconstruction of its spheres. Here, Honneth defines recognition as a multi-polar intersubjective practice (love, respect, and esteem) that takes place in different interactive contexts (love-relations and friendships, legal relations, and social and cooperative relations) and underlies three forms of undamaged practical identity (self-confidence, self-respect, and self-esteem). As we shall see, this investigation reveals some important issues, such as the tension between the symmetry and asymmetry of recognition and the anthropological justification of the paradigm (section 2.4).

The final section aims to summarize the essential features of the concept of recognition as it emerges in *The Struggle for Recognition* and to focus some of the issues that will accompany us thorough our investigations: the internal tensions within the concept of recognition, its relationship with the subject's formation and with the institutional reality (section 2.5).

2.1 Honneth's Hegel: An Intersubjective Social Ontology

With a certain discontinuity with the previous works, Hegel—and more precisely the so-called Jena Period—represents the main reference of *The Struggle for Recognition*, through which Honneth seeks to elaborate an original social theory that is able to encompass a persuasive account of the conflict as the engine and own dynamic of social change; the reasons behind this choice are multiple and would require a quite demanding historical, exegetical, and theoretical collocation of Honneth's work.[1]

However, the first pages of the text can already show *ex abrupto* what theoretical problem Honneth is trying to face by bringing up Hegel. Indeed, the aim of the book is to propose a *third* concept of sociality, which could overcome the opposition between the individualistic and the Aristotelian views. In this sense, as Deranty rightfully claims, Honneth's "focus is not on Hegel, but on the ontology of the social, even before any concept of subjective identity and agency" (Deranty 2009, p. 192). In other words, the aims of the re-actualization of Hegel's thought derive from a theoretical need, that is, that of offering an original proposal to the social-philosophical research of the twentieth century. For this reason, Honneth's quite freely and explicitly external interpretation of the "The Scientific Way of Treating Natural Law" (1802), the *System of Ethical Life* (1802), the *Systementwurf* (1803–04), the *Realphilosophie* (1805–06), and of the predominance of recognition among other forms of praxis should not, in my view, raise too many issues.[2] Rather, the problem would be to

---

1 As Deranty remarkably summarizes, the reference to Hegel is by no means a foregone conclusion on the part of Honneth. In *Social Action and Human Nature* and *The Critique of Power*, Honneth sees Hegel as an obstacle to the de-idealization that the critical theory had to operate to face the contemporary challenges. But especially in the first of Honneth's two early works, co-written with Hans Joas, one can find the main reason for the initial interest in Hegel. In fact, Honneth believes that the possibilities of a materialistic social theory can be developed through the formulation of an intersubjectivistic anthropology. This, together with the Habermasian interpretation of the Jena writings, can represent a first contextualization of Honneth's motivations. Moreover, another series of Honneth's publications show the interest in performing a critique of society based on the experience of moral damage. All these other studies prior to *The Struggle for Recognition* thus represent the basis for the delineation of suffering as misrecognition, i.e. for the placement in social contexts of the origin of normativity and expectations of justice. See, in particular, Honneth 1995b.
2 Without a doubt, as Petherbridge shows through a close comparison between the Hegelian texts and Honneth's reading of them, Honneth's move consists of a quasi-unilateral focus on recognition, which tends to identify it with intersubjectivity itself. See Petherbridge 2013, ch. 6.

show whether Honneth's original social-philosophical proposals will be able to respect their own claims or not. In fact, Honneth's interpretation of the Hegelian conceptual world is too original and far too aimed toward his own purposes: an analysis conducted exclusively through historical-philosophical criteria would risk reducing one author to another.

However, and with this in mind, Honneth's use of Hegel is clarified through the beginning of *The Struggle for Recognition*, which starts with the depiction of a theoretical bifurcation within social philosophy, embodied by the classical figures of Hobbes and Machiavelli, on the one side, and Aristotle, on the other. Hobbes proposes a model of society constituted through conflict resulting from individual purposes and motivations, from subjects' capacity to put on the field rationally calculated aims and ends, which conflagrate as they clash with another's. In a nutshell, we are in front of a depiction of sociality as an outcome that presumes the encounter between already formed persons, the purposive-rationality of which orients their own aims, demands, interests, and motivations. The other person is correspondingly conceived as a potential obstacle and as an effective interference in the realization of my aims. Aristotle represents the apex of a tradition of thought that is diametrically opposed to Hobbes, according to which human beings are properly social, by nature political animals (φύσει πολιτικόν ζῷον; Aristotle, *Pol.* 1253a). Community, for Aristotle, thus precedes the individual, both in a genealogical and in a conceptual sense, and the personal dimension becomes intelligible only if conceived as emerging from a pre-existing weave of relations. In this sense, the other does not represent an interruption from the outside, but rather a condition of possibility for the very process of individuation. Honneth himself clearly embraces this second hypothesis or perspective:

> every philosophical theory of society must proceed not from the acts of isolated subjects but rather from the framework of ethical bonds, within which subjects always already move. Thus, contrary to atomistic theories of society, one is to assume, as a kind of natural basis for human socialization, a situation in which elementary forms of intersubjective coexistence are always present (Honneth 1995c, p. 14).

This passage, that apparently relies upon the almost self-evident ascertainment that every human lifeform implies an already existing human context or set of practices, poses some compelling issues. Honneth's attempt at a response revolves around a conversion of the Habermasian communicative theory into a paradigm of recognition, which would be able to rephrase the idea of "ethical totality" (Honneth 1995c, 12). Thus, the Hegelian conceptual plexuses proposed in the Jena Period seems to be helpful in the elaboration of such a social theory. But, since the Honnethian reading of the Jena Period is quite free and certainly not locked in criteria of a philological inquiry, it may be useful to fathom such originality by mentioning the comparison between Honneth and some of his contemporary references. In fact, such an interpretation of the Jena works is in some way the result of some precursors' elaborations: Habermas, Ludwig Siep, and Andreas Wildt.[3] For this reason, my intent is to bring to light Honneth's self-comprehension through a comparison with such authors, for his own aims can become clearer when weighed against their presuppositions.

The first decisive point coincides with choosing the Jena Period as subject of analysis, instead of Hegel's later works. This choice, which certainly represents a quite original aspect of Honneth's work, is not arbitrary. As is well known, Habermas is of the opinion that the period preceding the *Phenomenology of the Spirit* represents the most fertile ground for a resumption of the Hegelian themes. At this time, the developmental formation of the spirit would be not considered as a monological self-manifestation through human forms, already destined to be subsumed in an all-encompassing metaphysical subject. Rather, "it is the dialectical interconnections between linguistic symbolization, labor, and interaction which determine the concept of spirit" (Habermas 1973, p. 143). In other words, spirit would represent the end of an open-ended unfolding formation process, which takes its moves from practical actions and interactions—or, better: the resulting spiritual dimension is anchored to the practical engagement, instead of, as in the later Hegelian works, the underlying self-moving totality that assumes particular manifestations in order to reach itself.[4]

For similar reasons, Ludwig Siep, in his *Anerkennung als Prinzip der praktischen Philosophie*,[5] looks at the Jena Period as the most apt Hegelian resource for the framing of a contemporary moral and institutional theory. Hegel's ethical theory would be able to overcome the difficulties emerging from the proceduralization of ethics and the reduction of such formal procedures to *one* type of social action. First, against the proceduralization, Siep finds in Hegel an indissoluble bond between principles and institutional realities, which mutually shape each other within historical evolvements. On the one hand, institutions "embody" (*verkörpern*) principles, which are in turn de-formalized and seen as shared praxis-orienting norms in the social world. On the other hand, principles themselves are "genesis," namely, "processes of significance-development" (*Prozesse der Bedeutungsentwicklung*), which clearly take place in the institutional world. In this sense, principles would possess a quasi-self-generative power, which is all but ahistorical and concerns the ongoing reflection and counter-reflection of practices that occur within and by institutions. Principles are in fact "genesis of their own meaning" (*Genesen ihrer eigenen Bedeutung*) and their definition comprehends both their belonging to the lifeworld and their inner evolution (Siep 1979, p. 17). To be sure, principles orient moral praxis within and through the institutional world and so set the concrete conditions for their own overcoming, development or refinement. Second, the "principle of recognition" (*Prinzip "Anerkennung"*) would be able to play an encompassing role, avoiding the

---

[3] In order to gain an overview on Honneth's collocation within the *Hegelforschung*, see Deranty 2009, pp. 206–15.
[4] See Robert Sinnerbrink 2007, pp. 105–11.
[5] All the following translations of Siep 1979 are my own.

reduction of the institutional and practical multiplicity to only one fashion of praxis — whether it is, for example, verbal communication, speech, or a social contract (Siep 1979, p. 17). As Hegel describes it, recognition is the deep dynamic that underlies a wide spectrum of (objectual and interpersonal) interactions, all unified by the subject's getting lost in the other and self-regaining, whereby it both gives shape to the world and forms itself, since it is constituted by and formed in the already-present otherness.

It is therefore not surprising that Honneth chooses or discovers these Hegelian texts as his source. In fact, precisely the outlining of such (formally conceived) principles and of their bond with the practical spheres of interaction is one of the main tasks of his normative social theory. But it is at this level that we find the originality of Honneth's reading, which—unlike Habermas and Siep—situates Hegel's most insightful purpose in the *System of Ethical Life* and in the corresponding attempt to describe social reality as a conflictual movement originating from an original ethical core. The aim, therefore, is to describe a theory of the social that dynamizes, so to speak, Aristotle through Hobbes: conflict does not coincide with a natural condition, but rather with a rupture-stage whose result is the evolution of the "elementary forms of interpersonal recognition" into "a state of social integration," which "can be conceptualized formally as an organic relationship of pure ethical life" (Honneth 1995c, p. 18). Two forms of recognition belong to the stage of natural ethical life, that is, love (love-relations and parent-child relations), characterized by its biologically-oriented attitudes, and the one concerning the exchange of goods, which introduces a certain legal universality thanks to the forms of contract. Hence, Hegel describes the stage of crime—although leaving aside a proper explanation both of the motives and of the social-historical situation of such acts[6]—as the moment where social partners are made "aware of underlying relations of recognitions" (Honneth 1995c, p. 26). The stages of crime Honneth individuates—natural devastation, theft, and that regarding the struggle for honor—are already highlighted and directed to the following distinction between three different spheres of recognition, which are quietly difficult to acknowledge in Hegel's own texts. Admittedly, Honneth asserts that such an interpretation of the *System of Ethical Life* as developmental social history of intersubjective relations of recognition represents a debatable thesis, above all because of the Aristotelian ontological ground that underpins the whole structure of the text.[7] Correspondingly, Honneth performs the more incisive interpretation effort of the struggle for honor, extrapolating from such passages a third stage of recognition against the unconvincing conclusion of Hegel's own discourse about the state. In order to grasp the motives behind such interpretative choice, it seems helpful to look at how Andreas Wildt's *Autonomie und Anerkennung* contributes to Honneth's interpretation.[8]

---

[6] See Honneth 1995c, pp. 19–22 and 26.
[7] See Honneth 1995c, p. 25.
[8] All the following translations of Wildt 1982 are my own.

Wildt focuses his interpretation of Hegel's moral thought on the attention paid to certain life-practices, which leads to the detranscendentalization of practical reason and its principles. In contrast with Kant, the relevance gained by "non-legalistic morality" (*nichtrechtsförmige Moralität*) and the consequent ethical "relativism of practical rationality" (*sittlichen Relativität der Vernünftigkeit*)—which has to be understood in a non-radical sense—requires a re-definition of moral obligations (Wildt 1982, p. 9). Hegel's starting point coincides therefore with a closer observation of the lifeworld, where the rightfulness of practical intercourses is determined mostly by "intersubjective motivations," "altruistic tendencies," "life-conceptions," and "moral intentions" (Wildt 1982, p. 15). Such phenomena, always at stake in those practical positions assumed by social partners in their vital interplay, cannot be completely embedded in an obligations-view determined by legal-conformity. In fact, such practices establish the idea of "undemandable obligations" (*nichtforderbare Verpflichtungen*), which clearly exceed the legal form in two specific dimensions (Wildt 1982, p. 17). First, the assumption of a moral standpoint has as its necessary precondition the immanence to certain vital relations—relations of recognition—which allow the subject to act according to criteria provided to her by this context.[9] In this sense, Wildt argues, the form of relativism that Hegel introduces in the moral sphere does not concern the correctness of practical actions, but coincides with a "relativism of moral motivation" (*Relativismus der rationalen moralischen Motivation*) (Wildt, 1982, p. 18, my translation). Correspondingly, and second, the validity of moral obligations does not disappear within the self-justification of legalistic morality, the precepts of which find their own explanation regardless of the ethical relations, but has to be relativized to the immanence to certain milieus. But to show that a moral standpoint can be adopted simply by membership in certain groups, whose relations are of recognition, consists precisely in the formulation of a "theory of non-institutional ethical life" (*Theorie nichtinstitutioneller Sittlichkeit*) (Wildt 1982, p. 18).

The second central point Wildt focuses on concerns the possibility for the subject to be in-itself and for-itself (*Anundfürsichsein*). The subject's self-certainty relies on the affirmation or confirmation of oneself achievable through recognition relations and can therefore always be unsettled anew and regained. In this sense, Hegel's description of self-consciousness concerns the concept of "qualitative ego-identity" (*qualitativer Ichidentität*), which refers both to the position assumed by the self toward itself and, almost directly, to the relational context, which serves as ethical condition of the possibility of such self-relation (Wildt 1982, p. 22). Personal identity

---

[9] "Hegel's fundamental thesis here reads: Only in ethical life-contexts are there convincing reasons to take this standpoint; but if the trans-subjective, ethical relations of recognition are hopelessly destroyed, there is also no longer any compelling reason to be moral. And then moral obligations, whether they can be legitimately demanded or not, have in principle the character of a groundless, mere 'ought'" (Wildt 1982, p. 18).

hence represents a qualitative concept, which is essentially dependent on the quality of relations that encircle the subject.

But a third point Wildt highlights reveals one of the most interesting aspects of Honneth's theory. This definition of qualitative practical identity would in turn hinge on a delineation of the "affective-emotional ego-identity" (*affektiv-emotionale Ichidentität*) (Wildt 1982, p. 23).[10] Such an issue sheds light on the decisive significance attributed by Honneth to the dimension of love, above all regarding child-caregiver relations. In fact, as Wildt emphasizes, the love-recognition cannot be addressed to the subject's personal features, performances, or abilities, simply because the child has not yet had the opportunity to develop them. Because of that, the object of recognition is the naturalness of the body itself, its particularity, and the consequent neediness, the affirmation of which represents a central step to the self-realization.[11]

Turning back to crime, it becomes clearer, given Wildt's interpretation, that Honneth's explanation hypothesis, which apparently reduces crime to a "pathology of recognition" and therefore functionalizes it into a "learning process," does not completely overlook the material or power-related grounds that can underlie such phenomena (Petherbridge 2013, pp. 97–98). In fact, as Wildt clearly shows, the formation of a qualitative ego-identity relies on ethical, social, and relational presuppositions. Therefore, within the lifeworld, the material reasons of criminal acts or the perception of domination always concern the destruction or obstruction of the "possibilities of individuation" (*Individuationsmöglichkeiten*), precisely because they represent a ripple within the best possible ethical conditions (Wildt 1982, p. 102). Honneth, inheriting this Wildtian perspective, does not therefore reduce the criminal motivation to a pathology of recognition, but rather to the perception of impediment that the subject experiences in the moment in which the conditions for his own self-realization are lacking.[12] Nor does Honneth cancel the material dimension. Rather, he brings it back to the social environment in which the object is value or instrument and not pure objectuality: objects are not reduced to a subject-centered perspective, but are comprehended as social objects. In this sense, it becomes even clearer that the struggle for honor concerns, first, the "integrity of the person as a whole" (Honneth 1995c, p. 22), that is as Wildt expresses it, the "self-assertion of the ego-identity" (*Selbstbehauptung der Ichidentität*) (Wildt 1982, p. 324). In this sense, such motiva-

---

10 Honneth emphasizes the importance of the recognition relations of love as dimension in which the "emotional conditions for successful ego-development" are realized, on the trail marked by Wildt (Honneth 1995c, p. 38).

11 See Wildt 1982, p. 356.

12 "[O]ne can also understand the disrespect said to be tied to the exercise of legal coercion in the sense of an abstraction from the material conditions for the realization of individuals' intentions. In this case, the 'individual will' would lack social recognition because the legal norms institutionalized together with contractual relations are so abstractly constituted that the individual opportunities for the realization of legally guaranteed freedoms are not taken into consideration" (Honneth 1995c, pp. 54–55).

tional background can be defined as 'pathology of recognition,' using a wide meaning of the concept.

All such factors come together in Honneth's definition of the struggle for honor, where the object of dispute is the "entirety" of the individual existence—that is: "the stance I take towards myself when I identify positively with all my traits and peculiarities." The subjects involved become more aware of the fact that the "possibility of such an affirmative relation-to-self is dependent" on the—partially underlying—"confirming recognition of other subjects" (Honneth 1995c, p. 22). The resulting conflict aims to regain the integrity of such confirmation from others and moves toward a better social framework, one more able to assure the person their self-position. In this sense, conflict would apparently represent a second or derived character, the interruption or disruption of a previous intersubjectivity.[13] The very idea of an always-previous ethical life—which would represent the originality of the *System of Ethical Life*—implies a twofold role assigned to struggle. On the one hand, it reveals the priority of the already-existing forms of intersubjectivity; on the other hand, it represents the "vehicle by which subjects articulate their unmet claims of identity" (Petherbridge 2013, p. 99). So, the central idea resides in the possibility of struggle opening new—ethical, and therefore relative—horizons of affirmation and self-affirmation, which branch out from the needs and demands that clash in the conflict.

At stake in the conflict there is therefore the subject's "need to self-affirmation, self-confirmation, and self-representation" (*Bedürfnis nach Selbstsetzung, nach Selbstbestätigung und Selbstdarstellung*), a desire that depends on the social condition, namely, on recognitional confirmation: self-affirmation follows social affirmation (Wildt 1982, p. 339). Yet the struggle reveals the already-underlying recognition, which at least allows the subjects to take each other as opponents. With respect to this, we shall ask a fundamental question: what are the motives to recognize the other, if not as necessary pre-condition of being recognized by someone already recognized as worthy of doing that?[14] How does Honneth conceive the nature of the non-legal moral obligations described by Wildt?

Although we will postpone an in-depth discussion of the issue to the sixth chapter, here we need only mention the symmetrical structure of recognition, which is one of the salient features of Ludwig Siep's inquiries. For, if recognition seems totally unbalanced—either because it is self-centered or because it is altruistic—nevertheless, one of its main features is precisely a certain mutuality.

Siep's analysis of—and criticisms against—Hegel's Jena works revolves directly around the idea of mutuality as central character in the principle of recognition. According to his reading, Hegel grasps recognition first and foremost as a process of mutual formation of the individual and the general consciousnesses. At the

---

[13] See Wildt 1982, p. 340.
[14] Exactly in such terms Honneth speaks of 'obligation to reciprocity.' See Honneth 1995c, pp. 37–38.

level of interpersonal relationships, self-consciousness arises through the various forms of recognizing oneself in the other as a unity of particularity and generality. In this sense, every individual concretization within action and interaction consists of the simultaneous being-determined and being-free from such determinations. The central role is therefore assigned to the terms "freedom-giving" (*Freigabe*) and "self-negation" (*Selbstnegation*), which describe the dialectic of getting lost and finding oneself in the other (Siep 1979, p. 279). Mutuality would not, therefore, be primarily about the "positive side" of recognitional attitude, but would concern self-negation attitudes, which are configured as contemporaneity of dispersion and leaving space to the other, a sort of game of dialectical mirroring through which individuality emerges. Yet, Hegel would see this interpersonal level as necessarily already subsumed in a "supra-subjective" level, that of the "trans-subjectivity of ethical life" (Deranty 2009, p. 220), which allows us to conceive such a process as a development: the "freedom-from" the natural determination coincides with a "freedom-in" the spiritual dimension, the "self-release" represents a "self-let in" (Siep 1979, p. 283).[15]

In this sense, three facets of Siep's interpretation are noteworthy for our present interests. First, Hegel's theory of recognition could serve as normative benchmark in the depiction of the different stages of personal and social identity. In any case, it remains difficult to conclude that Hegel develops a theory of "full-fledged individuation" (*vollständigen Individuierung*)—as Habermas and Honneth claim (Siep 1979, p. 24). Rather, Hegel's theory concerns the liberation of the particular from its own determination and the acceptance of the latter. Second, as already noted, this liberation implies a constellation of lifeforms, such that any freedom-from is always a freedom-in. This implies being theoretically involved with a concept of good life, which further derives from the fact that the development of the person occurs within concrete relationships that the subject immanently inhabits and the instantiation of principles in institutions.[16] The third and final observation from Siep brings to light several consequences of the structure of Honneth's thought. Siep considers the teleological evolution of the process of becoming-free as an injury of the reciprocity-principle of recognition.[17] In this respect, especially in the *Systementwurf*, from the struggle onward the individual is considered as "substitutable" (*substituierbar*) in his uniqueness and is exclusively seen as subsumable in the following and more general stages.[18] In the spheres of rights and above all of the state, an "asymmetrical relation" (*asymmetrischen Verhältnis*) where the self-negation of the individual does

---

15 In this case, it is worth quoting Siep's expressions: ",Freiheit von' [ist] zugleich eine ,Freiheit in,' das Sich-Lösen zugleich ein Sich-Einlassen."
16 See Siep 1979, pp. 232–33.
17 See Siep 1979, p. 285.
18 See Siep 1979, pp. 126–27; 282–83.

not correspond to a reciprocal self-negation within institutions, which, on the contrary, perform a conclusive function of the development (Siep 1979, p. 279). [19]

Siep identifies three main problems concerning Hegel's asymmetrical-teleological shortcomings. First, this asymmetry makes it difficult to identify possible sources of innovation or social change. If, in fact, the reciprocal formation of the individual and the general embody a theoretical framework capable of explaining the progress of the principles—and therefore of the practices—the teleologization of this dynamic, that is, its description according to an axis of the annulment of the particular in the general, this makes the detection of emancipatory resources at least problematic, using a more Honnethian lexicon.[20] Second, Hegel's teleological description implies the functionalization of the first acts of recognition in view of the subsequent and higher ones. In this sense, liberation from naturalness would coincide with an assimilation that eliminates the singularity of the individual or, using Honneth's terms, its "biographical uniqueness" (Honneth 1995c, p. 61). Third, this priority of the conclusion over the commencement also implies an asymmetry between the spheres of recognition themselves.[21] By justifying the "right" of the spheres of recognition not on the basis of their capacity to render the individual herself, but on the basis of their distance from naturalness and particularity, the higher spheres possess a priority that can also be considered coercive. In other words, observing the dynamic not in its development, but from its conclusion or from the outside, the necessary contemporaneity of the spheres does not coincide with an equal interplay.

Once he has defined these limits or risks, Siep proceeds to list a number of points programmatically. In fact, by rejecting this teleological approach, the possibilities for a moral theory centered on recognition would consist, briefly, in the description of "successful or unsuccessful identity-formations" (*gelungener oder mißglückter Identitätsbildungen*) within the institutional context and in the analysis of the interdependency between principles and institutions, spheres where recognition also represents a "framework for judgment" (*Beurteilungsrahmen*) of institutional contexts, without falling into relativism. Recognition is thus able to criticize pathological developments (Siep 1979 pp. 295 and 97).

When one turns to Honnethian interpretation, and especially to the tasks he assigns to the re-actualization of Hegel, it is not difficult to find the legacy he assumes from Wildt and Siep. His reading of Hegel is almost perfectly encapsulated in a rather long passage, which is worth is worth quoting at length in order to highlight several necessary observations:

---

[19] "Accordingly, the construction of the ethical sphere occurs as a process in which all elements of social life are transformed into components of an overarching State. This generates a relationship of asymmetrical dependence between the State and its members similar to the one that holds fundamentally between Spirit and the products of its manifestation" (Honneth 1995c, p. 59).
[20] See Siep 1979, p. 281.
[21] See Siep 1979, p. 284.

> The structure of any of these relationships of mutual recognition is always the same for Hegel: to the degree that a subject knows itself to be recognized by another subject with regard to certain of its abilities and qualities and is thereby reconciled with the other, a subject always also comes to know its own distinctive identity and thereby comes to be opposed once again to the other as something particular.... Since, within the framework of an ethically established relationship of mutual recognition, subjects are always learning something more about their particular identity, and since, in each case, it is a new dimension of their selves that they see confirmed thereby, they must once again leave, by means of conflict, the stage of ethical life they have reached, in order to achieve the recognition of a more demanding form of their individuality. In this sense, the movement of recognition that forms the basis of an ethical relationship between subjects consists in a process of alternating stages of both reconciliation and conflict. It is not hard to see that Hegel thereby infuses the Aristotelian concept of an ethical form of life with a moral potential that no longer arises merely out of the fundamental nature of human beings but rather out of a particular kind of relationship between them. Thus, the coordinates of his political philosophy shift from a teleological concept of nature to a concept of the social, in which an internal tension is contained constitutively (Honneth 1995c, p. 17).

First, the transition to the philosophy of consciousness by the *Systementwurf* and the *Realphilosophie*, while it provides Honneth with important insights into the motivations of conflict and the forms of recognition, is rejected mainly because of the subjection of the consciousness-constitution process to the totality of the spirit.[22] In other words, according to Honneth, Hegel's focus would no longer be on the evolution of the ethical primary relations into more sophisticated forms, but rather emphasizes the self-mediation of the individual consciousness, which, after all, would only represent a wave in the sea of the spirit. Thus, the main problem is that "communicative relations between subjects can no longer be conceived as something that in principle precedes individual" (Honneth 1995c, p. 29). In this sense, besides the problematic embedding of the individual in the spiritual, the starting point already seems to Honneth to be a misleading one, one which fails to bring carry out Hegel's original intuition, shifting the focus away from social theory.

Second, it is therefore understood that the priority assigned to the *System of Ethical Life* derives from two factors, both entailed in the genealogical and logical priority of intersubjectivity. On the one hand, the Aristotelian assumption of an original sociability of human beings would make it possible to justify the perception of an already-underlying normative consensus or threshold of evaluation, which emerges in cases of social pathology or in those of moral damage. Even conflict presupposes such a background: in fact, both in the cases of property or contract and in those concerning honor, the possibility of confrontation already presupposes the consideration of the other person as such, according to a degree of recognition that can always be perfected. In this sense, Honneth maintains that "theoretical attention must be shifted to the intersubjective social relations that always already guarantee a minimal normative consensus in advance" (Honneth 1995c, p. 42). Honneth also defines such previous "unity" by using an expression of Barrington Moore, accord-

---

22 See Honneth 1995c, pp. 27–29.

ing to which members of society move within a horizon of expectations, demands and attitudes defined by and instantiated in an "implicit social contract" (Honneth 1995c, p. 167). On the other hand, this intersubjective precedence also regards the generation of such expectations, namely, the constitution of the person. Not only does the precedence of certain forms of relationship allow for the elaboration of a normative social theory, but it also lets the development of a model in which individuation and social integration coincide, according to a dialectical process of objectification, identification, and liberation from determination. For every aspect in which the self is affirmed, it will know how to recognize itself and will be able, by way of this recognition, to distance itself from such determination. Therefore, without a determined idea of primary intersubjectivity, one would fall again into the impasse of the different atomistic perspectives on the person. Honneth thus claims that the first task of his own social theory coincides with a post-metaphysical—that is, formal and not substantive in the Habermasian sense—argument on such primary intersubjectivity, which could avoid a purely ontological or speculative justification,[23] and on the subject-formation within recognition relationships.[24]

Third, with the research subject thus structured—in particular the second and third tasks of the normative theory, that of structuring the three spheres of recognition and the delineation of a concept of progress anchored to conflict[25]—Honneth does not consider what precedes the natural ethical life in the Hegelian works and, in general, he does not consider the dimension of materiality adequately.[26] Nonetheless, I would here like to limit myself to arguing that this perspective does not coincide with a simple annulment of materiality, but rather with its re-comprehension within intersubjectivity, inherited primarily from Habermas's reading of Hegel. Habermas's arguments about the dimensions of language and labor within the *Systementwurf*, which precede the forms of the natural ethical life, can apparently allow a first sketching of the priority of recognition (*Anerkennen*) over cognition (*Erkennen*), albeit Honneth first deals this issue in *Reification*:

> As cultural tradition, language enters into communicative action; for only the intersubjectively valid and constant meanings which are drawn from tradition permit the orientation toward reciprocity, that is, complementary expectations of behavior. Thus interaction is dependent on language communication which has established itself as part of life. However, instrumental action..., as social labor, is also embedded within a network of interactions, and therefore depend-

---

23 Both Deranty and Petherbridge speak of a ontological concept of original intersubjectivity (cf. Petherbridge 2013, p. 88; and Deranty 2009, pp. 220–21). However, if the word 'ontology' itself represents a problematic issue and could be interpreted differently each time, it emerges quite clearly that Honneth means to avoid such level of discussion by producing a post-metaphysical account of Hegel's ideas, that is, by giving an empirical and psychological justification of the primary intersubjectivity.
24 See Honneth 1995c, p. 68.
25 See Honneth 1995c, p. 69.
26 See Joel Whitebook 2008, pp. 382–89.

ent on the communicative boundary conditions that underlie every possible cooperation (Habermas 1973, p. 158).

For the time being, we can therefore limit ourselves to arguing that Honneth—following Habermas—does not simply get rid of the material dimension or overtake it in order to facilitate his intersubjective foundation. Rather, he understands the material dimension or even language as always situated in an intersubjective horizon, with an almost phenomenological attention both to the ontogenetic and phylogenetic development of human beings.

The final point concerns the interactionist reading of Hegel Honneth performs,[27] which would lead to a "one-dimensional account of the concept of 'relationality' operating in Hegel's work" (Petherbridge 2013, pp. 100–101), namely, to a pure intersubjectivistic reading of recognition, incapable of entailing the complex dialectic between particular and universal. Moreover, such peer-oriented view on intersubjectivity and recognition, according to which they consist of a "horizontal dependency of each on each, not the dependency of each on all" (Deranty 2009, p. 220), would imply an inadequacy to account for the complex relationships between individuals and institutions, for crime and for the dynamics of power.[28] My claim here is that such a tendency, clearly taken on by Honneth, aims to avoid the risks Siep identified in Hegel's thought, both generally but in particular in his description of ethical life, where the subject merely emerges from and again is subsumed into the spirit, without enjoying a proper ontological independence. To avoid such characterizations, Honneth—at least in *The Struggle for Recognition*—describes institutions as a moment of intersubjectivity, depicting the latter primarily in terms of an I-you, rather than an I-we that is teleologically oriented.

On a first level, even if the dialectic between general and particular is not completely eliminated, it emerges distinctly that such horizontal forms of recognition derive from the intent to develop a normative social theory reconcilable with the non-prescription of certain goods or ends, transitions leading to which would only live as functionalized to them. Such a framework comes therefore from a concern oriented toward *detranscendentalizing* the theory of progress, now conceived as open-ended social change, driven by conflict, namely, by a negative and denying practice.

On a second level, the horizontal nature of recognition aims to keep the individual's own biographical uniqueness. This idea finds space in *The Struggle for Recognition*, primarily in the centrality assigned to the principle of self-realization, and in the importance given to the form of recognition of love, in which the subject knows and experiences itself, in its own particularity and corporeity, as a "vital subjectivity" (Honneth 1995c, p. 39). This idea is based on Wildt's interpretation, according to which Hegel links the foundation of the moral theory not to general principles,

---

27 See Deranty 2009, p. 218.
28 See, regarding Honneth's reading of Hegel, Petherbridge 2013, pp. 92–96.

but to the constitution of the person, where recognition in the form of love is the first fundamental level of affirmation. Indeed, in a rather radical way, Wildt argues that love is the form of recognition that supports all subsequent ones: a thesis that, despite the affirmed equality between the different spheres of recognition Honneth describes by, certainly makes its influence felt.[29]

On a third level, such a horizontalization of intersubjectivity plays its role not only at the end of the teleological route, but also at its beginning. In fact, one of the more compelling tasks of Honneth's own theoretical operation consists in substituting the ontological and holistic model of primary sociality, according to which individuality must always be traced back to a precedent substantial common element. Honneth intends to replace this model, centered on the Aristotelian metaphysics, with fundamental relational structures, in order to de-ontologize the concept of natural ethical life and to be able to conceive subjectivity from a practical perspective and not as a mere sub-category of a previous totality.[30]

To summarize the key points of this section, one can say that Honneth's reading of Hegel leads to five main theoretical points. The first is clearly the concept of recognition, seen as an interactional keystone-principle that constitutes the normative fabric of society, as it emerges in the experience of suffering. Regarding this, it is important to emphasize that Honneth takes on Siep's appreciation of the multipolarity of the principle of recognition, which therefore does not run into the shortcomings of the univocal proceduralizations of ethics. Moreover, Honneth uses this polysemanticity of recognition to place in its system, at the same time, non-legalistic and therefore unbalanced forms of recognition (following Wildt) together with symmetrical and mutual forms (following Siep). Second, recognition implies and relies on an intersubjective definition of the subject and of personal identity, the undamaged unfolding of which represents a normative standard—according to Siep's reading. Third, however, the analysis of the intersubjective conditions of the formation of an undamaged identity (following Wildt) is sociologized through the formal concept of ethical life. Honneth identifies the appropriate normative criterion not in a theory of the determined relationship between existing principles and existing institutions (following Siep), but in the much more modest—or more ambitious—idea of formally identifying the structural social conditions for the undamaged development of the person.[31] Fourth, the Hegelian idea of ethical life would be able to provide accounts of normativity and of the social that encompasses the embryonic sociability of

---

[29] "The fact that Hegel thematizes love as the first form of recognition implies the thesis that the rationality of legal, moral and ethical recognition is only possible on the basis of loving recognition.... The voluntative ego identity entails moral motivation as long as the experience can remain alive that the particularity of the individual is affirmed and acknowledged as such, not only as a case of general norms" (Wildt 1982, p. 356).
[30] See Deranty 2009, p. 197.
[31] On Honneth's taking distance from Siep and Wildt, see Honneth 1995c, pp. 189–90 ns. 2 and 3; and Deranty 2009, p. 258.

human beings with the dimension of conflict and struggle: social reality would be the disharmonic yet identifiable development of a primary intersubjective structure. Correspondingly—and finally—despite Honneth's (present) refusal of Siep's account of institutions, the account of the three spheres of recognition as instantiations of normative principles embedded in intersubjective practices must be traced back to the intention to inherit Hegel's perspective on the *Sitten*, while still avoiding the logical or metaphysical dimension of his thought. In this sense, Honneth's action-theoretical approach would lead to challengingly conceiving the objective implications of ethical practices without recourse to the concept of objective spirit.

2.2 'I' and 'me': Mead's Concept of Practical Identity

Honneth takes the first step in developing Hegel's concept of recognition in a post-metaphysical framework through the confrontation with George Herbert Mead. The idea that the American psychologist-philosopher offers the best approach to pursue such an operation is owed to the influence of Habermas and shows, despite the criticisms, that Honneth elaborates his original thought in close relation with the groove furrowed by his master.[32] As by the confrontation with Hegel, our interest here is not oriented to a verification of the correctness of Honneth's reading of Mead—even the very idea that Mead depicts a clear distinction between three spheres of recognition is debatable.[33] Rather we want to deal with Honneth's closest references in order to better understand his original intentions and conclusions. Thus, we try to approach Honneth's interpretation of Mead through Habermas's, so that—in the similarities and differences—we can identify the main traits of the so-called re-actualization and naturalization of Hegel's thought.

In "Individuation through Socialization," Habermas finds in Mead's works—and especially in the binomial 'I' and 'me'—the key to re-interpret the concept of individuation within the postmodern contexts of rationalization, differentiation and detraditionalization of society. Mead's merit is in the understanding that, in such a context of rarefaction and of autonomization of traditional bonds, even the process of individuation could no longer be based on the agency of a monologically understood subject able to express its sovereignty and aims in the external world. Thus, the very concept of individuality has to be re-conceived. Mead would therefore allow thinking autonomous individuation paths within the contemporary de-subjectification and, indeed, depict a model in which these two dimensions match. In addition to this theoretical need—and to the very identification of Mead as a suitable figure for rethink-

---

[32] On Habermas's engagement with Mead, and in addition to "Individuation through Socialization," see Habermas 1987, ch. 5.
[33] See Honneth 1995c, pp. 80–91; and Deranty 2009, pp. 264–68.

ing ego in inter-subjective terms—there are three main reasons why this essay of Habermas's can represent an interpretative basis for reading Honneth.

Even if Honneth wants to maintain a normative character in his discussion of Mead—that is, outlining the social constitution of practical identity and, through this, the depiction of the normative fabric of society—his account almost inevitably takes on different aspects, which will then lead him to abandon this philosophical reference. In fact, as Habermas notes, in Mead "the important distinction between the *epistemic* self-relation (*Selbstbeziehung*) of the knowing subject and the *practical* relation-to-self (*Selbstverhältnis*) of the acting subject" remains unclear and blurred (Habermas 1992, p. 178). These different levels of ego are, for Mead (as for Hegel), not separable from each other, because of a certain holistic conception of the experiential starting point, which is conceived through a pragmatist lens. From a certain point of view, this blurring represents one of the reasons for Honneth's appreciation, who often refers to diverse authors that first adopt a tentatively all-encompassing approach.

Apart from this issue, the first decisive point to understand the importance Honneth attributes to Mead consists in the conception of individuality, which (as with Hegel) is not conceived as a "singularity, nor as an ascriptive feature, but as one's own *achievement*" (Habermas 1992, p. 152). In this sense, 'subjectivity' would not be a mere starting fact, but a point of arrival or—better—an open-ended process; an unfolding that implies dynamism. By this process, individuation and social integration would run, so to speak, on the same track, inevitably intertwined with one another. Indeed, the subject is not seen as a substance, as a givenness already fulfilled in itself before any (cognitive or practical) relation with the world. Rather, the subject always comes-*from*, its provenance disperses into the social milieu from which it emerges and in which it is always situated: its always-actual origin coincides with the otherness in its social dimension, with interpersonal and gestural interactions, and with communicative gestures. Mead's insightful element is therefore represented by the identification of the constant origin of the self from the alterity that again appears in certain practices. More precisely, individuality would form itself through the communicative interactions, which disclose the very possibility of "intersubjectively mediated self-understanding" (Habermas 1992, p. 153), gained ever anew thanks to practical reactions in front of vocal gestures. Moreover, Habermas explicitly links such interpersonal dynamics through which the self emerges with the Hegelian idea of recognition:

> One organism can understand another organism's behavioral reaction that is triggered by the first's gesture as if it were an interpretation of this gesture. This idea of recognizing-oneself-in-the-other serves Mead as the key to his explanation, according to which the elementary form of self-relation is made possible by the interpretive accomplishment of another participant in the interaction (Habermas 1992, p. 175).

Relations with others are therefore the fundament for one's own self-relation.

This brings us to the second point, which goes beyond a purely normative level and concerns the very structure of the self: the I-me polarity. Here, the practical modalities of achieving one's selfhood are underlined according to different accents. In fact, Habermas and Honneth consider two different aspects through which Mead reaches the postulate of the I and the me: if Habermas focuses on communicative action, vocal interactions and the reflexivity allowed by the shared objectified meanings, Honneth focuses on the dynamics of internalization of the generalized other's norms through practical intercourse. However, the core of Mead's account is that, through practical interactions, the subject can have itself as object, namely, as me. In this possibility of shaping one's self from the otherness as otherness, the I—the proper singularity of the subject—emerges as beyond that is before: as memory of the singularity of the self that is implied in every gesture, which, however, is always the expression of me. In every practical attitude that is seen by me as gesture of the me, as an already socialized and objectified gesture, my I has to be implied as before such practical happenings. I encounters the acting me always as an alter-ego, a second person, but then, through the reactions of the actual partners in interaction, it can, so to speak, re-gain the never-objectified source of individual action, namely, the always-present I behind every action.[34] In this sense, the very reflexivity of the subject, that is, the possibility of the subject having oneself as object, would not primarily coincide with an intentional (and somehow transcendental) self-relation, but as a result of a social interaction. Thereby "the distinction between an originary self-relation" and "the reflected self-relation" would be neglected (Habermas 1992, p. 178). In other words, through this polarity, Mead describes the self-relation not as a transcendental, epistemological threshold of appearance, which also precedes any self-manifestation, but properly as a reflection of social interaction, which is implied in every practical attitude. Through the interaction and the reactions of practical partners, the I can re-gain itself as me not as an object observed through an inward-directed introspection, but as partner of the social partner.[35] Thereby, just as

---

[34] As Habermas notes, "Mead explicates the self of self-consciousness as this *social* object. In the first person of his performative attitude, the actor encounters himself as a second person. In this way there arises an entirely different 'me.' Even this 'me' is not, however, identical with the spontaneously acting 'I,' which ... withdraws from every direct experience; but the 'me' that is accessible in the performative attitude *does* present itself as the exact memory of a spontaneous state of the 'I,' which can, moreover, be authentically read from the reaction of the second person. The self that is given for me through the mediation of the gaze of the other upon me is the 'memory image' of my ego" (Habermas 1992, p. 172).

[35] Habermas clarifies this 'inner' yet 'inter-' structure in linguistic terms—which are not adequately considered by Honneth, at least in *The Struggle for Recognition*: "The idea that lets Mead break out of this circle of selfobjectifying reflection requires the transition to the paradigm of symbolically mediated interaction.... The 'me' casts off the reifying gaze, however, as soon as the subject appears not in the role of an *observer* but in that of a *speaker* and, from the *social perspective* of a *hearer* encountering him in dialogue, learns to see and to understand himself as the alter ego of another ego" (Habermas 1992, pp. 171–72).

the me is not conceived of as an internal object of consciousness, the I does not represent an internal core of consciousness, an inward-directed ego or a inward eye.[36] Rather, it would represent an instance that precedes every determination, "a shadow, because 'I,' as the author of a spontaneous gesture, am given to 'me' only in memory" (Habermas 1992, p. 177). In this sense, the logical priority of the two selfhood's poles is inverted: no longer would a gazing I objectify an observed me, but the always-already social me would disclose the I as implied memory. Such an understanding of selfhood is the key to the Honnethian elaboration of the concept of practical identity as derived from recognitional relations. In fact, Honneth describes certain possibilities of relating to oneself as dependent on being the addressee of recognitional attitudes, according to a scheme that can be easily understood when we— hitherto still generically—talk about the nexus of received esteem and self-esteem: a subject is able to relate positively to some aspects of its personality only when these are affirmed in the practical horizon of surrounding relationships. But this very possibility is rooted in a more fundamental one, which concerns the structure of the self, and that clarifies why Honneth proposes, in "Pathologies of the Social," the formulation of a formal and intersubjective anthropology as an actual possibility for the critical theory to accomplish its tasks. Through the mediation of Habermas, Mead's theory allows Honneth to explain in post-metaphysical terms an anthropology in which the 'self-' is such as a consequence of the 'inter-,' and the I is the undeterminable reflection of the social me.

The third aspect that Habermas illuminates, which influences Honneth's use of Mead, concerns, in properly normative terms, the paradigm-shift when moving to the practical dimension of self-relation.[37] As we have seen, Mead's pragmatist approach blurs the boundaries between epistemological and normative discourses. However, once one enters the world of reasons and moral acts, the I-me polarity takes on a rather different meaning, which Honneth adopts to justify various aspects and consequences of his paradigm. Assuming, as he does, that Hegel's interest in the Jena texts resides more in the discussion of the practical than the epistemic self-relation,[38] Honneth focuses on the former also with regard to Mead, but leaves the inevitable consequences that the latter continues to exert quasi-undetected. Just as the epistemic self-relation, the practical self-relation is similarly conceived as emerging from and through interactions with concrete partners, but the forms of adopting

---

36 In *Reification*, Honneth mentions such reified perspective on self-consciousness under the concept of 'detectivism.' As we shall see in chapter 3, the paradigm of recognition almost necessarily implies (or explicitly founds) a re-conceptualization of the structure of the self in intersubjective terms. See Honneth 2008, pp. 67–69; and Honneth 1999.
37 Focusing only on the late writings, Honneth focuses on Mead's social psychology and not on his pragmatic and functionalistic approach to the constitution of selfhood in problem-solving situations. In this way, he overlooks the rich possibilities that might arise from the Meadian analysis of the social constitution of material objects. See Petherbridge 2013, pp. 135–36.
38 See Honneth 1995c, p. 76.

the other's perspective no longer coincide with the acknowledgment of the other's reactions in front of shared communicative significances, but are "extended into *role-taking:* Ego takes over alter's *normative*, not his *cognitive* expectations" (Habermas 1992, pp. 178–79). In such a frame, me no longer represents the occasion of self-consciousness, but "an agency of self-*control*," which accomplishes behavioral tasks (Habermas 1992, p. 179). The behavior-controlling function of me derives once again from its alterity-related features: as soon as we conceive the relationship with the other in practical terms, me coincides with the resulting instance of the shared expectations toward the self among the partners in the interaction. The me as already-other represents the individual face of the existing institutionalized practices and norms: these are therefore internalized and act on the behavior of the subject as action-controlling promptings.

In *The Struggle for Recognition*, referring, like Habermas, to Mead's "The Social Self," Honneth introduces this dimension describing the constitution of the moral self through patterns of internalization: "the child can think about his conduct as good or bad only as he reacts to his own acts in the remembered words of his parents" (George Herbert Mead 1964, p. 146). In other words, only through the criteria that the self receives within its social context it can ensure itself a practical identity. In order to approach such an idea, Honneth sketches his post-metaphysical re-actualization of Hegel's recognitional account of practical identity through the categories of 'play' and 'game,'[39] found in *Mind, Self, and Society*.[40] Play presupposes the capability to assume different personal roles within the ludic activity, so that one can identify with concrete expectations and anticipations of action—that is, the ability to put oneself in another's shoes. But the stage that exemplifies and instantiates the internalization-dynamics that interest Honneth most is that of game:

> If we contrast play with the situation in an organized game, we note the essential difference that the child who plays in a game must be ready to take the attitude of everyone else involved in that game, and that these different roles must have a definite relationship to each other (Mead 1972, p. 151).

In games such as team sports, all participants must deal with a normative level that precedes and goes beyond them, consisting of the rules of the game, tactics, and concrete possibilities for shared action such that the actual game can develop. The capability of the players is not to know how to identify with each concrete other, but with a generalized other, which coincides with the shared pattern of elements that

---

[39] See Mead 1972, pp. 149–61. Habermas also plays a decisive role here, through his reconstruction of the binomial play-game in Habermas 1987, ch. 5.
[40] It is worth noting that describing the dynamics of internalization through which selfhood is constituted in terms of a theory of recognition involves a certain ambiguity, because of the one-sidedness inherent in the phenomenon, which might overlook forms of productive power and normalization. See Petherbridge 2013, p. 139.

actually shapes the game. This would lie in the child's own possibility to generalize or to abstract the shared norms in order to move into a collective field of action, and to conceive of herself within (or, possibly, also outside) the group that organizes itself according to these norms. As Deranty points out, the process of internalization is allowed by the previously mentioned configuration of the I as memory: *Er-innerung* coincides with the ability to internalize certain reactions and expectations that arise in the conversation of gestures and, therefore, create the capacity to anticipate them in future interactions.[41] Accordingly, the generalized other and the capacity of the subject to confront a wide horizon of expectations also underlie the very process of social integration as a whole, for it "involves the internalization of norms of action that result from a generalization of the action-expectations of all members of society" (Honneth 1995c, p. 78). In this sense, me coincides with the counterpart of the conventional expectations that can find a consensus among a generalized community or, put differently, the self-understanding of a subject that knows itself as included in a so shaped social milieu. And it is here that Honneth properly introduces the concept of recognition within his analysis of Mead's thought. The ability to abstract group norms and to adequately take part in them would prelude being recognized and self-recognizing as members of such a community:

> If it is the case that one becomes a socially accepted member of one's community by learning to appropriate the social norms of the 'generalized other,' then it makes sense to use the concept of 'recognition' for this intersubjective relationship: to the extent that growing children recognize their interaction partners by way of an internalization of their normative attitudes, they can know themselves to be members of their social context of cooperation (Honneth 1995c, p. 78).[42]

These dynamics of abstraction, generalization, internalization, and sharing of norms therefore describe the emergence of the practical me, as a socialized self that knows itself as an included member of a group. Thus, it is noteworthy that the concept of game—and the very expressions that Honneth uses in these passages—might suggest that the cooperating group is composed of peers, as well as in a team, thus drawing a model that would be inapplicable to social effective misbalances. Evidently, however, this same dynamic can easily be used to explain the different power relationships present in society through a de-generalization of the other, which could then be described as a more or less exclusive provider of social norms that, when internalized and shared, have different effects.

In this context, and also given this latest issue, the practical I also takes on a slightly different form. As far as the epistemic self-relation is concerned, it coincides with the withdrawal from any determination, being that shadow behind and beyond

---

41 See Deranty 2009, p. 251.
42 Honneth himself quotes Mead employing the term recognition: "It is that self which is able to maintain itself in the community, that is recognized in the community in so far as it recognizes the others. Such is the phase of the self which I have referred to as that of the 'me'" (Mead 1972, p. 196).

any objectification of the self. On a practical level, this instance of elusiveness presents itself under two faces, also originally highlighted by Habermas. The I represents at the same time "the onrush of" pre-social "impulses" and "the source of innovations" (Habermas 1992, pp. 179–180), which might transform the moral rules interiorized by the me—and, thereby, the context of the social game. Even if such a distinction is emphasized by Habermas—representing, on the one hand, the unconscious impulses placed under control by the me, but which continuously emerge, and, on the other hand, also a more conscious innovative capacity that might overwhelm the conventional norms[43]—Honneth puts together the two dimensions[44] and defines the I as "the unregimented source of all my current actions" (Honneth 1995c, p. 74).

Synthetically, Honneth's reading of Mead revolves around three main points: first, the description of an intersubjectivistic model of the emergency of the self, which is now clearly decentered; second, the I-me polarity as inner relationality, no longer conceived in intentional or transcendental terms, but properly social ones; and finally, the delineation of the practical self-relation as result of the internalization of behavioral and normative models and the overflow over them. There are three main, interconnected issues that rely on these conceptions and that significantly shape Honneth's paradigm of recognition.

First, the I-me relation concerns the process of social integration and the position of the individuality or singularity of the self within it.[45] In this sense, even if not dyadically determined as it is in Habermas, Honneth's interpretation of the I serves mainly to reserve a space of singularity and potentiality for the subject.[46] The peculiarity of the I, deriving from its inability to accept any objectification, is therefore not to be understood as a reintroduction of a sort of atomism, of a strict split between the social and the individual. Rather, it represents the deprivation of

---

43 "This distinction should account for the experience we have of the *difference* between the way in which institutionalized forms of social intercourse are placed in question by the revolt of split-off motives and repressed interests, and the way in which they are placed in question by the intrusion of a revolutionarily renewed language that allows us to see the world with new eyes" (Habermas 1992, p. 180).
44 "What [the 'I'] stands for is the sudden experience of a surge of inner impulses, and it is never immediately clear whether they stem from presocial drives, the creative imagination, or the moral sensibility of one's own self" (Honneth 1995c, p. 81).
45 As Deranty points out, such relation between singularity and sociality at stake in the internalization of the normative rules proper of the generalized other shows that Honneth's idea of recognition is not only "horizontal" (between an I and a you), but also "vertical," that is, facing with the society as a whole. The determination of such levels within recognition does represent one of the most problematic aspects in Honneth's paradigm, and will therefore discussed later. See Deranty 2009, p. 254; and Siep 2010, pp. 107–27.
46 See Patchen Markell 2007, pp. 107–14. Contrary to what Markell claims, I do not think that the one implemented by Honneth is a clear separation between the two poles, but rather the opposite: the co-implication of I and me shows in fact an inseparable binomial. I will discuss the application of the categories of potentiality and actuality to the concept of recognition later in chapter 6.

the socially determined, where its emergence-from the social has a founding character. Without me, I could not reach the surface as a reflected image, but without the latter, the self would not be as such: the subject would be totally ascribable to its social environment. In contrast to the actuality of the me, to its, so to speak, presence, the I represents a to-come, the sources of which can only coincide with the surrounding effectiveness. In this sense, the Aristotelian terms potentiality and actuality are overturned both in a logical and in a chronological sense, thus outlining an open-ended and indeterminate teleology, the definition of which represents one of the most challenging theoretical issues for Honneth.

The second element is quite implicit in *The Struggle for Recognition*, but is made explicit in *Decentered Autonomy*. For as the relation between I and me sketches a decentered subject, it also lays the foundations for an intersubjectivistic rethinking of autonomy that is able to positively include the dimension of otherness in its definition. For Honneth, this represents a particularly decisive issue because contemporary reflections on freedom require paradigms that enable the alterity to be conceived not as a heteronomous obstacle: after the crisis of the modern perspective of the self-posing subject, ipseity itself seems de facto overwhelmed on every side by an alterity that precedes it and that expropriates its own sovereignty, dissolving it in the social, environmental, psychological, and biological antecedents.[47] Given such a situation, that is, one in which the individual seems precluded from freely elaborating its own path of self-realization,[48] the I-me polarity apparently allows re-actualizing the Hegelian definition of freedom—being with oneself in the other—at an elementary level. Not only, then, is the Meadian perspective able to guarantee an intersubjectivist-founded definition of selfhood, but also, through its own dynamicity, a pattern of individuation. In fact, the absolutely singular creativity of the I can only be expressed within the objectivizing and objectified horizon of the me: the other is already present in the articulation of each individual initiative as a necessary condition of existence. The other—me, the language, the generalized other—represents an irreplaceable dimension for the I, since it provides modes of expression and contexts that are meant to be transcended. In this sense, the me constitutes the situations in which the I is enabled to elaborate, and elaborate itself freely, receiving space for action. Without this precedence of the other, without this provenance, the I would find itself in an inconceivable non-situation of total aphasia and immobility. Hence, the self is with oneself in the another as a non-objectified reality that objectifies itself in the beyond that precedes it, as antecedent traceable only afterward.

Such a definition of freedom implies not the merely given sociality, but one that must come, bringing us to the third point, that is Honneth's "non-utilitarian *moral sociological explanation* of social conflicts" (Mauro Basaure 2011, p. 264). By pointing out the motivational horizon of the conflict in the suffered misrecognition, Honneth

---

[47] See Honneth 1995a.
[48] See Habermas 1992, p. 184.

finds himself in the difficult position of having to found a potentially violent practice without running into a vicious circle, so that the expansion of the spaces of recognition coincides in turn with their negation (for other members of society).[49] I argue that it is mainly to avoid this difficulty that Honneth outlines his own theory of conflict specifically on the basis of Mead's I-me polarity. Conflict does not represent, first and foremost, a reaction to social domination or to power dynamics, but rather— even if these occur, as in the case of misrecognition—it takes place thanks to the structural sociality of the self,[50] that is, precisely from the creativity of the I and its consequent capacity to expand the normative concretions proper to the me. Being always beyond the forms of the me, the I would somehow succeed in anticipating social assets more suited to its moral expectations, which are inevitably formed and shaped through the process of internalization and the confrontation with the generalized other, but which may eventually lose their effectiveness and generate frictions with respect to the abovementioned expectations.[51] The initiative of the I is not, therefore, a setting outside the fabric of social relations, but the possibility of anticipating a better realization of that starting material which society, in one way or another, provides it with. In this sense, creativity, anticipation, abstraction, and imagination are decisive factors for the elaboration of a conflict conceivable in terms of moral progress.[52] In other words, this is about a "dialectic of conformity and uniqueness" (Deranty 2009, p. 263). Thus, the struggle for recognition is properly a conflict aimed at widening the spaces of recognition, aligning them with the expectations of the members of the social environment according to two vectors: the social inclusion of a larger number of members and the individualization of the forms of recognition, that is, the improvement of their ability to encompass ever more aspects of their practical identity.[53] These are also the most exemplary features of Honneth's conception of progress: struggle for recognition and the latter, in fact, cannot be separable from one another, because—at least in *The Struggle for Recognition*—it is precisely the conflict that represents the praxis in which progress can be discovered and traced in the historical path of the west. Accordingly, outlining a social world whose characteristics are able to correspond more adequately to the expectations shaped by society itself represents the other side of freedom: giving shape to institutions allows the self to recognize itself in them, that is to say, to ex-

---

49 As Aboulafia has points out, Mead himself proposes an exclusively positive and constructive understanding of social conflict. This view is evidently inherited from Honneth in order to avoid possible contradictions, which would emerge as such in the light of disrespect and moral suffering as critical starting point. See Mitchell Aboulafia 1991. Honneth's account on social conflict does not take a stand about violence because violence in social struggle can be justified a posteriori, under given conditions. See Honneth 1995c, p. 163; and Honneth, Jonas Jakobsen, and Odin Lysaker 2010, p. 168.
50 See Lonnie Athens 2012.
51 These expressions refer quite clearly to Searl's idea of collective intentionality. I discuss the relation between such accounts and the concept of recognition in chapter 6.
52 See John Rundell 2001.
53 See Honneth 2003d, pp. 184–89.

perience being with oneself in the other. In this sense, the dynamic of internalization and the corresponding creativity of the I would describe not only the development of the selfhood of the self, but the vary shaping of social reality.

As Petherbridge critically points out, with this depiction of social conflict, "Honneth seems to assume there is a seamless flow between internal psychic and external social world" (Petherbridge 2013, p. 143). This would imply two risky consequences: first, a naïve reconstruction of the relationship between the inner and outer worlds and, second, an excessively social determination of the psychic. However, although the first aspect may represent an effective objection to the current take on Mead, the discussion of the object-relations theory contained in *The Struggle for Recognition* already shows that such an unfolding of the I through the elaboration of new social forms is by no means without obstacles, possible constraints, or even frustrations and imbalances. Regarding the second point, and as we have tried to show, the richness of Mead's paradigm consists precisely in proposing a description of the psychological as socially determined, but not depleted within society. Therefore, the justification Honneth adopts for the conflict is, I would claim, certainly psychological, but not psychologistic, because the psyche itself is social. Conversely, the exposure from excessively socializing the psyche or reducing the singularity of the self (even in its unconscious elements) to the priority of the social is avoided by the centrality attributed to the pole of the I. Rather, this risk, if present, appears once Honneth abandons the Meadian model because of its excessive cognitivism. Moreover, this criticism overlooks the very pragmatist concept of the psychological at stake in Mead and Honneth,[54] especially regarding emotions. Referring to Dewey, Honneth intends to develop an action-theoretical idea of emotions as a spark that can potentially ignite social conflicts. Put in a schematic way, the heart of this subject coincides precisely with rejecting the perspective wherein emotions represent a bridge between an interior of consciousness and an exterior of the world. Rather, starting from the practical action and the expectations at stake by the anticipation of its developments and consequences, emotions would be characterized on the basis of their adherence or not to such individual anticipation. They would represent an aspect of practical gestures, marking individual reactions to the success or failure of actions. Thanks to this pairing of satisfaction and frustration, Honneth proposes again, at the base of the struggle for recognition, the same account as Wildt: the motivations for the struggle correspond to the perception of impediments, inhibitions or frustrations to one's own practical expectations (of self-realization).[55] The centrality of this action-theoretical perspective put into play by Honneth is not limited to the description of emotions —and therefore not limited to the psychological, showing a certain impossibility of

---

[54] "The 'psychical' represents, as it were, the experience that one has of oneself whenever one is prevented by a problem that emerges in practice from carrying out the action in the usual way" (Honneth 1995c, p. 72).
[55] See Honneth 1995c, pp. 136–38.

opposing internal and external in Honneth's thinking—but represents a key to his social theory in *The Struggle for Recognition*.[56]

The importance of Mead for Honneth's thought can be read in light of the concern that the individual would be subsumed into the social totality, proper to Siep's argument and that, according to the aforementioned interpretation, leads Honneth to horizontalize recognition relationships. As Deranty argues, the interaction between self and generalized other can already be read as the re-proposition of the dialectic between particular and universal, which at first glance seems absent from the re-actualization of Hegel. My claim here is that the intent not to subsume the particular in the universal, that is, the singularity of the self in the ethical totality, finds an interesting antithetical equivalent in the theory of social change based on the I-me polarity. In fact, where in Hegel the particular coincides with the individual and the universal with the spirit (objective, therefore social), and progress consists in a teleology that moves from the first to the second, in Mead the terms are reversed. The particular that is overcome is always the determined me—namely, the social—while the universal coincides with the undetermined I, that is the exclusively individual, driving force of an open-ended development. In this sense, progress is not vectorized to the attainment of a goal other than the individual, but itself possesses the character of singularity, which must, of course, find collective forms to change, via struggle, the particular forms of the me.

2.3 Disrespect as Misrecognition and Conflict

The account of emotions represents the best introduction to Honneth's argument about misrecognition. In fact, the idea that emotions represent the implication of actions, and thus coincide with frustration or the satisfaction of expectations, allows Honneth to consider different forms of violence as an impediment to well-founded normative demands. Although the chapter of *The Struggle for Recognition* on disrespect, moral injury, and injustice is meant as a sort of counter-evidence of the spheres of recognition he has already explicated—and the three forms of misrecognition are admittedly to be traced back to those[57]—it seems useful here to start our account of Honneth's re-actualization of Hegel from the negative point of view, namely, keeping with the perspective I sketched in the previous chapter. This will be useful for four main reasons. First, taking the negative starting point more readily shows the critical potential of the work, which otherwise would almost exclusively delineate a positive social theory;[58] thus, in a general way, Honneth's whole perspective emerges more clearly. Second, it is negatively that the connection between personal integ-

---

[56] See Deranty 2009, p. 335.
[57] See Honneth 1995c, p. 132. To claim, therefore, as a criticism, that the identification of these spheres of misrecognition derives exclusively from the spheres of recognition is incorrect.
[58] See Deranty 2009, pp. 310–11.

2.3 Disrespect as Misrecognition and Conflict — 61

rity, practical identity, and practical self-relation, namely, the core of the formal anthropology depicted in the book, is to be conceived, as an almost unapproachable idea circumscribable from the moral insights active within the experiences of suffered damage. In other words, focusing on the negative allows the gaining of a positive, yet unsubstantial perspective. Third, such an approach is an apt way to further distinguish Honneth's positions from those of Wildt and, above all, Siep. In fact, if the arguments that bring us to embrace recognition as the key of critique are anchored to negative experiences, it is clear that the positivity of the normative theory has to be both socially informed and more modest than an institutions-directed normative judgment, as if one was stopping at one step before reaching a conclusion. Finally, starting from the classification of disrespect sheds light on the positive spheres of recognition and the relative forms of self-relation. Indeed, many criticisms or observations about the spheres of recognition are—legitimately—aimed against or about their interplay, their dependence on each other, their capability to entail certain inter-practices or not. My claim here is that one can gain a precious insight through the lens of three forms of disrespect: physical violence, legal exclusion (denial or subtraction of rights), and social denigration.

Honneth's analysis takes its phenomenological anchor on the everyday language, where the experiences of injustice are seen by the affected as disrespect.[59] In other words, every injustice is perceived as lacking respect or apt consideration of the affected individual's personal worth. Without wanting to be redundant by repeating elements already highlighted in the previous chapter, it is nevertheless useful to underline two aspects. First, anchoring his thought to everyday language shows Honneth's intention to develop a theory that starts from an identification with suffering, its factuality, and concreteness. Second, the central element is personal vulnerability: just as every injustice coincides to a certain extent with disrespect, so every longed-for form of justice should refer to undamaged modes of relationships. These represent both the ground on which injustice can be felt as such as well as the end of any struggle for recognition. In other words, we are dependent on others—through recognition—for the formation of our practical identity: this means that any damage suffered is perceived not only as an external limitation of freedom, but also reflexively understood as a wound to one's own personal integrity. Thus, as we have already seen, conflict is understood not as an end in itself, but as a means,[60] thanks to which the already existing conditions of recognition are highlighted and the foundations for the elaboration of new and more suitable ones are laid. In this sense, the attention to "non-material forms of injury" (Johnathan Allen 1998, p. 450.) allows Honneth to fill what, in his view, was one of the most significant shortcomings in the paradigms of Hegel and Mead, namely, the motivational

---

59 See Honneth 1995c, p. 131.
60 See Jonathan Allen 1998, p. 461.

drive to conflict.⁶¹ If, in fact, the interplay of me and I represents the justification of the dynamics of the conflict, emotional reactions to misrecognition represent the socio-existential spark that *can* activate this dynamic.

But, before dealing with conflict, it is worth concentrating on the forms of disrespect, emphasizing again the centrality of vulnerability, that is, of intersubjective dependence. Although the aforementioned analogy with the biological diseases and the relative health of the body also plays a decisive role in *The Struggle for Recognition*,⁶² it is useful to stress that the violations to personal integrity highlighted here are not generally conceived social pathologies, but pathologies of recognition, that is, deficient forms of intersubjective relations, which undermine the constitution of the person. Therefore, a possible criticism emerges: the broader theme of social pathologies is reduced to the theme of pathologies of recognition, narrowing the horizon of the critique to intersubjective relationships. Honneth's idea, instead, is that misrecognition—as well as recognition—represents, for the social partners, the encounterable and experienced side of social dynamics. Therefore, in a nutshell, for social theory there can be no other credible access point to social complexity in all its dimensions, than a pre-theoretical one. Moreover, it is clear that the same category of suffering—if taken seriously—takes the discourse to a much broader level than that of identity politics, to which those who accuse Honneth of culturalism refer. The materiality of suffering and its corporal dimension, in fact, represent the heart of Honneth's critique at this point.⁶³ The fact that every form of misrecognition (not only physical violence) is analyzed in terms of suffering does not allow us to skip the material dimension. Consequently, it enables us to understand the bold claim of the critical project, that is, to highlight the most hidden folds of social dysfunctions.

What is at stake in the form of misrecognition represented by physical violence—such as torture and rape—is the undermining of the very possibility of *having* a body. Such violent acts, directed against a person's freedom of *being* a body, represent the "most fundamental sort of personal degradation," because of the combination of pain and the most elementary experience of subjection to another's will. Such experiences lead to damages in one's autonomous relation with its own body, which, "coupled with a type of social shame," has as its proper consequence "the loss of trust in oneself and the world" (Honneth 1995c, pp. 132–33).

Although Honneth is quite succinct about it, there is room for some further considerations. On the one hand, one could say that precisely these grievous consequences to the openness toward one's own corporeity, to others, and to the world can be caused also by psychological damage not included in physical violence.⁶⁴ On the other hand, some scholars have noted that Honneth would overstep damages caused by deficient forms of care and by "poor parenting" (Simon Thompson and Paul Hog-

---

61 See Honneth 1995c, p. 132.
62 See Honneth 1995c, p. 135.
63 See Deranty 2004.
64 See Piromalli 2012, p. 114; and Ricoeur 2005, pp. 190–91.

gett 2011, p. 43). This last observation clearly takes its cue from Honneth's positive discourse, which identifies the child-caregiver relationship at the center of the first form of recognition, that is, love. Moreover, Ricoeur criticizes Honneth's failing to identify that the more fundamental form of misrecognition should coincide with a sort of humiliation that withdraws the experience of being-with, by denying an essential-existential approval and therefore making the subject feel "insignificant" and "nonexistent" (Ricoeur 2005, p. 191). This remark comes from a certain priority Ricoeur gives, within the sphere of love-recognition, to the essential affirmation of the uniqueness of the person in friendship and in love relationships. Even if such a comment raises, in my opinion, an open point in Honneth's theory—which in fact he takes up later in "Invisibility" and *Reification*—both this criticism and the preceding one risk to be more focused on the form of acquiring (or denying) a certain self-relation, than on the features of self-relation itself. In other words, in analyzing the forms of misrecognition it is fundamental to focus foremost on *what* is damaged: in this case, the fundamental and minimal familiarity—confidence—that, through and with our body, allows us to relate to ourselves, to others, and to the world. Honneth's arguments concern the centrality of embodiment in social integration and any addition to this—also in light of the positive forms of recognition—represents, in my opinion, an over-interpretation of the issue at stake.[65] Our experience of injustice is indissolubly and inevitably tied to our having a body, which, even in its closest intimacy, always remains exposed, vulnerable, and potentially dependent. This impossibility of exclusive possession of one's own body—because violence has the potential to threaten it—is the first concept through which Honneth intends to show the intrinsic sociality proper to any experience of injustice, as well as its moral dimension. If, therefore, it is true that his attention is directed to the experience of non-material injury, it is useful to emphasize that such non-materiality represents—explicitly in the case of physical violence—an aspect of actual episodes, which concern the materiality of the corporal relationship with the world in all its dimensions, both internal and external. As for the first observation mentioned—namely, that Honneth does not consider certain forms of psychological violence that can actually cause the same impossibility of experiencing oneself and living in the world with confidence through and with one's own body—it certainly touches an open point. In any case, it is not useless to emphasize that Honneth's definition of the first forms of misrecognition touches the most fundamental experiences of damage, without excluding other forms, provided that they are actually directed to this type of self-relation.

---

65 See Bernstein 2005, pp. 313–14. Although Bernstein's argument is not explicitly addressed to Honneth, it may be to some extent useful to illuminate some aspects between the lines of *The Struggle for Recognition*. Moreover, Bernstein argues that Honneth, by developing a concept of formal ethical life, moves away from a necessary closeness that critical thinking should maintain in order to respond to injustice against the body (see Bernstein 2005, p. 305). In dealing with the first sphere, I intend to argue that the formality of Honnethian normative social theory is not in contrast with such proximity and concreteness.

The second class of misrecognition concerns rights and legal relations:

> What is specific to such forms of disrespect, as exemplified by the denial of rights or by social ostracism, thus lies not just in the forcible restriction of personal autonomy but also in the combination with the feeling of not enjoying the status of a full-fledged partner to interaction, equally endowed with moral rights (Honneth 1995c, p. 133).

Honneth's account therefore once again concerns the consequences of disrespect on the subject's self-perception, namely, its self-relation. Through the denial of rights, the individuals affected are threatened, first, in their own perception as rational-moral subjects, capable of moving autonomously within the social context, that is, in their self-respect. Such an account of misrecognition as legal injustice implies not a "'quantitative' (to receive what one is due)," but a "'qualitative' (to receive what one needs in order to be a full subject)" account on justice (Deranty 2009, p. 297). In other words, Honneth argues that the deprivation of rights—be they civil, political, or social—fundamentally undermines the experience of individuals, insofar as it hinders their ability to be considered equal, endowed with the same qualities and faculties as other citizens, according to a trajectory that can be increasingly expanded. In this sense, the reflected object of the denial of rights is clearly human dignity, which leads us directly to the third form of misrecognition.

In fact, since the American Revolution, the idea of dignity has been following a path of ever greater universalization, which implies ever greater individualization, that is, its ongoing particularization: the dignity of every human being coincides with its uniqueness. It is with the third form of misrecognition that, according to Honneth, we enter the dimension that in everyday language is indicated by terms such as disrespect, insult, or degradation. These "evaluative forms of disrespect" aim the "individual or collective ways of life," thereby downgrading certain manners "of self-realization within a society's inherited cultural horizon." Therefore, the addressee of such forms of denigration cannot "relate to their mode of life" as something that is at home within certain communities, as something worthy for the others, hence experiencing "a loss of self-esteem" (Honneth 1995c, p. 134).

The transition from such forms of disrespect and the depiction of social struggles is performed by the concept shame, the emotion that accompanies the particular response to every form of misrecognition. Given that "the injustice of disrespect does not inevitably *have to* reveal itself but merely *can*," Honneth considers such emotions as the "motivational impetus" for social struggles (Honneth 1995c, p. 138). Thus, Honneth sketches an original account of social struggle that tries not to detach "the emergence of social movements" and "the moral experience of disrespect" (Honneth 1995c, p. 161). In other words, Honneth aims to depict a model of struggle that avoids the "zero-sum game" of the Hobbesian-interest model of conflict (Zurn 2015, p. 56), by bringing to the foreground the emotional-moral component left aside by many academic sociologists.[66] In doing so, Honneth does not mean that the interest-oriented conflicts do not represent an actual feature of the modern and contemporary social struggle. Rather, referring to the historical-sociological studies of E. P. Thompson and Barrington Moore,[67] he intends to support the secondary character of interest-guided conflicts. That is, they would always be situated, and would always find their origin "within a horizon of moral experience that admits of normative claims to recognition and respect" (Honneth 1995c, p. 168).[68] In other words, the struggle-model Honneth outlines is intended to be a broader and more comprehensive one in comparison with those described according to the paradigms of purposive-rationality or identity politics, thanks to the conviction that these models also find their foundation or their adequate collocation in the primary experience of personal self-relation.[69]

But the transition from the experience of misrecognition and from emotional reactions to social conflict is far from immediate, despite the suspicions that the I-me dynamic may have brought out. What is required is a "moral insight" that allows affected individuals to grasp the "cognitive content" of the injury and its social nature (Honneth 1995c, p. 138). Such forms of disrespect have to be identified as group-directed and as socially caused,[70] otherwise any form of conflict they may bring about would remain confined to the private sphere, to the quarrel and to the dispute. Instead, the conversion of the (necessarily) individual experience of suffering into the sociality of struggle is allowed by a "semantic bridge," where such experiences of injustice can find adequate space for expression thanks to a "shared semantics." Only through such communicative practices can a "collective identity" based on misrecognition be developed (Honneth 1995c, p. 163).

Even if Honneth does not give a more precise account of how this communicative process is shaped,[71] it is rather clear that his intention is to propose at a theoretical level the structures and mechanisms that have developed and been effective (at least) in the experiences of struggle in the last centuries of the west. Despite the already mentioned intention of biographical identification with suffering and with the oppressed which is present in Honneth's early writings, the object of social theory he promotes in *The Struggle for Recognition* is a grammar of social conflicts: every step in characterizing how this semantic bridge develops coincides with a historiographical and empirical task. More than anything else, although such shared semantics clearly represent a necessary condition for the emergence of social groups of protest, the risk for the critique is to leave aside the instances that remain "in the shadow of

---

[66] For a brief, yet useful comparison between the different theoretical models of struggle, see Zurn 2015, pp. 57–59.
[67] See Honneth 1995c, pp. 166–68.
[68] See also the reference to Simmel and economic struggles in Honneth 1995c, p. 127.
[69] See Mariana Teixeira 2017, pp. 593–97.
[70] See Zurn 2015, pp. 66–67.
[71] See Pilapil 2011, p. 83.

the political public sphere" (Honneth 2003d, p. 122). Although this is a criticism that Honneth makes of Fraser and her model of struggles for recognition, which focuses on the public recognition of minority identities, it could be, once it has been pushed to the extreme, addressed to Honneth himself. In other words, the assumption of the experience of misrecognition as a starting point and of emotional reactions as a spark constituting the fight groups—that is, the whole metaphor centered on the binomial pathology/health—risks condemning the critique for its inability to exercise its tasks in the absence of symptoms. What position should the theory take with respect to suffering that has no voice, that is, which cannot be articulated more or less publicly? In addition, the absence of symptoms could be caused not only by the impossibility of establishing a semantic bridge of sharing, but also by the fact that the subjects themselves are not able to articulate the aforementioned moral insight, namely, they cannot acknowledge disrespect as such and therefore identify themselves as victims. In other words, how could the affected people escape (at least cognitively) from an ideological system?

Although Honneth does not engage directly these issues in *The Struggle for Recognition*, we can still make some observations. On the one hand, the matter concerns the general approach of Honneth's philosophy, which is always oriented toward the definition of structures and the identification of historical developments of pre-conditions: while admitting that the normative level always indicates an ought, it never goes as far as determining or predetermining how these conditions should be characterized in content. It always assumes, so to speak, the position of the owl of Minerva,[72] leaving the evolution of the identified tendencies to historical actuality. On the other hand, the problem of the (im-)possibility of catching the damage suffered concerns the ideological forms of recognition—which will be dealt with in more detail in chapter 5—represents a quite compelling problem. At this juncture, the central issue of the possibilities of critical philosophy, as Honneth understands it, is re-proposed. Not only for the theory, but also for the affected subjects, there seems to be a need for a hermeneutical threshold to go out from the inhabited context and its horizon, that is, from the reproduction of forms of domination that the subject would not be able to acknowledge and, therefore, to rebel against.

Even if Honneth does not directly answer this question regarding the oppression-without-symptoms, the problem allows us to read the concluding passages on the conflict in another light, where the main role is played by the concept of progress. In the struggle-communities, the disregarded subjects can newly find basic communicative conditions to relate to themselves in an undamaged way, thanks to the reciprocal respect and solidarity that, at least at a minimal level, must be accorded among the members. In such groups, the idea driving the praxis is represented by the "anticipation" of a future "communication-community," where the subjects should be recognized for the traits, abilities and features that are disregarded in the present sit-

---

[72] See, above all, the concluding pages of Honneth 1995c and Honneth 2015.

uation (Honneth 1995c, p. 164). Honneth's account that considers social conflicts as "struggle for recognition as a historical process of moral progress" (Honneth 1995c, p. 168), hinges precisely on the capability to anticipate a hypothetical future where recognition would be more fitting for the oppressed or disrespected. This implies a certain degree of hoped for progress: in other words, conflict would instantiate the emancipatory interest. Rather than indicating an evolutionary approach to morality and history,[73] Honneth introduces this idea to respond to a crucial problem, that is, the need to be able to anchor the mechanisms of struggles to evaluation criteria, by which it is then possible to condemn reactionary, hierarchical, or subjugating pressures originating in requests for recognition:

> moral feelings—until now, the emotional raw materials of social conflicts—lose their apparent innocence and turn out to be retarding or accelerating moments within an overarching developmental process.... [I]n order to be able to distinguish between the progressive and the reactionary [struggles], there has to be a normative standard that, in light of a hypothetical anticipation of an approximate end-state, would make it possible to mark out a developmental direction (Honneth 1995c, pp. 168–69).

If from the point of view of the subjects involved in the struggle the anticipation of this hypothetical end-state is elaborated in a negative way—as absence of misrecognition suffered—from the point of view of theory, the question is more complex. The idea of progress based on the image of health should not be conceived as an evaluation-yardstick outside history, on the basis of which historical phenomena shall be judged. Rather, it intends to anchor itself empirically in the historical development of forms of recognition and has the claim to enunciate, from within this development, the forms of its becoming.[74]

Before concluding this section, it might be useful to add an element that has not yet been clarified. Honneth's approach could be considered problematic not only because of the risks related to the psychologization or culturalization of (in-)justice, but also because of the very assumption of emotions as a starting point. In other words, not only would this assumption excessively reduce the critical theory's field of investigation, but it would also imply a reified treatment of the emotions themselves, which are considered as a given starting fact, as an unmediated realm of experience: that is, their social constitution would be bypassed.[75] That this is not the case emerges clearly from Honneth's positive account, because recognition expectations are only established within the recognition relations themselves. In this sense, a previously mentioned issue reopens: the conflict always throws light on the conditions of recognition that precede it. Put in more Honnethian terms, even the initial relation-to-self, by virtue of which the subject is entitled to perceive injustice as an im-

---

73 See Jeffrey C. Alexander and Maria Pia Lara 1996, p. 130.
74 See Nikolas Kompridis 2004, pp. 327–28.
75 See McNay 2008b p. 278.

pediment or damage and that triggers an eventual struggle to improve the present context, is not self-generated, but always follows the priority of the intersubjective relations. Even emotions, therefore, are always dependent on the social context.

We are therefore in a position to explain the factors that constitute a response to the four issues raised at the beginning of this section. First, the negative approach guarantees an understanding of the critical dimension of *The Struggle for Recognition*, which starts from the experiences of disrespect and—anchored in the binomial pathology/health—tries to determine the conditions for an ought. In this context, the idea of progress plays a fundamental role, which in some way restores the objectivity necessary not to close the possibilities of a critique to the subjective perspective, according to the idea of rational universal. Second, the main elements of a formal anthropology have been hinted at, but not yet defined. Honneth intends to negatively determine a constellation of concepts—such as practical identity, self-relationship, dignity, etc.—from injuries to the person, which, if defined on the basis of positive assumptions, could appear an excessively substantial idea. The different objects of misrecognition instead refer—perhaps only intuitively, but Honneth's discourse is based on this elusive link—to an idea of the person that is essentially structural. Thus, the wholeness (integrity) of the person is tied to their perception of themselves (self-relation), and thus to their identity. In addition, three spheres of this self-relation—self-confidence, self-respect, and self-esteem—have been negatively approached as having to constitute a minimal idea of dignity. Third, the attention to the experience of damage and the related account on the conflict further clarify Honneth's distance from Wildt and Siep. Turning the issue upside down in positive terms, one can say that the heart of the issue of recognition, as in Wildt, is the definition of a moral dimension based on the idea of practical identity. However, the negative access allows Honneth to sociologize his theory right from the start: the purpose of the text coincides with the mirror image with respect to the social forms of misrecognition and at which social struggles aim. Thus, the social conditions for the establishment of a non-damaged practical identity are put in the foreground, formulating a social (and not moral) normative theory. As far as Siep's thought is concerned, it is the combination of the concepts of practical identity and conflict that pushes Honneth to reject the idea that the normative standards acquired within (mis)recognition can lead to the development of a theory of institutions and their critique. Rather, the purpose is that of developing an idea of the end-state that guides the conflict not to the very determinations it ought to take on but stops at the genetic and formal conditions of its development, whose center is and remains the practical identity. Fourth, it has become clear—again via mirroring—what the focal point of the spheres of recognition should be. In fact, if the focus of the sections on misrecognition is the analysis of certain forms of damaged self-relation (and of related practices), Honneth's positive account revolves around the definition of the relational conditions necessary for an undamaged practical identity. With this focus on forms of relation-to-self in mind, it will be clearer—especially in the case of love, which includes phenomena of different kinds, and which in some respects has a broader claim than the other spheres—what Honneth states from sphere to sphere. In addition, the discussion about emotions and demands of recognition helps us to focus attention on another purpose of *The Struggle for Recognition:* dealing with the concept that ethical life cannot be separated from the *genealogical* tasks of recognition.

2.4 A Formal Conception of Ethical Life: An Anthropological Justification

Honneth's positive account revolves around the definition of three patterns of intersubjective recognition, which differ "from each other with regard to the 'how' as well as the 'what' of practical confirmation" (Honneth 1995c, p. 25). First, these patterns would be, philosophically, a re-proposal of Hegel's and Mead's theories, which respectively represent a threefold model of the social and of the constitution of personal identity. Second, sociologically, they would coincide with the scope of demands that emerge in the history of struggles. Finally, such forms of recognition would represent not merely the historical and social development of a not-further-definable idea of good; Honneth indeed intends, in a constant confrontation with the empirical hints, to distill a formal model that can explain the mechanisms of social change at a grammatical (and therefore structural) level. Thus, the main aim of *The Struggle for Recognition* is the delineation of a formal model of ethical life, which would lie halfway between the procedural and deontological ethical models and the substantial perspectives on the good.

However, before approaching these three intersubjective forms—and thus outlining our major object of interest, that is, the paradigm of recognition—we can turn briefly to the observations preliminarily listed in the first chapter: psychologization, culturalization, and teleology. Specifically, the first criticism claims that Honneth focuses his attention erroneously and excessively on the psychological side of suffering, thus giving a reduced image of justice; moreover, this focus would implicitly lead to an image of psychological health that compromises the formality the paradigm requires. This can be answered mainly through the account of emotions, which indissolubly links Honneth's paradigm to the practical dimension and expectations that are articulated in it. In this sense, suffering should not be characterized primarily in psychological terms (which are certainly present), but in practical, interactional, and intersubjective ones: in other words, in normative terms. However, it is true that Honneth relies decisively on psychoanalytical arguments to elaborate his theory. But even in this case, the shift from Freud's ego-psychology to an object relations theory would guarantee a recourse to psychology in constant dialogue with sociality, for the distinction between internal and external dimensions is not marked in atomistic or solipsistic terms. Second, during the discussion of the conflict, we can observe a topic that arouses the critics who charge Honneth of culturalism.[76] Honneth argues that every struggle, even that for a fairer distribution, finds its horizon within demands for recognition. With this claim, which seems to be a confirmation in favor of the criticism just mentioned, there are two factors that reduce its corrosive capacity. On the one hand, Honneth does not intend to reduce material social conflicts to those of a cultural nature: his model would equally concern both and would present itself as a basic structural model, which can then assume different specific connotations. Therefore, even if Honneth never performs a direct critique of the economic system, one could say, on the other hand, that his is not a reduction of the just to the cultural, but a constant *return* to the (even existential, one could say) instances and claims of the subjects (individuals or groups) that struggle. As such, what is at stake is a much broader concept of identity, as we have already seen by the forms of misrecognition regarding basic self-confidence and self-respect, which clearly cannot be reduced to a restricted account of cultural identity. The third point concerns the concept of progress and its link with the idea of good life, which together would characterize Honneth's thought in strongly teleological terms. As for the second factor, that of the good, we will soon see that Honneth does not intend to define a substantial idea of the good and by doing so assign a specific purpose to the vector of progress. However, the very idea of an end state and the capability to anticipate it on the part of the struggling subjects represents an elementary and essential normative standard, necessary in order to characterize the conflict in terms of the moral progress of society. It is therefore useful to emphasize that Honneth's claim is not to *assign* a predetermined progressive path or an end to historical progress, but to extrapolate the contours of such a dynamic starting from the effectiveness itself. In this way, the idea of progress would receive its characteristics from the evolution of the struggles themselves and their demands, with respect to which the task of the social philosopher would be that to distill a structure—a moral grammar—that plays the role of an always-open formal condition for the future.

All these issues converge in the definition of the 'formal conception of ethical life,' which would coincide with a minimalistic representation of what, at the present time, can be considered as the "provisional end-state" sought and pursued through social struggles (Honneth 1995c, p. 171). Again, Honneth's aim would be to unearth the emancipatory interest actually at stake in, and which shapes, the conflicts aimed toward social change: the identification of the structural normative level and its delineation would then guarantee the critique an apt evaluative standard to name social pathologies as such and to distinguish regressive and progressive dynamics in the context of pluralism. The attempt is therefore to define an ethical model that is equally distant from the Kantian morality and from the different substantive images of ethos, which can be found for example in communitarianism or

---

[76] As seen in the first chapter, Fraser and Thompson are those who move the criticism in the most radical way. I will address this issue in more detail in chapter 4.

2.4 A Formal Conception of Ethical Life: An Anthropological Justification

neo-Aristotelianism. The distance from the former is marked by Honneth's intention to derive ethical principles thanks to a phylogenetic and ontogenetic reconstruction, the directions of which are already present thanks to the analysis of the forms of misrecognition and of the grammar of the conflict, in addition to the confrontation with Hegel and Mead. Precisely for this reason, the paradigm that Honneth defines is that of the good, not of the just or of the right, as an ideal that subjects seek for the purpose of their own realization. It must be noted, though, that Honneth distances himself from substantial perspectives on the good of "concrete tradition-based" communities (Honneth 1995c, p. 172). This is basically for two reasons: first, there is the intention to retain the universality of Kantian morality and, second, in order to outline a model capable of withstanding the challenges of liberal pluralism. The characters of the depicted ethical life have therefore to "be formal or abstract enough," but, at the same time, "have sufficient substantive content" in order to give a broader insight into the self-realization paths of individuals (Honneth 1995c, p. 173). Such a balance between the formality and consistency of the good then allows us to define an ethical framework, not through the description of a substantive content nor through procedures, but through the delineation of "the structural elements of ethical life, which, from the general point of view of the *communicative enabling* of self-realization, can be normatively extracted from the plurality of all particular forms of life" (Honneth 1995c, p. 172, my emphasis). Honneth's account therefore relies on the "intersubjective structure of personal identity" (Honneth 1995c, p. 173), depicting three concentric and progressive spheres of recognition, which must be understood primarily as bundles of practices aimed at the formation of an undamaged personal relation-to-self—that is, actual freedom—and not as realities of institutional nature:

> The forms of recognition associated with love, rights, and solidarity provide the intersubjective protection that safeguards the conditions for external and internal freedom, upon which the process of articulating and realizing individual life-goals without coercion depends. Moreover, since they do not represent established institutional structures but only general patterns of behaviour, they can be distilled, as structural elements, from the concrete totality of all particular forms of life (Honneth 1995c, p. 174).

A central way to achieve this balance between structure and good concerns the empirical accountability of Honneth's genealogical reconstruction of the spheres of recognition as dimensions of the constitution of an undamaged self-relation. The explicit aim is in fact to re-actualize the Hegelian model in accordance with an "empirically supported phenomenology" (Honneth 1995c, p. 69): this use of empirical data—which is concretized in referring to psychoanalysis for the reconstruction of the first phases of the child's life and to historical-sociological inquiries—would accomplish the precise purpose of accessing the content without presupposing a substantive perspective.

Before analyzing the respective forms of recognition and the modes of self-relation they enable, it is necessary to address three general points, which provide an adequate condition for reading. The first concerns the relationship between the spheres of recognition, the second involves the use of empirical sources as means for justification of the theory, and the third relates to the anthropological character of Honneth's discourse.

Regarding the first point, critical literature is divided by assigning a certain priority, hierarchy, or order to the different spheres. While it is true that Honneth (following Wildt) argues that love represents the most fundamental form of recognition—both in logical and chronological terms[77]—it is not clear whether this coincides with the idea that the three spheres should actually be considered as steps of a progressive logic.[78] This thesis would be supported by the Hegelian insight that accompanies Honneth's model: the three spheres concern practical modes of affirmation and confirmation of three different aspects necessary to an undamaged personal self-relation, so that the subject can know itself in its particularity (love), universality (rights) and individuality (esteem).[79] However, one could argue that the priority-sphere is the recognition of legal rights because of its ability to fit into the others' domain through the universal character of laws,[80] and for the degree of equity that the other forms of recognition also need in order to be articulated according to a logic of symmetry. Equal access to recognition would therefore be a pre-condition for all spheres and the very idea of equality must be conceived as the core of the universality of law.[81] Third, one could also claim that the last sphere has to possess a certain priority because of its focus on the uniqueness of the person. Merging Siep's worries about Hegel's asymmetrical tendencies and Ricoeur's observation on misrecognition, according to which the more fundamental form of disrespect coincides with the withdrawal of the person, one could say that the core of recognition should be represented not by the affirmation of certain characters, but of the person as such for how she is and because she is. Clearly, in Honneth's model, this type of recognition could be found above all in the sphere of social esteem—not without some overlap with love, where the uniqueness of individuality is at stake. Moreover, the analysis of misrecognition has already made it clear that everyday language means 'recognition' precisely in this connotation: if the analysis is to be phenomenological, this aspect should not be ignored. Although it is useful not to overlook the multipolarity of recognition and of its spheres—an element through which Honneth intends not to fall into the risk of unilateralizing the ethical discourse—it seems to me correct to argue that all spheres are equally subdued to the purpose of individual

---

[77] See Honneth 1995c, p. 176. This goes together with the fundamental character that physical violence possesses in terms of damaging the personal self-perception.
[78] See Zurn 2000, p. 117.
[79] See Zurn 2015, p. 40.
[80] See Honneth 2007a, pp. 144–62, for what concerns the priority of legal recognition on love-relations within the family; regarding a certain priority of equity on social contribution, see Honneth 1998.
[81] See Piromalli 2012, pp. 121–22.

self-realization, which has to be understood first and foremost as the "ontological possibility of subjective identity before the ethical notion of the good life" (Deranty 2009, p. 275). The very fact that one can reasonably argue in favor of the priority of each sphere over the others, and the tensions between them, shows nothing more than that each of them—according to ways and balances that depend on social developments and configurations—illuminates a fundamental dimension of how the concept of the *person* can be conceived in terms of identity, integrity, and dignity under contemporary conditions. Given this priority accorded to personal identity on the singular spheres and their interplay, a main problem arises: why should the idea of self-realization be considered *the* critical normative standard? Is it sufficient to say that the reason relies on its being the structural abstraction-result of the particular aims of recognitional relations and social struggles?[82] Why does Honneth choose *this* value among others? The question leads us once again to the idea of suffering and moral damage. Honneth's most ambitious intent is to outline a critical theory that, at the structural level, lays the foundations for the elimination of individual suffering. In these negative terms, the priority of self-realization seems to me less arbitrary, and in fact is capable of describing a universal and effective principle at the same time: the unacceptability of pain.

But the fact (and here we move to the second issue) that Honneth resorts to determined ideas of the good does not represent, in my opinion, a threat to his theoretical framework. In fact, it is precisely Honneth's intention to find the substantial content of good life in social reality and then to strongly distinguish it—via means of formalization—from the structural conditions that only historical progress can fill with—for the theory, unpredictable—new content. In any case, this theme leads us to address, once again, the relationship between Honneth's critical social theory and its effectiveness and empirical data, which are conceived at the same time as a starting point and as the means of testing the theory. Are such values or, more generally, Honneth's setting supported by a plausible empirical reconstruction? This issue, which seems unresolvable, is omnipresent, since critical thinking finds itself dependent on its object. I do not claim to find a definitive answer here, which in my view would be impossible to provide,[83] but I intend to discuss Honneth's attitude toward historical-sociological effectiveness, rather than the conclusions he draws from it. It seems useful to emphasize that Honneth's approach is primarily philosophical and his analyses are conducted in a "half-speculative, half-empirical" way (Ricoeur 2005, p. 187). The use of empirical data provided by psychoanalysis, historiography, and sociology is intended as a tool for the re-actualization of Hegel's theory, not as its raw material. However, some criticisms levelled at the formulation of the spheres of recognition, and more particularly at the centrality assigned to the

---

[82] See Zurn 2000, p. 120.
[83] For an insightful account on the relationship between Honneth and empirical data, see Deranty 2009, pp. 277–86.

family—that sphere in which the purpose to verify Hegel's model empirically is widely implemented through the object relations theory—allow a more general discussion of Honneth's setting. The assumption of the family as a starting point can be criticized from three different perspectives. First, this empirical testing would possess a tautological structure. In fact, the empirical reconstruction of the child's development already implies and assumes that the environment that should be tested is a justified form of recognition. Second, the context of the family, as historically contingent, should also be tested and not taken uncritically as a starting point. This would imply the theoretical possibility of accessing the issue of recognition from other phenomena.[84] Third, this starting point would move naively in the capitalist context, without considering the dissolution and functionalization that the bourgeois nuclear family undergoes, as the first cell of power and assimilation of the individual into the consumerist system.[85]

Generalizing the heart of these criticisms, one could say that there is an ambiguity in Honneth's thought, namely, a lack of theoretical distinction between facticity and legitimacy. Keeping the example of the family, one could dispute that the mere existence of such an institution—and its currently intersubjectively constituted subjects—is a sufficient prerequisite to justify its role in an ethical model, even more so when this institution itself performs functions of power. This is certainly due to two elements. On the one hand, the approach proper to critical theory cannot fail to assume a starting point proper to present reality: in this sense, even the intention of formulating a formal and minimal model could only be determined through the intersubjective relationships actually lived. To think of another starting point would also lead to the same conclusion and to what would no longer be a problem: a both timely and culturally determined access:

> What can count as an intersubjective prerequisite for a successful life becomes historically variable and is determined by the actual level of development of the patterns of recognition. The formal conception loses its ahistorical character in that, hermeneutically speaking, it winds up dependent on what constitutes, in each case, the inescapable present (Honneth 1995c, p. 175).

On the other hand, Honneth's Hegelianism plays a significant role here, because, as we have seen, the decisiveness assigned to the actual life-contexts in the justification and formulation of an ethical theory is precisely one of the fundamental elements of Hegel's criticism of Kant. However, within Hegel's system, this starting point finds its premise in the conviction that the real is rational, that is, that the practical and institutional forms, by their unfolding, embody and better realize rationality in its universality in an ongoing process. Honneth inherits this idea, stripped of its metaphysical habit, through the Hegelian Left and the Frankfurt School under the name of emancipatory interest.

---

[84] See Paul Cobben 2012, p. 132.
[85] See Thompson 2014, pp. 783–85.

But it is precisely this point that leads us to the third issue, namely, that Honneth's philosophical proposal lies on an anthropological justification:[86] "The concept of 'ethical life' is . . . meant to include the entirety of intersubjective conditions that can be shown to serve as necessary preconditions for individual self-realization" (Honneth 1995c, p. 173). The normative significance of the forms of recognition is not justified solely on the basis of their actual existence—and thereby through the nexus established with emancipatory interests—but because they are identified as the conditions for an undamaged person-formation. Both normativity and, therefore, the possibilities of critique hinge on the intersubjective conditions of human self-realization, the intact image of which represents the guiding idea of healthiness for the whole paradigm. Consequently, the very idea of progress—which represents the other normative set of evaluative criteria—instantiates or not depending on dynamics capable of leading to personal self-realization. It is important to note that Honneth describes the concept of self-realization sparingly, precisely to avoid falling into a substantial definition of the good. However, this normative idea clearly embraces a certain,[87] albeit broad, concept of freedom proper to the historical, cultural, and social development of the west. In fact, in Honneth's eyes, self-realization is that minimalistic good that is represented by the possibility to freely articulate a "successful life" (Honneth 1995c, p. 174), namely, an undamaged life, which could be further reduced to a generic idea of "human well-being" (Zurn 2015, p. 75).

We can derive three further consequences from this type of justification of the theory. First, Honneth would depict a "maximalist conception of self-realization" (Allen 1998, p. 462), which seems presupposed rather than demonstrated.[88] So, the alleged priority of emotions and moral injury would represent a consequence of the positive idea. This apparent short circuit, however, corresponds perfectly to Honneth's approach, symbolized by the pathology/health pair: through the symptom, the wound, the damage, it is possible to find its opposite, by virtue of which the symptom emerges as such: the "first" shows itself as "second" and vice versa. Both ideas—that of pathology and that of self-realization—therefore oscillate on the threshold of perceptibility of the emancipatory interest. Second, if the justification of social forms and practices relies on their contribution to subject-formation, then the anthropological and social levels cannot be separated from each other.[89] And here, third, the tension between the normative and generative dimension of recognition comes to the surface.[90] In fact, the primacy of the normative idea of self-realization as the aim of emancipatory interests—Honneth also says: "'quasi-transcendental interests' of the human race" (Honneth 2003d, p. 174)—is almost totally based on the

---

86 See Zurn 2015, p. 94; and Petherbridge 2013, pp. 162–63, 167–69.
87 One could reasonably argue that Honneth's anthropological depiction is not formal, but "essentially contested" regarding certain embraced values (van den Brink 2011, p. 174).
88 See Kompridis 2004, p. 333.
89 See Kompridis 2004, p. 328.
90 See Deranty 2009, p. 463.

intersubjective anthropology outlined through recognition. And this modest, formal anthropology cannot, despite the intentions of the author, be enclosed in the normative idea of personhood, which concerns integrity, personal identity, and autonomy by acting. In fact, the tendency to use psychoanalysis to reconstruct the steps of subject-formation brings Honneth's discourse to a much broader level, which has anthropological and, perhaps, ontological claims: the subject's constitutive vulnerability and its dependence on relationships with others are the basis for which a normative account of personhood can be grounded on recognition. Thus, I argue that the motility implicit in the concept of self-realization, that is, a concept of freedom not enclosed in the idea of free will, but describable through the idea of possibilities to develop a harmonious biographical path, finds its justification in the dynamics of the I-me polarity and in the tension between selfhood of the self and the annulment of the ego-boundaries, which are proper anthropological ideas and not merely normative.

2.4.1 Love and Self-Confidence

As we have seen, the core of the physical violence is the injury to the basic self-confidence that allows the person to experience herself and the world "without anxiety" (Honneth 1995c, p. 104). The experience of being denied the intimacy, closeness, and usability of one's own body would therefore represent such a fundamental experience of "breakdown" that it would not open up a conflict for recognition that could change the essential characteristics of this sphere, as opposed to what happens with legal forms of respect and social esteem (Honneth 1995c, p. 133). This is because of the historical invariance of the harmfulness of violence, which would, despite cultural and social changes, embody the same degree of danger for one's relation-to-self. Correspondingly, Honneth claims that the first form of recognition, love, possesses "trans-historical and trans-cultural" characters that concern the socialization of every human being (Deranty 2009, p. 288). Given that, Honneth interprets the form of recognition of love as an almost unchanged constant throughout history—although of course the struggles for recognition that affect other spheres lead to consequences in this as well. But, in addition to the anthropological dimension concerning socialization, another aspect leads to this conclusion: the impossibility of universalizing ingroup instances—through the so-called semantic bridge—dynamics connoted by a marked moral particularism.[91]

Moreover, this fundamentality comes together with the fact that, in this sphere, Honneth has two purposes: on the one hand, he intends to re-actualize the concept

---

[91] Honneth significantly changes his own view in the debate with Nancy Fraser, claiming that this sphere of recognition is also subjected to social changes able to re-phrase the ways and the practices of recognition themselves. See Honneth 2003d, pp. 138–39.

of primary intersubjectivity; on the other hand, he aims to depict the intersubjective conditions of self-confidence. Correspondingly, two main features of the genealogical reconstruction of this sphere of recognition are, first, the role and ambiguity of the concept of symbiosis inherited from Winnicott and, second, the centrality of the capacity of being alone as main character of the positive self-relation here described.

Before reconstructing (in a quasi-phenomenological way) the steps by which the person is constituted through love-relations, Honneth proceeds to define the first sphere of recognition by considering the environmental scope of the subjects involved, namely, the object of recognition and its expressive mode. Love-recognition is in fact, first, "strong emotional attachments among a small number of people," which cannot be expanded indefinitely to include larger groups or even all of humanity. Taking inspiration from the Hegelian treatment of sexual love, Honneth next argues that, in such intersubjective practices, "subjects mutually confirm each other with regard to the concrete nature of their needs and thereby recognize each other as needy creatures." Finally, such confirmation of the other's (foremost biological and corporal) needs would be accomplished via "affective approval or encouragement" (Honneth 1995c, p. 95). The form of recognition is defined by "care" (Honneth 1995c, p. 107), since the circle of involved subjects is restricted to concrete others because of the emotional and affective character of the bonds (*who* are the recognizers/recognizees); the "independence" (Honneth 1995c, p. 107) of the other in its needs (*what* is recognized) is therefore implemented through the affective taking care of the other, and is motivated by feelings and attachment (*how* the subject is recognized).

Moving to the genealogical analysis Honneth carries out, the first issue, the concept of symbiosis (also called 'absolute dependence') describes the first phases of the child's life, in which the practical identities of newborn and caregiver are completely assimilated to each other. Honneth opens his analysis with this concept, first, to re-elaborate the Hegelian idea of a primary intersubjectivity in post-metaphysical terms, that is, the structural intersubjectivity of human beings. This aim is pursued foremost by moving away from the *intra*-psychic focus of the Freudian ego psychology to the *inter*-psychic dimension, thus showing that the constitution of the person depends on their innate exposure-to and dependence-on interpersonal relationships; in other words, to show that the intersubjectivity precedes the subjectivity. A second aim of this starting point is to take distance from the Habermasian model through a focus on "prelinguistic interactive experiences" (Honneth 1995c, p. 97): just as the normative thresholds operating in society are not realized in discursive practices but in the instances of recognition, in the same way the structuring of such demands is found, above all, in modes of relationship that precede the rational-symbolic expression of language, and that hence possess the claim to be more original. It is precisely from these purposes that the numerous ambiguities that have arisen around this sphere of recognition derive.

The first aspect to note coincides with the possibility opened by the interpretation of the Meadian I as the seat of the unconscious impulses: this allows Honneth to develop a psychological model that is totally inscribed within an intersubjective philosophical model and, therefore, to use the object relations theory as a paradigm for the constitution of the psyche.[92] In this sense, Honneth's explicit intention to formulate an account that exclusively concerns the moral personality has its roots in a larger dimension that, even if only between the lines, has much greater demands: the depiction of a general account of subjectivity.[93] In this regard—and also taking into account the centrality of the corporal dimension in the correspondent sphere of misrecognition—the centrality of the phase of being-held is noteworthy. With Winnicott, Honneth claims that a coherent development of embodiment and spatial orientation is allowed only as the newborn is held in its mother's arms.[94]

The second problem concerns how one is meant to conceive this state of "symbiotic oneness." Honneth describes it as a state of undifferentiated practical intersubjectivity in which the two interactional poles are completely merged, "incapable of individually demarcating themselves from each other" (Honneth 1995c, p. 99). Even for the mother, the perception of the child's neediness would be felt as her own and thus capable of defining the totality of her practical identity. First, Honneth tends to describe a phase in which subjectivity cannot exist in intersubjective terms, given the lack of distinction between the interactional dyads, thus confusing interrelation and sociability with intersubjectivity.[95] Without the experience of being-with,[96] in which necessarily two egos are involved, one cannot speak of intersubjectivity and therefore also cannot speak of recognition. Second, since one has to exclude the intersubjective dimension, the practical dimension of this phase of the relationship could be questioned, insinuating that what Honneth proposes is an ontological description of the primary nature of the intersubjective.[97] The third issue concerns the problem of describing this symbiotic phase, but more generally parenting itself, in mutual and symmetrical terms. On the one hand, the submission of the care to the rules of reciprocity would undermine the idea that caring for the other should be a gesture aimed primarily at its uniqueness and tendentially free, unbalanced, without wanting anything in return;[98] on the other hand, to describe parenting in mutualistic terms would imply a serious gap, that is, to not consider the implied asymmetrical power relations and roles adequately,[99] and a devaluation of the independence of the caregiver.

Although Honneth never speaks of proper recognition for the phase of symbiosis, these observations are useful to explicate two main features of his paradigm of

---

[92] See Whitebook 2001, pp. 276–78; and Petherbridge 2013, p. 148.
[93] See Deranty 2009, p. 291.
[94] See Honneth 1995c, p. 99.
[95] See Whitebook 2001, pp. 279–80.
[96] See Johanna Meehan 2011.
[97] See Petherbridge 2013, p. 150.
[98] See Petherbridge 2013, p. 154.
[99] See Iris Marion Young 2017, p. 207.

recognition, which are derived from the intent to ground the theory of recognition on the Aristotelian idea of the natural sociability of the human being. First, to the overlap between intersubjectivity and recognition already mentioned, one can now add also an assimilation between interactivity and intersubjectivity. By describing a non-personal interactive phase through intersubjective-interactional terms, Honneth is led to over-expand the characters of recognition by giving them an all-encompassing capacity and thus de-powers the specificity of the concept toward a more generic concept of practical inter-personality.[100] Second, the focus on parental relationships reveals a lack of theoretical clarity about the terms reciprocity, mutuality, and symmetry, which are often used as synonyms, but which cannot find the same space if applied to the reality of the relationship between caregiver and newborn. In any case, Honneth seems here to propose a model of recognition that affirms, in milder terms, the Hegelian assumption of the biunivocity of recognition, opening up to a more unbalanced model, where reciprocity and symmetry do not coincide.[101]

In any case, the heart of Honneth's account coincides with the analysis of the steps that lead to the development of a form of relation-to-self that can be described as basic self-confidence. Here, the central concept is the child's capacity of being alone and its paradox: it depicts indeed "the experience of being alone while someone else is present" (Donald Woods Winnicott 1990, p. 30).[102] The discussion focuses on two phenomena, that of destruction and aggression and that of transitional objects that allow the progressive detachment from the symbiosis and the acquisition of an individuality by the child (and the caregiver). According to Winnicott's analysis, the phase in which the mother gradually moves away from the newborn and acquires a form of life closer to that before childbirth marks the transition to relative dependence. In this phase, the child is subjected to pressures, due to the progressive awareness of its own distinction from the mother and the world, which are not immediately available. Thus, the aggressive gestures of the child toward the mother would represent, first, gestures testing the resistance and independence of reality, which shows itself in all its impertinence:

> In this sense, the child's destructive, injurious acts do not represent the expression of an attempt to cope negatively with frustration, but rather comprise the constructive means by which the child can come to recognize the 'mother,' unambivalently, as 'an entity in its own right.' If she survived the infant's destructive experiments as a person capable of resistance—indeed, if she, through her refusals, even provided the child with occasion for fits of temper—then the child will, by integrating its aggressive impulses, become able to love her (Honneth 1995c, p. 101).

---

100 See Deranty 2009, pp. 467–79; and Piromalli 2012, p. 246.
101 See Lucio Cortella 2008; and Arto Laitinen 2010. I discuss this issue at length in chapter 6.
102 See Winnicott 1990, pp. 30–38.

Thus, two elements are noteworthy. First, these aggressive acts of the child constitute a structural moment of subject-formation,[103] whose constructive character must not obscure the centrality of the "infant's painful compulsion to break with the merely momentary states of symbiosis with the primary care-giver and become an independent entity" (Honneth 2011b, p. 394). Although Honneth undoubtedly paints a rather positive anthropological image, such a statement cannot but consider that at the basis of individuality itself there is an experience of fracture that connotes all the successive steps of the constitution of the person. Second, these aggressive gestures of testing the independence of the outside world—and as a consequence, of the child itself—may imply a step toward individuality and relationship only if the mother's response is marked by a renewal of affective confirmation. In other words, only if the caregiver resists the attacks of the child, can he or she be perceived by the latter as an independent entity, and only if the response to these attacks is affectively charged will the child know to be confirmed in its own agency. If these transitions succeed with a certain balance, "then mother and child can acknowledge their dependence on each other's love without having to merge symbiotically" (Honneth 1995c, p. 102).

The second decisive step in establishing a personal identity is characterized by interaction with transitional objects. These objects, loaded in a strongly emotional way by the child in an attempt to relive experiences of symbiotic union, find their ambiguous ontological realm in the intersubjective acceptance of their semantic versatility. By playing, the way of relating to objects corresponds to an over-signification that is possible only via the encouragement or the tacit agreement by others. In other words, "out of a basic confidence in the care of a loved one," the child is "capable of being 'lost' in interaction with the chosen object" (Honneth 1995c, p. 103), which accomplish the task of bridging the inner and the outer realities, because of the emotional meaning assigned to the object itself. Being unbalanced toward objectual reality by playing without merging with it is allowed by a self that is kept—guaranteed—by the affection of other loved ones. This dynamic, the consequences of which in the adult's relations with cultural object are only mentioned by Winnicott and Honneth, represents the theoretical key that describes the positive self-relation here at stake and its link with recognitional relations:

> Only a refracted symbiosis enables the emergence of a productive interpersonal balance between the boundary-establishment and boundary-dissolution that, for Winnicott, belongs to the structure of a relationship that has matured through mutual disillusionment. There, the capacity to be alone constitutes the subject-based pole of an intersubjective tension, whose opposing pole is the capacity for boundary-dissolving merging with the other (Honneth 1995c, p. 105).[104]

---

103 See Deranty 2009, p. 291.
104 The German expressions Honneth uses for "boundary-establishment" and "boundary-dissolution" are "Abgrenzung" and "Entgrenzung," which effectively show the complementarity of the two dynamic moments of the "Alleinseinkönnen" (Honneth 1992b, pp. 169–70).

In other words, in being emotionally tied with someone, the subject can find its space of independence and the capacity of interacting freely with otherness, without being embedded in it. Likewise, the contribution of friendships and love relationships to the formation of an undamaged relation-to-self is interpreted by Honneth as an intimacy that affectively guarantees this balance of confidence, a being-with-oneself or being at home in the world.

We are now able to summarize the main features of this sphere of recognition that Honneth has reconstructed genealogically through a focus on the subject-formation's steps. First, as physical violence causes the long-lasting damage of denying an immediate access to one's self, the others and the world, so the positive basic self-confidence has to be conceived as a freedom from anguish gained and instantiated in the experience of being alone thanks to the others. The practical relation-to-self here described revolves around a delicate and fragile balance between merging with the otherness and keeping one's selfhood. As such, it is noteworthy that Honneth describes the interaction with the objectual world as derived from a certain self-relation guaranteed by the affective affirmation from others: the access to objects is therefore always mediated. Second, the description of the subject as a "ruptured symbiosis" has not only the purpose of placing the first piece of a normative concept of personal integrity (Petherbridge 2013, p. 158), but also the broader one of defining independence as conceivable only within patterns of dependence, namely, to depict the particularity of the individual without falling back into atomism or subjectivism. Third, we need to emphasize that this independence within dependence primarily concerns the corporal dimension and physical interactions: through being held, aggression-testing, transitional objects, affection from others, the subject is formed by developing an immediate sense of familiarity with the world, which friendships and sexual relations confirm even in adulthood. Every other dimension of love relationships or friendships—in *The Struggle for Recognition*—can be traced back to the sphere of social esteem. The object of recognition is the subject's biological neediness and corporal vulnerability, which relies on "an affective confidence in the continuity of shared concern" (Honneth 1995c, p. 107), through which the self can achieve the balance necessary to avoid re-falling into merging with the other. Fourth, recalling Wildt's arguments, one can deduce a first form of undemandable obligations from Honneth's account: it is the vulnerability of the other to establish unbalanced moral commitments, which fall outside the Kantian legal-form paradigm.[105] This imbalance implicit in the forms of recognition of love and the moral particularity of care and affection profoundly calls into question a symmetrical model of recognition.

---

[105] See Honneth 1997.

2.4.2 Respect and Self-Respect

Also in the second sphere, Honneth proceeds in the first instance with a theoretical definition of the form of recognition, and then genealogically traces the respective characters in their unfolding.

The core distinction that Honneth introduces in approaching his discourse on the sphere of recognition of respect is between Hegel's and Mead's views on the system of rights. Indeed, if Mead, focusing on the experience of actual recognition relations, defines the sphere of rights as first belonging to a community of rights-bearers, Hegel embraces within his own perspective some Kantian assumptions that are fundamental for the understanding of the modern system of law. On the one hand, the limit of Mead's perspective is to conceive a traditional system of rights in which the main aspect is that of group-belonging. The Kantian perspective, on the other hand, introduces a universal concept of moral responsibility tied to criteria of rationality, which would find its most immediate social concretion in the rights expressed at least since the Enlightenment and the French Revolution, according to a scheme of progressive decoupling of human dignity from belonging to value communities that represents a criterion of distinction—only possible in modern societies—between the second and third spheres of recognition. However, Honneth maintains a certain tension between the universal dimension of moral rationality and group-belonging, and tries to harmonize them by focusing on the possibilities of recognizing a subject as capable of rational morality.[106] In fact, such universal moral accountability is not approached as transcendental feature, but as primarily disclosed through recognitional acts, that is, through recognizing a person as bearer of the rights and the obligations proper to a given community. Therefore, keeping the community dimension guarantees, in the first place, a de-formalization of the Kantian idea, in an attempt to show that the concept of the moral responsibility of every man can only be effectively implemented through an extension of the legislation of given communities. In this sense, even the partner of the interaction would know herself as morally responsible only when she is recognized as one from whom it is expected to adhere to certain legal obligations and as bearer of rights, both—evidently—valid in the definiteness of a community. Moreover, this approach is aimed at responding to a cognitive issue, that is, the necessity for a context in order to claim whether the subject before me is a concrete bearer of universal rights:

> In legal recognition, two operations of consciousness flow together, so to speak, since, on the one hand, it presupposes moral knowledge of the legal obligations that we must keep vis-à-vis autonomous persons, while, on the other hand, it is only an empirical interpretation of the situation that can inform us whether, in the case of a given concrete other, we are dealing with an entity possessed of the quality that makes these obligations applicable (Honneth 1995c, pp. 112–13).

---

106 See Allen 1998, pp. 454–55.

2.4 A Formal Conception of Ethical Life: An Anthropological Justification

Honneth therefore argues that the concrete recognition of a human being as a person (endowed with moral accountability) is dependent "on background assumptions about the subjective prerequisites that enable participation in rational will-formation" (Honneth 1995c, p. 114). However, if this process of contextualization seems to weaken the universality of Kant's perspective and, thereby, sketches a risky relativistic account of human dignity, it is also true that, conversely, the inscription of such an idea in the concreteness of a given community indissolubly binds the sharing of underlying normative standards and their possible questioning through rational criteria of justification.[107] Such an account—present in Hegel, but not in Mead— prevents the process of social integration from being uncritical and equivalent to social assimilation, precisely because belonging to a community endows the subject with a universal insight on its moral rationality, which can affect the subversion of unjust law systems.

Given this speculative account, Honneth moves to reconstruct the evolution of this social form genealogically, namely, by explicating why it has become a dimension within which personal integrity forms itself under contemporary conditions. Nonetheless, contrary to what we saw in the sphere of love, Honneth maintains that an empirical verification cannot be carried out in proper terms.[108] However, the distinction made by T. H. Marshall between civil, political, and social rights provides Honneth with two arguments, which are therefore related, albeit mildly, to matters of a historiographic nature.[109] Since these different types of rights characterize instances of social change in successive periods, they would be able to show the link between rights and demands "for full-fledged membership in the political community" (Honneth 1995c, p. 116). Throughout history, different categories of rights— civil, political, and social—have been required as determined instruments of affirmation of one's universal dignity. Moreover, this historical evolution suggests a vectoriality already underway, a path of progress that can be identified along two axes: the de-formalization of rights, that is, their ever-increasing acquisition of content and the opening up of possibilities through material means; and the universalization of rights, namely, the increasingly inclusive expansion of their spectrum to include— ideally and not without contradictions—every human being. It is noteworthy that this second direction cannot be fully realized without the first, which is the effective instrument of de-abstraction of the Kantian perspective.

Having briefly sketched the theoretical situation of recognition and its historical evolution, a rather intricate matter arises: the relationship between rights and recognition. Honneth first argues that the different forms of rights are tied to demands for recognition, as mentioned above. Therefore, second, social partners experience rights as "depersonalized symbols of social respect" (Honneth 1995c, p. 118):

---

107 See Deranty 2009, p. 295.
108 See Honneth 1995c, pp. 110 and 120.
109 See Honneth 1995c, pp. 115–18.

through rights, subjects relate to themselves with regard to their moral responsibility and accountability. However, third, this process of symbolization is also thought of as an abstraction in legal form of an effective gesture of personal recognition. But, finally, the system of rights and obligations—the outcome of the depersonalization of recognizers—represents the concrete precondition that enables recognition within a given community; only thanks to the social assumptions of moral accountability can the concrete other be considered worthy of recognition under this respect. This apparent vicious circle, in which the result of the depersonalization of recognition is also the precondition for the personal recognition of the concrete other, can be reconciled if we focus on the relationship with the social effectiveness inherited from Hegel and on the importance of progress: this coincidence of result and condition of possibility must be conceived in diachronic and progressive terms, where the initial situation is never—not even conceptually—an absolute. Moreover, it should be noted that, at this point, the discourse on law could shift the axis of recognition from the interpersonal to the institutional level. However, Honneth does not seem interested in further detailing this process of depersonalization, thus leaving the structural contours of the institutional world vague but suggesting a first aspect to be established: institutions are instantiations of principles and, even more, of practices of recognition.

However, this process of depersonalization not only concerns the recognizers, but also the recognized and the mode of recognition, since the Kantian insight leads the depiction of the sphere. First, the form of recognition of respect is not graduated or differential (within the community where the laws are valid) and, second, it considers the subject neither for its needs nor for its peculiar traits, but as end-in-itself (given the assumptions of moral accountability).[110] Respect, unlike love, is therefore not motivated by emotional reasons and is not articulated according to particular modalities of caring, but has a strongly cognitive character aimed at the mutual affirmation of an "equal status" (Deranty 2009, p. 294). Second, in relation to this, respect outlines a principle of equity between the recognizing partners, which forms a moral obligation of a properly legal nature: contrary to the imbalance of the principle of love, the attitudes of the subjects involved are articulated according to symmetrical forms of relationship. Third, the second form of recognition represents an affirmation of the person—of her status as bearer of rights—that implies, however, at the same time, a distancing, a step back from the other. This connotation—implicit in the German term for respect: *Achtung*, which also means "watch out!," "danger," or "attention"[111]—is fundamental for the delineation of the universal dimension that otherwise seems to be taken for granted: it is by means of such a cognitive distance—the idea that one is in the presence of someone that should remain untouched—that respect can be addressed to every human being.

---

110 See Zurn 2015, p. 35.
111 See Wildt 2010, p. 197.

Having clarified the *what* of respect—the dignity of human beings according to their moral accountability—and its *how*—equal and mutual cognitive perception, which presupposes a certain distance—the positive form of self-relation of this sphere remains to be determined, which, according to Honneth, becomes intuitively more graspable through the negative method, namely, by observing the reactions before the denial of rights. However, the elements already enumerated allow for an understanding of self-respect as reflection of respect. The first would therefore coincide with that relation-to-self in which the subject looks at itself from a general point of view and knows itself as deserving legal rights by means of its participation in a universalizable community in which the granting of such rights affirms and confirms its moral accountability and responsibility.[112] In other words, its dignity.

2.4.3 Esteem and Self-Esteem

The emergence of the third sphere of recognition is closely tied, from a historical point of view, with a decoupling to which the concept of human dignity has been subjected throughout the course of modernity. Though the sphere of law has assumed the universal element of the idea, this dynamic is not able to accommodate the singularity of the individual. But, Honneth claims, besides the forms of love and rights, subjects need "a form of social esteem that allows them to relate positively to their concrete traits and abilities" (Honneth 1995c, p. 121), in order to develop an undistorted relation-to-self. Then, if the neediness of the person finds its context of affirmation in the relationships of love and her moral responsibility in the sphere of rights, those demands that are not yet included can find their own dimension thanks to evaluative criteria tied to ethical ideas, images of the good, and so on, which take place in a social horizon of shared values, namely, always group-mediated:

> This task of mediation is performed, at the societal level, by a symbolically articulated—yet always open and porous—framework of orientation, in which those ethical values and goals are formulated that, taken together, comprise the cultural self-understanding of a society (Honneth 1995c, p. 122).

One could say that the definition of this mode of recognition starts from the phenomenological ascertainment, supported by the observation of the acts of misrecognition, that people see themselves, in specific contexts, evaluated, esteemed, or degraded for their uniqueness, which is always related to evaluative criteria. However, it is precisely here that the ambiguity of this sphere emerges. In an attempt not to superimpose a substantive value framework, the structure Honneth describes is much broader than those of love or law and tends to embrace many different aspects and phenomena. Such a "context-dependent" (Zurn 2015, p. 41) form of recognition is

---

[112] See Honneth 1995c, pp. 118–19; and Zurn 2015, p. 37.

indeed considered as addressing the person's unique "traits and abilities," "accomplishments," achievements, "integrity," "ways of life", "manner of self-realization," "forms of life and manners of belief," etc. (Honneth 1995c, pp. 125–134). In other words, Honneth's account seems to oscillate between three dimensions. First, the focus is on the individual's qualities and abilities that are worthy of esteem in light of their representing a contribution "to the practical realization of society's abstractly defined goals" (Honneth 1995c, p. 126). Second, the reference to cultural conflicts between different value-groups and ways of life legitimizes the inclusion of a broader dimension in this sphere of recognition, one that cannot be reduced to the concept of contribution, but that instead properly concerns the idea of cultural identity.[113] Finally, keeping our eyes on the third form of misrecognition, where insult, degradation, and downgrading coincide with the daily understanding of the concept of disrespect, it can be understood that the spectrum of this form of recognition embraces a dimension that coincides with what could be defined as the dignity of the person in its most immediate sense: the integrity of the person per se, that is, my being who I am and how I am. Even if, from an extremely functionalized perspective of the social groups' interplay, cultural identity could be seen as a contribution to the realization of the ends of society, it seems to me that certain instances of identity and requests for recognition of one's own personal integrity cannot be exclusively traced back to the "way in which the individual fulfils social functions" (Deranty 2009, p. 301), but also concerns the elementary level in which one can see one's worthiness in the eyes of others, not for particular contributions or achievements, but also for one's own particular presence.

This three-dimensionality (contribution, cultural identity, and singularity) of the third sphere of recognition is due to the genealogical analysis that leads Honneth to root the idea of esteem in that of honor, inherited prima facie from Hegel and identified as that pole of human dignity left aside by the universalization of legal rights.[114] This concept expresses a traditional idea of personal integrity and esteem totally attributable to group belonging. Honneth claims that, as long as the value system maintained an objective validity, the degree of esteem accorded to the subject depended strictly on its place in the classification of the different groups, which constituted, therefore, the authentic object of esteem: the individuals were only participants in group-pride.[115] However, because of the compactness and cohesion of these social groups, relationships of solidarity were able to develop within them. The latter

---

[113] See Honneth 1995c, p. 127.
[114] This description is not exempt from future reworkings, indeed: it is precisely the definition of the third sphere of recognition that fluctuates the most in Honneth's works. In *Redistribution or Recognition?*, Honneth defines the principle characterizing the third sphere as 'achievement,' while in *The Pathologies of Individual Freedom*, *Freedom's Right*, and *The Idea of Socialism* (due to the greater influence of Hegel's *Philosophy of Right*) the third sphere of recognition coincides with the dimension of the democratic state.
[115] See Honneth 1995c, pp. 127–28.

represents "not just passive tolerance" (Honneth 1995c, p. 129), but the way through which subjects sympathize with each other based on symmetrical, mutual esteem. It is noteworthy that it is in this sphere of recognition that Honneth uses the attribute of symmetry for the first time to describe recognitional interactions, and above all to describe the authentic form of esteem. This insistence is due to Honneth's reading of Siep and is intended to keep the dynamic of recognition—and especially its third sphere—in the field of horizontality, avoiding a subsumption of the individual into totality. The multipolarity of objects of esteem in contemporary societies thus becomes comprehensible in light of the fragmentation and multiplication of groups within the modernization of society, which leads to the individualization of the idea of honor and to its openness to all social classes, according to an equalization dynamic: personal integrity is no longer structurally ascribable to any belonging, but depends on a myriad of factors, which hinge on the multiple contexts that a contemporary subject may find herself living within. If esteem is granted according to eclectic and multifaceted standards, the primary task for the theory is to elaborate a general collaboration-context and value-horizon in which relationships of solidarity (as a full-fledged form of esteem) can develop under contemporary situations for all members of society, according to the axes of individualization and equalization. In Honneth's view, this operation cannot be prescribed by the social theory, but only be carried out by future struggles for recognition.[116]

In any case, Honneth's historical-speculative reconstruction allows us to define the characters of the third form of recognition. The object of esteem is represented by what can be synthesized through the individual's *singularity*—that is, the individual's traits, abilities, achievements, and forms of life—which is affirmed through symmetrical forms of social esteem, that is, solidarity. Thanks to this form of recognition, which always assumes its dimension in relation to the context of reference and its evaluation standards, the subject is able to relate to itself with self-esteem, that is, looking positively at its own singularity as something worthy.

2.5 Some Open Issues: Recognition, Subject-Formation, and Social Ontology

The formal conception of ethical life Honneth outlines is therefore a structural concept of good that defines the conditions for the development of an undamaged practical identity in which recognition practices, principles, and spheres of interaction

---

[116] See Honneth 1995c, pp. 178–79. I think that this idea of openness and the dependence of theory on practice shows quite clearly that Honneth's paradigm, which also concerns issues of justice (especially in *Redistribution or Recognition?* and *Freedom's Right*), is to a certain extent open to the "to come" (*à-venir*), contrary to what Bankovsky claims. The normative dimension derives its traits from a genealogical reconstruction that allows structural proposals from the present perspective, but future evolutions are not pre-determinable. See Miriam Bankovsky 2012.

are closely intertwined. For the sake of clarity, these levels can be schematized as follows:[117]

Table 1: Honneth's first paradigm of recogntion

Mode of recognition	Emotional support	Cognitive respect	Social esteem
Dimension of personality	Needs and emotions	Moral responsibility	Traits and abilities
Forms of recognition	Primary relationships (love, friendship)	Legal relations (rights)	Community of value (solidarity)
Practical self-relation	Basic self-confidence	Self-respect	Self-esteem

In any case, there are some theoretical knots that still need to be investigated.

The first set of questions concerns the definition of the concept of recognition. Honneth embraces Siep's idea, according to which one of the theoretical advantages found in the principle of recognition consists in its multipolarity. As we have seen, this would allow the foundation of an ethical theory that approaches social reality in a non-unilateral way. This idea, which certainly brings benefits, also has its drawbacks. First, Honneth does not clarify how a uniform concept of recognition could be unearthed from such diversity, one that would be able to comprehend the different faces of the three forms. In fact, Honneth's account lacks a common definition of practical acts that actually differ from one another with regard to their aims, practical modalities of accomplishment, and consequences. Surely the idea of affirmation or confirmation allows us to understand a certain unity, but, second, this lack of clarity has an even greater impact when looking at the conceptual consequences implied by the different forms of recognition. Beyond the immediate differences seen when observing affection, respect, and esteem, the biggest problem concerns the idea of mutuality. While reciprocity is affirmed as a characteristic of all three forms, we have seen that love-recognition possesses a structural imbalance, resting on undemandable obligations in the face of the other's vulnerability, while legal relationships and esteem require equity and symmetry, without which we would witness their own collapse qua recognitional acts. Therefore, it would become even more difficult to gather, under a single concept, forms of relationship that respond to different logics. Third, one could argue that recognition has a functionalistic character because such a unitary concept could be provided by the efficacy of the intersubjective gestures to the possibility of the person's formation. Here, however, another binomial opens up, that is, the simultaneous presence of generative and normative dimensions in Honneth's paradigm of recognition. Regarding this, one could say that what constitutes recognition is its person-generative character, according to the different dimensions that 'person' possesses under contemporary conditions. But this

---

[117] See Honneth 1995c, p. 129.

solution is apparently not completely suitable for a normative account of recognition, such as Honneth's. Fourth, in *The Struggle for Recognition*, it is not particularly clear whether such gestures of recognition—which have first and foremost to do with aspects of the person and not with the person per se—play an *attributive* or *perceptive* role, that is, whether they actually grant personal features or, rather, acknowledge them. Finally, a problematic aspect of the text is that the concept of recognition is dealt with almost exclusively from the point of view of the recognized. This perspective, which finds its motivation in the focus on misrecognition and on the purpose of individual self-realization, however, provides a partial definition of the idea, which strongly characterizes Honneth's entire paradigm. In other words, while the reason for being recognized is clarified, the reason for recognizing is not. Although I will postpone an in-depth discussion of these issues to chapter six, it is useful here to briefly outline two further unclarified issues.

First, we have seen that the formal concept of ethical life is based on the idea of self-realization, which in turn has anthropological connotations that cannot be eliminated. Despite Honneth's intention to keep his discourse on a normative level, I believe that his paradigm of recognition has—even in its development, and therefore not limited only to *The Struggle for Recognition*—some relevant guidelines for the formulation of a post-modern anthropology. Besides the centrality of the problem of the justification of the critical theory, this anthropological problem concerns the concept of recognition in more general terms: since the Hegelian description, this peculiar form of intersubjective relation has been presented as the basis for the generation of self-consciousness in the broad sense. One could therefore argue—as a first phase of Honneth's thought shows—that the concepts of recognition and of personhood are complementary.

Second, the confrontation with Siep and the issues at stake in the sphere of legal recognition have brought to light a very problematic issue: the relationship between intersubjective practices of recognition and institutional reality. Honneth develops this theoretical dimension above all in later works, but it is useful to emphasize that a link between recognition and the process of generation of institutions is already central in *The Struggle for Recognition*, especially with regard to the mechanisms of social change. However, an analysis of the relationship between the horizontality of recognition and the verticality of the individual-institution relationship is (perhaps voluntarily) overlooked, and the ways in which recognition practices can instantiate in spheres, the nature of the latter and their interplay remain implicit. Therefore, even if the aim of the work is a re-actualization of the Hegelian idea that conflict leads to the evolution of primary forms of sociality, many details of such a theory applicable to contemporary reality are missing.

Chapter 3
Reification and the Antecedence of Recognition

Reification (2005) is the more comprehensive and in-depth expression of a series of ongoing changes in Honneth's paradigm of recognition after *The Struggle for Recognition*.[1] Before dealing with the text and the new outlines of the concept of recognition contained therein, it seems useful to focus briefly on these changes, summarized in six nuclei, that enclose a certain perspective or a second phase in Honneth's thinking.

A) First, the tripartition of recognitional forms and the relative multidimensionality of the subject are left aside. Consequently, the investigation is directed toward "individuality itself, taken as a normative fact" and described as an indivisible phenomenon (Deranty 2009, p. 442); similarly, recognition is considered within a certain unitariness, and theoretically deepened as a conceptual and existential whole, within dimensions other than the normative one.[2]

B) Honneth also departs from Mead's social psychology because of the "tendency toward cognitivism" that characterizes the internalization of the behavioral models of the generalized other (Honneth 2008, p. 42).[3] This feature would in fact hinder an adequate understanding of the role played by recognition during the processes of constitution of selfhood and social integration. In this way, Honneth moves further away from Habermas and from a possible explanation of the recognition that includes the dimension of language, accentuating the role assigned to the pre-linguistic and reciprocal "expressive gestures" (Honneth 2001, p. 117).

C) Entering the twenty-first century, Honneth's link with psychoanalysis is deepened and broadened, with numerous consequences—an example of this tendency being "Postmodern Identity," but also "Appropriating Freedom." In *Reification*, however, the reference to Winnicott is considerably reduced in favor of the empirical results of different researchers in the field of developmental psychology, which lead Honneth to describe the first phases of the child's life in a different way from *The Struggle for Recognition*.[4] From a genealogical and logical point of view, a theoretical priority is assigned to a type of interaction defined as "antecedent act of recognition" (Honneth 2008, p. 52), affectively or empathetically characterized. This concept—at least in the first instance—seems irreconcilable with the Winnicottian symbiosis.

D) The differences from *The Struggle for Recognition* mentioned above are largely due to a re-evaluation of Adorno's thought and above all to the influence exerted by the concept of mimetic reason.[5] With the marked and explicit adoption of some

---

1 See Deranty 2009, p. 461.
2 See Honneth 2001.
3 See also Honneth 2002.
4 See, among others, Honneth 2011b, p. 393.
5 See Deranty 2009, p. 461.

Adornian accounts, Honneth acquires new tools to unveil the unfulfilled promises of modernity,[6] as well as the pathological effects of paradoxical modernization, of the "dialectical intertwinement of enlightenment and power" (Theodor W. Adorno and Max Horkheimer 2002, p. 138). that is. Honneth redefines these contradictory and detrimental outcomes for personal integrity through Lukács's concept of reification.

E) A further peculiarity of *Reification* concerns the "indirectly normative character" of the inquiry (Honneth 2008, p. 21). The original or genuine form of recognition sought after in fact "draws its justification much more strongly from social ontology or philosophical anthropology than from the sphere customarily termed moral philosophy or ethics" (Honneth 2008, p. 26). The description of recognition as "existential engagement" with otherness thus marks a profound distance with the social-theoretical and political connotations of the struggle for recognition (Honneth 2008, p. 32),[7] and it also possesses more theoretical insights thanks to the references to authors such as Heidegger, Dewey, Cavell, and Sartre, which make the tone of the arguments wide-ranging and comprehensive.

F) A last notable difference between *The Struggle for Recognition* and *Reification* concerns conflict. If conflict was considered a dimension intrinsically inherent to the intersubjective interactions of recognition—which represents the very core of Honneth's account on social reality—in the latter work it is completely set aside. From a certain point of view, this absence could find its explanation in the very attempt to describe a level of recognitional interaction that precedes "all other, more substantial forms of recognition" (Honneth 2008, p. 90, n. 70.)—love, respect, social esteem, with their respective spheres—and, by so doing, to ground the aforementioned anthropological justification. In this sense, this originality or primacy of recognition would precede, even in a chronological sense, any form of recognition or misrecognition and consequently any struggle aimed at correcting such distortions in social interaction. However, the aspect of conflict that *Reification* seems to lack most is not so much the political one—which concerns the moral progress of society—as the genealogical one. In fact, the tension or balance between autonomy and boundary described by the object relations theory played an essential role in the constitution of the subject, since it allowed for the coexistence of the two selves necessary for the very existence of relationships and thus of recognition itself.

Although all these issues are apparently in contradiction with some of the focal points of *The Struggle for Recognition*, *Reification* embodies a certain continuity with the instances left in abeyance in the first work and, with this, is a bold attempt to base normative social theory on social-ontological and anthropological structures aimed at showing the priority of *recognizing* (*Anerkennen*) over *cognizing* (*Erkennen*). However, it is precisely because of the criticisms received by this admixture of nor-

---

6 See Alessandro Ferrara 2011, p. 372.
7 See Anita Chari 2010, p. 601.

mative and onto-anthropological dimensions that Honneth, after this work, decisively abandons these levels of investigation.

Therefore, before analyzing and focusing on the novelties that the definition of recognition contained in *Reification* brings with it, it is useful, first, to briefly mention some articles in which Honneth focuses on certain aspects—the epistemological dimension of recognition, the problematization of the idea of self-realization, and the Adornian concept of mimetic reason as key for social criticism—that lay the foundations for the work and show its relationship with *The Struggle for Recognition* (section 3.1). Second, discussing the concept of reification will be useful for introducing new determinations of recognition and, especially through the criticisms aimed at Honneth's approach, for deepening his critical perspective and setting (section 3.2). Subsequently, the focus will be on the concept of antecedent recognition or emotional identification, which constitutes the heart of the re-definition of the concept of recognition, as well as on its triple declination: toward others, toward the world, and toward one's own self (section 3.3). Finally, we will try to condense some critical points to relaunch the discussion for the following chapters (section 3.4).

3.1 Some Premises: Visibility, Authenticity, and Mimesis

The purpose of this chapter is to show how *Reification* represents the outcome of Honneth's elaborations of recognition in the early 2000s, still strongly determined by the attempt to elaborate a formal and intersubjective anthropology, conceived as a normative pivotal principle and enabling-threshold for critical thought. In fact, some of the criticisms levelled at the idea of 'antecedent' recognition—and, consequently, at the new description of the first phases of the infant's life[8]—lack what could be called a 'continuity-perspective,' that is, they fail to take *Reification* as a further step in an ongoing research project. However, leaving these themes aside for the moment, we want to focus on three articles published by Honneth between 2001 and 2003 that focus on several issues left unresolved by *The Struggle for Recognition:* the epistemological character of recognition, the apparent unproblematicity of the work's core concept—namely, the idea of individual self-realization—and the almost immediate link made in identifying moral injury with misrecognition.

The first of these attempts, "Invisibility" (2001), plays a crucial role in widening the concept of recognition,[9] since it is in this writing that Honneth considers the relation between *Erkennen* and *Anerkennen*. Once again, Honneth's starting point is the experiences of disrespect and moral damage, examining Ralph Ellison's novel *The Invisible Man*, where racial discrimination is described as the experience of being

---

8 Here I primarily have in mind Judith Butler's and Jonathan Lear's comments contained in the English edition of *Reification*, where Honneth is reproached for not giving sufficient weight to the symbiotic phase of the newborn-caregiver relationship. See Butler 2008; and Jonathan Lear 2008.
9 See Zurn 2015, p. 43; Petherbridge 2013, p. 177.

looked through, as the impossibility of being seen. Honneth's argument can be summarized in the following four points.

First, Honneth takes his cue from the definition of physical visibility, the core of which is the idea of "individual identifiability" (Honneth 2001, p. 113). The possibility of acknowledging an object as such, that is, to identify it visually, would be—trivially expressed—allowed by its manifestation within a perceptive space-time horizon, namely, within situational parameters. This "represents a first, primitive form of what we call 'cognizing' (*Erkennen*)" (Honneth 2001, p. 113).However, second, the experience of being looked through clearly cannot be defined in such physical terms, but rather implies that they exist, and relies on a performative aspect: the affected subjects would be able to perceive being overlooked because of the absence of certain intersubjective practical reactions that are, under normal social conditions, signs or expressions of consideration, respect, and affirmation:

> The 'making visible' of a person extends beyond the cognitive act of individual identification by giving public expression, with the aid of suitable actions, gestures or facial expressions, to the fact that the person is noticed affirmatively in the manner appropriate to the relationship in question; it is only because we possess a common knowledge of these emphatic forms of expression in the context of our second nature that we can see in their absence a sign of invisibility, of humiliation (Honneth 2001, p. 116).

Social visibility hinges on an evaluative framework, within which gestural and symbolic expressions become capable of accounting for the performative seeing or ignoring the other. And thanks to these evaluative criteria, the subject can know itself as recognized: recognizing is always originally both a perceiving and an expressing, both of which actions are in some way formed within the normative context of second nature.[10] Therefore, just as physical visibility depends on the space-time horizon that allows the identifiability of an object, a person's social visibility depends on a moral horizon, within which perception and expression represent two phases of recognition. Conversely, making the other invisible through the deprivation of gestures that publicly attest to affirmation would be an essential element of misrecognition and, thus, a cause of moral suffering.[11]

Third, Honneth defines recognition as a "meta-action" (Honneth 2001, p. 120), that is, as adoption of a public stance, testified and instantiated in expressive gestures, through which we make the other aware of our attitudes. In this sense, recog-

---

[10] See also Honneth 2002. Although this article represents a decisive turning point in the definition of recognition, we will focus on it—and on "Recognition as Ideology"—in chapter 6, where the concept will be addressed as such.

[11] This argument, which in fact seems to anticipate Ricoeur's criticism of the form of misrecognition of love, represents, according to Zurn, a considerable difference with *Reification*, where primary recognition would not possess a normative character. However, in my view, the fact that Honneth repeatedly emphasizes the non-normative character of the antecedent recognition does not coincide with the amorality of suffering due to its deprivation. See Zurn 2015, p. 217 n. 11.

nition would not only coincide—as could be synthetized from *The Struggle for Recognition*—with punctual affirmational acts toward the personal dimensions of others, but would at the same time depict a stance, within which we are able to bring to expression the character of the others being perceived. In other words, recognition is fundamentally a position toward the interacting partner, which acts as a condition of possibility for the active manifestation of determined and positive practical gestures of affirmation.

Finally, one could therefore say that, in addition to the epistemological dimension, a notable passage concerns the expressivist model of recognition, according to which its content and its mode of expression cannot be unrelated.[12] The inseparability of these two dimensions—the *how* and the *what* of recognition—is found in the developmental account showing the relation between recognition and expressive gestures. Drawing on Daniel Stern's account, Honneth emphasizes the gestural and reciprocal component of the child's process of social development. The key to this process revolves around the caregiver's facial expressions—which are affectively charged and reveal his or her "readiness to interact"—and the infant's "spectrum of reflex-like activities that, in reaction to the gestural stimulation of the caregiver, can develop into the first forms of social response" (Honneth 2001, p. 117). In such a relationship, the affective character of certain gestures immediately expresses the other as recognized. Thus, it is important to make two observations. First, such a reciprocal practical interaction between infant and caregiver—whose core would be represented by the smile and similar affective interactions—is at least partially in contradiction with the concept of symbiosis, which excludes any form, albeit primordial, of agency on the part of the child, because any nuclear form subjectivity would have not yet emerged: as we have already seen, the idea of symbiosis cannot be accompanied by the experience of being-with.[13] Or, in any case, one could argue that the experience of symbiosis cannot be established on a reciprocal level; the two poles of interaction overlap each other.[14] Second, the "dependency of recognition on expressive gestures" and its consequent definition as meta-action gives us a greater clue about the very nature of the concept and, in particular, its difference from verbal expressions (Honneth 2001, p. 120). In fact, the practical gestures of affirmation, even in adulthood, coincide with symbolic abbreviations, which "express in abbreviated form the totality of the actions that are supposed to be accorded" to the other in view of his or her situation within the evaluative horizon of the second nature (Honneth 2001, p. 118). In other words, if by linguistic articulation the signifier conveys the signified and can be separated from it, in recognitional affirmation acts the *how* and the *what* of expression are co-extensive and co-immanent to each other because of their expressive structure. This holistic character of recognition, as we shall

---

12 See David Owen 2010.
13 See Meehan 2011, p. 98.
14 See Franco Crespi 2008, p. 39.

see, is one of the main features of *Reification*'s redefinition of the concept, as well as its determination as an epistemic stance.

Moving to the second article, "Organized Self-Realization" (original German, 2002), our object of interest changes. In this paper, Honneth does not focus on the concept of recognition, but on the idea of self-realization, highlighting the problematic nature of individualization within capitalistic society. The main idea of the paper revolves around the fact that sociology has from the very beginning considered the process of individualization as an enrichment and an impoverishment of personal freedom. Drawing on Simmel's account, Honneth highlights the ambiguity of the term, which hinges on four different meanings: the increasing external biographical possibilities, the "growing isolation of individual actors" in metropolitan contexts, the "increase in individuals' powers of reflection," and individual autonomy (Honneth 2004b, p. 466). Given this great multiplicity of meanings, the causal (or consequential) element of such ambiguity is represented by a "paradoxical reversal," whereby self-realization claims are institutionalized and therefore "the particular goals of such claims are lost" and "transmuted into a support of the system's legitimacy" (Honneth 2004b, p. 467). Referring to numerous sociologists, as well as to dynamics such as the purification of family relationships, the experimental exploration of one's own personality in leisure activities, and the consumption of luxury goods, Honneth comes—always together with Simmel—to the conclusion that a so-called "individualism of irreplaceability" (Honneth 2004b, p. 471), rather than expressing an effective instance of a subject coming to its own self-realization, represents an effective and pervasive mechanism of a system aimed at its own maintenance and social reproduction. It is an organized self-realization, which provides contemporary social actors with "pre-given templates for individuality" (Zurn 2015, p. 110). One example is that of the entrepreneurial employee, an idea that favors the deregulation of work by means of an earned flexibility, conceived as measure and result of the worker's willingness. Another example concerns the advertising industry, whose strategies tend more and more to propose representations according to which the consumers would be able to find in the purchase "an aesthetic resource for both the presentation and the heightening of the originality of their own chosen life-styles" (Honneth 2004b, p. 472):

> the individualism of self-realization, gradually emergent over the course of the past fifty years, has since been transmuted—having become an instrument of economic development, spreading standardization and making lives into fiction—into an emotionally fossilized set of demands under whose consequences individuals today seem more likely to suffer than to prosper (Honneth 2004b, p. 474).

After this rather stringent synthesis, we can still highlight two points for which "Organized Self-Realization" is noteworthy. On the one hand, it probably represents the clearest example of the escape from Honneth's moral-theoretical monism. To explain the reversal from the search for authentic individual self-realization to an institutionalized demand, Honneth refers to various factors of social and cultural change ranging from the productive system to the social movements of the 1960s and 1970s, from mass education to celebrity culture.[15] This seems significant because, although this is not a major work, such a willingness on Honneth's part to question one of the fundamental concepts of *The Struggle for Recognition*—that of self-realization—through a non-monological approach makes us understand that the latter—explicitly formulated only a year after the publication of "Organized Self-Realization" in the debate with Nancy Fraser[16]—is not to be understood in a radical way. On the other hand, the questioning of the concept of self-realization further clarifies that Honneth's notion of freedom concerns both autonomy and authenticity. Although Honneth never uses this second term unilaterally and plainly, because of the substantial consequences that would result and of the "profound tension between" it and the "demands of autonomy" that characterize contemporary societies (Honneth 2004a, p. 15),[17] it represents a key through which many aspects of his thought are connoted. The weight that this concept assumes, from the beginning of 2000 onward, is always greater and concerns the effects of recognition, understood as an intersubjective condition of the self's actualization,[18] and the definition of self-realization, understood as the proximity to one's own inner contents and as "biographical continuity" (Honneth 2014b, p. 36). Such an idea evidently converges in a significant way in *Reification*, where—also through the reference to Heidegger—the attempt is to describe an original form of praxis.

Our last introductory reference concerns "A Physiognomy of the Capitalist Form of Life" (original German, 2003), where Honneth focuses on Adorno's social critical theory. Also in this case, the intention is not to engage the text or the relationship between Honneth and Adorno in depth, but to highlight the elements that allow us to better contextualize and understand *Reification*. In this sense, two aspects are of major interest: the first is methodological, while the second concerns the concept of mimesis or imitation.

From a methodological perspective, Honneth points out, Adorno's work never takes the form of an explanatory social theory, but is rather unsystematically configured around ideal-types, which emerge, by means of critical questioning, as expressive of social formations: social analysis-critique would therefore coincide with a "materialistic hermeneutic of the capitalist form of life" (Honneth 2009e, p. 55). Keeping the strong persuasion—discussed in chapter 1—that social forms, rational capacities, and suffering are deeply intertwined with each other, Honneth argues that the apt method of social hermeneutic would then be that of physiognomy: with regard to the body, such approach aimed at considering the physical appearances and features as epiphenomena or symbolical concretions of the person's character. In the same way, sociological physiognomy purposes to induce "the social defor-

---

15 See Zurn 2015, pp. 111–12.
16 See Honneth 2003d, p. 157.
17 See also Ferrara 2004; and Ferrara 2015.
18 See Honneth 2002, pp. 509–10.

mation of our rational endowments, by means of a stylized, ideal-typical construction of its surface appearances," that is, distilling an idea of a form of life through the theoretical engagement with literature, music, art, but also through "gestures, mimicry, modes of practical intercourse in and with the world" (Honneth 2009e, p. 63). In this sense, always referring to Freud, this deeply practical-hermeneutical methodology—through which potentially every practical form is traced back to its socially constituted form of life—would disclose suffering-symptoms that would otherwise be imperceptible, namely, the deformations of rationality.[19]

This brings us to the second relevant point of this article, that is, the idea of mimetic reason. Given Adorno's persuasion that every form of social domination systematically causes a diminishment of one's rational capabilities and, therefore, even physical suffering, critical thought cannot avoid sketching out a form of undamaged rationality. Here, the relation between Adorno and Lukács plays an important role, as it does in *Reification*. In fact, even if Lukács and his *History and Class Consciousness* represents an unavoidable point of reference regarding this issue, the idealistic legacy concerning the subject-object relation and the consequent Lukácsian delineation of an undamaged praxis decidedly represents, according to Adorno and Honneth, a relapse into identity-thought, that is, the domination of the otherness. The re-appropriation of the object by the subject in an authentic way, would not per se be able to re-assess the rational capacity *and* to avoid the social pathology of reification.[20] Adorno's counterproposal revolves around the idea of imitation or mimesis, that is a re-definition of rationality itself: "The human is indissolubly tied with imitation: a human being only becomes human at all by imitating other human beings" (Adorno 2005, p. 154). An undistorted form of rationality would be therefore re-constructible through the observation of the first phases of the infant's life,[21] where it emerges that our rational faculties are structured through intersubjective relations. This formation process would imply that even in adult life the human way of knowing is determined by an "attitude of non-conceptual affinity that escapes and lies beneath the subject-object relation shaped by the cognitive-instrumental way of seeing" (Somogy Varga 2010, p. 26). In imitational acts, rational domination would therefore be avoided and,[22] indeed, the priority within the knowing-process is given to otherness: in other words, one could say that imitation represents a pre-cognitive stance in which a nuclear form of self-decentering guarantees a practical attunement to the other, and through this attunement cognizing would be opened and at-hand, always mediated by the decentered perspective furnished by the imitated:

---

19 See Honneth 2009e, pp. 68–70.
20 See Honneth 2009e, p. 60.
21 It is noteworthy that it is precisely in this passage that Honneth refers to Tomasello, Hobson, and Dornes, who represent, here but also in *Reification*, the researchers who provide Honneth's account with empirical confirmations. See Honneth 2009e, p. 61, 201, n. 22.
22 See Martin Seel 2004.

Only through imitative behavior, which for Adorno originally goes back to an affect of loving care, do we achieve a capacity for reason because we learn by gradually envisioning others' intentions to relate to their perspectives on the world. For us reality no longer merely represents a field of challenges to which we must adapt; rather, it becomes charged with a growing multiplicity of intentions, wishes, and attitudes that we learn to regard as reasons in our action.... He is therefore convinced that any true knowledge has to retain the original impulse of loving imitation sublimated within itself in order to do justice to the rational structure of the world from our perspective (Honneth 2009e, p. 61).

Therefore, the abandonment of imitation as affective and non-conceptual form of relation with otherness would lead to identity-thought and social pathologies such as collective narcissism and, by the process of organization, the becoming ends-in-themselves of purposes.[23] These phenomena within capitalist societies, "just as 'typical' as the suffering they generate" (Honneth 2009e, p. 69), would show that an original stance toward the other—imitation, mimesis—has been lost or forgotten in social life. As we shall see, both this methodological approach and the concept of imitation are decisive in Honneth's elaborating *Reification*.

3.2 Reification as Forgetfulness of Recognition

Honneth's account of the concept of reification has raised numerous criticisms, which have led him to later abandon some of these theoretical issues. For this reason, we will focus briefly on the salient features and criticisms of the concept reification, and then move on to the idea of recognition proposed in the Tanner Lectures of 2005. In doing so, we do not intend to engage in a direct confrontation with Honneth's interpretation of Lukács. Indeed, Honneth's interpretative approach, once again, is rather free, based in fact on a so-called "unofficial version" of *History and Class Consciousness* (Honneth 2008, p. 29).[24] Distilling this non-linear relationship with Lukács, we can summarize Honneth's original thesis on reification by identifying five main traits.

First, as for the Hegelian recognition theory, Honneth's aim is to re-actualize the concept of reification, maintaining, so to speak, its critical core, but reshaping the respective paradigm of justification. Accordingly, Honneth attempts to maintain three principal features of Lukács's concept of reification. First, the starting point coincides with the definition of the concept, according to which reification consists of "a cognitive occurrence in which something that doesn't possess thing-like characteristics in itself (e. g., something human) comes to be regarded as a thing" (Honneth

---

[23] See Honneth 2009e, pp. 65–66. Interestingly, the pathological dynamic of independentizing and fixing of the ends represents the first pattern of reification of the other described in *Reification* through the example of the tennis player; see Honneth 2008, p. 59.
[24] One can also consider Habermas's colonization thesis through these lenses, namely, those of a re-actualization of Lukács's core idea; see Konstantinos Kavoulakos 2017, pp. 75–77.

2008, p. 21). Second, Honneth wants to keep Lukács's totalizing tripartition, even if only to a certain extent, according to which:

> Subjects in commodity exchange are mutually urged (a) to perceive given objects solely as "things" that one can potentially make a profit on, (b) to regard each other solely as "objects" of a profitable transaction, and finally (c) to regard their own abilities as nothing but supplemental "resources" in the calculation of profit opportunities (Honneth 2008, p. 22).

Third, according to Lukács, this attitude would derive from the actor's participation in the commodity-exchange process. Precisely because of the incessant expansion of the latter, the subject would be led to assume a contemplative and detached perspective toward her surroundings. This contemplative stance clearly does not concern the un-emotionality of the practical acts. To be sure, Lukács, and Honneth with him, does not claim that forms of instrumental reason could not "themselves become forms of passion, modes of attachment, sites of emotional investment and excitation" (Butler 2008, p. 105).[25] To raise the issue of contemplative attitude and instrumental reason by contrasting coldness, absence of emotions, on the one hand, and emotionality, on the other, can lead to misunderstandings of the Honnethian argument—and in general of the discourse on reification—which cannot be reduced to this simple juxtaposition. Rather, such a detached, reifying perspective is not "simply cognitive," but is a systematical misinterpretation that is "emotive and encompassing: it affects all aspects of life" (Lear 2008, p. 132). In other words, the detached and contemplative stance would coincide with an "abstraction" of the "qualitative singularity" of the otherness (Kavoulakos 2017, p. 68), so that even emotions themselves could have a reified form.

Second, given these first three points, Honneth proceeds by ascribing one more feature to this social pathology. Deriving from the pervasiveness of the system of exchange of commodities, this distorting attitude cannot be conceived as mere moral misconduct or a simple categorical error. Rather, the reifying gaze has to be considered "as a form of praxis that is *structurally* false" (Honneth 2008, p. 26). On the one hand, Honneth manages to show quite easily why reification cannot be a categorical error. It is precisely because of its pervasiveness and constancy: it is not merely a matter of mistakenly and occasionally confusing a non-thing for a thing, but is rather the systematic replacement of ontological characters. On the other hand, the distinction between reification and moral error is more problematic because Honneth's argument always presents a normative character, such that reification can be considered as "morally criticizable" (Todd Hedrick 2013, p. 183). Moreover, at a rather simple level, regarding the interaction partner as thing-like clearly represents a form of misrecognition and disrespect; indeed, probably their most radical forms. As Jütten points out, the fact that such forms of reification of others can lead, in an obvi-

---

[25] The quotation is borrowed from a criticism Butler addresses to Honneth: according to the first, an error of the latter would be to describe the reifying attitude as "emotionally arid."

ous way, to moral suffering on the part of the affected should require a certain accountability of the reifying subject; thus, we should imply a concept of moral responsibility that is incompatible with Honneth's statement that reifying gestures and moral misconduct do not coincide.[26] I think that, when Honneth says that reification is not a moral error, he means not so much that the acts of reification do not lead to moral injury, but that any reification, by the performers, is also ideology, that is, essentially unfreedom.[27] It is indeed caused by and instantiated in a second nature, an ensemble of habits, behaviors, and attitudes that structurally "obscure the practices in which they originate" (Andrew Feenberg 2011, p. 110). In this sense, social subjects would find themselves living in a world that systematically proposes itself as fixed by naturally endowed laws that leave no room for individual practices in terms of responsibility or options. Reification, for those who carry it out in relation to others, would therefore not be a moral error, but the consequence of an ideological bias that finds its origin and concealment in social structures. In other words, it is not a matter of individual choice. However, reading "Organized Self-Realization"—and the focus on social pathologies I proposed in chapter 1—gives us one more factor: in that text, Honneth claims that social pathologies possess a second-order disorder character. In fact, what is problematic is not the pursuit of individual self-realization, but rather the reflective and practical ways in which this ethical content is pursued under the influence of social structures. Therefore, to conceive reification also as second-order disorder allows us to reconcile the moral imputability of the acts of misrecognition with the essential unfreedom of social pathologies.[28] What Jütten's criticism seems to forget is that reification is "a name for both a process and a result" (Honneth 2008, p. 53), which leaves no room for full moral responsibility. In other words, there is something wrong or unjust about reification, but this factor is rooted in a dimension that goes beyond individual responsibility: specifically, it lies in the social mechanisms and structures of second nature. If, therefore, reification can be considered a structurally false form of practice, Honneth maintains that it cannot be totally free from normative connotations and that—always following the pathology-health pair—on the contrary, it announces the presence and "the existence of a 'true' or 'genuine' praxis over and against its distorted or atrophied form" (Honneth 2008, p. 26), which allows the identification of the latter as deviation or misdevelopment.

Third, it is only now that Honneth explicitly distances himself from Lukács, referring to a so-called unofficial version of *Reification and the Consciousness of the Proletariat*. The reasons for the divergence are found in the reception of the Lukácsian work through the tradition of the Frankfurt School and in the consequent detection of an "idiosyncratic coexistence of materialist and idealist motifs" in Lukács's thought (Hedrick 2013, p. 182). Two points can be identified. Following Adorno,[29]

---

26 See Timo Jütten 2010.
27 See Dirk Quadflieg 2011, p. 701.
28 See Zurn 2011; Titus Stahl 2011; and Laitinen 2015.
29 See Kavoulakos 2017, pp. 72–73; and Honneth 2009e.

Honneth argues that Lukács's image of undistorted human praxis, configuring itself as a harmonic coincidence of producing subject and produced object, is unable to escape from identity-thought and therefore idealism.[30] Following Habermas,[31] Honneth rejects Lukács's totalizing attitude, which seems to lead to the equalization of every objectification through reification.[32] If reification is merely defined as an abstraction from the qualitative characteristics of otherness in favor of the objectifying attitude of instrumental reason, then the numerous spheres of social action that require this type of objectification or "depersonalization" (Honneth 2008, p. 76)—such as any technical practice or natural-scientific inquiry—should be considered as manifestations of reification, which could not be acceptable.[33] According to Honneth, therefore, what is required is a new and more sophisticated definition of reification, which could remain closer to the "literal meaning of the term" (Honneth 2008, p. 149). This would also be required as a final point of distance from Lukács, and could be considered as a rejection of Habermas's colonization thesis.[34] As far as Lukács is concerned, Honneth intends to distance himself from the totalizing tendencies with regard to a certain economic monologism, according to which "the effects of a capitalist free-market society" lead *automatically* "to a generalization of reifying behavior in all three dimensions" (Honneth 2008, p. 76), and *only* the commodity exchange system could be the cause of reification. Such a unilateral explanation leads to further consequences. On the one hand, it would result in Lukács not considering brutal practices of de-humanization such as "racism or human trafficking" (Honneth 2008, p. 78). On the other hand, it does not regard those elements that, in the sphere of the market, guarantee the person a minimal defense against being hypostatized as a thing. In the case of the "protective power of law" (Honneth 2008, p. 80), which Lukács disregards as an expression of the reified and reifying capitalistic institutions, Honneth sees them rather as a form of recognition and respect, a form of safeguard against the de-humanization of the person.[35] Therefore, forms of reification should be sought in the weakening of the labor contract, which corresponds to ends-autonomization and to the consequent identification of others as instruments and means. The argument against the unilateralization of the economic sphere as totally reified is also significant in relation to Habermas. The problem with the colonization thesis

---

30 See Honneth 2008, p. 27.
31 See Ferrara 2011, pp. 374–75.
32 On Honneth's unwillingness to reject modernity as a whole because of its historical-normative significance, see Deranty 2011.
33 See Honneth 2008, pp. 54–55.
34 See Habermas 1983; and Jütten 2011. These brief observations echo Honneth's arguments against Habermas's perspective; see Honneth 1991, esp. ch. 9.
35 It is important to emphasize that Honneth—as we will see in the next chapter—is well aware that it is not the legal form per se that represents an embankment to the phenomenon of reification, but its being a modality and expression of intersubjective relations. In fact, following Hegel, Honneth reads the unilateralization of this sphere of action as an imbalance or sclerotization, which itself produces reification. See Daniel Loick 2015; and Hedrick 2013.

is the loading of the functionalist distinction between system and lifeworld "with a normative burden of proof that they cannot possibly shoulder" (Honneth 2008, p. 55). In other words, the separation of two spheres of action and the idea of one colonized by the other would not be able to justify the normative perception one has of reification as a false praxis. Reification cannot be described merely phenomenologically, precisely because of its normative implications.[36] Moreover, the idea that the employment contract represents a normative element, as recognition relationship, within the market's systemic sphere shows that Habermas's functionalistic argument does not take into account even the fact that the system is to a certain extent delineated by normative expectations, and is not a norm-free realm.[37] Therefore, although one can certainly argue that Honneth inherits Habermas's rejection of an economic-systemic explanation in favor of an intersubjective paradigm,[38] which accounts for reification in terms of a thinning or a veiling of an intersubjectively understood social freedom,[39] one could at the same time argue that Honneth's claim is even more radical: he intends to show the (not total) referability of the system to the normative sphere, not to separate one from the other.

Fourth, Honneth intends to provide a new concept of reification, again taking into account its relationship with the idea of authentic or genuine praxis. Starting from this concept, one can stress the impossibility of a totalizing idea of reification, which would definitively eliminate any possible non-reifying attitude. In other words, Honneth intends to argue that the original form of praxis is somehow also present in the acts of reification, albeit in, so to speak, an inactive way: the perception of reification as false would announce the persistence of a true praxis, which cannot therefore be totally dissolved. It is therefore necessary to find a definition that reconciles these two poles of praxis according to a reciprocal non-exclusivity,[40] which would lead to the aporia just mentioned. Hence, Honneth defines reification as "forgetfulness of recognition":

> We have, on the one hand, forms of knowledge sensitive to recognition, and, on the other, forms of knowledge in which every trace of their origin in an antecedent act of recognition has been lost.
>
> ... it is prima facie most advisable for us to distinguish between two modes in which these two kinds of stances relate to one another: they are either transparent to each other or obscure, accessible or inaccessible. In the first case, the act of cognition or detached observation remains conscious of its dependence on an antecedent act of recognition; in the second case, it has freed itself of the knowledge of this dependency and deludes itself that it has become autonomous of all non-epistemic prerequisites. By further pursuing Lukács' intention at a higher level, this kind of "forgetfulness of recognition" can now be termed "reification." I thereby mean to indicate the process by which we lose the consciousness of the degree to which we owe our knowledge and

---

[36] See Honneth 2008, p. 55; Jütten 2011, pp. 703 and 711.
[37] See Hedrick 2013, p. 183.
[38] See Chari 2010, pp. 594–98.
[39] See Quadflieg 2011, p. 708.
[40] See Hedrick 2013, p. 182; and Butler 2008, p. 100.

cognition of other persons to an antecedent stance of empathetic engagement and recognition (Honneth 2008, p. 56).

Although the definition of the antecedence of recognition has not yet been addressed, the characterization of reification as forgetfulness can be understood in its essential character. The concept of reification concerns first of all the nature of action and then its social sources.[41] Therefore, the reifying attitude coincides with a form of detached, contemplative knowledge that—at a social-ontological level, but with normative implications—attributes to the other a thing-like character, which does not merely unlearn the latter's qualitative features, but, under the pressure of binding social formations, acquires a habit of non-attentiveness to its own process of formation.[42] Correspondingly, this structurally false praxis implies a genuine form, which cannot therefore be considered as completely absent or removed by means of objectification or depersonalization, but rather must always be—with a certain permeability—combined with reification itself. Thus, rejecting Lukács's idealistic assumptions, Honneth follows the same solution attributed to Adorno in "A Physiognomy of the Capitalistic Form of Life":[43] by abandoning the subject-object binomial, an original praxis must be found in intersubjectivity.

Finally, although I will leave a full analysis the concept of recognition developed in *Reification* to the next section, it is necessary to anticipate some elements in order to be able to summarize a comprehensive definition of Honneth's methodology. As already mentioned, recognition acts are identified as the genuine form of praxis that can be forgotten when a reifying habit is being assumed. Therefore, a detached and de-humanizing position would coincide with the overshadowing of the previous knowledge of the other as a human being, opened within primary recognition gestures, particularly evident and significant—as we have seen in "Invisibility"—in the early stages of the child's life. In contrast to contemplative detachment, recognition would indicate an involvement that finds its main trait in the affective dimension: it would be an openness that allows the receptivity of the qualitative traits of otherness in all its forms and informs an attitude that allows the decentering of the ego. At this point, Honneth not only intends to propose an alternative explanation to that provided by Lukács's economic monologism, but believes that the identification of reification with recognition-forgetfulness would allow for avoiding Lukács's idea that the three forms of reification—of the other person, of the world, and of oneself—necessarily manifest themselves as intrinsically co-dependent, due to being caused by the same phenomenon: the commodity exchange. To avoid this further consequence of Lukács's totalizing tendency, Honneth thus provides a heterogeneous explanation of the emergence of reifying practices,[44] in which, however, the link between the lat-

---

41 See Feenberg 2015.
42 See Honneth 2008, pp. 58–59.
43 See Honneth 2009e, pp. 60–61.
44 See Quadflieg 2011, p. 708.

ter and the relative social sources is "non-essential" (David T. Schafer 2017, p. 424). What Honneth provides is therefore not a sociological-explanatory theory of the causes of reifying acts, but rather, I argue, a critique of the reifying and reified form of life, which refers to emerging epiphenomena, so that even attitudes, behaviors, and gestures that may appear as episodic shed light on the system that lies behind them.

Although Honneth does not talk of a critique of the capitalist form of life explicitly—and the very concept of 'form of life' is indeed unfamiliar with his vocabulary—I believe that there are three main reasons for supporting this interpretation, at least regarding *Reification*. The first is represented by Adorno's influence on the text, which, as we shall see, plays a fundamental role in the definition of recognition as the genuine form of praxis and in the description of forms of reification. Already in "A Physiognomy of the Capitalistic Form of Life," Honneth sees in Adorno's methodology, which addresses non-systematic and quasi-episodic aspects of everyday life, an incisive way to implement a critique of capitalism. If the main effect of reification is to annihilate the understanding of economic structures as based on human practices,[45] then a legitimate starting point for critique—not reified in turn—may be to question structures out of practices, that is, to remove the latter from concealment, showing their blindness, opaqueness and discrepancy,[46] and then to show that they are the basis for the system.

Second, the concept 'form of life' is applicable to the kind of critical theory that Honneth wants to carry out. If, from a minimal point of view, we can consider a life-form as a set of practices that possess a certain continuity, reproductive independence, and identifiability,[47] then a critique of it satisfies Honneth's need to expand the normative theory beyond the issues of distributive justice. Honneth's critical aim—in general, but perhaps even more so in *Reification*—is to reverse a trend that has been established since the 1970s in social normative theories, namely, that of "evaluating the normative order of societies according to whether they fulfill certain principles of justice"; and, by so doing, such theories would lose "sight of the fact that a society can demonstrate a moral deficit without violating generally valid principles of justice" (Honneth 2008, p. 84). Critical theory's need is therefore to broaden its own understanding-horizon in order to address social pathologies, which coincide, one could argue, with socially caused dysfunctional forms of life.

Finally, this association with the idea of a critique of the forms of life provides the slightest justification for Honneth's disregard for an explicit questioning of the systemic factors of the phenomenon of reification. In other words, this lack of consideration would not coincide with a separation between lifeworld and system or lead to a lack of understanding of the structural causes or systemic factors at

---

45 See Chari 2010, p. 589.
46 See Jaeggi 2005.
47 See Jaeggi 2018, chs. 1–2.

stake. Rather, and as already noted, Honneth rejects a monological and all-encompassing economic explanation: as mentioned with regard to "Organized Self-Realization," a sociological explanation is by no means extraneous to his interests, rather the key to the critique of social pathologies can only be found through broad normative criteria, which, in *Reification*, are found in the formal anthropology proposed in "Pathologies of the Social" and in *The Struggle for Recognition*.[48] In other words, Honneth appears to demand that even the critique of the economic system requires criteria for its own justification that cannot be found in the system itself.

In any case, *Reification* was almost unanimously negatively received, leading Honneth to concentrate on and further develop other aspects of his own thinking, those considered more appropriate to justify critical theory. These criticisms, which can be summarized in three groups, indirectly show that *Reification* represents the most radical attempt of anthropological justification of critical theory and of intersubjective reductionism carried out by Honneth: rather than trying to engage in a close confrontation with each of them, mentioning some issues opens the possibility to focus further on elements that have gone unnoticed or have not been properly evaluated.

The first criticism concerns the fact that Honneth considers the concept of reification exclusively in its literal meaning.[49] The fact that reification means to know, encounter, or interact with a human as thing-like also seems to legitimize an observation by which this phenomenon is reduced to a "cognitive process" (Chari 2010, p. 600), an epistemic problem,[50] or even to a "psychological pathology" (Schafer 2017, p. 422). The "Rejoinder" added to the 2008 English edition of *Reification* shows that Honneth acknowledges the problem of such an assumption. Here, Honneth maintains and clarifies that "Reification annuls the form of elementary recognition that ensures that we existentially experience other humans as the other of our self" (Honneth 2008, p. 154). In this sense, it has to be distinguished from the instrumentalization of the other,[51] precisely because, in order to instrumentalize someone *as if* he or she were a thing, one must have already recognized someone as someone, with characteristics that allow one to instrumentalize him or her. But then, even one of the most explicit cases of de-humanization of the human being, slavery, cannot be considered as a reification in the literal sense.[52] These difficulties lead Honneth to admit "how improbable true cases of reification are for the social lifeworld as a whole" and to introduce a distinction between real reification (which is difficult to trace socially) and "fictive reification," which would include all those cases of instrumentalization or de-classification of the other, such as racism, exploitation, slavery, and so on (Honneth 2008, p. 157).

---

48 See Kavoulakos 2019, p. 42.
49 See Feenberg 2011, p. 102; and Jütten 2010, p. 236.
50 See Quadflieg 2011, p. 707.
51 See Honneth 2008, pp. 148–49.
52 See Owen 2010, p. 101.

A second criticism concerns Honneth's methodological path, which follows "the anthropological scheme 'primary–secondary'" in order to address recognition and reification as genuine and distorted forms of praxis (Kavoulakos 2017, p. 77). Consequentially, reification, as false, would be reduced as a "morally objectionable form of intersubjectivity" (Hedrick 2013, p. 183), losing thereby the critical scope of the concept. This second aspect of the criticism can be answered by the argument already mentioned, according to which reification does not involve a moral error and therefore does not represent the violation of positive moral obligations. Rather, as Honneth explains in the "Rejoinder," it means a "violation of necessary presuppositions of our social lifeworld" (Honneth 2008, p. 149).

So, third, Honneth is accused of not being able to consider the historical-social factors of reification,[53] that is, that reification represents the other side of the capitalistic production-system, commodities exchange and consumption. In other words, the claim is that Honneth fails to consider the possibility that reification not only possesses a subjective dimension, namely, the distorted fashions of praxis, but also, and more fundamentally, an objective one, namely, the consolidation of social systems that carry out such distortions.[54] This involves three intertwined implications. First, Honneth's approach would bring a *"methodological individualism"* (Kavoulakos 2019, p. 54): Honneth in fact explains reification as an attitude that always belongs to an individual subject. Second, this lack of consideration of the systemic and material factors leading to the adoption of certain reifying attitudes could be considered as the effect of an idealistic approach.[55] In this sense, Honneth's perspective would not be individualistic, but his intersubjectivism would suffer from an excessive ahistoricity by overly opposing system and lifeworld. Third, such an a-sociological approach would lead to blindness with respect to the concept of second nature, which is one of the cornerstones of Lukács's concept of reification. Honneth therefore overlooks the fact that the persons may appear as thing-like only because of their being encountered in certain social structures and contexts,[56] the "naturalization" of which enables the self-reproduction of forms of power and ideology (Thompson 2017, p. 208). Summarizing these (quite different) criticisms at the heart of Honneth's approach, one could even say that his own definition of reification is reified because the purely anthropological approach,[57] which refuses to consider the systematic mechanisms and powers as the basis for the individual praxis, would itself lead to obscure the real relationships that lead subjects to suffer.[58]

While stressing that these criticisms do not do complete justice to Honneth's argument, this concept of reification seems unable to respond to its own premises and,

---

53 See Chari 2010, pp. 598–601; Stahl 2011, p. 737; and Quadflieg 2011, pp. 707–8.
54 See Kavoulakos 2017, p. 69.
55 See Chari 2010, pp. 598–600; and Thompson 2011, p. 235.
56 See Hedrick 2013, p. 183.
57 See Kavoulakos 2019, pp. 55–56.
58 See Quadflieg 2011, p. 702.

in this sense, fails to offer a useful tool for the unfolding of critical theory. In the same way, the fact that reification in a strict sense rarely happens in social reality calls into question the normative potential of the concept of primary recognition. Although such concepts therefore seem to be a blunt tool for the purposes of a critical theory of society, I believe that the concept of recognition described in *Reification* represents a significant step in Honneth's paradigm.

3.3 The Priority of Recognition

The redefinition of recognition therefore starts from the need to outline a form of genuine praxis, which would in some way persist even in acts of reification as a forgotten, according to a criterion of mutual non-exclusivity of both practices. Although Honneth now addresses very different authors,[59] such as Lukács, Heidegger,[60] Dewey, Adorno, and Cavell, the aim is quite clear: to outline a holistic form of knowledge involved with the world, which attests before the subject-object polarization at the basis of identity-thinking and the detached reifying attitude[61]—or, better: a practical stance through which "the world is" foremost "disclosed to us as an inhabitable reality" (Ferrara 2011, p. 378). Thus, Honneth's main aim is to outline the genetic and conceptual priority of recognition (*Anerkennen*) over cognition (*Erkennen*).[62] This aim is pursued through four steps, which can be summarized as follows.

First, drawing on Lukács's concept of empathetic engagement and on Heidegger's concept of care, Honneth intends to show that the most genuine way of relating to the world coincides with a practical involvement, from which the emotional and affective dimensions are not excluded.[63] Even turning to some contemporary philosophical proposals, which see the possibility of assuming the perspective of the participant as alternative to detached knowledge, Honneth argues that the concepts mentioned above cover a broader horizon and, above all, are able to embrace within themselves a "nonepistemic character" (Honneth 2008, p. 151), which would precede even the faculty to take the other's perspective.

---

[59] See Bart Van Leeuwen 2006, p. 237.
[60] Although the interest in Heidegger may raise some perplexities, especially in a work that should mark Honneth's rapprochement with Adorno, it is important to stress that Marcuse had already tried to translate the thought of *Being and Time* into Marxist terms, precisely to address the dispersion and sclerotization experienced in the capitalist system. See Feenberg 2013; and Feenberg 2011, pp. 113–15. But Honneth and Marcuse are not the only ones who retrieve Heidegger's account of *das Man* and inauthenticity for critical purposes; see William Koch 2015. Moreover, Honneth shows, albeit indirectly, an engagement with Heidegger's *Mitwelt* in a writing that precedes by little *Reification*: see Honneth 2003a.
[61] See Varga 2010, p. 21.
[62] See Honneth 2008, p. 36.
[63] See Honneth 2008, pp. 33–36.

The second step is represented by the reference to Dewey. Here, Honneth intends to show that "every rational understanding of the world is always already bound up with a holistic form of experience, in which all elements of a given situation are qualitatively disclosed from a perspective of engaged involvement" (Honneth 2008, p. 36). Reification would therefore coincide with forgetting the primacy of the qualitative dimension of our interaction with the world in which we live and with which we have always been in tune. And in this sense, Honneth clarifies that detachment represents a derived possibility, rather than an annihilation of the genuine interaction with the world. Taken together, empathetic engagement, care, and involvement describe a certain form of knowledge, but even more so, a relationship with the world that is not "self-centered" or "egocentric" (Honneth 2008, p. 37):

> our actions do not primarily have the character of an affectively neutral, cognitive stance toward the world, but rather that of an affirmative, existentially colored style of caring comportment. In living, we constantly concede to the situational circumstances of our world a value of their own, which brings us to be concerned with our relationship to them (Honneth 2008, p. 38).

It is precisely this character of decenteredness and care, proper to our primordial way of being open to the world, that constitutes the bridge through which Honneth comes to the concept of recognition. This transition from care and the Deweyan concept of interaction to the idea of recognition, besides appearing not fully justified, brings with it a central problem: Honneth's discourse oscillates several times between an idea of openness to the world and the delineation of primal intersubjective relationships. This is where Honneth's claim actually resides: to bring openness to the world back to intersubjective relations of recognition, indicating that "what defines the ideal of genuine praxis is a norm of reciprocity" (Butler 2008, p. 101). However, as we will see in the next two passages, the discourse seems to be developed exclusively on human relationships and therefore to represent a basis only for taking the perspective of the participant. Moreover, this unmediated shift from care and interaction to recognition entails an additional consequence. As Varga brilliantly points out, Honneth hesitates between two alternatives concerning the intentionality of cognition: on the one hand, this antecedent form of recognition seems to represent a pre-intentional openness to the world, which structures, on a (quasi-)transcendental level, our experience as a whole; on the other hand, recognition itself seems to require an intentional object,[64] which tends to coincide with an other with human features, whether it be the other person or our own mental contents. However, here it seems helpful to maintain that recognition so far would be the condition of thinking itself, and that too on a pre-epistemic level.[65]

We can now move to the third step of Honneth's argument, namely, the genetic priority of recognition over cognition: here the conceptual shift from care to intersub-

---

64 See Varga 2010, p. 24.
65 See Deranty 2009, p. 462.

jectivism mentioned earlier appears immediately clear, because Honneth narrows his focus on the self's possibility for decentering its own position by taking on the perspective of the participant. It is useful to focus on three relative steps. The first step consists in referring to those thinkers—including Mead—according to whom the child's ability to develop a symbolic thought hinges on the possibility of taking on the perspective of the other. However, this view seems to be marked by a "tendency towards cognitivism" (Honneth 2008, p. 42), which would be discredited also by more recent studies in developmental psychology.[66] Thus, Honneth not only rejects this perspective, but argues that the very possibility of taking on the other's perspective—instantiated in the Meadian phases of play and game—depends on an earlier stage of emotional attachment between infant and caregiver. This passage, which at first glance seems to contradict Mead's central role in *The Struggle for Recognition*, does nothing more than reaffirm in different terms and redefine the phase of symbiosis and primary interactions described through the use of the object-relations theory —and this in an attempt to avoid the ambiguities of the concept of symbiosis, giving a greater weight to reciprocity.[67] Hence, second, referring to Hobson and Tomasello's research on autism, Honneth continues to outline the centrality of emotional identification. The child's cognitive progress is made possible by the presence of an "emotional attachment to a psychological parent, for it is only by way of this antecedent identification that the child is able to be moved, motivated, and swept along by the presence of a concrete second person in such a way as to comprehend this person's changes of attitude in an interested way" (Honneth 2008, pp. 43–44). What is at issue is precisely the gestural-expressive reciprocity already described in "Invisibility," that is, a first form of pre-linguistic recognition. Before moving to the last step, it is useful to make two observations. On the one hand, it seems problematic to affirm that, here, subjectivity is a product of recognitional acts,[68] precisely because this type of attachment and gestural reciprocity presupposes or requires a certain form of ipseity—albeit minimal—even on the part of the infant. This solution therefore seems to sweep away the ambiguities and problems inherent in the concept of symbiosis. On the other hand, implying a nuclear form of subjectivity in the young child apparently denies the priority of the intersubjective over the subjective, since the interaction would be allowed by an implicit distinction, that of the partners being determined as selves. One would then fall into a modern concept of subjectivity, which would precede entering into a relationship with the other. Although one could argue that the idea of symbiosis already represents a primacy of interaction on the two poles —and not a meta-subject in which the ontological boundaries of the two selves are confused and opaque, but rather referring to their practical identities—it is clear that the only way out this deadlock is to think about the antecedence (of sub-

---

66 For a concise but enlightening overview on Honneth and developmental psychology, see Somogy Varga and Shaun Gallagher 2012.
67 See Tommaso Sperotto 2017.
68 See Schafer 2017, p. 424.

jectivity on intersubjectivity or vice versa) outside of merely temporal patterns. This would, in fact, lead to a vicious circle, which would force us to indicate whether the egg or the chicken came first. Rather, it seems more fruitful to conceive of the "*equiprimordiality* of subjectivity and inter-subjectivity" (Varga 2010, p. 24) with vital consequences concerning the very concept of recognition too. According to this perspective, subjectivity arises within interpersonal interactions of which and in which it is itself actor and partner. It is only with the last step that Honneth demonstrates the genetic priority of recognizing over knowing. Drawing on the Adorno's concept of imitation or mimesis, Honneth reaffirms the centrality of affectively-charged primary interactions for our access to the world and for our knowledge of objects. But, once again, this access to the world is seen as intersubjectively mediated. The qualitative knowledge of surrounding objects and their different facets would hinge on the possibility of assuming the different interaction-partners' perspectives on them. Thus, by generalizing this multiplicity of views, the knowledge of a world consisting of constant and independent objects would depend essentially on decentering the ego's perspective.[69] However, such a possibility of taking the other's perspective on objects is, in the first instance, only allowed by an "involuntary openness, devotedness, or love" toward the other: that is, imitation. Without such an attachment, the child would not be able to place him- or herself in the triangular relationship with the object, which is always seen in some way through the other's eyes:

> it is from the perspective of a loved one that small children first gain an inkling of the abundance of existential significance that situational circumstances can have for people. Therefore, it is through this emotional attachment to a "concrete other" that a world of meaningful qualities is disclosed to a child *as* a world in which he must involve himself practically. Genesis and validity—or in Marxist terms, history and logic—should not be torn apart to such an extent that the conditions under which a child's thinking originates lose their relevance for the categorial significance of our knowledge of the world (Honneth 2008, pp. 45–46).

As we have already seen in *The Struggle for Recognition*, that genesis and validity are inseparable from each other is a characteristic trait of Honneth's normative theory. Thus, as far as knowing is concerned, the fact that the cognitive process starts from intersubjective relations would provide a justification for the notion that a correct, genuine interaction with otherness, even in adulthood, must retain within itself the memory of this intersubjectively-marked process of development: recognition, to a certain extent, *should* precede cognition.

With the fourth and final step, Honneth attempts to depict the conceptual priority of recognition, drawing on Stanley Cavell's account of acknowledgment. But here again, the argument is narrowed to the intersubjective dimension or, more precisely, to the issue of the possibility of gaining access to "other minds" (Honneth 2008,

---

[69] See Deranty 2009, p. 462. As Petherbridge points out, Honneth here seems to draw an object-relational account of Adorno's concept of mimesis. See Petherbridge 2013, p. 178.

p. 47). The issue at stake coincides with the investigation of the ways in which the mental states of the other are accessible to the interaction-partner. Since they do not possess the same characteristics of material objects, they would not be accessible according to a simple cognitive relationship based upon the subject-object polarity. In order to avoid skeptical conclusions about the existence of other minds, Cavell draws two arguments. According to the first, we can conceive our relation to the other's mental states in the same terms as we grasp this other's relation with its own inner contents.[70] In other words, cognition of the other's mental state would be disclosed primarily by the awareness of ourselves as the other's alter-ego: this would bring us in such a position, thanks to which we can conceive the other's inner life as comparable with our own. However, the knowledge of the other's interior state is not grounded on a contemplative gaze, but on the verbal indications through which the other makes us aware of its own emotions and thoughts. These indications require the "listener's 'sympathy'" to be intuited, approached, and understood, leading to a form of knowledge that is characterized more as proximity than as observation. Therefore, "a certain stance, in which a subject feels existentially involved in the emotional world of another subject, must precede all possible cognitive knowledge of that other subject's mental states" (Honneth 2008, p. 49). Even if this argument displays a certain validity solely regarding "the sphere of interpersonal communication" (Honneth 2008, p. 51), Honneth believes it has provided sufficient arguments to justify his "recognition-precedes-cognition claim" (Jütten 2010, pp. 239–40).

However, two aspects concerning the very nature of this form of recognition need further clarification. First, it is noteworthy that this notion of antecedent recognition oscillates between numerous connotations, which find their unity more in the concepts of imitation, attachment, engagement, or identification than in the idea of mutual recognition, as it is normatively conceived in *The Struggle for Recognition*. Second, the pre-epistemic emotional identification, above all with regard to the genetic argument, can lead to some ambiguities, that is, to overburden positive emotions—such as love, caring, etc.—and to leave aside any contribution to the development of negative intersubjective forms and thus provide an unrealistic model of intersubjectivity.

As for the first issue, even if only in a footnote, Honneth explicitly refers to "Invisibility" and clarifies the relationship between this form of recognition and the concepts of love, respect, and esteem outlined in *The Struggle for Recognition*: "I now assume that this 'existential' mode of recognition provides a foundation for all other, more substantial forms of recognition in which the affirmation of other persons' specific characteristics is at issue" (Honneth 2008, p. 90 n. 70). This antecedent form of recognition would thus constitute the threshold that allows us to grasp the other as a human being and therefore as an appropriate addressee of those gestures of recognition indicated as substantial because they are connoted from the historical-

---

70 See Honneth 2008, pp. 48–49; and Ferrara 2011, p. 379.

cultural point of view: love, respect, and esteem. In other words, the possibility of normatively recognizing the other would be disclosed by the fact that he or she is already recognized as such, in a non-reified way, as a human being.

The answer to the second question—the presumed 'positivity' of emotional identification or empathetic engagement—proceeds in the same direction as well.

> Thus the adjective "positive," ... mustn't be understood as referring to positive, friendly emotions. This adjective instead signifies the existential fact—which certainly has implications for our affects—that we necessarily affirm the value of another person in the stance of recognition, even if we might curse or hate that person at a given moment.... [E]ven in cases where we recognize other persons in an emotionally negative way, we still always have a residual intuitive sense of not having done full justice to their personalities (Honneth 2008, p. 51).

After having clarified at least partially these issues, which I will examine in more detail in the next section, it is now useful to turn to those passages in which Honneth once again devotes himself to the concept of reification and its threefold dimension. In doing so, the main interest that guides us is not questioning the attempt to re-actualize the Lukács's concept again, but focusing rather on the threefold dimension attributed to recognition: toward others, the external world and one's own self. In fact, it is only through such an explanation that one can fully understand how Honneth redefines recognition in this work. To this point, however, we have focused almost exclusively on its precedence over other practical forms.

3.3.1 Recognition as Apperception of Human Features

As we approach the concept of the reification of others, we can briefly say that it coincides with those cases in which "a person unlearns something he or she previously and intuitively mastered" (Honneth 2008, p. 79): to consider the other as a person. At a fundamental level, this facet of reification could be plainly named "*misrecognition*" (Ferrara 2011, p. 383). Honneth depicts two different dynamics. First, just as by Adorno's explanation of organization, the matter concerns the making themselves independent on the part of the ends. In our practical interactions, we can pursue an aim so energetically that what is different from it—the others around us—become abstract from their human characteristics. This can be expressed by the example of the tennis player, who, fossilized in the purpose of the victory, forgets that her opponent is her best friend.[71] In the "Rejoinder," responding to Butler's criticisms, Honneth rejects this example and maintains that independent aims do not always lead to reifying attitudes. Rather, mentioning the case of a soldier about to annihilate the enemy and the Holocaust,[72] he retracts his thesis, claiming that only "the independence of

---

[71] See Honneth 2008, p. 59.
[72] See Honneth 2008, pp. 156–158.

3.3 The Priority of Recognition — 113

those practices whose successful execution demands that we ignore all the human properties of our fellow human beings can lead to intersubjective reification" (Honneth 2008, pp. 156–57). However, I argue that it already emerges clearly from the distinction between reification and objectification that not every abstraction of purpose coincides with a reifying act. Moreover, including the aims of acting in the consideration of the matter—albeit comprehensible—exacerbates the tension and the overlap between the normative and socio-ontological/anthropological dimensions.

The second case of misrecognition taken into consideration is not so intimately embodied in practical acts, but rather concerns the consequences that certain models of thought may have on our evaluation of social facts, groups, or people.[73] This is the case with discrimination of all kinds in which, through the assumption of ideological models, "antecedent recognition is retroactively denied" (Honneth 2008, p. 81). Here, too, however, the normative implications are quite clear: it emerges that reification in the form of misrecognition causes moral suffering.

But these observations, rather than reopening the discussion of reification, are useful for a better understanding of what Honneth means by primary recognition and to highlight some respective problems. In fact, although Honneth intends to characterize this previous form of recognition in pre-normative terms—so that it precedes the forms of love, respect, and esteem—when such acts of recognition are denied they lead to cases of clear normative matrix, such as racism, exclusion, or even the annihilation of other human beings.

> this stance itself has no normative orientation. Although it compels us to take up some sort of position, it does not determine the direction or tone of that position.... Therefore, this type of recognition is still far from the threshold beyond which we can speak at all of norms and principles of reciprocal recognition. Normatively substantial forms of recognition such as are embodied in social institutions ... represent instead various manners in which the existential scheme of experience opened up by elementary recognition gets "filled out" historically. Without the experience that other individuals are fellow humans, we would be incapable of equipping this schema with moral values that guide and limit our actions. Therefore, elementary recognition must be carried out, and we must feel existential sympathy for the other, before we can learn to orient ourselves toward norms of recognition that compel us to express certain specific forms of concern or benevolence. The implication for the structure of my own theory of recognition is that I must insert a stage of recognition before the previously discussed forms, one that represents a kind of transcendental condition (Honneth 2008, p. 152).

This long quote from the "Rejoinder," in addition to providing the clearest definition of antecedent recognition, illuminates its relationship with the normative dimension.

---

73 See Honneth 2008, p. 59.

3.3.2 A Triangular Relationship with the World

Lukács's concept of reification, however, also concerns the relationship with material objects. Honneth therefore has the difficult task of providing an account of genuine interaction with the 'external' world through the "narrow basis" provided by recognition (Honneth 2008, p. 61). In contrast to what could be defined as *"technical fetishism"* (Ferrara 2011, p. 383) the need is to describe a mode of interaction with the world that is able to let objects emerge in their independence and qualitative peculiarities: this authentic mode of interaction—as opposed to a calculating detachment and instrumentalization—must therefore be able to coincide with an acknowledgment of the objects' autonomy (for example, of nature), but at the same time with a practical involvement with them. Honneth's argument revolves around the pivotal role played by the infant's mimetic and gestural interactions in structuring the experience itself,[74] and so again refers to Adorno. As we have already seen, if, on the one hand, the primary interactions constitute the condition of possibility for the mentation itself, the child gradually learns to distinguish attitudes toward objects from the objects themselves, generalizing the multiplicity of perspectives. On the other hand, this mediation of the figures of attachment to objects would be maintained by the subject, who would then relate to them according to those facets that are considered worthy by relevant partners. Through the imitation of other persons, we relate to the object "by endowing it with additional components of meaning," which are triangulated by the perspective of the loved ones (Honneth 2008, p. 62).

One could then say that Honneth fails to describe a "non-anthropocentric value" of nature and the physical world (van Leeuwen 2006, p. 239). In other words, he seems to claim that, *for us*, "objectively given objects are those that are intersubjectively given" (Butler 2008, p. 116), namely, that we gain our access to the world solely through culture and social facticity. However, although this later dimension is surely a logical consequence of his view, I think that the argument is slightly different here:

> With Adorno, we could add that this antecedent recognition also means respecting those aspects of meaning in an object that human beings accord that object. If it is indeed the case that in recognizing other persons we must at the same time recognize their subjective conceptions and feelings about nonhuman objects, then we could also speak without hesitation of a potential "reification" of nature.... We then perceive animals, plants, or things in a merely objectively identifying way, without being aware that these objects possess a multiplicity of existential meanings for the people around us (Honneth 2008, p. 63).

What Honneth argues here is therefore not a phenomenological or hermeneutic argument, nor does he intend to reduce cultural mediation—which can be understood both as a transcendental condition of possibility for cognitive processes, and as influential mechanism of power—to the intersubjective dimension. Even less does he

---

74 See Butler 2008, p. 112.

seek to pursue an idealistic view whereby objects are enclosed within an anthropocentric perspective. Rather, and much more modestly, the issue at stake concerns the fact that our apperception of the objects' qualitative value is inevitably mediated by the figures around us, proposing what could be named as an Adornian account on Habermas's intersubjectivistic turn. This does not mean that all forms of interaction with the world are reduced to this dimension. If, therefore, from a genetic point of view it is true that Honneth attributes a fundamental role to the antecedent recognition for the structuring of the experience itself, the recognition of objects represents only an indirect form; in recognizing the other we are compelled to consider the meanings (even personal, affective) that our partner attributes to physical objects. However, this argument does not seem to do complete justice to Honneth's assumption that recognition precedes cognition. Rather, the use of Adorno seems to concern a single dimension of experience, not its totality: the relationships of recognition, besides allowing a harmonic structuring of the cognitive faculties in the child, allow us to deal with objects, perceiving their qualitative value according to an attitude of respect, through which objects manifest themselves as concerning, engaging and involving *us*. Such an attitude would be borrowed triangularly from the stance we live in relation to our interaction partners. Recognition toward the world is therefore an asymmetrical *reflection* of the recognition we perform toward others: whereas the terms reification and antecedent recognition can be used in a direct sense when referring to intersubjective relations, they can be meant only indirectly when referring to physical objects or non-human living beings.[75]

3.3.3 Self-Recognition as Inner Proximity

The last dimension of reification, and therefore of recognition, to be dealt with is that which concerns the relationship with one's own self. In this case, it seems legitimate to use the binomial "*inauthenticity*"–authenticity (Ferrara 2011, p. 383). Although these expressions can be problematic for various reasons, especially in the context of a critical theory of society, letting ourselves be guided by the conceptual constellations evoked by these terms is enlightening for three main reasons. First, the anthropological connotations with which the concept of reification is described—a constant decay from a more original mode—allows us to glimpse a deeper connection with Heidegger's thought than what appears in the written word.[76] Second, "Organized Self-Realization" represents an interesting point of contact between the concept of self-realization and that of authenticity. Although in negative and critical terms, this testifies that Honneth approaches a comparison between the two terms: they could coincide if the latter were to be interpreted at a formal level, as a possibility

---

[75] See Honneth 2008, pp. 63–64.
[76] See Schafer 2017, p. 424.

of harmonic self-expression within a certain biographical continuity. Third, the term authenticity can summarize a series of Honneth's contributions around the time of *Reification*, which testify to the intention to deepen the idea of undamaged self-relationship expressed in *The Struggle for Recognition*. In this case, therefore, it should not come as a surprise that this form of recognition toward one's own self, while attesting to a socio-ontological and anthropological level, has normative implications, given the effective closeness with concepts such as self-confidence,[77] "inner aliveness" (Honneth 1999, p. 239), "self-appropriation" (Honneth 2009b, p. 128), "inner freedom," or "inward tolerance" (Honneth 2009c, pp. 160 and 164). The surprising aspect of Reification, however, is that this undamaged self-relation is described in terms of a recognition relationship.

Again, Honneth proceeds negatively. First, Honneth considers two reifying forms of relationship with one's own inner contents, both of whose shortcomings—even though they are diametrically opposed modalities—is that of considering the relationship with the latter as comparable with the relationship with physical objects. The first form of reification toward oneself is derived from the concept of detectivism developed by David Finkelstein. According to this view, the subject would act as "a detective who possesses privileged knowledge of his own desires and feelings," who encounters and discovers his own mental states as if their existence preceded the gaze of an "inward eye" (Honneth 2008, p. 67). Honneth criticizes this through the lens of the second form of self-reification and which is called constructivism, or, again referring to Finkelstein, constitutivism. This view takes its clues from the statement that our "mental states generally possess a rather diffuse and highly indeterminate substance that cannot be grasped" by the cognitive stance outlined by detectivist approaches (Honneth 2008, p. 68). If, therefore, mental states, desires, and sensations appear to us as not perfectly defined, it implies an active role for us in their constitution through linguistic elaboration. However, this solution, which in Honneth's opinion presents fewer problems than detectivism, "transforms our desires and feelings nevertheless into products of our own free decision" (Honneth 2008, p. 69). Simplifying, one could say that the shortcoming of detectivism coincides with considering mental states as prior to reflexive activity, while the limit of constructivism lies in conceiving them as products, and therefore subsequent to reflexive activity. Sociologically speaking, both these forms of reifying one's inner contents would be detectable in those institutionalized practices, such as job interviews or interaction through social media, in which subjects are constantly urged to exhibit and elaborate themselves through forms of self-portrayal.[78] In this sense, the concepts of detectivism and constructivism could be used for the aims of an ideology critique, since they could be considered not "as deficient descriptions of the original

---

[77] See Zurn 2015, p. 45; and Piromalli 2012, p. 247.
[78] See Honneth 2008, pp. 82–83; and Honneth and Gonçalo Marcelo 2013, pp. 218–19.

mode in which we relate to our mental life, but as appropriate descriptions of deficient modes of self-relationship" (Honneth 2008, p. 72).

Conversely, the original or undamaged form of self-relationship is depicted by mentioning different figures and concepts: Winnicott's idea that psychic health hinges on a playful dealing with desires; Aristotle's concepts of self-friendship and self-love; or Bieri's account on appropriation of one's own desires.[79] But above all, Honneth tries to outline a middle way between detectivism and constructivism. While the constructivist emphasis on the role of the linguistic articulation is an element to be valued, the passivity of the detectivist approach does justice from a phenomenological point of view to the fact that the reflexive elaboration of mental states always has a starting material. The relationship with the inner contents is therefore characterized by an activity that can only be articulated toward a *something*, which in fact can appear to us even as extraneous and uncomfortable. In this sense, self-recognition would coincide with an inner proximity, which approaches the inner contents as something worthy of expression. To this primary mode of self-relation Honneth gives the name 'expressionism':

> According to this model, we neither merely perceive our mental states as objects nor construct them by manifesting them to others. Instead, we articulate them in the light of feelings that are familiar to us. A subject who relates to himself in this original manner must necessarily regard his own feelings and desires as worthy of articulation (Honneth 2008, p. 75).

Such a giving expression to one's inner contents would therefore represent a form of freedom in the relationship with oneself: the essential mode of self-recognition.

3.4 Some Open Issues: Ontology or Normativity, Recognition or Identification

The concept of recognition as described in *Reification* is also the subject of numerous criticisms. That many of these criticisms contradict each other reveals a certain ambiguity in Honneth's argument. If, however, *Reification* seems to represent a dead end for the purposes of a normative and critical social theory, I believe that it contains some important indications for the definition of the concept of recognition both in Honneth and in general.

In this case, the criticisms can be summed up in three groups: the first concerns the ahistoric and asocial nature of the argument; the second involves the all-encompassing account of recognition; and the third is the relationship between antecedent recognition and normativity.

The first set of criticisms is therefore inextricably tied to those aimed at the redefinition of the concept of reification. In fact, the bonds of recognition described

---

[79] See Honneth 2008, pp. 65–66 and 74.

by Honneth seem to be exclusively interpersonal, a "purified"—because it is independent of history—"concept of intersubjectivity" (Chari 2010, p. 588): in this sense, the anthropological investigation seems to be superordinate to the sociological one,[80] since even in this work every normative implication is derived from the singular I-Thou relation,[81] to which the role of institutions (in the broadest meaning of the term) is external, even up to being marginal.[82] The references to institutionalized practices—which in any case concern reification and not recognition—seem to be episodic and do not flow into the process of defining the concepts at stake.

Second, Honneth would propose an "overstretching" concept of recognition,[83] which serves as the basis for the unfolding of every human faculty. This raises a problem possessing two facets. On the one hand, the "transcendental and genetic exclusivity placed on recognition" (Deranty 2009, p. 464), beside not seeming very plausible, diminishes the contribution of other dimensions and dynamics that contribute to the development of human beings and other modes of interaction that go beyond the spectrum of intersubjective gestures of recognition. Therefore, if, on the one hand, recognition does not seem to be a sufficiently broad concept able to encompass all these dimensions, the concept itself seems, on the other hand, to be distorted. In fact, although the modest account of recognition toward the physical world can avoid such criticism, it does not fully respect the assumption that recognition precedes cognition. More than one perplexity can also be raised about the adequacy of using the term recognition as far as the self-relation is concerned. Although (Sartre's and) Cavell's argument may possibly provide a justification in this direction, since it shows a connection between our recognition of the other and the relationship between the other and its own inner contents, the same cannot be said about Honneth's. With *Reification*, therefore, one can raise the doubt that Honneth blurs the characteristic traits of recognition in the direction of a more general and generic idea of identification or, more simply, interaction, reducing the latter accordingly.[84]

The third group of criticisms concerns the relationship between the concept of antecedent recognition and normativity. We can state the first criticism as follows. This form of recognition should be neutral from a normative point of view: affective involvement in the early stages of childhood would not imply any stance of respect for the other or for his autonomy.[85] But, if so—that is, if it represents an all-encompassing foundation for every intersubjective stance regardless of moral principles (and therefore also for hatred, disrespect, instrumentalization, and racism)—it is rather unlikely that such an intersubjective form could be a basis for ethics or social criticism.[86] How-

---

80 See Butler 2008, p. 101.
81 See Deranty 2009, p. 464.
82 See Chari 2010, p. 598.
83 See Varga 2010, p. 23; and Piromalli 2012, p. 246.
84 See Deranty 2009, p. 463.
85 See Lear 2008, p. 134.
86 See Raymond Geuss 2008, p. 127.

3.4 Some Open Issues: Ontology or Normativity, Recognition or Identification — 119

ever, because of the constant tension between description and prescription in Honneth's texts,[87] this concept of social-ontological recognition seems to imply some normative account[88]—Honneth in fact admits that this form of identification urges subjects to assume a certain stance. Then, as a second criticism, the delineation of the antecedent recognition would coincide with the position of an a priori ethical good, which prevents, among other things, the development of a multipolar account of intersubjectivity.[89] Moreover, the third criticism is that if such an essential involvement were at the basis of some normative value, this would certainly not be due to the fact that involvement per se possesses some relevance from this point of view:[90] that is, even if antecedent recognition possibly conveyed any normative value, it would not itself represent one of them.

Certainly, Honneth proposes a two-level account of recognition in this work.[91] As Lear insightfully points out, on the one hand there is *"recognition-as-sine-qua-non* for any real development at all" and on the other there is *"recognition-as-paradigm* of healthy human development" (Lear 2008, p. 134). If by the first form Honneth means recognition as a (quasi)transcendental condition for the entry of subjects into the web of intersubjective relations and the social world itself (also with its objects)[92]—which seems to be the object of *Reification*—the second definition of recognition would describe the normative and institutionally instantiated dimension depicted in *The Struggle for Recognition*, which would help to constitute the conditions for an undamaged practical identity and for a free path of self-realization. This distinction, although admitted by Honneth, brings with it numerous problems. In fact, we might think of such a separation in three ways. The first two coincide with two criticisms already mentioned: either it is a sharp distinction, and the antecedent recognition has no normative implication, or it constitutes an ethical good, but its original character seems to cast a substantial shadow on its normative character. There is a third possibility, which I think is the one Honneth embraces: the normative constraint proper to antecedent recognition invites us to take a certain position in front of a human being, recognized as embodying human features through this precise form of recognition. Accordingly, this anteriority of recognition should not be conceived in ahistorical terms, since such awareness of the other as a human being is instantiated in every gesture of recognition within our social, determined world; even hate toward someone presupposes a preliminary recognition, for the simple fact that we cannot hate a chair or a bookshelf—unless it is the object of a triangular relationship in which our position toward someone is projected on it. In this sense, and in response to Geuss's criticism, the usefulness of this concept for

---

87 See Koch 2015, p. 313.
88 See Petherbridge 2013, p. 179.
89 See Petherbridge 2013, p. 180.
90 See Butler 2008, p. 104.
91 See Varga 2010, p. 20.
92 See Ferrara 2011, p. 380.

the purposes of social criticism is clearly indirect: it does not in itself set any stringent normative criteria—given, among others, the unsuccessful consequences of Honneth's re-elaboration of reification. However, it does pose a fundamental element to be able to develop a critique of society through the concept of recognition because it clarifies the structure of this very concept.

However, it is precisely at this conceptual level that most of the problems condense, and tensions emerge in the use of the term recognition.[93] In fact, by describing the concept of antecedent recognition by referring to ideas such as care, involvement, imitation, and emotional attachment, Honneth describes a non-mutual and non-reciprocal praxis. Moreover, when referring to self-relation, such an attitude of familiarity with inner contents seems to have the traits of a (albeit affective and participatory) cognition (*Erkennen*) more so than of a recognition (*Anerkennen*). Moreover, as already mentioned, the fact that Honneth refers to Heidegger and Dewey makes us question whether this form of recognition possesses an intentional character or not. In fact, on the one hand, the very concept of recognition would imply an intentional (human) object, thus describing a certain knowing-stance with a precise addressee; on the other hand, Honneth's depiction of the genuine praxis seems more to describe a pre-intentional openness to the world, that is, a stance that lets otherness in general emerge in all its qualities and independence. According to Varga, embracing this second interpretative hypothesis would be more fruitful, precisely because antecedent recognition does not possess a precise addressee, but rather opens up the very horizon of the experience. Thus, it would be preferable to replace the expression "primary recognition" with "affective attunement or 'aquaintedness,'" which have the merit of maintaining the priority of the intersubjective over the subjective, while avoiding the normative and conceptual implications proper to the concept of recognition (Varga 2010, p. 23). This solution effectively solves many of the contradictions highlighted by critical literature, avoids the improper stretching of the concept of recognition and dissolves the tension between it and the idea of identification, while maintaining what could be considered the main thrust of the work: interpersonal interactions have a major, indeed primal role in the constitution of the cognitive faculties of the subject and the human person and thus in their relation with the world. However, I would argue that the concept of antecedent recognition should be maintained at least in its epistemological dimension, thus drawing closer to how it is described in "Invisibility." Every normative act of recognition can be articulated on the basis of a cognitive potential that, at the same time, is both instantiated within it and represents its foundation. As Honneth points out in an interview in 2010, "before we, in a society, can even begin to differentiate between different forms of recognition, we must recognize each other as human beings" (Honneth, Jakobsen, and Lysaker 2010, p. 165). Therefore, in Honneth's view, this two-level conception of recognition, despite the aforementioned ambiguities, must be maintained.

---

93 See Deranty 2009, p. 463.

Chapter 4
Freedom's Right and the 'Historical Turn'

To take a new step in reconstructing the unfolding of Honneth's thought, it is necessary to turn to the fundamental work published in 2011, *Freedom's Right*. This work contains numerous variations and represents a shift in the equilibrium proper to Honneth's paradigm. In general, it more explicitly deals with contents and issues closer to political philosophy, such as the theory of justice and freedom, to the extent that one could say Honneth himself has changed his aims, moving from a theory of recognition to a theory of freedom,[1] outlining not a paradigm of social change, but one of social reproduction.[2] In my opinion, these expressions mark this change of perspective too sharply, since Honneth himself describes the shift as a learning process of an almost implicit nature.[3] This means that it is rather difficult to categorize his thought into distinct and different phases that would correspond to reconsiderations or explicit retractions; rather, it seems more useful to highlight the continuity of the evolution, contextualizing and characterizing the actual changes as the taking shape and unfolding of dimensions largely already present not only in *The Struggle for Recognition*, but even previous to the paradigm of recognition itself. In fact, it remains almost impossible, in Honneth's thought, "to separate social reproduction and social change, just as freedom and recognition are deeply intertwined with each other, starting from the concept of self-realization.

However, Honneth certainly changes the infrastructure of his own thought, proposing what he himself calls a "historical transition" (Honneth, Jakobsen, and Lysaker 2010, p. 166): in exposing a social theory of justice referring mainly to Hegel's *Philosophy of Right*, the main focus shifts from the *practices* of recognition and the related moral grammar of conflict to the *spheres* of recognition and their institutionalized normative principles. As we have already seen—especially in our discussion of "Invisibility"—the definition of recognition practices requires a previous dimension of reference, which Honneth defines as second nature. That is, a gesture of recognition receives its own evaluative guidelines only within a normative, qualitative, social horizon, which also opens up the epistemological possibilities of such intersubjective practices. Certainly, this conceptualization is not absent in *The Struggle for Recognition*, a work in which, however, the action-theoretical approach leaves the institutional context in the background, making recognition appear as an act that takes place exclusively between individuals. In this new phase of his thought, and closer to Siep's positions, Honneth elaborates a theory of institutional spheres, whose already-given principles of recognition play a historicizing role for the entire paradigm of rec-

---

[1] See Teixeira 2017, p. 600.
[2] See Teixeira 2017, p. 605.
[3] See Honneth and Morten Raffnsøe-Møller 2015, pp. 265–66.

ognition, to sharpen the universalistic drifts and ambiguities of *The Struggle for Recognition* and *Reification*,[4] which in turn are tied to the so-called anthropological justification. This shift can be grasped by referring to the following quotation from *Redistribution or Recognition?*: "Before I can attempt to interpret distribution conflicts according to the 'moral grammar' of a struggle for recognition, a short explanation is required of what it can mean to speak of capitalist society as an institutionalized recognition order" (Honneth 2003d, p. 137). In other words, in order to analyze the normative and motivational logics that trigger social movements, that is, the emancipatory drives that the critical theorist must be able to unearth, it would be necessary to focus on the set of normative principles within which these movements act. In fact, they perform both an informative function—that is, they necessarily form the expectations and aspirations for recognition, which can only be based on an already present ethical ensemble—and an emancipatory one—because their institutional realization can always be questioned and perfected from within.

Clearly, the extent of the matter at stake prevents a detailed analysis of all the issues, which can be addressed from multiple points of view. As such, we will focus on the changes the paradigm of recognition undergoes, which is inevitably influenced by the enrichment of the normative-institutional framework that Honneth faces with greater determination.

In the first section of this chapter, we will focus on *The Pathologies of Individual Freedom*, a text that contains the Spinoza Lectures held by Honneth in 1999. In a theoretical context similar to that outlined in *The Struggle for Recognition* and "Pathologies of the Social," Honneth turns for the first time to Hegel's *Philosophy of Right*, taking its first steps in structuring a theory of justice in terms of social freedom. Here, the analysis will focus on the characteristics of the social spheres of recognition, and in particular on the dimension of education (*Bildung*), and on the concept of right (*Recht*), which clarifies the relationship between individual expectations and the principles of recognition, that is, their justification, their right to be (section 4.1).

The focus of section two is instead oriented toward the exchange with Nancy Fraser contained in *Redistribution or Recognition?* The analysis of this text, rich in its implications, finds its fulcrum in the concept of surplus of validity, which effectively shows the change of emphasis of the Honneth's theory: the historically institutionalized principles of recognition would have a normative significance able to transcend the contingent, providing a new evaluation apparatus with respect to the claims of social movements, thus allowing an elaboration of an idea of progress that should not refer directly to an anthropological theory (section 4.2).

The last section turns to *Freedom's Right*, specifically to Honneth's attempt not only to re-actualize Hegel, but to take up his theoretical challenge in the contemporary philosophical context. In this case, our attention will be drawn to recognition relations, whose specific characteristics seem at times generalized in the direction

---

4 See Honneth and Marcelo 2013, pp. 210–12; and Honneth, Jakobsen, and Lysaker 2010, pp. 167–68.

of a more neutral theory of intersubjectivity. In the course of this analysis, the two key concepts are certainly those of normative reconstruction and social freedom, which represent the aforementioned fulcrums of this second phase of Honneth's thought: the reconstruction of the recognition order and its institutionalized normative principles and an outline of recognition in terms that strongly distinguish Honneth's theory from identity politics; the affirmation of the other through recognition does not concern already-formed cultural identities, but represents the mutual condition for the realization of freedom, that is, for being oneself with the other (section 4.3).

4.1 Ethical Life as Place of and for Freedom

The Spinoza Lectures held by Honneth in 1999, then published under the title "Suffering from Indeterminacy,"[5] represent his first attempt to deal with Hegel's *Philosophy of Right*. And if, on the one hand, Honneth now states that, even in this mature text, we can find the original intention of Hegel's Jena period,[6] on the other hand, taking this work as an object of confrontation inevitably alters certain aspects of Honneth's perspective.[7] It is therefore useful not to take this new subject of re-elaboration for granted: in fact, if Honneth's view remains almost unchanged with regard to the assumption of suffering as starting point for critique, to the action-theoretical approach, and to the identification of the spheres of recognition as social condition for individual self-realization, the main focus seems to shift to a definition of the Hegelian enterprise as a theory of justice concerning freedom and a greater concentration on the structure of the social spheres. As Siep puts it, the interest that the Hegelian work can represent for contemporary thought is constituted by the fact that the theory exposed in the *Grundlinien* would harmonize a theory of social differentiation—suitable for interpreting the complexity of modern-contemporary societies—with a paradigm of normative integration—thus providing an alternative to systemic sociological views.[8] By sharing this persuasion, Honneth states that the notion of *Sittlichkeit* would be capable: a) to provide a socio-ontological model for the coordination of anti-atomistic and anti-utilitarian social action; b) to describe its own reproduction and development as necessarily anchored to relationships of recognition; and c) to develop—and this is the real novelty—a theory of justice deeply tied to the diagnosis of time,[9] according to which the normative guidelines of society (and of

---

5 Hereafter, we will refer to the 2010 edition *The Pathologies of Individual Freedom*.
6 See Honneth 2012d, pp. vii–viii; Honneth 2010, pp. 18 and 50; Pippin 2000 p. 155.
7 For a detailed overview of Honneth's relationship to Hegel, see Andreas Busen, Lisa Herzog, and Paul Sörensen 2012, pp. 251–58.
8 See Siep 2014a, p. 144.
9 Honneth explains in an interview that "a necessary first step" in the enterprise of drawing a theory of justice "is a diagnosis which informs us whether or not the understandings of freedom are some-

social theory) must be derived from the analysis of the conditions of the instantiation of freedom, which is in turn defined as leading an unharmed autonomous existence.[10]

In any case, it is important to emphasize that these lessons are precisely an internal and indirect comparison with the *Philosophy of Right*. In other words, it is difficult to distinguish the inside of the reading of Hegel and the outside of Honneth's original intentions—as happened in *The Struggle for Recognition* and *Reification*—and also to understand which aspects of his exegesis Honneth actually endorses in his own thought.[11] Without entering in an intricate and potentially overwhelming confrontation between the two works, we can summarize Honneth's text according to four subsequent steps.

First, Honneth proposes an external access to the text, which derives from the refusal to use Hegel's *Logic* as a necessary presupposition for the structuring of ethical life and from its consequences on how the relationship between individuals and state is conceived, as well as the teleologically-oriented hierarchy between the different spheres.[12] Already is not difficult here to see that Honneth's intention is not to provide a faithful interpretation of the *Philosophy of Right*, but to filter and re-propose those Hegelian elements that can play a significant role in the contemporary philosophical horizon.[13]

Second, Honneth sets the ambitious goal of defining a concept of objective spirit without resorting to the idea of spirit. This would imply the assumption according to

---

what justified, and in that sense I see a clear link between the two kinds of enterprise.... As long as the understanding of freedom is to some degree an incorrect one, a one-sided one, then the concept of justice, which is in a sense an expression of our search for freedom would not be sufficient; it would also be somewhat diminished. And only if we can get a clearer understanding of freedom, only then would our understanding of justice be sufficient. So in order to prove whether or not our understanding of freedom is correct, one has to undertake something like a time diagnosis.... I think the direction that such a diagnosis should take today would be to make clear that there are narrow understandings of what individual freedom means. There is, on the one side, a kind of legal understanding of freedom. There is, on the other side, a kind of romantic understanding of freedom in the sense of self-realization (*Selbstverwicklichung*), authenticity, and those understandings of freedom taken separately and only one-sidedly would lead to social pathologies" (Honneth and Gwynn Markle 2004, p. 384). See also Honneth 2010, pp. 23–24 and 49.

10 See Deranty 2011, pp. 65–66.
11 See Antti Kauppinen 2011, p. 295.
12 See Honneth 2010, pp. 3–5.
13 Honneth is certainly neither the first nor the last in the contemporary context to defend such philosophical approach to Hegel's *Philosophy of Right*. See, among others, Allen W. Wood 1990; and Frederick Neuhouser 2000. In the specific case of Honneth, the reason is not to be found exclusively in the rejection of Hegelian ontology or metaphysics, which are considered as no longer usable and inadequate. The concept of spirit is put aside because its implications seem to lead to the undermining of the very purpose of outlining the actualization of individual freedom. See Honneth and Markle 2004, p. 386. Moreover, the idea that recognition relationships play a fundamental role in the *Philosophy of Right* is also echoed in contemporary literature. See Robert R. Williams 1997; Williams 1992.

which "all social reality has a rational structure" and that failures to fulfil this rationality in the carrying out of social functions would lead to detrimental effects on social life (Honneth 2010, p. 6). Clearly, the idea at stake here is that of *mis*developments and social pathologies. More specifically, Honneth takes as a pivotal issue the concept of freedom, determining in its realization the criterion through which a theory of justice can be exposed: therefore, the lack of actual or realized freedom would lead to social suffering and in turn to an unjust society. Put in positive terms, Honneth maintains, Hegel's aim would coincide with outlining a "general principle of justice that would legitimize those social conditions under which each subject is able to perceive the liberty of the other as the prerequisite of his own self-realization" (Honneth 2010, p. 8). In this context, as we shall see, how Honneth interprets the concept of right plays a central role.

A third step concerns the structure of ethical life. Having rejected the metaphysical foundation due to Hegel's logical accounts, Honneth derives the institutional forms of ethical life—here the action-theoretical perspective comes into play—from the defective and realized modes of freedom described in the Introduction to the *Grundlinien*. In this way, the forms of *Sittlichkeit* are represented as institutional concretions (in the broad sense) of intersubjective attitudes concerning freedom. For our purposes, the description that Honneth proposes of the ethical spheres is of particular importance, the characteristics of which shed new light on the concept of recognition.

Finally, in the light of his analysis, Honneth emphasizes the main limits of the Hegelian theory concerning the institutional spheres of family, civil society, and state. Unsurprisingly, the main criticism is that of an over-institutionalized account of ethical life, with an overloaded role and scope assigned to the state that is: this shortcoming of the Hegelian theory results in each institutional concretion that makes up the *Sittlichkeit*. As far as the family is concerned, Honneth argues that the exclusion of friendship relationships from this sphere is due to an excessive consideration of the forms determined by the positive law. In other words, friendship—which according to its practical-communicative modalities and its being one of the most simple ways of being with oneself in another could rightly fall into this sphere of ethical life—is excluded because of the shaping role already granted to legislation in this sphere. Clearly, friendship could not be a legislative object, while the sphere of love is occupied by the bourgeois nuclear family.[14] This would also imply a devaluation of the first sphere, which would not receive its definition from within—that is, from the practices that constitute it—but from outside, that is, from the framework predetermined by the state.[15] The second set of consequences concerns the sphere of civil society and in particular the role assigned to corporations. The presence of this institutional form—besides representing a description that would be already

---

14 See Honneth 2010, pp. 67–69.
15 See Honneth 2010, p. 71.

badly adapted to the industrial development of Hegel's time—determines the outline of a further practical mode within the second sphere than that of commodities exchange, which in turn implies the recognitional forms tied to individual rights. Hence this co-presence of two forms of intersubjective interactions unbalances the principle according to which each sphere is determined by a practical form, thus constituting its institutional concretion.[16] That this appears problematic in Honneth's eyes must not appear contradictory with what has been said about the sphere of love. In fact, contrary to the possible duplicity of the first sphere, which could accommodate both family and friendship, the forms of recognition proper to the commodity exchange and corporations would respond to two different logics—which could be briefly explained from within Honneth's perspective using the distinction between the second and third spheres contained in *The Struggle for Recognition:* legal respect and esteem as basis for cooperative interactions. It is important to emphasize here that Honneth is therefore sympathetic to the idea that each sphere corresponds to a single bundle of practical modalities: not a single type of action, but a practical and meta-practical horizon, which concerns instrumental actions, linguistic relations, and intersubjective relations of recognition.[17] In this sense, the practical univocity of each ethical sphere is not understood in exclusive terms, but rather on what practical forms could represent the essence of a social context: clearly, family is constituted within a legal and cooperative context, but without love there would not be an identifiable institutional form, distinguished by others. Moreover, the limit of corporations strictly concerns the shortcoming of the third ethical sphere. In fact, even if we are to support Hegel's solution as it proposes a context of public freedom for the individual that is able to stem the potentially disruptive aspects of the market and the exchange of goods for social life,[18] the need that Hegel feels in inserting this dimension already in the second sphere derives, according to Honneth, from the fact that the sphere of the state turns out not to be able to fulfill such a task. In fact, sharing Siep's reservations,[19] Honneth argues that the idea that inside the sphere of the state the individual is raised to its universality represents an unequivocal sign that "a horizontal relationship"—that of recognition—is replaced "by a vertical one" (Honneth 2010, p. 78)[20]—of subsumption. That would inevitably lead to a loss of individual autonomy and thus to a perspective that would betray the original intention of determining a theory of justice that outlines the conditions for personal freedom—at least according to the liberal pre-comprehension of the idea, which Hon-

---

[16] See Honneth 2010, pp. 75–77.
[17] I therefore find it problematic to say, as Teixeira does, that Honneth's idea of market in this text becomes differentiated and can no longer be exhausted in its being normatively embedded. See Teixeira 2019, pp. 188–89. In any case, I discuss Honneth's idea of market in the next section.
[18] In order to comprehend the relationship between cooperative action and democracy within Honneth's perspective, see Honneth 1998.
[19] See Deranty 2009, p. 232.
[20] See Hegel, *Philosophy of Right*, § 258.

neth does not intend to renounce. Instead of being a sphere of public freedom, the state represents a sphere of universal subsumption: therefore, Hegel seems compelled to throw back this essential dimension of actualized freedom in the realm of civil society.

4.1.1 Justice as Non-Discursive Justification

Having briefly framed the different passages of the Spinoza Lectures, it is now useful to focus on the two cornerstones on which Honneth builds his argument:

> Hegel's *Philosophy of Right* represents a normative theory of social justice that, by reconstructing the necessary conditions of individual autonomy, tries to determine what social spheres a society must comprise or make available in order to give all its members a chance to realize their self-determination. In this program it is also easy to recognize the second intention that Hegel has kept alive since his youthful phase in Jena and revived in the mature shape of his practical philosophy: …[…] the central intention of the *Philosophy of Right* is seen to be the development of universal principles of justice in terms of a justification of those social conditions under which each subject is able to perceive the liberty of the other as the prerequisite of his own self-realization (Honneth 2010, p. 18).

Before we move on to analyze the link between the concepts of justice and justification, it is essential that we address Honneth's understanding of personal freedom, which is deeply related to these terms. This idea can be approached, first, through two opposite criticisms addressed to Honneth's account. On the one hand, one can say that the Neo-Hegelian perspectives on freedom do not leave room for emancipatory freedom, that is, for modes of dissent and critique, as well as the basis for practical transformation.[21] On the other hand, Vetlesen, for example, views Honneth's interpretation as inspired by an excessively individualistic reading of Hegelian thought, and thus proposes a surplus of indeterminacy.[22] In other words, founding personal freedom on given ethical ideas would constrain individual freedoms—or their scope of possibilities—or, conversely, a too individualistic description of social freedom would not be able to solve the problem of indeterminacy, that is, abandoning individual autonomy to itself, thus providing it with insufficient orientational and motivational grounds. One could say that these two critiques, at the same time, both hit and miss the target. For, as claimed in the *Zusatz* to § 7 of the *Philosophy of Right*, "freedom lies neither in indeterminacy nor in determinacy, but is both at once" (Hegel, *Philosophy of Right*, § 7Z).[23] Once again, Honneth proceeds negatively. Writing about the Introduction of Hegel's text, he describes two partial (because

---

21 See Brian O'Connor 2012.
22 See Arne Johan Vetlesen 2015.
23 See Honneth 2010, pp. 18–19 and 25–26.

one-sided) modalities of freedom with which Hegel is confronted. On the one hand, there is a negativistic paradigm and, on the other hand, an optional model.

According to the first, freedom would consist of the "exclusion of all specific inclinations or purposes" (Honneth 2010, p. 11), or a subject can be considered free "to the extent that there is a certain external space within which his activity can unfold without any interventions by other subjects" (Honneth 2016, p. 161). Combining these two different characterizations, we arrive at the classic definition of negative freedom or freedom-from: autonomy is guaranteed when the subject is faced with an empty space in which it can freely articulate its initiative, without being bound to ethical and social constraints.

The optional model concerns instead the so-called positive freedom or freedom-to, as traditionally defined by Rousseau and Kant. Its emphasis is on the reflexive dimension of autonomy, that is, on the subject's ability to opt for reasons of action that are not in turn determined by desires, inclinations or impulses that "are themselves beyond the subject's control" (Honneth 2010, p. 12). The central intuition here is that the individual could be considered autonomous only insofar as she is bound by moral laws that she gives to herself.

The third mode of freedom is one that does not have to exclude otherness from its definition in order to articulate itself: to this mode, Hegel assigns the famous definition "being with oneself in the other." Honneth, drawing from the Addition of § 7, where Hegel speaks of friendship to explain this third form of freedom, interprets this definition in purely intersubjectivistic terms.[24] The doctrine of freedom does not therefore coincide with the analysis of an individual faculty or possibility, but with a normative social theory in which the communicative and social conditions that allow the subject to enjoy his or her own freedom are outlined: that would mean the realization or actualization of freedom, that is, its liberation from the solipsistic dimension that considers otherness as external. Given that the negative and the optional model concern the relation between subjects and reasons for action, the actualization of freedom also involves the idea, as Robert Pippin emphasizes,[25] that only a communicative sphere would allow the person to recognize herself in her own desires and acts, providing her, so to speak, with a starting material for her own moral considerations and therefore with the capability to acknowledge her accomplishments as her own; that is, enabling her reflective endorsement for the reasons of her own practical agency and the possibility that the externalization of acts would not coincide with alienation. Therefore, to participate in social institutions with ethical character has a *transformative* and a *formative* effect on the individual:[26] on the one hand, it allows the subject to transcend her own indeterminacy through acts that

---

[24] See Deranty 2009, p. 230.
[25] See Pippin 2007.
[26] See Pippin 2001, p. 8.

possess a consistency and, on the other hand, the institutions educate the individual, allowing her to recognize the orientation of these acts as her own.

Therefore, the outlining of a social infrastructure would correspond with a theory of freedom: here, the concept of right plays a fundamental role and allows us to understand why the delineation of institutional forms of freedom can be considered a theory of justice. The issue can be dealt with in three steps.

First, Honneth links an action-theoretical approach with a social-ontological account, deriving the sections of the *Philosophy of Right* on Abstract Right, Morality, and Ethical Life from the three forms of freedom mentioned above:

> in the course of the discussion, in parallel with the levels occupied by the different concepts of freedom, a sequence of action models, characterized by ascending degrees of theoretical complexity and social appropriateness, comes into being.... [I]f the final aim is to bring together, under the concept of "ethical life," the sum of communicative spheres characterized by specific forms of intersubjective action, it makes sense to carry out the analysis in action-theoretical terms right from the outset.... In addition, such a procedure offers Hegel a further advantage ...: since the individual concepts of freedom are reconstructed in terms of a theory of action, the step-by-step argumentation can also be understood as an attempt to outline a kind of social ontology; with each element that is added to the initially primitive concept of action, in parallel with the increasingly complex models of freedom, the set of concepts used by Hegel moves closer to the point at which it can finally be employed to describe the complexity of social realities in a fully adequate way (Honneth 2010, p. 32).

By doing so, Honneth proposes an account according to which social integration would possess a normative character and would be implemented on horizontal relations of recognition, thus excluding the vertical integration proper to Hegel's concept of the state. A concept of objective spirit (without spirit) would also be given: the spheres of social life would relate with the normative core of freedom embedded in its practical-individual dimensions, thus providing rational standards within social reality itself: hence, put negatively, "social reality" would not be "indifferent to the use of those false or incomplete definitions of human existence" (Honneth 2010, p. 24), that is, of one-sided perspectives and practices concerning freedom. The idea of objective spirit corresponds therefore to the institutional and historical unfolding of that intersubjective form of freedom—being with oneself in the other —which alone would guarantee the realization of autonomy.

Second, as we have already seen in the previous chapters, the burden of proof rests once again on the emergence of negative phenomena within social life, i.e. social pathologies. Referring especially to the *Zusatz* of the *Philosophy of Right*,[27] Honneth highlights the profound link that Hegel establishes between his social theory of justice and a diagnosis of time. Thus, following in the footsteps of the Hegel's notion of disease in living organisms, according to which one organ "establishes itself in isolation and persists in a particular activity against the activity of the whole"

---

[27] See Hegel, *Philosophy of Right*, §§ 136, 141, and 149.

(Hegel, *Philosophy of Nature*, § 371), Honneth affirms that the autonomization of negative and/or optional freedoms would lead individuals to suffer from indeterminacy.[28] In a nutshell, the atomized subject, left in the negative freedom of law or in the optional freedom of morality, would be deprived of an orientation-context and incapable of committing itself,[29] thus remaining blocked in the mere possibility.

This idea of social pathology could be subject to a criticism similar to that applied to the idea of reification. On the one hand, if pathology is identified as a second-order disorder, that is, as a reflexive dysfunction experienced by social actors, one could charge that suffering from indeterminacy lies purely within psychological dimension. On the other hand, if we want to emphasize, with Honneth, that unilateralization of freedom in these ways represent "conflicting rationalities *embedded in society*" (Honneth and Markle 2004, p. 385, my emphasis), one could ask whether this idea does not represent a "reduction of the institutional to the moral" (Deranty 2009, p. 235), given that socially normative integration seems to be the only social-ontological model at stake. Considering the difficulty of distinguishing the analysis of Hegel's text from the actual evolutions of Honneth's thought, it seems fruitful not to deal directly with these issues, which go to the heart of the social ontology possibly outlined by the author. However, it seems reasonable to me to embrace Deranty's interpretation, according to which Honneth's perspective settles at a radical level:[30] as Honneth repeats several times throughout the text,[31] the concept of justice Hegel defends throughout the *Philosophy of Right* is strongly egalitarian and the ethical spheres would thus enable individual freedom at a cultural, psychological, and material level.[32] Reducing the social pathology of indeterminacy to only one of these dimensions would at the very least be a misreading of the text.

The third and final step explicates the idea of right. Through this concept, Honneth intends to argue that the one presented in the *Philosophy of Right* is characterized as a theory of justice insofar as it proposes the right to exist that certain practical modalities and ethical spheres possess within the social world: "Hegel enlightens us about the exact position that legally and morally determined freedoms must hold in a comprehensive concept of modern justice, and he does so by diagnosing the negative effects that are bound to follow if either kind of freedom becomes detached from our social lifeworld" (Honneth 2010, pp. 30–31). In this sense, "the term *right* has the double meaning of a 'necessary condition' and a 'justifiable claim'" (Honneth 2010, p. 15): therefore, the institutional spheres, as actual bearers

---

[28] See Honneth 2010, pp. 23–24 and 44–45.
[29] See Max Pensky 2011, p. 140. Significantly, the only Hegelian criticism to the Kantian categorical imperative Honneth embraces is precisely that of context-blindness. See Donald Loose 2014, p. 179; and Honneth 2010, pp. 39–40.
[30] See Deranty 2009, pp. 236–38.
[31] See Honneth 2010, pp. 15, 25–26, 46, and 49.
[32] See Kauppinen 2011.

of rights,[33] can or must occupy a certain position within the social world that is in harmony with a rational—that is, non-pathological—development of society. This also constitutes the link between justice and justification mentioned above: the degree of justice within a society depends on the latter's justifiability (or not) in the eyes of the actors who inhabit it, which in turn relies on the capacity of institutional concretions—taken individually and in their mutual relations (i.e. in occupying their right place)—to provide actual conditions of freedom. However, one could say, following Pippin, that this concept of right is ill-suited to the idea of ethical life Hegel proposes: in fact, the communicative spheres could not be subjected to processes of justification, precisely because one of their tasks is to form and transform the individual capacities useful in weighing if and how the institutions are justified. In other words, what would be the interlocutor "under an obligation" or the right-claim of the spheres (Pippin 2001, p. 11), if they represent an unavoidable world of reasons for the social actors' practical agency? Although *Redistribution or Recognition?* will provide us with more insights in this regard, I believe that we should read this concept of right according to two conceptual cores.

The first concerns social ontology. The idea of right place of ethical spheres concerns the need—perceived by Honneth—to avoid a non-normative premise to the provided social-ontological image.[34] A non-normative assumption would in fact be incompatible with the conviction that in the Hegelian concept of *Sittlichkeit* social differentiation and normative integration are co-dependent, thanks to the evolution and expansion of relationships of recognition. Consequently, the resulting institutional concretions of these intersubjective practices must always be open to questioning.

This brings us to the second point, which concerns freedom, and more precisely the aforementioned critical alternative between determinacy and emancipatory freedom. I intend to argue that the concept of right outlined by Honneth has the dual task of describing, on the one hand, the establishment of a recognition order capable of ensuring an actualized freedom for all its participants and, on the other, to justify critique: the dimension that enables social actors to question and refine the principles underlying their social integration is outlined in the balance between determinacy and indeterminacy. In this sense, recognition orders and social struggles would not be in conflict—and would not represent the concepts around which Honneth constitutes two distinct phases within his thinking—but would essentially depend on each other. Thus, on the one hand, excessive determination would not afford the communicative space in which normative principles can be questioned as to their realization and, possibly, reworked. On the other hand, excessive indeterminacy would lead to pathological outcomes for both society and individuals. As already noted, the idea of right embraces the necessity of the ethical spheres as a normative,

---

33 See Honneth 2010, p. 17.
34 See Neuhouser 2016.

formative, and orienting context that allows for the concreteness of freedom, but this concreteness is also realized in the freedom of critique, that is, in the possibility of overcoming the punctual realizations of the principles institutionally realized. Here, clearly, right concerns the justifiability of the institutions.

4.1.2 Overlapping and Noncoincidence of Ethical Spheres and Practices

Since, therefore, the theory of freedom coincides with a theory of ethical life, it is now necessary to briefly address the characterization of the ethical spheres that Honneth extrapolates in his confrontation with the *Philosophy of Right*. This proves interesting for two main reasons. First, more plainly than ever before or after, Honneth states in just a few lines the characteristics that must pertain to the ethical spheres. This might obviously be an advantage for the clarification of some aspects, but also a disadvantage for others: some elements seem to contrast with what will emerge in *Redistribution or Recognition?* and it is not clear if such differences represent an effective rethinking or if Honneth's intent in *The Pathologies of Individual Freedom* is simply to interpret how a Hegel purified-from-metaphysics could explain the nature of the spheres of recognition. Second, this definition of the spheres enlightens a second phase of reflection on the concept of recognition, which has already been met in "Invisibility." It could be summarized under the title of 'expressionist account' and strongly connotes Honneth's thinking of institutions.[35]

Honneth highlights four characteristics of ethical life:

> If we are to list the conditions in brief key phrases, the sphere of ethical life must consist of interactional practices that are able to guarantee individual self-realization, reciprocal recognition, and the corresponding processes of education; and the three aims must be closely interwoven, since Hegel seems convinced that their relationship is one of mutual conditioning (Honneth 2010, p. 56).

The first, minimal condition of the ethical spheres concerns their accountability in terms of the liberation of individual freedom.[36] Sketching Hegel's account, according to which, in duty, "the individual liberates himself so as to attain substantial freedom" (Hegel, *Philosophy of Right*, § 149), Honneth describes the ethical horizon as the necessary condition within which the three forms of freedom described in the Introduction find their right place and concur to form the preconditional setting for individual self-realization. Therefore, regardless of the specific recognitional quiddity of each sphere—be it love, right, or social esteem—what should connote the ethical as such is its ability to relieve the social actors from indeterminacy, thus providing them the tools or opportunities for seeing the actualization of their own freedom.

---

35 See Deranty and Renault 2007.
36 See Honneth 2010, pp. 43–49.

The second characteristic concerns the intersubjectivistic interpretation of Hegel's "being with oneself in the other." In a nutshell, if freedom can only be realized when the other-of-freedom is also endowed with freedom, and if the free otherness is necessarily another subject with whom to enter into a relationship while keeping oneself, then it follows that the realization of freedom on an ethical level must, so to speak, run on intersubjective tracks.[37]

The third condition that the ethical spheres have to satisfy "is that the intersubjective actions that constitute it should express certain forms of reciprocal recognition" (Honneth 2010, p. 52). If, on the one hand, there are no great differences with the definition provided in *The Struggle for Recognition*, because Honneth there defines recognition as "an effortless mutual acknowledgement of certain aspects of the other's personality, connected to the prevailing mode of social interaction" (Honneth 2010, p. 51), on the other hand a further element, the behavioral component of recognition, accounts for an ampliation of the concept as described in "Invisibility":

> mutual recognition means not only meeting each other in a certain affirmative attitude but implies, also and indeed above all else, treating the other in the way that the relevant form of recognition morally demands.
>
> The fact that reciprocal recognition has a behavioral dimension, and that implies a certain form of intersubjective treatment, does not mean that it is a special, free-standing type of action; rather, Hegel seems to assume that it is more like an extra dimension that certain actions have. Certain actions, that is, have recognition built into their character as the subject engaged in them relate to each other in such a way as to express a specific form of recognition (Honneth 2010, p. 51).

In this sense, recognition is once again described as a meta-action, that is, as a stance within which and through which different affirmative gestures toward the other can be articulated *as* recognition; such gestures, in order to be classified as recognition, must be able to *express* evaluative qualities that are reflected in a context of values, to which Honneth gives the name second nature. But these lines of thinking enlighten another facet of this perspective. In fact, not only can some gestures be acknowledged as gestures of recognition if they express certain qualitative instances, but their character of recognition would be identified in an extra-dimension that somehow goes beyond the particularity of the affirmations toward the other, showing itself within the behavioral intersubjective treatment.

This dependence of recognition acts on the surrounding value context leads us directly to the fourth characteristic of *Sittlichkeit*, that of education (*Bildung*). Hegel does indeed adopt the concept of second nature to describe the necessary non-extraneousness that the ethical subject must live within its own impulses and desires for the purposes of the concreteness of freedom: in this sense, even the starting material of moral considerations must not be considered as a pure datum—an objection that is wrongly made against Honneth as far as moral injury is concerned (see section 2.3

---

[37] See Honneth 2010, p. 50.

above)—but as a 'what' that is already culturally formed. Thus, the intersubjective gestures of recognition have to be "able to initiate processes of education that produce, for their part, the practical habits that constitute the foundations of the ethical life" (Honneth 2010, p. 55).

Therefore, there is a complex interweaving of recognition practices and their spheres. In fact, if recognition, in order to be articulated as behavior, needs to be informed by the evaluative horizon given in the second nature, the formation of such a horizon would belong precisely to the educational scope of the gestures of recognition. However, if the formation and transformation of needs is obtained through the broader dimension of culture, it is not clear what the relationship between the latter and the gestures of recognition would be: in other words, although Honneth grants recognition a further shaping component, it is not clear how it relates to the totality of the institutionalized sphere. Despite the action-theoretical approach, according to which each ethical sphere is determined by its prevailing practical form, Honneth's argument does not seem able—or willing—to provide an explanatory argument for the structuring of such spheres. Moreover, it is clear that the institutionalized dimension of the spheres represents a *context* of recognition practices, which always remains intersubjective. Institutions, thus, can be conceived as expressions, concretions, or coagulations of recognition practices, but not as recognizer or recognizee. However, the thesis according to which Honneth's idea of social freedom could account for social, psychological, and material conditions of freedom becomes problematic: the link between culture and recognition, and between the latter and the materiality of institutions, that is, their independence, remains unclear.

But this refusal to consider the institutional world in its genealogical independence from intersubjective practices has also to do with a rejection of the hierarchy that the ethical spheres clearly possess in the *Philosophy of Right*. According to Honneth, Hegel prioritizes the spheres in the name of their formative capacity, that is, in accordance with the fact that "in each of the three partial spheres the subject undergoes an enhancement of his own personality in proportion to the degree of the rational transformation of an initially inchoate, natural individuality" (Honneth 2010, p. 61). Nevertheless, by rejecting the so-called verticalization of recognition that is expressed in this dynamic of the universalization of the individual, Honneth seems to opt for de-hierarchizing the spheres, describing them as equally necessary conditions, quasi-sociologically identified,[38] for individual self-realization, social reproduction and the actualization of freedom. One might argue that, as far as a theory of justice is concerned—which is characterized as free access for all citizens to the social possibilities of the realization of freedom—the principle of equity (and therefore the relating sphere) has a certain priority, because it follows that each actor must be able to enjoy other forms of recognition in the same measure as others.[39] In any

---

[38] See Honneth 2010, pp. 56–57.
[39] See Piromalli 2012, pp. 116–22.

case, Honneth seems oriented—as we have seen in the previous criticism concerning the Hegelian over-institutionalization—to maintain the paradigm of *The Struggle for Recognition*, thus re-elaborating the principles of love, respect, and esteem as plural and equally fundamental goods, which are articulated at the level of intersubjective practices and within spheres of recognition. In this way, the elaboration of a theory of justice could not be separated from an adequate paradigm of recognition and from a relating concept of ethical life.

In any case, this analysis of the 1999 Spinoza Lectures allows us to get closer to three focal points on which Honneth's own reflection hinges and that open the doors to the so-called historical turn.

The first element is represented by a deeper conceptualization of the ethical spheres within which recognition practices take place—though, at the same time, the former would be shaped through and by the latter. The *how* of such shaping represents one of the most controversial points in Honneth's entire corpus and one of the major sources of misunderstandings, as we will see in the next section.

Second, the delineation of a theory of plural justice is configured as a theory of justification on the part of social actors of the historical and institutional instantiations. Accordingly, the principles of recognition through which the social actors are integrated in the lifeworld are used as a criterion to evaluate the grade of justice realized in society. Thus, the relationship between recognition practices and principles (which in turn seem to assume a certain autonomy from the relative practices) takes on a fundamental role: that is, in this polarity, not only would the principles of recognition be a result of the practices, but these would be oriented with respect to the former. It follows from this that the principles are not completely embedded in the intersubjective interactions, precisely because they are oriented by them: one could argue that there is an essential irreducibility of one to the other.

Finally, on my reading, Honneth's elaboration of "being with oneself in the other" is best understood through the lens of this polarity between recognition practices and principles. The individual possibility of freely orienting oneself practically by adhering to or distancing oneself from the principles that constitute the ethical horizon of the contemporary western social context is revealed according to a fragile balance between determinacy and indeterminacy. All this is translated into a paradigm of freedom in which the social conditions (determinacy) are shown as inescapable presuppositions for a free individual self-realization (indeterminacy). As we will see in the next section, these three conceptual guidelines represent a key to the debate with Nancy Fraser.

4.2 Surplus of Validity: from Interaction to Principles

The double exchange between Nancy Fraser and Axel Honneth contained in *Redistribution or Recognition?* encompasses a rich multiplicity of elements that make it difficult to completely reconstruct the subjects it deals with.

First, it is a comparison between two authors who see themselves belonging to the same tradition of thought: that of critical theory, and who more specifically consider Habermas as the inevitable starting point for the elaboration of a philosophical agenda that aims to question contemporary capitalist societies.[40] However, given this common ground, Honneth and Fraser seem to be enveloped in a series of mutual misunderstandings that compromise an effective solution to the initial differences of perspective, leaving the debate open even today.[41] The point of greatest misunderstanding is precisely about how the concept recognition is conceived.[42] On the one hand, Fraser's view is strongly influenced by Charles Taylor, and thus relates recognition, rather immediately, to the demands of ethnic-cultural minorities, that is, in the framework of the problems of pluralistic societies and identities: hence, recognition is to be understood precisely as recognition of difference.[43] On the other hand, Honneth's paradigm, as we have seen, focuses on the constitution of practical identity and the normative fabric of the lifeworld in a more general sense. One could say that the different solutions that the two authors find and the relative criticisms levelled at one another spring from this unexplained fundamental difference.

Leaving aside an in-depth analysis of the numerous cues offered by the text, which range from political and social philosophy to critical thinking via moral philosophy and ethics—and on which critical literature is abundant[44]—we presently have three main aims: a) to re-propose the salient aspects of Fraser's argument, in order to better contextualize Honneth's positions in this text from 2003; b) to illuminate the continuity and differences between the latter and *The Struggle for Recognition*, as well as the peculiarities of the so-called moral-theoretical monism; and c) to highlight the role of the discontinuities in our reconstructive path of the recognition paradigm.

Nancy Fraser's core position derives from the persuasion that theories of recognition such as Honneth's cause an over-culturalization of redistribution issues. Relatedly, focusing exclusively on economic issues would prevent an adequate consideration of identity related matters. Inequalities of an economic matter cannot and should not be reduced to social facts that instead concern cultural identity and vice versa. Hence the two issues—redistribution and recognition—though they can be strongly intertwined, cannot be assimilated.

They are intertwined, according to Fraser, because discrimination or social exclusion, as well as denigration, often bring with them economic inequalities. The most suitable example in this case is that of gender discrimination: the stigmatiza-

---

40 See Nicholas H. Smith 2011, pp. 323–29.
41 See Zurn 2015, p. 140; and Honneth and Markle 2004, p. 388.
42 See Kompridis 2007, p. 278; and Susanne Schmetkamp 2012, p. 182.
43 See Zurn 2003b; and Emil A. Sobottka and Giovani A. Saavedra 2009.
44 See, among others, Simon Thompson 2006; Simon Thompson 2005; Zurn 2003b; Zurn 2003a; Zurn 2005; Thomas McCarthy 2005; Saul Tobias 2007; Terry Lovell 2007; McNay 2008a; and McNay 2008b.

tion of a slice of the population, or its labelling, entails an unequal division of labor, which in turn leads to economic dependence. Fraser thus aims to avoid both reductionisms (economicism and culturalism) by arguing that "*every* practice" is "simultaneously economic and cultural" (Fraser 2003b, p. 63). However, misrecognition and injustice cannot be assimilated because they respond to two different logics, which have to be *analytically*, and not *substantially*, distinguished.[45] The example Fraser offers in this case is that of the "skilled white male industrial worker who becomes unemployed due to a factory closing resulting from a speculative corporate merger" (Fraser 2003b, p. 35). In this case, the loss of work is not the consequence of discriminatory gestures, but to a systemic logic concerning the capitalistic global market.[46]

Fraser therefore proposes a perspectival dualism,[47] which thus contrasts with the monism advocated by Honneth. The former coincides with a bifocal standard that would dissociate from an analytical point of view the two types of (in)justice, which at a social level present themselves concomitantly. This would make it possible to avoid confusing and overlapping the perception of injustice and injustice, so much as to avoid the reductions entailed in economicism and culturalism: considering the being intertwined yet distinguished of the cultural and the economic would lead neither to an "unbridgeable chasm" between the two dimensions nor to their mutual assimilation (Fraser 2003a, p. 218).

This position would then guarantee a deontologically effective criterion for distinguishing between justified and unjustified social instances and demands. That is, the criterion would not be determined by subjective experiences of injustice, but by the identification of certain phenomena as obstacles or impediments to the aim of democratic societies, which Fraser calls parity of participation. As Fraser says, the "existence of either a class structure or a status hierarchy constitutes an obstacle to parity of participation and thus an injustice" (Fraser 2003b, p. 49). From this principle of justice, which concerns the right and not the good and already presupposes a certain account of autonomy, for social participation is considered a consequence of the latter,[48] we can derive the objective forms of injustice that prevent social actors from being full-fledged members of society. This would make it possible to identify, without having to theoretically depend on further reductionism—the psychologiza-

---

[45] See Simon Thompson 2005, p. 94; Nicholas H. Smith 2011, pp. 330–31.
[46] "This market order is culturally embedded, to be sure. But it is not directly governed by cultural schemas of evaluation. Rather, the economic logic of the market interacts in complex ways with the cultural logic of recognition, sometimes instrumentalizing existing status distinctions, sometimes dissolving or circumventing them, and sometimes creating new ones. As a result, market mechanisms give rise to economic class relations that are not mere reflections of status hierarchies. Neither those relations nor the mechanisms that generate them can be understood by recognition monism. An adequate approach must theorize both the distinctive dynamics of the capitalist economy and its interaction with the status order" (Fraser 2003a, p. 214).
[47] See Fraser 2003b, pp. 62–64.
[48] See Kauppinen 2011, p. 294.

tion of injustice—which presents itself as an obstacle to a free form of life in contemporary societies, that is, restrictions on individual freedom due to economic unavailability or ethnic-cultural denigration or segregation.

Even the very concept of recognition is to be thought of differently. Fraser indeed proposes that we interpret recognition as recognition of status, which does not entirely depend on interpersonal relations,[49] but on the subject's belonging to social groups,[50] which can therefore be identified from the outside depending on their positioning within the social totality:[51]

> The recognition dimension corresponds to the *status order* of society, hence to the constitution, by socially entrenched patterns of cultural value, of culturally defined categories of social actors —statuses—each distinguished by the relative respect, prestige, and esteem it enjoys vis-à-vis the others (Fraser 2003b, p. 50).

To take up the example cited above, the skilled white male industrial worker belongs, independently of his effective interpersonal interactions of recognition, to a certain segment of society and holds a certain status, which, because of a hierarchical organization of society, guarantees him un-discriminated access to the public dimension. If so, his inability to participate equally in democratic life in a full-fledged manner depends on economic issues, but not on his ethnic-cultural affiliations. This concept of status is hence considered as the cultural counterpart of the social class, by which the decisive and essential aspects do not regard the economic condition, but the recognition (determinable at a general level) enjoyed in a given society. As already noted class and status are not to be distinguished from each other substantially, but, as Fraser herself states, "one cannot infer class directly from status, nor status directly from class" (Fraser 2003b, p. 54).

This brief summary of Fraser's positions enables us to better understand Honneth's positions, which seem to be in conflict in certain points, precisely because the two authors are seemingly addressing two different levels of inquiry. I want to highlight three nuclei in Honneth's answers: the phenomenology of social movements, where the core issue is to the determine critical perspective's possibilities to access to social reality, and the priority of good over right (section 4.2.1); the distinction between cultural and economic (section 4.2.2); and the justification of demands for justice (section 4.2.3).

---

[49] See Edoardo Greblo 2009, pp. 340–41.
[50] See Schmetkamp 2012, pp. 180–81.
[51] See Zurn 2003b, pp. 522–23.

4.2.1 The Unavoidability of Moral Experiences

As far as the phenomenology of social movements is concerned, Honneth believes that Fraser's analysis is essentially flawed because of its total reliance on a description of (American) new social movements, which characterize our "post-socialist era" (Honneth 2003d, p. 124). There are three errors, in particular, inherent in this reading. First, Honneth re-proposes what was already expressed in *The Struggle for Recognition* through the studies of Thompson and Moore: even the working class's struggles of the nineteenth century were deeply characterized by instances of recognition. Distinguishing requests for justice from demands for practical identity would therefore constitute a "misleading—indeed false—" historical reconstruction (Honneth 2003d, p. 123). Certainly, the increase in social conflicts over the recognition of difference can be interpreted as a historical novelty that characterizes the contemporary occidental horizon, but that would, in Honneth's eyes, confirm the point, rather than deny it: what is as stake are "'indivisible' conflicts" (Honneth 2003d, p. 120), where material and symbolic aspects cannot be distinguished.

Honneth's second criticism concerns social movements as a given starting point for social critique: the mistake here lies in using what is already the outcome of a certain process as a starting point without considering the process itself. In fact, the social movements to which Fraser refers are those that have already passed the filter of the public. This would imply, on the one hand, a certain unawareness of the ideological components that may actually be at the base of the shaping of the public mind: "Today, such a—surely unintended—complicity with political domination can only be undone by introducing a normative terminology for identifying social discontent independently of public recognition" (Honneth 2003d, p. 125). Hence, on the other hand, this can lead to our failing to consider those forms of opposition that do not have sufficient strength to arrive at such a space of expression, which would represent an acute shortcoming for a critical theory of the social.[52] Such an approach would exclude basing the development of critical thinking on the moral experience of social actors, whose moral intuitions, injuries, and normative demands cannot simply be surpassed, on pain of the loss of adherence to social reality in all its complexity. One may indeed wonder what would be critical about a social theory that appears disinterested in the experience of suffering,[53] thus proposing an objectivist approach to social analysis: "If the adjective "social" is to mean anything more than "typically found in society," social suffering and discontent possess a *normative* core. It is a matter of the disappointment or violation of normative expectations of society considered justified by those concerned" (Honneth 2003d, p. 129). It is clear that Honneth is directing the criticisms of psychologization and idealism at

---

[52] See Kompridis 2007, pp. 281–83.
[53] See Zurn 2003b,

this renewed stance, whereby critical theory cannot allow itself to abandon the social actors' moral point of view in a fundamental way.

And it is precisely on this last point that Honneth's argument of the priority of the good over the right is based. Taking the social partners' moral experience as starting point would allow us to better understand, from within the lifeworld, the normative horizon on which they move, act, and interact. Such a horizon, which is, according to Honneth's reading, intersubjectively shaped, is characterized by a plurality of ethical principles (love, equality, achievement, or merit) that find their right place in the name of their ability to form and respond to the tendency toward self-realization. This last principle, conceived at a formal level, and therefore potentially open also to radical changes, represents the ambit within which various historically instantiated principles would find their justification, so that Honneth considers them as "'quasi-transcendental interests' of the human race" (Honneth 2003d, p. 174).

Clearly, the so-called anthropological justification still holds a certain priority in this work. However, from the point of view of the theory of justice, Honneth believes that a certain perspective on the good is at least inevitable, so much so that he even conceives Fraser's principle of participatory parity in such terms.[54] That is, even the deontological procedures of justification presuppose an ethical orientation that both precedes and informs the justifying procedure.[55] Thus, even participatory parity could not actually boast of the aimed non-substantivity or non-sectarianism: it would represent a pre-figuration of the good as much as of the concept of individual self-realization because it would presuppose a spectrum of values and images of individual freedom. In fact, that economic and cultural exclusion represent a hindrance to social participation cannot be stated without referring, even minimally, to social actors' moral experiences[56]—as Fraser argues[57]—and thus to a certain ethical good, which in turn forms the right.

Contra such a perspective, the theory of justice Honneth describes here is characterized accordingly with an embracing of the ethical good as object of the justification, which, however, does not constrain itself within the limits of a rational-argumentative procedure. The problem with this justification is that of not comprehending—and thus not entailing—the multiple dimensions at stake in the social world, which instead would be normatively permeated by expectations, demands, and therefore by injuries and experiences of injustice. In other words, the "restriction to only a form of justification seems to entirely lose sight of the normative

---

[54] "Put in terms of an ethics of particular goods, Nancy Fraser defines the 'why' or 'what for' of equality with reference to the good of participation, whereas I understand this 'what for' as the good of personal identity-formation, whose realization I see as dependent on relations of mutual recognition" (Honneth 2003d, p. 176). See also Christopher Lauer 2012, pp. 27–29.
[55] See Jacob Held 2008, p. 82.
[56] See Kompridis 2007, p. 280.
[57] "One can show that a society whose institutionalized norms impede parity of participation is morally indefensible *whether or not they distort the subjectivity of the oppressed*" (Fraser 2003b, p. 32).

perspectives from which individuals decide how far they can follow the established principles of public justification in the first place" (Honneth 2003d, p. 130). If, therefore, the aim is to develop a critical theory of contemporary society, it would be necessary to observe which principles have proposed themselves through its historical evolution, that is, which have such *validity* in the eyes of social actors that they can be considered as principal and effective goods in the framework of a theory of justice, precisely because "social injustice is experienced the moment it can no longer be rationally understood why an institutional rule should count on agreement in accordance with generally accepted reasons" (Honneth 2003d, p. 130).

As we already know from *The Struggle for Recognition*, these principles correspond to three spheres of recognition, which are distinguished respectively by the practical modalities of intersubjective interaction, by the partners involved in them, and by the personal dimensions that are thereby affirmed or confirmed, according to the development of a practical, undamaged practical identity. However, Honneth does not leave the triad of principles described in the 1992 work unchanged. In *Redistribution or Recognition?*, they coincide with love, equality, and accomplishment. There are three aspects worthy of being noted.

The first is that Honneth's attention, rather than being drawn to recognition practices, is focused on its principles. There is in fact no further account about intersubjective relations or what recognition *is*, while the emphasis is placed on the definition of the principles that inform and guide such practices: as Honneth puts it, the aim of his interventions in the work is "to reveal the moral 'constraints' *underlying* social interaction" (Honneth 2003c, p. 249, my emphasis). In other words, the aim is to describe a plural theory of justice anchored on a recognition order.

Thus, second, contrary to *The Struggle for Recognition*, the principle of love is described as subject to internal progress, that is, to a process of reformulation and remodulation of the understanding of the principle itself, and therefore of its intersubjective practical realization. Although Honneth therefore speaks of a certain trans-historicity ("quasi-transcendental interests") of the recognition principles, they are nevertheless considered fully historicized in their evolutions and instantiations.[58] Honneth therefore makes a step forward in the definition of the recognition principles: in *Reification*, the three forms of recognition were attributed a certain degree of cultural-historical substantivity (as opposed to existential recognition), while here he is convinced that the dimensions of reference of the principles of love, equality, and esteem have a scope wherein they are, to some extent, able to transcend historical punctuality. However, such trans-historicity coincides with the historicity and the immanency of the realizations and understandings of such principles, that is, with their substantivity. Clearly, the matter does not coincide with the realization of some ahistoric principle within history, but, on the contrary, with the possibility of discovering tendencies from within social life in its different and open-ended tra-

---

[58] See Honneth 2003d, pp. 138–41.

jectories. Hence, even the dimension of love would not be exempt from evolutions and changes.

Third, the shift in the third sphere is significant: where in *The Struggle for Recognition* it was described through the concept of esteem, in this work such esteem is strongly tied to the principle of merit or accomplishment—which, even if it is almost always ideologically shaped, would not represent as such a false principle.[59] This shift is to be understood according to two issues. On the one hand, Honneth attempts to resolve the ambiguity present in the 1992 work, where the third sphere described esteem as regarding individual contributions in cooperative frameworks, but also cultural forms of life in the context of pluralism. Honneth therefore narrows the spectrum of this sphere, which previously covered an excessively wide range of phenomena: what is at stake in the third sphere is labor, the conceptualization of its normative boundaries, and the possibilities for individual self-realization in terms of their contribution to society. On the other hand, Honneth seeks to distance himself from Fraser's position, in which recognition has a purely cultural matrix, and from identity politics in general. With respect to such conceptualizations, Honneth believes that those instances of social movements Fraser takes into consideration can actually be included at a higher degree of abstraction through the principles of equality and merit: in this sense, "the overwhelming majority of demands now being made by means of" the identity-politics "formula do not really transcend the normative horizon of the dominant recognition order" (Honneth 2003d, p. 169). In other words, even the consideration of the new social movements would show that the experience of injustice and the required political changes were oriented toward the questioning of the normative constraints through which—taking as an example feminist instances—some performances were not considered as contributions to society (and therefore not worthy of merit) and were not considered equal from a legal point of view.[60] In this case, recognition is anything but cultural, if the term is understood to possess the meaning that Fraser endows it with. Although Honneth admits a certain historical shift from conflicts oriented toward the reconciliation of differences through equal treatment to those directed toward an equal consideration of the difference itself, such a transition would not be sufficient to hypothesize a fourth principle of justice and a related fourth sphere of recognition. In the present context, which is neither extraneous nor immune to possible evolutions, such instances can be traced back to the principles of equality and recognition of one's contribution to the reproduction of social life.[61]

---

[59] See Honneth 2003d, p. 148.
[60] See Honneth 2003d, pp. 161–69.
[61] See Honneth 2003d, pp. 161 and 169; and Lisaker and Jacobsen 2015, pp. 172–73. For an attempt to translate Honneth's account into group-identity dynamics, see Benno Herzog 2015.

4.2.2 Between Norms and Facts

We come therefore to the third general point of Honneth's criticisms, that is, the distinction between economic and cultural dimensions—regarding the first two the nature of social movements and the priority of good over right. First, Fraser's dualism would not be able to comprehend certain dimensions that are fundamental to *our* conception of justice, such as rights and legislations, which can be reduced neither to the economic nor the cultural.[62] The decisive issue is once again that of guaranteeing the critical thought's possibility of unfolding, which would be secured by the depiction of an anti anti-normativist perspective.[63] And the target is precisely Fraser's bifocal approach: indeed, if the distinction between matters of justice and issues of recognition were exclusively analytical, as Fraser argues, it would not be able to support the cogency it was meant to with respect to social reality.[64] Although Fraser understands her perspectival dualism as a mere interpretative distinction, that is, as an analytical tool for distinguishing two dimensions that are actually undivided and thus better at formulating philosophical-political proposals, the distinction also suggests a de facto difference between economic and cultural facts, as if the first would coincide with an autonomous sub-system:[65] if this were not the case, Fraser's distinction would be purely arbitrary.[66] The perspectival dualism, therefore, implies the decoupling of systemic and social integration. As her example of the white specialized worker shows, social reality would be constituted, on the one hand, through market logics that possess their own autonomy, thus avoiding being at the disposal of individuals and operating at their back, that is, being independent from individual choices (systemic integration) and, on the other hand, social reality would also be shaped by another domain in which the perspectives about values and norms, subjective and intersubjective praxis, as well as the moral expectations of individuals or groups play a fundamental role (social integration). It is therefore the Habermasian distinction between system and lifeworld that Honneth, as we have already seen, intends to question, if not set aside. And such an account of social ontology concerns, above all, the possibilities of critical thinking.

What is rejected is the idea of a norms-free system,[67] precisely because the absence of a normative horizon would hinder the aims of critical thought. Fraser's

---

[62] See Greblo 2009, p. 340; and William E. Scheuerman 2017.
[63] See Nicholas H. Smith 2011, p. 339.
[64] See Carl-Göran Heidegren 2004, p. 367.
[65] See Nicholas H. Smith 2011, p. 332.
[66] See Honneth 2003d, p. 156.
[67] See Deranty 2009, p. 420; Heidegren 2004, p. 367; Teixeira 2017, pp. 597–99; and Teixeira 2019, p. 184. According to Thompson, Honneth's attempt to derive the normative role of recognition relations and principle from the dynamics of social integration would represent a logical shortcoming, for facts and values could not be tied necessarily one another. See Simon Thompson 2005, pp. 99–100. However, even these two dimensions are certain mutually irreducible, one can wonder

shortcomings would therefore be twofold: at first, the breadth of recognition would be narrowed to a cultural matter and, consequently, this would leave economic issues without normative criteria for justification and critique. Hence, Honneth does not reject the idea that the economic sphere somehow possesses some autonomous dynamic, but argues that normativity also has a say in that matter: that alone would show that a system cannot be explained just by referring to its self-sufficient logics. What Honneth rejects is precisely the idea that the economic system is to be conceived as norm-free, as oriented by self-sufficient logics: this, in his view, would not only respond to an inaccurate reading of social reality—since social actors in their moral facticity would be excluded from the focus of inquiry—but would risk placing the market beyond the range of critique. Conversely, the perspective Honneth introduces is that of a "moral-theoretical monism" (Honneth 2003d, p. 157):

> it is not a matter of an external relation—of applying normative criteria to a theory-independent reality—but rather of revealing this reality guided by normative criteria.... The three-fold "point" of the category of recognition ... should consist precisely in establishing such an internal connection: social reality is revealed (social theory) by means of the same conception that, owing to its normative content, can be used to evaluate social change (a conception of justice) in a way that allows the perspectives of those affected to be articulated (moral psychology) (Honneth 2003c, p. 265).

Although there is some lack of clarity on Honneth's part, it seems to me correct to argue that his aim is not to explain the constitution of contemporary societies through a single principle, as the term monism could legitimately allow us to think. In the same way, the explanation (and the critique) of institutional formations could not be implemented by resorting to the idea of recognition alone. Two aspects need to be highlighted here.

First, Honneth points out that his account is to be understood in terms of a moral, not cultural, monism.[68] His theoretical proposal cannot therefore be regarded as an attempt to bring economic issues back to an indeterminate sphere of culture—a term that is used above all by Fraser and to which Honneth rarely resorts.[69] The idea is not to water down the specific characteristics of the market and its systemic functioning by use of the truism that every sphere of society is cultural. This alone would be enough to understand the external character of the criticism of culturalism directed at him, precisely because Honneth does not provide any account of culture and does not seem to refer to any specific idea of it. Rather, greater difficulties arise in

---

which form of ought derives its features with no regard to an is: thereby there may not be any logical cogency, but even deontological principles cannot help to possess certain substantive contents.
68 See Honneth 2003d, p. 157; and Honneth 2003c, p. 254.
69 A quite misleading example is represented by the idea that the theory of justice would require an account of the cultural values that shape the economic sphere. See Honneth 2003d, pp. 155–56. However, the fact that Honneth acknowledges this (rather indisputable) point does not seem to me to serve as the main connotation according to which to interpret his monism.

facing the more general criticism of idealism, according to which his approach would not be able to critically address the sphere of economics in itself. And it is here that the fluctuations in the Honneth's account highlighted by Zurn become problematic.[70]

The *moral* character of Honneth's monism—that is, the conviction that normative principles are immanent to every social sphere—would result phenomenologically from the analysis of social conflicts and would be also necessary in order to develop a critical thinking that sets itself in contact with the society's emancipatory drives. Consequently, a certain social-ontological view is at stake, in which normative integration precedes systemic integration. Certain moral principles, which are closely tied to the requests for recognition expressed in social conflicts, play a primary role in the contemporary differentiation in social spheres; in accordance with these principles themselves—which, it should be stressed, do not coincide with recognition, but represent its directions and respective contents—it would therefore be possible to develop a theory of justice. Such priority of the normative over the systemic, besides unfolding the critique's possibilities, would also constitute a key to interpreting the social ontology of contemporary societies, whose constitution (and opportunities of progress) is presided over by certain normative principles, which in turn are at stake in intersubjective relations of recognition:

> From the perspective of their members, societies only represent legitimate ordering structures to the extent they are in a position to guarantee reliable relations of mutual recognition on different levels. To this extent, the normative integration of societies occurs only through the institutionalization of recognition principles, which govern, in a comprehensible way, the forms of mutual recognition through which members are included into the context of social life (Honneth 2003d, p. 173).

> As long as we hold onto the idea of a normatively substantial social theory, we must always try to discover principles of normative integration in the institutionalized spheres of society that open up the prospect of desirable improvements (Honneth 2003c, p. 254).

However, the lack of clarity begins just when one intends to detail the relationship between the normative and the systemic, that is, between the plural principles of justice and the mechanisms of the capitalistic market (but more generally of societal forces, such as media and power).

On the one hand, in fact, this idea of normative integration suggests that such principles represent an exclusive logic of social differentiation.[71] The systemic aspects, apparently, would not play any role. Such a perspective, as Zurn argues, would be correct at a very high level of abstraction:[72] it is indeed conceivable arguing that the social sphere can ultimately be traced back to the interaction between its actors and that the economy, as well as other institutional formations, could in the last instance be tied to

---

70 See Zurn 2005, p. 113.
71 See Nicholas H. Smith 2011, pp. 341–42.
72 See Zurn 2005, p. 105.

an at least implicit consensus by the participants, which can be withdrawn potentially at any time: "It is true that some socially generalized media, like money or political power, can in fact coordinate social interaction relatively automatically, but even they depend on some belief in their legitimacy that can weaken or disappear altogether at any moment" (Honneth 2003c, p. 255). In other words, a) social reality (and the market within it) would consist of an institutionalization guided by the core principles at stake in intersubjective relations of recognition; b) with respect to these principles social actors could or could not (ought or ought not to) give their consent to such social formations (justification); and c) that such justification would have to be accomplished in accordance with those principles should result from their ethical validity; this, in turn, would emerge historically and with respect to their attainability concerning individual self-realization.

If this were to be understood as Honneth's idea, his account of institutional reality would precisely lack an adequate idea of culture: the description of social spheres as instantiation of principles would in fact require a wider medium than that which can be provided by the intersubjective interactions of recognition alone. Honneth had already hinted to the idea of such a medium in *The Pathologies of Individual Freedom*, adopting the Hegelian idea of *Bildung*, but even in that case it was not specified in detail. A thick account of culture is not in Honneth's interests, most probably because it could not be supported by the idea of recognition and because, as we have seen, the reconduction of economics to culture would not represent anything but a truism, and indeed a very abstract one.

On the other hand, pressed by Fraser's criticism, Honneth seems to emphasize another possible view in "The Point of Recognition." Here, he claims that his account has no "explanatory purpose"and that the immanence of the normative in the systemic is to be understood in the sense of the market's moral "constraints" (Honneth 2003c, p. 255).

The first assessment would therefore mean that the structuring of the social sphere would not be realized exclusively with reference to the relations of recognition and its principles: institutions, therefore, would not be exhausted in being concretions of practices, but would possess a certain consistency on their own. Hence the principles would be decisive not for a social theory aimed at reconstructing the constitution of contemporary societies, but for a critical social theory. From a social-ontological point of view, the systemic character of the market would not be excluded, but it in turn would not represent a norms-free social realm. In fact, as Zurn emphasizes and as we have already seen in *Reification*, legal arrangements would represent an essential precondition for the market itself: without that form of recognition relations, the sphere of the economic could not exist as it actually does, but that would not imply a reducibility of the latter to the former.[73]

---

[73] See Zurn 2015, p. 134.

However, everything is played out in how one interprets the term 'constraints': in my view, these cannot be conceived as external, that is, as mere boundaries, on pain of a return to the division between system and lifeworld that Honneth intends to bridge. Therefore, such constraints or preconditions must be conceived as limits of justification, which would possess a thin (but present) social-ontological role, and a thick (but not exclusive) critical and normative one.

In this matter, Honneth's interpretation of market as sphere of labor plays a decisive role. As the Hegelian civil society represents above all an ethical sphere of interaction among subjects—whereby the invisible hand is surely at stake, but the fundamental and peculiar character of interactions is an ethical one—Honneth understands the economic sphere as labor sphere, where (systemic) facts and norms happen to be indissolubly intertwined one another. Albeit briefly, it is here noteworthy to mention Honneth's ideal of social democracy. Honneth refers to Dewey as saying that the formation of a (healthy) democratic public sphere requires a just division of labor and that social differentiation and coordination proceed according to a certain learning process in which differences among the participants would enrich the social problem-solving through multiple perspectives and approaches.[74] While this latter point represents a first, partial hint on how recognition relations and institutionalization proceed on the same track, the main interest here is represented by the idea that economics is determined primarily by the division of labor and that the latter contains normative indications. Therefore, the comprehension of the peculiar normative core of work experience would be decisive for the depiction of a social-political theory over democracy. To this aim, the Marxian anthropology would be of little use, because it is constrained by a narrow instrumental view of rationality.[75] Rather, social reproduction (and its evolution according to criteria of justice) would be made possible, not by work intended as instrumental action, but by its social division, which would take place by following and expanding those normative criteria according to which subjects have been socialized. That would in turn clarify the extent to which the intersubjective standards of justification shape the economic dimension because the latter would be framed through normative perspectives regarding what counts as labor in the wider horizon of social reproduction. But this hypothesis, while allowing a better understanding of Honneth's position, would seem to reinvigorate the reasons of those who criticize him for idealism, that is, of a one-sidedness by his considering only norms and not social functions.[76] Indeed, the assumption of the pervasiveness of normativity often brings Honneth's attention away from the technical, instrumental, and non-subjective elements of work,[77] as well as the systemic and impersonal components of the economy.

---

74 See Honneth 1998; and Zurn 2005.
75 See Honneth 2003d, p. 127.
76 See Teixeira 2017, p. 598.
77 See Christophe Dejours *et al.* 2018, pp. 94–109 and 137.

If, therefore, this second interpretation of monism—which would be mostly critical and partly explanatory—seems to offer a way out with respect to an excessive burden that the concept of recognition alone would not be able to carry, it seems to presuppose and require social-theoretical explanations that Honneth does not seem intent on providing. Moreover, this interpretative hypothesis seems to be strongly in contradiction with Honneth's definition according to which institutions *are* concretions of practices and expressions of recognitional acts.[78]

In both cases, therefore, it seems to be a dead end. The first hypothesis—which could be defined as a thick monism—besides already being partially abandoned by Honneth in the same work, seems not to be able to bear the weight of its own aspirations, because it is not able to establish a persuasive explanatory link between principles of recognition and institutional formations. Conversely, the thin monism, while being more convincing at first glance, strongly reduces the scope of Honneth's thinking (could one even speak of monism?), leaving in any case its side uncovered with regard to an inquiry of market as such. Moreover, it seems to be in contradiction with a definition of institution that Honneth does not abandon in more recent works.

A double way out of this stalemate could be represented by the interweaving of these alternative hypotheses. On the one hand, it is necessary to interpret monism as a *theoretical* necessity felt by Honneth in the problematization of the possibilities of critical theory: only in this framework does the rejection of the market's conceptualization as a norms-free space become comprehensible and sharable. On the other hand, it is necessary to enrich from a social-ontological point of view the perspective according to which institutions are concretions of practices, that is—using the terms from the previous section—it would be necessary to make more explicit how to outline a theory of the objective spirit without spirit.[79]

---

[78] It is noteworthy that Honneth emphasizes that "we also need to avoid Fraser's repeated misunderstanding that I would claim that the institutionalized spheres always fall under just one principle of recognition. Just as today public schooling is normatively integrated by two competing principles of social recognition, the family has for good reasons long been governed not only by the normative principle of love, but also increasingly by legal forms of recognition" (Honneth 2003c, p. 255). Therefore, the critique levelled at Hegel in *The Pathologies of Individual Freedom*, according to which one problem of the civil society would coincide with its institutional plurality has to be understood as an internal critique; that is, Honneth is convinced that, according to Hegel's premises, the ethical spheres should entail one and only one institutional formation, which in turn would be shaped by one and only one recognition principle. That the idea according to which institutions are shaped by multiple recognition principles is not a transition within Honneth's thought is shown by his analysis of the family in "Between Justice and Affection" (Honneth 2007a).

[79] See Deranty and Renault 2007.

4.2.3 Justification, Validity, and Progress

The last step of the analysis concerns the criteria of justification, an issue that plays a central role both in structuring *Freedom's Right*, and in clarifying the implications for the concept of recognition contained in *Redistribution or Recognition?*. For, as we have seen, Honneth intends to develop a theory of justice *as* theory of justification. The first way to deal with the issue is to answer the question: justification *of what?* Here the peculiarity of Honneth's position emerges, revealing the interweaving of multiple levels and aims.

First, the issue at stake is the justification of current institutionalizations of the principles of recognition by social actors, that is, of the adequacy of concrete social realizations of love, equality, and merit in comparison with the expectations of the participants of the respective spheres. From this point of view, the flaw of proceduralist approaches would be that of conceiving such evaluative processes as hinging on an argumentative-rational model, while the decisive role would be played by the more articulated complex implied by the concept of practical identity. Therefore, the legitimacy of the institutional order would be more effectively described through a reference to the normative expectations for recognition.

But justification also means the justification of this first type of justification. In fact, given that Honneth intends to base his critical project (also) on the moral experience of the social actors, one issue that arises is that of which criteria the theory uses to discern justified social drives and demands from the unjustified ones. Clearly, not all requests for recognition, justice, or identity can be considered as being on the same level: social theory must be informed by social actors striving for justice, but it cannot confuse itself with them. Rather, it should possess a certain distance that would consequently enable the critical perspective.

Finally, justification coincides with the justification of the recognition principles that represent the heart of Honneth's plural theory of justice. Love, equality, and merit must be put through a process of justification and continuous revision, implemented both by social actors and the theory.

What Honneth proposes is therefore a complex theoretical framework that is articulated on multiple levels. For the aim is precisely not to apply an external criterion to social reality and then establish procedures that can lead to right outcomes, on the part both of social actors and social theory. Although in *Redistribution or Recognition?* Honneth reiterates his anthropological justification—that is, he once again claims that love, equality, and merit manifest themselves as goods for a theory of justice because of their capacity to respond to the quasi-transcendental interests of human beings with respect to their self-realization—it is rather interesting that he objects to Fraser overloading the moral-psychological account with excessive implications.[80] The experience of moral injury by social partners would indeed represent an

---

[80] See Honneth 2003c, p. 258.

essential point for critical theory, but only as adequate access point to the normative horizon that constitutes the actual fabric of social reality, not as a foundationalist starting point.[81] Since the latter is Honneth's real aim—because only a theory that has achieved this perspective can subsequently exercise the critique of society itself—in this work we can see the emergence of a historical-normative justification alongside the anthropological one. Here, in the context of the threefold meaning of justification, the concepts of surplus of validity and progress play a pivotal role. While the former concerns the justifiability of principles in the eyes of the theory and of the participants in the social spheres, the latter concerns the justifiability of social movements and institutions in the eyes of the theory, as well as the adequacy of institutions to the requests for recognition.

The process of justification starts from the nexus between genealogy and validity that characterizes Honneth's theory from the very beginning. In fact, one might say that deriving the ought from the is represents a logical incongruence,[82] but that is precisely the core of the whole paradigm: there could be no access to normativity and no theoretical delineation of it except from the present.

In the heart of the triple plan of justification there is the concept of "surplus of validity" (*Geltungsüberhang*), which implies two issues.[83] On the one hand, Honneth is persuaded that certain normative principles—love, equality, and merit—have been able to show their centrality through the historical evolution of modern and contemporary societies. This priority of their validity would appear foremost with respect to the social actors, that is, as goods they have pursued and are still striving for: from this point of view, their validity would count as phenomenological and social-theoretical evidence. On the other hand, surplus of validity also represents a normative orientation for a theory that does not intend to embrace a deontological or a proceduralist perspective. These principles would have proposed themselves with a certain forming (and formed) normative authoritativeness,[84] both for the social actors and consequently for the social theorist. Honneth, therefore, evidently embraces a certain value realism, which derives from his Hegelianism and, respectively, from the need to conceive second nature as an evaluative dimension and a condition of possibility for gestures of recognition.[85]

However, this retrospective scope of the validity of recognition principles does not extinguish what Honneth means with *Geltungsüberhang*. For their acquired priority would also suggest a certain ability to transcend the determinateness of the historical context, that is, representing the intramundane transcendence that the tradition of the Left Hegelians has always identified as an essential concept for a

---

[81] See Fraser 2003a, pp. 206–9; and Kompridis 2007, p. 284.
[82] See Simon Thompson 2005, pp. 99–100.
[83] See Honneth 2003d, pp. 186–87; Honneth 2003c, pp. 263–64; and Honneth and Fraser 2003, pp. 219 and 302.
[84] See Tristram McPherson 2018, pp. 253–77; and Stahl 2017, pp. 505–22.
[85] See Honneth 2002.

4.2 Surplus of Validity: from Interaction to Principles — 151

conceptualization of progress. The current validity of the principles would be able to exceed (surplus) the prevailing normative horizon, even though it is bound to it: once again, recognition order and social change are presented as concomitant and mutually dependent:

> that this "transcendence" must be attached to a form of practice or experience which is on the one hand indispensable for social reproduction, and on the other hand—owing to its normative surplus—points beyond all given forms of social organization…. "[T]ranscendence" should be a property of "immanence" itself, so that the facticity of social relations always contains a dimension of transcending claims (Honneth 2003c, p. 244).
>
> [E]ach of the three recognition spheres is distinguished by normative principles which provide their own internal standards of what counts as "just" or "unjust." In my view, the only way forward here is the idea, outlined above, that each principle of recognition has a specific surplus of validity whose normative significance is expressed by the constant struggle over its appropriate application and interpretation. Within each sphere, it is always possible to set a moral *dialectic of the general and the particular* in motion: claims are made for a particular perspective (need, life-situation, contribution) that has not yet found appropriate consideration by appeal to a general recognition principle (love, law, achievement). In order to be up to the task of critique, the theory of justice outlined here can wield the recognition principles' surplus validity against the facticity of their social interpretation (Honneth 2003d, p. 186, my emphasis).

Thus, even if transcendence should be conceived as immanence's germinal capability to overrun itself—then as an over with respect to *a given* context, not to *the* contextuality itself—the result is that the dialectic between generality and particularity depicts: a) a certain autonomy of the principles from the relative practices; and b) a certain noncoincidence between the "social value" (*soziale Geltung*) and "normative validity" (*normative Gültigkeit*) of the principles (Busen, Herzog, and Sörensen 2012, p. 265, my translation). This is not, of course, intended to support a reciprocal detachment from each other—because principles exist only as they are instantiated in praxis. Yet they emerge as not totally assimilated to the latter and almost as condition of possibility, thus enabling not only social conflicts, but social critique and vice versa. This guiding and informing role no longer allows principles to be interpreted as mere overflows that result from the affirmation of certain dimensions of individual practical identity.

Clearly, the idea of a surplus of validity proceeds together with a certain idea of progress that Honneth intends to defend. As we have already seen in *The Struggle for Recognition*, a *thin* concept of progress represents the key that the theory has to distinguish between justified (progressive) and unjustified (regressive) demands for recognition:

> the … theory of justice must be embedded within the comprehensive framework of a conception of progress that is in a position to determine a directed development in the moral constitution of society. Only on this basis can it be shown with more than a merely relativistic claim to justification to what extent certain social demands can be regarded as normatively justified (Honneth 2003d, pp. 183–84).

However, there are three significant differences from the perspective outlined in *The Struggle for Recognition*. The first aspect, already mentioned, is the retraction of the idea that the sphere of love is not subject to progressive re-modulations and re-interpretations. This is because, second, progress was considered as the exclusive domain of the spheres of right and cooperative contribution, characterized respectively by the trajectories of universalization or generalization (of rights) and de-formalization (of the esteem attributed to the individual, and no longer to the group to which she belongs). Third, this historical-social dynamic would find its anchorage, on an individual level, in the conflicting polarity between I and me, that is, in the possibility of socialized subjects to creatively transcend their normative context.

From this perspective, Honneth tries to define a logic of progress that would be internal to the practices of recognition and in line with the characteristics of the respective principles. Its justification would not be anthropological as in the I-me case,[86] but could be defined as normative, for it is grounded on the surplus normativity of the principles. That is, the instantiations of recognition relations run along the axes of individualization and inclusion.[87] With these two terms, Honneth claims that the social formations of recognition have historically been able to include more and more subjects and different identities (similar to the idea of the universalization of rights) and to concern more and more aspects and facets of the person, thus becoming intrinsically more adequate and adherent to it (as well as to the de-formalization that would have made the relations of esteem progressively deriving from individual and not group characters). If, then, this aspect effectively remains almost unchanged with *The Struggle for Recognition* except for the terminological choices, what constitutes the greatest difference is that these dynamics represent an internal criterion to the recognition relationships and to the ongoing social re-elaboration of their principles: equality and merit, as well as love, in their institutional forms, would require an increasingly perfect (and always perfectible) application, which spreads along paths of inclusion and individualization. Once again, it emerges clearly that recognition order and social change are not in contradiction with one another, but the former represents the condition of the latter, just as this gives rise to new institutionalizations via remodulations. As Laur notes, for Honneth, "social recognition is never something merely given, but is always *won*" and struggled for (Lauer 2012, p. 34). And it is therefore clear that Honneth's idea of progress has an extremely cautious teleological content, and for this reason his conception can be considered *thin*.

---

[86] Even if, after abandoning the binomial I-me, Honneth focuses on the omnipotence-fantasies of the child as a framework of justification for the individual tendency to conflict, it never represents how he intends to justify progress, that is, the transcending of the given situation according to certain vectorialities and trends. Hence, what the I-me represented—that is, the same basis for individual conflict and possibilities of progress—is somehow split here on a justification level. For what concerns the idea of child's omnipotence, see Honneth 2002, pp. 503–4; Honneth 2011b; and Honneth and Whitebook 2016.

[87] See Honneth 2003d, pp. 184–86; and Honneth 2003c, p. 260.

The task of the theory, in this case, is not to prescribe aims (this belongs to social conflicts from time to time), and thus to endorse substantive societal goals, but, as Zurn observes, to acknowledge that "social learning process" at stake in normative re-elaborations (Zurn 2015, p. 78), to identify trends that can at most be projected as trajectories on the future of social conflicts. Thanks to these trends and trajectories, theory and social actors would be equipped with the (internal) criterion that enables them to evaluate and eventually justify certain struggles for recognition, and not others.

Before proceeding to the analysis of *Freedom's Right*, we should emphasize that the concepts of surplus of validity and progress represent a multiplicity within Honneth's monism. Although both can be traced back to recognition practices and cannot exist outside of them, they certainly stand as some form of third instance to the I-Thou polarity at stake in intersubjectivity. The exceeding and overrunning character of the recognition principles informs and shapes the relations—and vice versa—while the concept of progress signifies a possible threshold of historical justification for the institutionalizations of these principles, as of the conflictual requests. Thus, if in the first case, without the acting validity of the principles, the gestures of recognition could not take place, in the second case, without the criterion of progress, it would not be possible for the critique to derive an ought from an is, that is, it would be impossible to depict a normative social theory as Honneth himself conceives it.

4.3 Being with Oneself in the Other: Social Freedom in Modern Societies

Freedom's Right (original German: 2011) certainly represents the second pillar of Honneth's thought as it has evolved to date: in addition to the impressive bulk of the text, what makes it the second "magnum opus" is the number of levels and issues that this work addresses from a normative, social-philosophical, and philosophical-political point of view, as well as the resulting multiplicity of approaches that can be employed in dealing with it (Zurn 2015, p. 155). Another aspect that contributes to the importance of the text is the numerous innovations it contains when compared to Honneth's previous works. They can be summarized according to three nuclei.

First, the focus is shifted from the practices and principles of recognition to those of freedom, whose link with the former is certainly present, but not so linear: this transition implies a disharmonious overlay between the social-institutional model presented in *Freedom's Right* and in previous works, above all *The Struggle for Recognition*.[88] Second, the critical-justifying approach seems to have changed completely. The normative principles in which the theory is rooted are not justified by their

---

[88] See Anita Horn 2018.

capacity to contribute to the constitution of an undamaged identity: no longer at stake is the so-called anthropological justification.[89] Rather, the method Honneth puts in place—the normative reconstruction—aims to provide an internal justification for the principles conveyed in and through the institutionalized practices of personal relationships, the market and the democratic public sphere. In other words, the whole question no longer concerns a formal theory of the good, but a historically informed theory of ethical life: in this shift from anthropology to normative history, the concept of self-realization is relegated to the background.[90] Finally, and almost as a consequence, this different methodological approach coincides with a shift from the analysis of experiences of injustice to a more general plane of historical-normative and socio-political investigation.[91] Thus, the great absences of Honneth's text seem to be, precisely, misrecognition, moral injury, suffering experiences, and social conflicts—in general (and at a first glance), the negative is apparently considered exclusively as pathological or as misdevelopment and no longer as propulsive motility.[92]

As we shall see, most of the criticisms in the secondary literature are directed at the last two of these three innovations, which are inevitably tied together: on the one hand, the normative reconstruction would present numerous limits and, after all, would not be able to provide any justification; on the other hand, the tone of Honneth's work would be excessively affirmative,[93] leaving aside what should represent the real object of critical theory: structural relations of power and domination, social homogeneity, ideology, and reification. In my view, most of these criticisms are flawed in exaggerating the discontinuity of *Freedom's Right* with respect to Honneth's previous works: thanks to the just completed analysis of *The Pathologies of Individual Freedom* and *Redistribution or Recognition?*, we will be able to better contextualize these conceptual innovations, so as to better understand their scope and to address the critical aspects of the work more precisely.

However, the richness and size of the text prevent a detailed analysis, at least here. For this reason, we will limit our focus to the methodological approach of normative reconstruction and on the concept of social freedom (section 4.3.1), and to the three ethical spheres of freedom in their basic structure, trying to emphasize the (unsatisfyingly addressed) tension between mutual recognition relationships and institutional entities (section 4.3.2). Finally, it will be useful to address the (numerous) criticisms directed at Honneth's methodological approach, which concern the identification of social freedom as "arch-value of modernity" (Karen Ng 2015, p. 7). On a general level, these criticisms concern a justificatory insufficiency and a critical deficiency of the accounts presented in *Freedom's Right*. Furthermore, as in the previ-

---

[89] See Busen, Herzog, and Sörensen 2012, p. 265; Freyenhagen 2015, p. 140; and Rutger Claassen 2014, pp. 79–80.
[90] See Honneth and Raffnsøe-Møller 2015, pp. 265–66.
[91] See Claassen 2014, p. 67; and Thomas Nys 2013, p. 12.
[92] See Teixeira 2017, pp. 605–6; and Luiz Gustavo Da Cunha De Souza 2016, p. 23.
[93] See Lysaker and Jakobsen 2015, p. 9.

ous chapters, we intend to critically examine some of the issues that concern the paradigm of recognition more closely: indeed, the very concept of recognition is apparently blurred in the direction of a vaguer account of intersubjective interaction or collective action,[94] and one could be at pains unearthing the specificity of recognition in the revisited framework of ethical life here proposed by Honneth (section 4.3.3).

4.3.1 Normative Reconstruction as Critical Method

The first issue regarding *Freedom's Right* undoubtedly concerns its methodological approach, namely, normative reconstruction. Although Honneth dedicates the Introduction of the work to the depiction of this methodology, he also clarifies that the "premises of such an endeavor cannot be so easily justified in advance, rather they can only be revealed in the course of the investigation" (Honneth 2014b, p. 3). In other words, *Freedom's Right* does not itself represent the mere application of a given or pre-elaborated method, but rather its unfolding, as if a formal methodology could only be distilled a posteriori. This preliminary precaution is decisive to understanding Honneth's self-comprehension by the inquiry and exposes its Hegelian soul. As is well known, Hegel feels a certain unease—or even aversion—toward those philosophical approaches that consider their own operation as discernible from the respective objects they observe, almost as if methodologies were considered as self-standing toolboxes. To mention the (probably) most renowned example, in the Preface to the *Phenomenology of Spirit*, Hegel, with a certain amount of irony, states that the existence of a preface to a philosophical work "seems not only superfluous, but in light of the nature of the subject matter, even inappropriate and counterproductive" (Hegel, *The Phenomenology of Spirit*, § 1). Honneth's adoption of such an approach clearly does not follow Hegel in its justification, which depends on the spirit's logical structure and ontological life, as much as on a clear conception of philosophy itself. However, it is easy to acknowledge a meaningful kinship between Honneth's and Hegel's approach.

In fact, Honneth's efforts are directed to the outlining of a theory of justice which cannot, on the one hand, be confined by the abstractedness of pure normative theories or, on the other hand, be exhausted by the hermeneutic acceptance of given moral facts. The leitmotif is thus represented by the renewed attempt to posit critical theory's possibilities on a third path between Kantian proceduralism and communitarianism. By this philosophical intention, Hegel's *Philosophy of Right* would represent a noteworthy—and indeed unavoidable—resource for its capability to not falling prey to the flaws of both positions.

---

94 See Claassen 2014, p. 77.

First, with respect to Kantian political theories, Hegel's approach would re-harmonize theoretical elaboration and "analysis of society" (Honneth 2014b, p. 1), that is, without decoupling normative principles and moral facts. Such theories would in fact: a) run into a certain abstractedness because of their persuasion that norms could be defined out of their immanence to the social world; b) face the difficulties of identifying an apt procedure for applying those norms to social reality; c) be characterized by a certain superfluity or redundancy. For, from a genealogical or hermeneutic point of view, it is clear that such normative principles are rooted in certain moral facts and are not purely intellectual or speculative matters. However, such superfluity is revealed only when—and Honneth's claim here is quite compelling—it can be shown that "the prevailing values are normatively superior to historically antecedent social ideals" (Honneth 2014b, p. 5).

Second, Honneth distances himself from communitarianism to the extent that the latter's recourse to moral facts and social facticity would turn out to be unsuccessful. That is, by flattening the philosophical-political elaboration to a hermeneutics of the present and forcing the potential scope of the first to a mere contextualism, merging or even confusing the analysis of social reality with its justification. With respect to this second point, the Hegelian concept of right would indeed respond to the rational need for justification: as he does in *The Pathologies of Individual Freedom* and in *Redistribution or Recognition?*, Honneth uses this concept by translating it into the dynamics whereby historically contingent institutional realizations find their (eventual) justification in the comparison with the surplus of validity of the principles that these institutional spheres should instantiate. This type of internal justification—and critique –, which takes into account the actual normativity expressed in institutional practices but requires a standard of rationality, is the heart of the normative reconstruction and, in fact, the real object of *Freedom's Right*.

Given Honneth's position, outlined in the introduction by only four methodological premises and shown during the course of the work via his normative reconstruction, it seems useful to outline this methodology by also making some conclusions of the investigation explicit.

The first premise states that the possibilities of succeeding in the project of integrating a theory of justice with an analysis of society depends on the assumption that "social reproduction hinges on certain set of shared fundamental ideals and values" (Honneth 2014b, p. 3). Several implications are entailed by such a claim, but the major point is that social formations can reproduce themselves only if they are justified by social actors with regard to the norms and values that the first should instantiate according to their supposed aims.

Such a "'transcendental' necessity of normative integration" (Honneth 2014b, p. 4) is a perspective that, on closer inspection, was already at the basis of the concepts of moral grammar and surplus of validity. Since *The Struggle for Recognition*, Honneth believes that social conflict is triggered when social spheres of interaction are no longer able to respond adequately to the normative demands of their participants. In this sense, conflicts lead to the formulation of new instantiations oriented toward greater harmonization with respect to the principles by which the subjects themselves have been socialized—love, equity, and merit. Moreover, already in *Redistribution or Recognition?*, rejecting functionalist views on norm-free sub-systems, Honneth had argued that even generalized media such as money need a renewed assent on the part of social actors for their reproduction. The difference here is that Honneth does not focus on the moral experience of the participants, but on the institutions themselves. And, as Laitinen points out, the idea that the legitimization of these institutions represents the conditio sine qua non of social reproduction seems to be aligning with the collective acceptance approaches to social ontology of John Searle or Raimo Tuomela. Consequently, social participants must to a certain extent be clear-sighted with respect to the normative contents and legitimacy of institutions: the participants' assent to the institutions would indeed represent an intentional act. Honneth would (more or less implicitly) embrace a constructivist account because the collective intentionality on the part of the subjects would possess some foundational power concerning the reproduction—and even existence—of the institutions.[95] Clearly, Honneth would reject such an approach, if understood in such quasi-contractualist terms. Rather, following Hegel, the aim is to conceive of the belongingness of subjects to social spheres as prior to their acceptance or consensus.[96]

With the intention of re-actualizing Hegel's *Philosophy of Right*, Honneth does not intend to inherit the logic of the concept and its various implications related to the ontological status of the *Geist*. However, he would not give up the idea that moral facts embedded in social reality entail a certain rationality. It is on such socially embedded rationality, in fact, that normative reconstruction hinges, but, even more profoundly, it would be vital for the success of critical theory: indeed, an unearthed rationality would represent the intramundane transcendence that necessarily informs a critical theory of society.[97] According to Honneth, a certain class of spiritual entities—namely, norms and values—would be able to reshape social reality to the extent that the normative claims they entail are embedded in institutions and are refined through social conflicts.[98] The risk of an anachronistic idealism would be mitigated by the fact that this historical rationality is not the result of a spiritual self-movement, but of the continuous polar tension between institutions, norms, and social actors. Thus, regarding the rationality of institutions, the spirit is replaced by the involvement of actors by means of critical justification.[99] In this way, Honneth certainly departs from Hegel to the extent that reconstructive thinking does not play the decisive role that reflection has in constituting institutional rationality itself: in other words, normative reconstruction would not be the moment when the latter becomes for itself. However, I would argue that, from that argument, we cannot draw

---

95 See Laitinen 2016, p. 269; and Andrew Buchwalter 2016, p. 59.
96 See Honneth 2014b, pp. 58–59.
97 See Piet Strydom 2013, p. 531.
98 See Honneth 2013, p. 38.
99 See Claassen 2014, p. 71.

the consequence that the philosopher plays the role of a simple external observer: certainly, the task of normative reconstruction is not to shape ontological realities, but finds itself (according to its own claims) on the same level as the emancipatory interests that it intends to make explicit and contribute to make clearer. This clearly emerges according to the triple level of justification already explained with regard to *Redistribution or Recognition?:* of the institutions by the social actors, of the demands of the latter by the theory, and of the institutionalized norms by the former and the latter in the name of the surplus of validity.[100]

The second aspect to be considered is the pragmatic matrix of such a perspective on social reproduction. Through the idea of normative integration, Honneth depicts a holistic account on social action, thus bridging the gap between praxis and ideals that would be involved in a functionalistic vision: conversely, praxis and ideals are in a reciprocal and dialectical relationship, where the latter would constitute reactions to the different structural changes (*Strukturwandlungen*) that take place in social practices and vice versa.[101] This would be visible in the course of *Freedom's Right* through the use of the so-called "founding documents" (Honneth 2014b, p. 136), that is, those intellectual and philosophical productions that conceptualize their respective ethical spheres, shaping and being shaped by the intersubjective practices realized within them. Thereby, the vitality of the actors' engagement with the institutions and their understanding of them would count as proof of their historical and normative relevance only if this holistic account of social action is accepted.[102] And only from such a perspective does Honneth's idea of progress as learning process become conceivable, precisely because interaction and action are not decoupled from their normative self-understanding. Thus, Hegel's transcendental "confidence" in historical progress could be more aptly conceived of as a not-pre-written path, but rather as an always-to-write evolution that could result only ex post (Honneth 2014b, p. 59).

That being said, the next three premises qualify almost as consequences. The second is that the theory's normative point of reference should draw on those values or ideals that "constitute the conditions of reproduction of a given society" (Honneth 2014b, p. 4). According to Honneth—for the object of his reconstruction coincides with western modernity—no value can compete with the role played by the concept of freedom. As a proof of its significance and generality, individual autonomy has been invoked by political perspectives often in contradiction among themselves and according to different meanings. It also plays such a fundamental role that any philosophical or political perspective on justice that did not take individual freedom into account would not be acceptable. Therefore, normative reconstruction must

---

[100] Here I disagree with Buchwalter and Pippin, who argue that Honneth's reconstructive approach leads, respectively, to an external attitude on the part of the philosopher and to the impossibility of understanding the idea of a self-constituting collective subject. See Buchwalter 2016, pp. 57–88; and Pippin 2014.
[101] See Honneth, Busen, and Herzog 2012, p. 275.
[102] See Buchwalter 2016, p. 68.

take the role played by freedom in social reproduction into account,[103] and the method can be further characterized as a hermeneutics of the ethical self-conception of modern societies.[104]

The third premise concerns *where* freedom has to be analyzed: via social analysis, those institutionalized spheres that, as a necessary feature, realize that the idea of individual freedom must be addressed. Following the Hegelian model and their role played within social reproduction, these spheres are identified as personal relationships (friendship, intimate relationships, and family), the market, and the democratic public sphere. On the one hand, clearly, the reconstruction differs in several respects from the actual situations of these spheres, precisely because of its normative character, but, on the other hand:

> The point is not simply to outline a certain desired state of affairs, and thus to follow a purely normative approach, but to examine contemporary reality in terms of its potential for fostering practices in which universal values can be realized in a superior, i.e. a more comprehensive and suitable fashion (Honneth 2014b, p. 8).

The reconstructive analysis neither outlines pure normative structures nor it concerns the evaluation of specific practices or values; rather, its aim is to delineate a critical investigation of the socio-structural (and intersubjective) conditions of their instantiation.[105] If, therefore, the reconstruction of the spheres includes within itself the ability of outlining the possibilities of their development—that is, the conditions of possibility of a better realization of freedom—it follows that the fourth premise concerns the critical nature of the project: "The point cannot be merely to uncover and reconstruct instances of already existing ethical life, rather it must also be possible to criticize these findings in light of embodied values" (Honneth 2014b, p. 9). It is hence clear that the critical potential disclosed by normative reconstruction lies in the counterfactual dimension provided by the distance between the principle of freedom and its instantiations.[106] Honneth's internal critique hinges on the idea that, even when they do not exert an actual influence on the social spheres—say, the capitalist market—values and norms would represent a counterfactual basis of validity.[107] Thus, the assumption that freedom represents the logic of social reproduction may not represent immediate evidence, and could therefore raise the suspicion that this is more of a methodological assumption.[108] However, according to Honneth, only once the values and norms by which social actors are socialized are understood will it be possible to criticize the inadequacies and misdevelopments of the institutions,

---

103 See Honneth 2014b, pp. 15–19.
104 See Honneth 2013, p. 40.
105 See Busen, Herzog, and Sörensen 2012, p. 267.
106 See Hans Arentshorst 2015, pp. 142–44.
107 See Honneth and Marcelo 2013, pp. 216–17; and Honneth 2012e, p. 67.
108 See David A. Borman 2019, p. 114.

precisely in light of the normative promise of which those same institutions should be the bearers.[109] As Pedersen observes,[110] even if Honneth's reference to Habermas—above all for what concerns the sphere of democratic life—regards mainly the early work *The Structural Transformation of the Public Sphere*, such a critical project does possess similarities with *Between Facts and Norms*, where the key of the critical method is identified in the "tension between the normative self-understanding" and "the social facticity" (Habermas 1996, p. 288). As already stated by the first methodological premise, the heart of the matter is precisely this normative self-understanding, on the horizon of which the discrepancy between standards and facticity emerges. At closer look, this counterfactual method of criticism does not differ much from what Honneth said in "Pathologies of the Social," where the possibilities of critical theory were anchored in the metaphorical binomial of pathology and healthiness. Unlike this juvenile text, however, the image of health evoked by social pathologies and misdevelopments is not, in *Freedom's Right*, related on a weak intersubjective anthropology, but on the principles that govern social integration via institutionalized practices. Moreover, precisely because the institutionally instantiated principles represent the (counter)factual rationality, and therefore the foundation of the possibilities of critique and progress, Honneth argues that misdevelopments cannot be "engendered or promoted by the corresponding system of action" (Honneth 2014b, p. 128). If the structure of such institutional practices is in fact that of realizing principles whose counterfactually grasped completeness represents the content of justice—thus the motivational source of social conflicts and the criterion of critique—the roots of misdevelopments are to be found elsewhere or outside. Contrary to "Pathologies of the Social," therefore, Honneth distinguishes misdevelopments and social pathologies, which, as we will see shortly, are characterized in line with *The Pathologies of Individual Freedom* and *Reification:* that is, as second-order disorders.

As already noted, the other great methodological difference, which casts a shadow over the tone of the entire work, concerns negativity in general. Indeed, Honneth has used the pathology-healthiness metaphor to access the normative horizon through negativity. Even in the present analysis, the starting point was represented by misrecognition and reification, to then define recognition and the related moral grammar or normative implications. As far as *Freedom's Right* is concerned, such access to the text would be difficult to defend. However, I argue that such a shift by Honneth, who embraces the affirmative aspect of a normative social theory, should be read in continuity with previous works. In fact, the negative experiences (moral suffering or social pathology) were regarded as opening an already present normative horizon, thanks to which the negative could emerge as such, and social critique could implement its own aims. Honneth's interest, particularly in this text, is to make

---

109 See Busen, Herzog, and Sörensen 2012, pp. 266–67.
110 See Jørgen Pedersen 2015, pp. 239–45.

explicit that social actors suffer or feel misrecognized exclusively because of a defective instantiation of society's normative structures. Quite simply: if, for example, in *The Struggle for Recognition*, the negative was the primary factor of the analysis that revealed, afterwards, the antecedence of a moral grammar, in *Freedom's Right*, the primary factor of the analysis coincides with this antecedence of the normative horizon.

Stressing the matter one more time, the methodological premises of *Freedom's Right* could be sketched as follows: a) social reproduction is guided by the normative assent of social actors to some institutions, in accordance with some ethical values; b) a theory of justice that is itself led by social analysis—thus avoiding formalism or contextualism—should orient itself to socially embedded, general values, that is, freedom; c) this embeddedness instantiates through and within certain spheres, which therefore are ethical: they coincide with the personal relations, the market, and the democratic public sphere; and d) normative reconstructing of the history of such institutions will highlight the tension between their self-understanding and their facticity, which presents certain misdevelopments: this gap represents the dimension proper to critical thinking.

4.3.1.1 Three Modes of Freedom
Since instantiations of freedom represent the object of normative reconstruction, it is first necessary to understand what we mean with this concept or, better, what its multiple dimensions are. Referring again to Hegel's *Philosophy of Right*, Honneth's account possesses many similarities to the view already defended in *The Pathologies of Individual Freedom*. However, two differences are easy to notice. First, the attempt to de-psychologize the idea of social pathology is evident as result, I believe, of the exchange with Nancy Fraser: if the focus in the Spinoza Lectures was on suffering from indeterminacy and on the therapeutic task of ethical life, in *Freedom's Right* Honneth describes for the first time social pathologies as second-order disorders, that is, as misunderstandings, at a reflexive level, of the norms of action, which may also not involve any suffering on the part of the subject who is inhabited by such distortions. However, ethical life represents a more jagged panorama compared to *The Pathologies of Individual Freedom*, not exempt from misdevelopments that counteract the realization of the right. The second difference consists in the fact that, in *Freedom's Right*, Honneth does not limit himself to dealing with the three modes of freedom from the point of view of a theory of action, but, in each case, extrapolates the connection that between a certain (eventually experienced) conception of freedom and a respective theory of justice.

The first mode of freedom that is depicted by Honneth is negative freedom, together with its parallel, legal freedom. Also referring also to Jean-Paul Sartre and Robert Nozick, Honneth points out that all the fundamental elements of negative freedom are already described by Hobbes, who identifies autonomy with the absence of external impediments. According to Honneth, the key of the attractiveness of this definition lies in describing "the purpose of freedom" as entailing "protected freespace for egocentric action, unimpeded by the pressures of responsibility towards others" (Honneth 2014b, p. 23). In other words, the central idea of negative freedom is a sort of guarantee of the individuality of the individual, within which the subject is able to suspend moral relations with others, bracketing any type of constraint and any reference to a moral content.

Over and above the different contractual perspectives that modernity has provided, the figure of justice implicit in such an idea of freedom would, according to Honneth, be particularly evident in Nozick's *Anarchy, State, and Utopia*. On Nozick's view, such a form of freedom is embodied in individual rights, which are so "far-reaching," as the well-known opening sentence of the work says, "that they raise the question of what, if anything, the state and its officials may do" (Robert Nozick 1999, p. ix). Consequently, any contact, any interest, any approach that intercepts the pomerium of individual freedom would represent, in fact, an abuse. With regard to the life-projects of others, therefore, an *epoché* must be performed, since no individual can dare to interfere. In this sense, such individualism also goes along with a certain perspective over value pluralism, whereby the only criterion that regulates interpersonal relations is based on a principle of non-interference. However, the limits of negative freedom are quite evident and coincide with the unavailability of resources useful for self-determination: excluding from its definition an analysis of the motives and moral directions of action, this form of freedom would be almost unable to express itself.[111]

In the second section of *Freedom's Right*, The Possibility of Freedom, Honneth considers the institutionalization of negative freedom that, as already explained through the reference to Nozick, concerns individual rights and the legal system more in general. This institutionalized form would have precise consequences regarding the modalities of intersubjective relations and would guarantee a peculiar self-relation:

> Externally, [the sum of subjective rights] grants subjects a merely purposive-rational form of decision-making, while protecting their ability to ethically form their will all the more effectively. As individuals who encounter each other in legal relationships, they represent for each other subjects that are free to act 'at will' and thus in accordance with their individual preferences. But from the internal perspective of subjects whose motives remain opaque to each other, the rights they reciprocally grant each other represent a kind of protective shell behind which they can explore the depths and shallows of their subjectivity without fear of reproach (Honneth 2014b, p. 73).

With regard to the internal self-relation, Honneth follows Hegel in identifying property right as the cornerstone that discloses certain possibilities. According to Hegel, the right to own external objects meets the human need to guarantee oneself consistency: in this way, the inconsistency of the will would find a way to express itself and

---

111 See Honneth 2014b, p. 28.

4.3 Being with Oneself in the Other: Social Freedom in Modern Societies — 163

thus gain continuity. Therefore, the role of private property would be that of granting the subject an objective expression (*Entäußerung*) before which she can ascertain and be certain of herself. Thanks to the ownership of external objects and through the "existential meaning" that they assume over time (Honneth 2014b, p. 75), the legal person has a criterion through which to question external relations and the different orientations of action. Consequently, the private space guaranteed by the property would open the doors to a fundamental horizon of self-examination, self-problematization, self-exploration, and self-assurance.[112]

Given this fundamental dimension of self-relation, the limits of legal freedom emerge in the type of intersubjective interaction it implies, symbolized by the contract. In fact, in the contract, two subjects meet, recognizing one another with respect to their ability and capability to maintain contractual constraints and obligations; therefore, according to the recognitive logic of respect. In this dynamic, however, motivations and goals remain in the background, only allowing the plot of interests strategically oriented to purposes to emerge. Thereby the "schema of behaviour thus imposed by the system of the law is that of isolated actors with ostensibly strategic aims" (Honneth 2014b, p. 83). In this case, the only normative obligation required of the individual is that they not infringe on the rights of the other, which explicitly implies a certain type of recognition, beyond which, however, no other type of bond or cooperation is assumed and the subject is not required to justify or publicly express their reasons. The legal person, therefore, can be depicted as the isolated result of the "neutralizing effect of the law" (Honneth 2014b, p. 83).

And it is here that the main limit of negative/legal freedom emerges, that is, an insufficiency, which can be interpreted as a contradiction between the external relationship and the internal one guaranteed by rights. In fact, individual rights, since they lack of concern for motivation and content—which conversely allows an instrumental depiction of individual's motives to emerge—cannot direct the ethical self-interrogation for which they themselves represent the condition of possibility. In this way, "legal relations enable a kind of freedom for whose successful exercise it cannot provide the basis" (Honneth 2014b, p. 83). But, more importantly for Honneth's purposes, it is clear that legal freedom presupposes a) a form of mutual recognition (contract), b) a normative status that is mutually granted (contractual accountability), and c) a particular of individual relation-to-self (self-confirmation through the objects, private sphere).

Honneth sees this estrangement from the ethical horizon of negative/legal freedom as the element that leads to the formulation of the reflexive/moral concept of freedom. If the previous notion of freedom was derived from (quasi-)physical determinations, this new articulation of the concept identifies the essential characteristics of autonomy—intentionality, self-determination, and authenticity—through an investigation of the psychic dimension of the subject: "individuals are free if their actions

---

[112] See Honneth 2014b, pp. 76–77.

are solely guided by their own intentions" (Honneth 2014b, p. 29). Reflexive freedom therefore does not concern the relationship between social actors and deeds, but their self-relation. The search for inner contents that are not subject to any heteronomy suggests that this type of self-relation has, in Honneth's eyes, some resemblance to the detectivist attitude outlined in *Reification:* the subject would have unlimited access to their inner contents and would be able to discern objectively which motives express it authentically and which instead would represent a submission of the will to external factors.

Honneth's discourse is more complex here and is divided into two different concepts of reflexive freedom, namely, the idea of autonomy (which responds to the Kantian tradition) and that of self-realization (which instead has in Herder and in the idea of authenticity its roots). In any case, according to Honneth, the modern progenitor of such prospects is Rousseau, who places the concept of free will at the center of the analysis of freedom, and introduces the contrast between the free will and passions, that is, the difference between autonomy and heteronomy. Thus, Rousseau would identify the nature of the free gesture in an uninterrupted continuity between will and action: self-legislation.[113]

Without reproposing every step of Honneth's argument, we can explain the first concept of reflexive freedom, focused on the idea of autonomy, through the trajectory that goes from Kant to Habermas and Apel. The subject's self-relation is conceptualized in relation to universal moral norms, through which the individual can orient her deeds and ask for reasons, as well as question the surrounding context about its correspondence with such universal maxims. Thus, the relations with others require respect, which in turn implies a moral judgment expressed in conformity with the universality of norms.[114] And even if Kant's transcendental perspective of the subject fades historically, giving and requesting reasons is fundamental for the communicative processes of collective self-legislation: the idea of equal respect for each participant in an interaction is based on their moral accountability.[115]

The second current that stems from Rousseau is that which reads reflexive freedom in terms of self-realization, whereby Honneth draws primarily from Herder. According to this view, freedom consists in articulating the will, so that our deeds would allow the expansion and deepening of the original core of the self, via a "diachronic process of self-discovery" (Honneth 2014b, p. 35). Freedom, then, represents the process and the end thanks to which the individual can realize her own most intrinsic nature, whereby the nexus with the idea of authenticity could allow speaking of self-realization in terms of self-actualization. Clearly, the contemporary deconstruction of the self as independent substance makes such an argument highly problematic: thus, if "there is no primal, 'true' self, then self-realization cannot be under-

---

[113] See Honneth 2014b, pp. 30–31.
[114] See Honneth 2014b, pp. 31–33.
[115] See Honneth 2014b, pp. 34–35.

stood as a process of self-discovery, but only as an essentially constructive process that demands standards other than those of reflection or identity with oneself" (Honneth 2014b, p. 36). A splitting of authenticity and self-realization follows from this, where the former would correspond to a closeness or familiarity between the subject, its inner contents, and its deeds, while the idea of self-realization would have to meet standards of biographical continuity, as Honneth claims following Harry Frankfurt's thought.

Trying to outline the implications of such reflexive concepts of freedom in terms of his theory of justice, Honneth insists on the idea of self-determination proper to the Kantian view. It would lead to a proceduralist vision, where justice would have to be found in the collective exercise of certain communicative processes of self-legislation, but whereby, conversely, the result of these processes would not be embedded within them, thus remaining external or posterior: "the substance of this system is not determined in advance, because for conceptual reasons the theory cannot anticipate decisions that autonomous subjects must make on their own" (Honneth 2014b, p. 37).

As for the reflexive freedom understood as self-realization, political theories are compelled to assume at least a certain type of knowledge or anthropological assumption on what or how the individual self-unfolding could be. In this case, Honneth identifies two macro-directions: one individualistic and one collectivistic. In the first case, the task of the state would be to provide the individual with the (material and cultural) resources necessary to freely articulate its own biographical path—and the exemplary case mentioned by Honneth is John Stuart Mill. In the second case, the various collectivist perspectives could be interpreted as similar to Hannah Arendt's or Michael Sandel's liberal republicanism. In these theoretical proposals, the main idea is that the nature of the self is socially shaped in a way that an expression of one's own nature, in order to be fruitful or free, could not exclude the collective dimension. Therefore, the individual could unfold its nature only in shared democratic practices oriented by a commonality of aims.[116]

In contrast to negative freedom, which has been formalized throughout history through individual rights, reflexive freedom, being essentially a certain type of self-relation, results as moral autonomy in "a weakly institutionalized cultural pattern" (Honneth 2014b, p. 96). However, even this kind of autonomy possesses certain characteristics that do not allow it to be reduced to a mere symbolic system of orientation:

> Just like legal freedom, the institutionalization of moral autonomy is accompanied by certain practices of mutual recognition; here as well, subjects ascribe to each other a certain normative status and expect a specific individual relation-to-self. Just like the private autonomy guaranteed by the modern legal system, the principle of moral autonomy, which is also organized as a system of action, only enables freedom and does not realize it institutionally. Here as well, individ-

---

[116] See Honneth 2014b, pp. 38–39.

uals are only given the opportunity, granted by the culture though not enforced by the government, to retreat from intersubjective obligations in order to then reconnect, in the light of a specific moral perspective, to a lifeworld previously experienced as divided (Honneth 2014b, p. 96).

Honneth thus highlights two major articulations of moral freedom. The first could be described as a critical moral freedom. In fact, the transcendental horizon of the norms allows each individual, regardless of his or her situation, to appeal to universal norms that guarantee them a perspective from which to question the social environment. The second aspect of moral freedom is positive and more closely concerns the Kantian imperative: in the name of this access to transcendental norms, which does not represent some individuals' prerogative but is proper to every rational being, it follows that other human beings are due recognition as ends in themselves, according to a logic of respect. Therefore, individuals who emancipate from the laws of nature and from their ethical context via an appeal to universal norms are enabled, in the name of freedom, to assume a perspective from which they can critically oppose the existing norms and, at the same time, work constructively in favor of new normative systems through a rational self-legislation: "As a generally shared body of knowledge, moral freedom is relevant to every individual as an independent authority that grants individuals the opportunity to legitimately question given norms of action and, if necessary, to overstep them" (Honneth 2014b, p. 105). If, therefore, the legal person could ask for an external confirmation of its own identity thanks to a comparison with objects of its own possession, for the moral personality, this type of self-relation would be realized through cognitive reference to universal(izable) norms. Without focusing on Honneth's analysis of Dewey, Schiller, Korsgaard, and Habermas's reflections,[117] it is useful to underline one more aspect. The fact that the consideration of every other individual as an end in itself can be based on human nature—that is, on the innate rational faculties that allow it to refer to a universal normative horizon—is strongly questioned by the last century and by the destructuring of the modern subject. At the same time, it has become a highly problematic assumption that universal norms have their own consistency regardless of the socio-cultural perspectives in the field. Consequently, Honneth comprehends the contemporary contribution of such views mainly in Habermasian terms. "Exercising moral freedom means taking part in a sphere of interaction that has emerged on the basis of shared and internalized knowledge—a sphere that is regulated by norms of mutual recognition" (Honneth 2014b, p. 105). The dignity of the individual, in fact, although universal, always has a decisive link with his or her partners of interaction and with the culturally institutionalized forms that allow them to perceive themselves prior to every role or social situation, and therefore with rational tools useful to their criticism. As in the case of legal freedom, therefore, moral freedom involves: a) certain practices of recognition (respect), b) a specific status granted to one another (dignity), and c) a particular form of self-relation (the

---

117 See Honneth 2014b, pp. 98–104.

cognitive possibility of referring to rules that are to some extent unrelated to the context).

Despite the significant contribution made by these forms of freedom, particularly with respect to the forms of self-relation that they disclose (the confirmation of oneself as independent from the social context and the possibility of questioning that context), the almost exclusively suspensive nature also indicates their main limit. Indeed, their "postponing and interruptive function" shows their insufficiency (Honneth 2014b, p. 94). The limitations of legal and moral freedom could therefore be understood as a genealogical inversion that causes the failure of a possibility.[118] Briefly, these two forms of freedom are based on normative and intersubjective conditions that do not fall within their own definition. On the one hand, the legal or moral subject's freedom status depends on intersubjective relationships of recognition that are then suspended via ethical self-interrogation; on the other hand, the normative contents to which the latter refers cannot be the result of these forms of freedom. They therefore represent a fundamental possibility of putting the context in parentheses, but, considered as self-standing, they can remain exclusively indeterminate, confined—and here Honneth follows Hegel—to a mere faculty or empty possibility.

However, we should stress that, according to Honneth's reading, these forms of freedom are not simply "ontologically tainted" (Joel Anderson 2013, p. 20). They represent a fundamental contribution to the constitution of modern subjectivity and its institutionalized forms. Moreover, the very form of ethical life would be unthinkable without such frameworks of legal and moral freedom. Legal and moral freedom essentially belong to social life,[119] but do not possess the necessary self-consistency to bridge the gap between individuals, making social life exist. To be sure, Honneth does not sufficiently emphasize these elements,[120] and he does not provide an account of the necessary capabilities that a contemporary person would need in order to master such different and everyday modes of freedom,[121] a fact that would justify the criticisms that have been levelled at him.[122] However, one could say that, following the first methodological premise, the existence of renewed consensus and assent to these ideas of freedom would to some degree justify their normative demand. To mention two examples of the relevance of such forms of freedom in the section on ethical life, it is enough to think of the normative meaning of labor

---

[118] See Honneth 2014b, pp. 81–86 and 104–13.
[119] "Hegel obviously intends thereby to integrate the other two forms of freedom dealt with above into his system of ethical life.... They are intended as a supplement to the ordered system of ethical institutions, granting individuals the right to legitimately renounce the demands these institutions make, without representing the source of a new order. Whether Hegel would have been prepared to include the rejection of the system as a legitimate exercise of legal and moral freedoms, provided this renunciation is shared by a sufficiently large portion of the population, is an interesting question" (Honneth 2014b, p. 58). See also Honneth and Raffnsøe-Møller, pp. 262–63.
[120] See Buchwalter 2016, p. 71.
[121] See Anderson 2013, p. 20.
[122] See Nys 2013; and Beate Rössler 2013, pp. 14–17.

contracts—which pertain properly to legal freedom—or of the critical attitude in general (both on the part of the theorist and on the part of social movements), which coincides with the stance of moral freedom, departing from the surrounding context to compare it with general norms. Conversely, their limits are to be interpreted in line with what Honneth has already said in *The Pathologies of Individual Freedom*: these forms of freedom are not self-sufficient and they need to be embedded in the broader horizon of institutionalized ethical life in order to be expressed according to their own characteristics. If such a reconciliation does not take place, that is, when these norms of action autonomize themselves, social pathologies would emerge.

In *Freedom's Right*, Honneth endorses the definition of social pathologies as second-order disorders for the first time, thus considering them social developments that significantly impair "the ability to take part rationally in important forms of social cooperation" and that "impact subjects' reflexive access to primary systems of actions and norms" (Honneth 2014b, p. 86). Since these are impediments whose emergence is attested on a reflexive level, these phenomena are difficult to ascertain from a sociological point of view, which is why Honneth also resorts to aesthetic expressions.

This is the case of the first form of pathology of legal freedom, where Honneth takes the movie *Kramer vs. Kramer* as an exemplary case of the juridification of relationships:[123] in a dynamic similar to that described in *Reification*, the totalization of juridical claims would lead to forget the communicative dimension that the relationship with the other could have.[124] The second pathology, instead—which Honneth depicts referring to the novel *Indecision*[125]—rather than finding its origin in the legal system and in the proliferation of legal forms of public interaction, would concern the very essence of the interruptive gesture that concerns the private sphere, and therefore its emulation within other social spheres of action. The suggestion that Honneth intends to offer is that the increasingly widespread perception that the maintenance of long-term obligations or commitments would be futile somehow hinges on the atomization of legal subjects. Within the private horizon obtained via the suspension of all intersubjective obligations, the self would not be provided with an apt horizon of motivation and aims of action: in other words, it would suffer from indeterminacy.[126]

Honneth also identifies two different cases of the pathologies of moral freedom, where both derive from an autonomization of the bond between the individual and the moral norms to which it refers. If, on the one hand, there is the rigid moralism

---

123 It is an iconic movie from 1979, written and directed by Robert Benton. It tells the story of a couple's case of divorce, and its impact on their young son.
124 See Honneth 2014b, pp. 88–92.
125 Benjamin Kunkel's novel from 2005. The protagonist, Dwight B. Wilmerding, leads an anonymous existence, burdened by a chronic inability to make decisions and commit.
126 See Honneth 2014b, pp. 92–93.

4.3 Being with Oneself in the Other: Social Freedom in Modern Societies — 169

that derives from an insensitivity to the pre-existing context and bonds,[127] on the other hand, a certain political absolutism could be explained in the consideration of oneself as absolute (moral) lawgiver[128]—and here Honneth's depiction possesses many similarities with Hegel's account on Revolutionary Terror provided in the *Phenomenology of Spirit*.[129] Such depictions are thus aimed at criticizing an agent-neutral morality,[130] so as a context-neutral one, whereby the implementations of moral values and norms are considered to unfold without any regard for each involved actor or situation.

Social pathologies do not constitute—as has already been said about *Reification*—psychoses, moral errors, or rational defectiveness that depend on individual choices or personally grounded stances at all. Rather, Honneth leads a critique of certain socially established forms of life (which, in this case, coincide with different facets of individualist atomism) that social actors find themselves living (tendentially unaware), thus misunderstanding from the outset some norms of action and contributing to the social reproduction of distorted patterns. As grounding factor of social pathologies there is therefore a general or socially widespread misunderstanding, which, to be defined as such, requires a definition of not-misunderstood norms of action: otherwise, pathologies could be identified only on the basis of what are the majority values and norms within a given social environment, with ruinous consequences for the goals of critical theory.

From what has been said, such a not-misunderstood norm of freedom must, like the two previous forms, include in its definition a) certain relations of recognition, b) specific normative statuses, and must enable c) peculiar modes of self-relation. Contrary to legal and moral freedoms, however, such freedom must entail in its own definition the respective orienting contents (remedying the mere possibility character) and must not be subject to the logic of genealogical inversion (thus remaining in the domain of its phenomenological shaping, intersubjective relations, that is). In other words, it must be a form of freedom in which otherness does not represent heteronomy, but the objective dimension through which what, if considered only for part of the individual (free will) remains bound to the emptiness of possibility, can be comprehensively actualized. For Hegel, notoriously, the realization of freedom coincides with the experience of being with oneself in the other, which concerns not only a social dimension, but also the general level of subject-object polarity and the dynamics according to which the latter would become subject in turn, generating a dialectic identity between the two poles of cognition, traditionally separated by a hiatus. Clearly, Honneth attributes an intersubjective or relational character to this definition, translating this third model of freedom proposed by Hegel with the

---

[127] See Honneth 2014b, pp. 114–18; and Honneth 1995a.
[128] See Honneth 2014b, pp. 118–20.
[129] See Hegel, *The Phenomenology of Spirit*, §§ 582–595.
[130] See Laitinen 2016, p. 274.

expression social freedom,[131] whereby the dimension of otherness in which one can be with oneself clearly has precise features: it consists of other persons or at least of the second nature. Thereby, such yet to clarify freedom would decisively not invert the phenomenological priority that intersubjectivity possesses before subjectivity: "Our dealings with others, our social interaction, necessarily precedes the act of detachment captured in relations of negative or moral freedom. Hence we must define that antecedent layer of freedom located in the sphere in which humans relate to each other in some way" (Honneth 2014b, p. 60). The central element for which this form of freedom should be superior to the models illustrated above concerns the need for complementarity ("Ergänzungsbedürftigkeit") (Honneth 2011a, p. 86) that *acting* would require for its own being free: in order not to succumb to the indeterminacy of contents (legal freedom) or to the heteronomy not of intentions, but of acts (moral freedom), it is necessary to meet another "whose aims complement our owns" (Honneth 2014b, p. 45). Now, according to Honneth, such complementarity can be understood in a weak sense, whereby the first would constitute a horizon of conditions for the free expression of the individual, or in a strong (ontological) sense, according to which social objectivity itself is proposed as identical—and not simply conciliatory—to the reflexive intentions of the self.[132] If, therefore, the idea that the interdependence of each person's freedom should not coincide with an interdependence of aims can be read as a weak view on social freedom,[133] Honneth's more demanding view claims that, even the determined purposes of ego and alter must coincide: and this is where the concept of mutual recognition comes into play. In the logic of mutual recognition, in fact, subjects meet by implementing an identical purpose: to recognize each other.[134] Hence, those of mutual recognition are the norms of action that *should* inform social reality so as to realize social freedom.[135]

Given that social freedom in the strict sense can only result from—or even coincide with—recognition interactions and provided the interest of normative reconstruction in not untying the elaboration of a theory of justice from a social analysis,

---

131 See Neuhouser 2000, p. 6.
132 See Honneth 2014b, pp. 47–48.
133 See Laitinen 2016, p. 271.
134 Although Honneth does not mention this, it is difficult not to notice a similarity between this perspective and the pure concept of recognition outlined in the *Phenomenology*: "Each is the mediating middle to the other, through which each mediates itself with itself and integrates itself with itself. Each is, to itself, and in that of the other, an essence immediately existing for itself which at the same time is for itself in that way only through this mediation. They *recognize* themselves as *mutually recognizing each other*" (Hegel, *The Phenomenology of Spirit*, § 184). As the Hegelian discussion of self-consciousness shows well, however, this purity of recognition (and therefore, in the specific case of social freedom, the identity of the aims) represents a phenomenologically difficult case to find and a highly demanding theoretical standard.
135 See Claassen 2014, pp. 69–70.

Honneth provides a thin concept of institution that can match the intersubjective character of freedom practices:

> For Hegel, institutions belong to the concept of freedom because the intersubjective structure of freedom must be relieved of the necessary task of coordinating subjects: In the routine practices objectified in an institutional structure, subjects can almost automatically recognize which contribution they need to make in order to realize their aims, which is only possible in concert. . . . The category of recognition, which for Hegel is the key to determining the intersubjective nature of freedom, is also the decisive foundation for his notion of institutions: Because such complexes of regulated behaviour must provide subjects with social conditions that allow the reciprocal realization of freedom, institutions must constitute congealed forms of mutual recognition (Honneth 2014b, p. 53).

Institutions would then be considered as coagulations of recognition practices and, precisely because of the link between the latter and the former, they can be conceived as institutions that foster social freedom.

It follows that the theory of justice relating to social freedom should result—as we have seen—from an analysis of intersubjective practices that are formed and form certain institutional spheres along lines of mutual recognition: personal relations, the market, and the democratic public sphere. The analysis of these spheres should provide internal criteria (i.e. concerning the ethical self-understanding of the spheres operating in the respective participants) to determine their correctness with respect to the principles that they should realize.

4.3.2 The Spheres of Social Freedom

In the exposition of the theory of justice that derives from the concept of social freedom, Honneth implements the normative reconstruction, that is, provides a counterfactual version of three institutional contexts that should realize—with respect to their own constitutive promises—their participants' freedom through the recognition practices they inform. In other words, Honneth presents the institutional spheres as ideal actualities,[136] that is, he follows Hegel in elaborating a social analysis that creates "an equilibrium between historical and social circumstances and rational considerations" (Honneth 2014b, p. 56). In this way, the reconstruction of institutional practices is not flattened on historical analysis or context-determined values: rather, Honneth can articulate the theory of justice with respect to a sociologically distilled intramundane transcendence, which entails a precise critique of the respective misdevelopments, too. As already mentioned, the institutional spheres correspond (in broad terms) with the subdivision made by Hegel in his *Philosophy of Right:* personal relations, market, and democratic public sphere. In considering such institutional frameworks, Honneth's primary aim is not to define the latter's function or function-

---

[136] See Ng 2015, p. 14.

al structure, but to illuminate which forms of intersubjective freedom they can (or should) foster in order to be considered just:

> The consequence of reconnecting freedom to institutions is that a conception of justice is based on the value of freedom cannot be developed and justified without simultaneously giving an account of the corresponding institutional structures. It is not enough to derive formal principles, rather theory must reach out to social reality; only there do we find the conditions that provide all individuals with the maximum individual freedom to pursue their aims. . . . To elucidate what it means for individuals to be free necessarily implies determining the existing institutions in which they can experience recognition in normatively regulated interaction with others (Honneth 2014b, p. 65).

In fact, despite the increased generality of Honneth's theory—which no longer focuses on the experience of individuals, but on social-political issues—this investigation of institutions does not concern what could be defined as their structural or ontological character: it does not analyze the actual functioning of the market or the laws that regulate it,[137] nor does it consider the relationship between individuals and government, legislation, political power, or the administration of justice, nor schooling.[138] In other words, neither institutions, as the term is usually understood, nor the relationship between individuals and these social spheres considered as a whole are addressed.[139] Rather, Honneth does not abandon the action-theoretical approach that has characterized his view since at least *The Struggle for Recognition* and considers intersubjective relationships that occur the contexts of our second nature, where subjects are led to assume certain attitudes toward each other. And it is precisely from within such perspective that the centrality of the idea of collective action takes its own importance for *Freedom's Right*. Thus, Honneth gives us hints about a somehow differently accentuated concept of recognition:

> These systems of action [i.e. institutions] must be termed 'relational' because the activities of individual members within them complement each other; they can be regarded as 'ethical' because they involve a form of obligation that does not have the contrariness of a mere 'ought.' ... The behavioural expectations that subjects have of each other within such 'relational' institutions are institutionalized in the shape of social roles that normally ensure the smooth interlocking of their respective activities. When subjects fulfill their respective roles, they complement each other's incomplete actions in such a way that they can only act in a collective or unified fashion (Honneth 2014b, p. 125).

---

[137] See, among others, Thompson 2015; and Thompson 2019b. I will address these issues in more detail in relation to the market and then regarding the more general criticisms to the approach of *Freedom's Right* in the next sections.
[138] See Bert van den Brink 2013, p. 25. In his reply to van den Brink's observation, Honneth admits that he would speak about schooling in an eventually new edited version of *Freedom's Right*. See Honneth 2013; and Honneth 2015a.
[139] See Horn 2018, p. 29; and Honneth 2013, p. 42.

The centrality of "role obligations" within the relational-ethical institutions shows once again and in an evident way that, for Honneth, the definition of recognition cannot prescind from elements of second nature.

4.3.2.1 Personal Relationships

In *Freedom's Right*, Honneth proposes a more complex differentiation of the sphere of personal relationships than in previous works. If, in fact, friendship has always been mentioned, as well as sexual relations, the focus always seemed to be on the infant-caregiver relationship, which was one of the main axes of the anthropological and social-ontological priority accorded to intersubjectivity. Here, the latter relational form is almost absent and emphasis is placed on mutuality and equality within frameworks in which the involved partners are simultaneously recognizers and recognized, that is, able to assume and grant each other normative statuses and fulfil "complementary role obligations" (Honneth 2014b, p. 133). Just as by legal and moral freedom, this kind of social freedom also a) depicts a kind of mutual recognition relations; b) exposes certain moral statuses that are reciprocally granted; and c) discloses specific relations-to-self enabled by the partaking in the first.

The three relational spheres here considered by Honneth are friendship, intimate relationships, and families. For each of these institutions of recognition, which involve not only the logic of love or emotional support, but also mutual respect and esteem, Honneth highlights, through his normative reconstruction, a tendency to increasing purification of the normative expectations from external motivations to their subsistence.[140] Almost to emphasize the clear distance with the positions expressed in *The Struggle for Recognition*, therefore, progress in personal relationships is seen as one of the fundamental aspects that base their legitimacy in the eyes of the participants, so that forms of friendship, intimacy, or family that find their motivation in reasons other than the relationship itself would no longer be acceptable. In other words, through such historical-normative reconstruction, Honneth claims to have distilled the implicit norms that participants share and through which these very relational forms could be (and are actually) evaluated: the historically emerging standards are an increased generalization or democratization, a finer differentiation in institutional roles, and an increasingly mutual and equal performing of the respective role obligations.[141]

In friendship one is free to entrust to the other those dimensions of ethical interrogation and self-exploration that legal and moral freedom confined to private space. Through the medium of esteem, those involved in friendship would be free to share in a way that the absence of the other would prevent:

---

140 See Honneth 2014b, pp. 134–38, 141–50, and 154–62.
141 See Zurn 2015, pp. 174–76.

> The complementary role obligations that define friendship today enable the mutual display of feelings, attitudes and intentions that would find no expression without a concrete other, and thus could not be experienced as something capable of being expressed. So much do we take for granted this experience of having our will 'freed' in friendly conversation and togetherness that we can hardly use the term 'freedom' to describe it, even though it is the only term that explains our primary interest in cultivating friendships, and that captures the place of friendship occupies within our social life (Honneth 2014b, p. 139).

> When it comes to friendship, being with oneself in the other means entrusting one's own desires in all their diffuseness and tentativeness to another person without compulsion or fear (Honneth 2014b, p. 140).

It is clear that, in these cases, "other" does not represent a potential limit or obstacle, but rather a condition of freedom, which above all concerns the possibility of entering into a relationship with oneself, thus expressing a greater familiarity with one's inner contents. Besides a certain form of expressionism—according to which a non-reified attitude toward one's inner contents consists in considering them as givennesses worthy of expression[142]—such types of relationality would favor forms of ego-boundary dissolution that Honneth considers as means and manifestations of inner vitality and freedom, rather than irrational regression.[143] In general, one could say that the "balance between boundary-establishment and boundary-dissolution" (Honneth 1995c, p. 106) is at the heart of the relationship between infant and caregiver as described in *The Struggle for Recognition*. Hence, one might say that the key idea regarding social freedom within personal relationships is precisely disclosing one's own frailty and vulnerability, thus handing them over in the presence of another, thanks to whom the dissolution of egoic boundaries is not perceived as a potential threat. Therefore, the possibilities of self-relationship constituted by these forms of social freedom concern the demolition of egoic rigidity and the acceptance of one's own vulnerability or self-insufficiency, according to three dimensions: inner contents (friendship), corporeity (intimate relationships), and the finiteness of life (family).

Intimate relationships, which have been shaped throughout history by an ever-increasing unilateralization of affection as the basic reason for their existence—even though, unlike friendship, they are more consistently structured by a legal framework—are built on a temporal community between two partners who can identify with such a relational structure: "such a self-reinforcing history of a retrospective 'We'" represents "a crucial element of love" (Honneth 2014b, p. 147). However, the distinctive factor for which they can be considered a form of ethical life concerns the physical-sexual dimension:

> What distinguishes love from all forms of friendship and what makes it a unique form of personal attachment is the mutual desire for sexual intimacy and the comprehensive pleasure in the

---

142 See Honneth 2008, pp. 67–75.
143 See Honneth 2009a.

other's physicality. There is no other place, perhaps with the exception of the intensive care unit or rest homes, where the human body is so socially present in all its uncontrollable independence and fragility as it is in the sexual interactions of two loving partners (Honneth 2014b, p. 147).

To be with oneself in another therefore means to regain, in the intimacy of love, one's natural incompleteness through bodily communication, without having to fear that this could compromise or hurt us. The moral rules implicitly in force today in the loving relationship aim to guarantee mutual trust or confidence, which allows us to reveal ourselves physically in front of a concrete other. Also in this case, freedom from fear is the essential element of the We of personal relationships: only trust in the other who encourages and approves allows one to expose oneself in all its most intimate vulnerability. Such depiction of the bodily dimension lets us grasp the deep connection with *The Struggle for Recognition*: the polarity of love and physical violence.

Moving on to the third institutionalized context of intersubjective freedom, the first distinctive element in comparison to friendship and intimate relationships consists of the fact that "families represent triadic rather than dyadic relationships" (Honneth 2014b, p. 154), that is, the triangular relation parent-parent-child (or children). Honneth argues that, from the decay of the model centered on children's obedience and on a rigid division of roles between parents, families today possess a degree of intersubjective discursiveness and equality no longer comparable with the image it offered at the beginning of modernity. Also, in the relationship with children, an orientation toward confrontation, rather than control, becomes more and more possible. Honneth thus reads the formation of "multi-locational cross-generational families [*multilokale Mehrgenerationenfamilie*]" (Honneth 2014b, p. 162) as result of the increasing divorce rates, in the continuity of natural relationships between parents and children even at the end of partnerships, and in the maintenance of ties between the generations even in geographical distance. Contrary to friendships and intimate relationships, family relationships would show a resistance to dislocations and temporality: "Parent-child relationships are not only legally and normatively interminable, in the last fifty years they have even undergone a process of 'structural solidification,' making them the central focus of the life-long attentiveness and concern of the parents" (Honneth 2014b, p. 163). The moral core of this institution must be grasped in the greater communicative understanding required by the relations, in the greater equality among its members and in the fact that the union is generated exclusively by an affection that does not require external factors to be realized. Honneth thus outlines a model in which conflict and power relations within the family seem to have no place, based on the persuasion that like never before families have become a free social concretion, both from the external point of view of the legal guarantees for different forms of family "(married/unmarried parents, biological/'social' children, heterosexual/homosexual parents)" (Honneth 2014b, p. 163) and from the internal one of the confrontation of the various members, centered on the dedication to the other.

This position can, of course, be criticized in many respects. First, according to Foster, Honneth fails to take into account the constitutive role played by socio-economic factors in the formation of contemporary families.[144] According to this criticism, Honneth is not able to avoid a certain idealism or, at least, naivety, even if he refers to social phenomena such as relationships' fluidification or to the time subtracted from family intimacy by the division of labor.[145] But moreover, Honneth does not seem to take into consideration that today's families, rather than having become pure relations justified only on the basis of mutual affection and care, are constituted by pervasive systemic processes that are less coercive than in past ages, but equally binding. And it was precisely the first generation of the Frankfurt School that claimed that families had been disjointed and reformulated under the imperatives of a capillary domination.[146] On the liberal side, proposing what seems a certain model of family would represent a to substantive account for a theory of justice.[147] Precisely because the one Honneth presents is *a* family model, he thus also excludes different types of family and therefore different modernities from his normative reconstruction.[148]

In response to the first criticism, one could respond by appealing to the resources Honneth explicitly provides in *The Struggle for Recognition* and, I argue, more implicitly in *Freedom's Right*. The fact that the critical method is no longer justified in anthropological terms does not mean that the anthropological and phylogenetic contribution of recognition should be set aside—keeping in mind its normative significance, though. This level is simply left in the background in *Freedom's Right*, but it is not absent.[149] In fact, the whole of Honneth's discourse about personal relationships is centered on the vulnerability and inadequacy of the individual. The primacy of intersubjectivity over subjectivity cannot but result in a certain normative positivity attributed to the phenomenological forms in which this antecedence manifests itself. Thompson correctly indicates that the reference to Mead is the cause of a general disregard of the close interconnection between socialization and domination by the last generations of the Frankfurt School,[150] whereby social integration could also be considered as homologation, but one that triggers the fundamental I-me polarity and that represents an unavoidable condition of self-relation. From this point of view, however, the non-consideration of the infant-caregiver relation represents a shortcoming in *Freedom's Right*, where the relationship between parents and children is

---

[144] See Foster 2017, p. 458.
[145] See Honneth 2014b, pp. 151–52 and 163.
[146] See Thompson 2014, pp. 783–86.
[147] See Piromalli 2012, p. 275.
[148] See van den Brink 2013, p. 26.
[149] See Horn 2018, p. 27; and Busen, Herzog, and Sörensen 2012, p. 265.
[150] See Thompson 2015, p. 157.

described in a more mutual way to avoid the difficult implications that the difference between symmetry and reciprocity pose to the concept of recognition itself. As far as the liberal criticism is concerned, the model offered by Honneth seems, on the one hand, to be sufficiently broad and comprehensive to be able to respond to a sociological datum that is present in western societies and, on the other hand, capable of understanding other perspectives on the family. Moreover, he underlines that families do not represent "a biological constant of human history" (Honneth 2014b, p. 155), and therefore should be considered only as institutional concretions, therefore porous and open to further evolutions and modifications.

Beyond these considerations, the possibility of being with oneself in the other in the family relations thus configured would be articulated, once again, as overcoming of one's own boundaries. In particular, Honneth finds the distinctive element of family relationships in the instantiation of parent's love in the child, and in the possibility of the child to be reflected in them. Nowadays more than ever before, given the multigenerational permanence of these relationships, the "core of this mutual mirroring" would concern "the temporal dimension of human life, in its biological course as a whole" (Honneth 2014b, p. 170). Moreover, children and parents "reflect for each other the life phases that are either past or still to come," thus gaining a sense "of the uncontrollable element of their own biologically determined lives" (Honneth 2014b, p. 170).

But even if such experiences would be decisive, the ethical core, that is, the experience of social freedom of the family is represented by *play* and the related "experimental role-switching" (Honneth 2014b, p. 171):

> In both directions, this dedifferentiation at work not only in the family members' imaginations, but also in their practical interaction with each other, represents a kind of emancipation, because it enables them to take a more relaxed perspective on the periodicity of our organic life and suspend it for the duration of their play with each other. In these moments, we can move forwards and backwards in our organic existence as if our external and inner nature imposed no limits upon us (Honneth 2014b, p. 171).

It thus clearly emerges that it is not enough to say that personal relations represent the possibility of expressing one's inner nature,[151] since such statements regarding playing and mutual mirroring of parents and children profoundly relate to the fading of ego's boundaries into an approving intersubjectivity, also as far as organic life, loneliness and death are concerned.[152] Then, if "freedom signifies our experi-

---

151 See Zurn 2015, pp. 173 and 186.
152 "This is not to say that this caring return to the start of the parents' life can remove the solitude and fear surrounding death, but perhaps this peculiar force of de-realization [*Derealisierung*] can create the healing and consoling illusion that our life within the circle of the family will return to its beginning and thus find a proper conclusion. If we see an element of freedom here, a measure of relief from the oppressive solitude and fear of death, then this is also due to the intersubjective practices that were initially institutionalized in the modern family. This has become one of the few places

ence of being free from coercion, of unfolding our personality" (Honneth 2014b, p. 61), it clearly emerges that the very sense of social freedom appears in the depiction of personal relations.[153] In fact, here the coincidence between modes of relationship and self-relationship is almost without discontinuity—with the risk, however, of providing an all too idealized image. However, it is evident that in personal relationships it is only the presence of others that can satisfy the need to complement our actions and goals: freedom coincides with the mutual satisfaction of inherent normative role tasks, which the involved subject must be able to master.[154] Within friendship, the individual can explore and express his or her inner contents, even the most indefinite: in love it is free because its own corporal vulnerability is exposed to the other without fear; within the family—and especially in the relationship with children—the subject is freed from anguish in virtually transcending even its organic boundaries.

However, one problematic aspect is the fact that all these relations are dyadic. It is true that families are described in terms of triangular relationships, but the reduction of this institution to the parents-child(ren) polarity seems to make the third collapse on the I-Thou. On the one hand, this would represent an utopian deficit on the part of Honneth, which would not consider present forms of non-monogamic love and relations.[155] On the other hand, it is a sociological deficit, which in turn can be divided into two levels: first, he does not consider groups of friends, which are no less significant precisely because of the factors that Honneth himself highlights with regard to friendship. Second, the exclusive consideration of duality in personal relationships would prevent us from taking into consideration the role of the third point of view in the constitution of the social spheres and the socialization of the participants.[156]

4.3.2.2 The Market (Society)
Moving on to the second ethical sphere, which, following the model proposed by Hegel in the *Philosophy of Right*, is identified in the *market*, Honneth immediately raises the question of how it could be possible to pinpoint here a dimension of social freedom, given the evident distortions that the neoliberal deregulation of the global economy brings with it. Indeed, since its birth, the capitalist market has been considered a fierce promoter of negative freedom, and therefore a place of unbridled competition, whereby "exclusively purposive-rational, self-interested calculations seemed to free this system from any individual considerateness or value-orienta-

---
where subjects can receive secular consolation, since they are able, at least in their imaginations, to see themselves as a part of an eternal whole" (Honneth 2014b, p. 172).
153 See Horn 2018, p. 29.
154 See Pedersen 2015, pp. 253 and 258–59.
155 See M. T. C. Shafer 2008.
156 See Strydom 2013, p. 541.

4.3 Being with Oneself in the Other: Social Freedom in Modern Societies — 179

tions" (Honneth 2014b, p. 179), thus causing "a spreading intellectual disquiet about" its "social consequences" (Honneth 2014b, p. 180). Two particular problems seemed to occupy the understanding of the capitalist market during the seventeenth and eighteenth centuries: the Adam Smith problem and the Marx problem. On the one hand, we need to explain whether and how the spontaneous harmonization of all individual aims according to the so-called invisible hand model is possible; on the other hand, market seems a context in which not only social freedom, but also negative freedom would not be guaranteed, since workers, because of exploitation, low wages and so on, would not have genuine contractual alternatives. The identification of areas of social freedom must therefore be able to answer this twofold question: how market coordination becomes conceivable and what standards should the latter respect in order to provide worthy conditions for its participants. The path Honneth takes is defined as moral economism.

Drawing from Hegel and Durkheim, Honneth argues that systemic integration as described by Adam Smith would not be comprehensible without forms of normative integration, that is "without taking account of an antecedent class of non-contractual moral rules" (Honneth 2014b, p. 181) that regulate the market and legitimize its interactions in the eyes of the participants. Not unlike what he already claimed in *Redistribution or Recognition?*, Honneth binds the economic to norms of (not only legal) recognition, which would be necessary for social actors considering themselves as "members of a cooperative community". In other words, according to this view "an antecedent sense of solidarity" (Honneth 2014b, p. 182), that is, a reciprocal recognition already operating among the subjects, represents the central feature of market's being an institutional actualization of social freedom:

> There is an intrinsic connection between the conditions of competition on the market and the norms of the lifeworld, because market competition can only be viewed as legitimate and justified on the condition that it take these norms into account…. [D]ifferent markets must be able to reflect the rules prevailing outside the market to a certain degree in order to be able to fulfil their function of coordinating economic action. If this reflection on the prevailing, generally accepted norms no longer takes place, then we can expect not only a disruption of the market mechanism itself, but also a subtle or publicly articulated withdrawal of legitimacy on the part of the population (Honneth 2014b, p. 191).

Via normative reconstruction, Honneth therefore aims to unearth the stages through which and in which the idea has been affirmed on the part of the participants, that the market could (or should) represent "a suitable means for the complementary realization of their own respective purposes" (Honneth 2014b, p. 192). In other words, focusing on social contexts that are aware of the constitutive role played by antecedent non-contractual forms of recognition allows one to respond to the Adam Smith problem and to the Marx problem. Concerning the first, comprehending the market as a cooperative sphere on the part of participants would clarify how the individual purposes are harmonized; concerning the latter, if the market appears as a cooperative sphere, constituted by relations of solidarity (and therefore of recognition), then such explicitly moral and social founded market would be able to guarantee contractual freedom and the right to human labor. Honneth's reconstruction takes the sphere of consumption and the labor market into account, rather than *the* market in the strict sense. That is, the perspective of normative integration does not consist in focusing on how the economy actually functions, but rather on the normative conditions that accompany (or constitute) its reproduction.[157]

As far as the sphere of consumption is concerned, Honneth draws his arguments from Hegel's system of needs, thus insisting on the reciprocal interactions that are required between producers and consumers in order to make the market function. Hence, the aim is to find an answer to the Adam Smith problem, thus providing normative criteria that could clarify how an individuals' purposes find a coordination within the market. Through the reconstruction, which focuses primarily on protest movements and social conflicts, such as bread riots, for example, Honneth tries to show the dependence of the system on the lifeworld: more properly, he proceeds by identifying the limits that moral norms impose on goods exchange through discursive communities and legal reforms. Four normative criteria are then distilled in order to show the market's non-independence on the non-contractual cooperative horizon.

First, "it is not at all self-evident which objects or services should be permitted to be exchangeable commodities at all" (Honneth 2014b, p. 209). Today, perhaps more than ever, there are many moral issues raised by the commodification of certain categories of goods. In addition to the blatant cases of human trafficking or the organ market, surrogacy and prostitution often raise many issues, as they could not, or should not, represent something that can be bought. Beyond the commodification of the human being, the sale of products such as drugs, weapons, and counterfeits is also strictly regulated by legal measures. Second, the pricing of certain goods is almost never abandoned to an absolute deregulation. Third, Honneth argues that different voices—religion, socialism, and ecologism—question "how extensive, luxurious or private the needs satisfied on the general market for goods should be" (Honneth 2014b, p. 209). Finally, in the nineteenth century, with the spread of cooperative systems, the mode of purchase and consumption also changed, because they were no longer conceived as the prerogative of the individual buyer, but rather of solidarity communities. Through these criteria, Honneth not only shows that all the elements of the demand and supply mechanism—products, prices, consumption, and purchase—hinge on normative rules, but he also highlights the fact that such limiting factors are determined through and within solidarity spheres of complementarity and recognition.

But the identification of such normative criteria also allows the critical detection of misdevelopments within this sphere of cooperation. Since the 1950s, an "increasing atomization of the consumer" (Honneth 2014b, p. 212) more easily made in-

---

[157] See Arentshorst 2015, p. 140.

dividuals object of market imperatives through the imposition of pre-given models, disguised as means of greater individual freedom. In fact, this individualistic fragmentation prevents the development of discursive mechanisms, places of negotiation, and spaces for discussion that already in the nineteenth century contributed to creating oases of social freedom in the sphere of consumption. Nowadays, a "moralization of the market from below" is therefore almost inconceivable (Honneth 2014b, p. 220), since every possible area of cooperative coordination between consumers seems to have dissolved due to dynamics—that of market itself—that, however, have no room for justification in Honneth's text, and therefore remain as mere observations of fact. In fact, all that relates to the prevalence of systemic integration or strategic orientations seem to be generated by and within an indeterminate and unexplained sphere,[158] which certainly is beyond the sphere of consumer cooperation and the sphere of labor.

Labor market represents the second dimension Honneth analyses, by which the recognition principles of respect (labor contract) and, primarily, esteem (contribution) constitute a fundamental feature of social freedom. If the reconstruction of the consumption market has aimed at providing normative criteria through which it is possible to respond to the Adam Smith problem, here the aim is to unearth resources to outline a theory of justice capable to answer to the problem posed by Marx —that is, unjust labor and exploitation—caused by "structural problems" and resulting in "social deformations" (Honneth 2014b, p. 223). Honneth's reconstruction focuses precisely on such elements, depicting the discomforting picture of working conditions and counter-movements.[159] Conversely, the model proposed by moral economism would strongly insist on the institutionalization of cooperative entities and their normative role within the market. Honneth's analysis then focuses on social concretions that possess many similarities with Hegel's account of corporations:

> the establishment of social freedom in this sphere, that is, the expansion of the labour market into a 'relational institution,' demands that it be institutionally equipped with discursive mechanisms that allow participants to influence the interests of the others and thus gradually give shape to the overall cooperative aims of the group. On both sides, wage labourers and employers, institutional rules must take effect that can anchor the social, cooperative meaning of economic activity in the minds of the participants (Honneth 2014b, pp. 231–32).

Honneth's reconstruction then focuses on social welfare measures aimed at improving working conditions, which were from the very beginning characterized by a certain ambiguity. If, on the one hand, they reduced the length of the work day and increased the basic forms of protections and guarantees (paid sick leaves, injury insurances, and so on), the unilateralization of these measures in the form of individual legal rights, on the other hand, has immediately compromised the possibility

---

[158] See Piromalli 2012, p. 278.
[159] See Honneth 2014b, pp. 223–29.

of realizing those relational areas of cooperative management that represent the nucleus of social freedom. The consequent individualization of the worker was exacerbated by Taylor's Scientific management system, production chains, and the emerging of the employee as professional figure. In this context, trade unions have never succeeded in their task of humanizing labor's conditions, also because their role was seriously diminished by the increased intervention of state welfare. Moreover, Honneth claims that, after WWII, welfare weakened collective drives that could have achieved social freedom in work. The last stage of the normative reconstruction consists in the deregulation processes, which leads us to the analysis of the present time, which is clearly outlined as a *misdevelopment:*

> Under the increasing pressures of globalization, political actors began to change their economic interpretations and policies, calling for lower taxes and fewer regulations on the financial markets; at the same time, the composition of the stock exchange was dramatically altered by the fact that a growing number of large institutional investors had taken the stage, marginalizing the more passive small investors and, with the aid of their widespread investments, pushing for rapid returns. Furthermore, intensifying sales competition on the world market drove many companies to restructure for the sake of maintaining their competitiveness, economizing on wages and production at the cost of the employees. Finally, the demand for company executives underwent a qualitative shift, placing less and less weight on a manager's experience within the company or on traditional management values, instead looking for purely 'objective' financial knowledge (Honneth 2014b, p. 245).

The picture appears even more disconcerting when one considers the demands for biographical flexibility that push individuals to conceive themselves as isolated from each other and to reify themselves in the consideration of their own attitudes and characteristics. Yet, this condition, considered almost universally unjust, does not provoke collective indignation or widespread protests, which would virtually represent a first step to subvert these dynamics. Thus, an emancipatory interest in the Habermasian sense is not at hand. The absence of a public dimension of conflict would show the definitive eclipse—at least up to now—of the possibilities for the realization of social freedom in the world of labor: in fact, not only has the possibility of organizing production cooperatively been precluded over time, but the very self-perception of individuals seems to have been totally atomized:

> Conscience seemed to dictate that the market should be understood as an institution of social freedom. If it is true, for which there are many indications, that over the last few decades the responsibility for success in the market economy has been strongly individualized, such that it is no longer 'we,' but *he* or *she* who is responsible for his or her own economic success, then this would suggest that precisely this background normative conviction has been abandoned (Honneth 2014b, p. 250).

It therefore seems that a marked pessimism represents the inevitable downside of normative reconstruction. However, Honneth, as he did in *Redistribution or Recognition?*, emphasizes the submerged version that the rejection of this state of affairs can take on in the contemporary context: the need to anchor critical theory to emancipa-

4.3 Being with Oneself in the Other: Social Freedom in Modern Societies — 183

tory interests must not be bound to their public manifestations.[160] Nevertheless, such mentioning of implicit conflict seems to be, more than an attempt to take moral suffering and hidden moralities as a founding factor for critique, the ascertainment of a misdeveloped outcome of the extreme individualization taking place in the neo-liberal labor market. But if normative integration were taken seriously, then these singular gestures of rejection would also already represent the germs delegitimization, even if minimal. Honneth identifies more solid ground is identified once again in cooperative forms of market limitation, namely, "transnational unions and non-governmental organizations" (Honneth 2014b, p. 253): they represent a possible way through which conflict for the affirmation of social freedom in waged work can be articulated. Their attempt to affirm the justice of freedom in the context of globalization, however, is only a feeble hope.

As we focus on the critical potential of Honneth's proposal, a series of interwoven problems emerges. First, the fact that Honneth does "not want to merely reduce the market to economic transactions in the narrow sense" (Honneth 2014b, p. 202) would lead his critical theory to overlook the systemic factors that should be its actual targets. In other words, rather than being a criticism of the capitalist market and its global mechanisms, it seems to expose the normative resources external to it. This would be evident in the fact that most of the phenomena described as causes or consequences of misdevelopments originate outside the discursive and cooperative contexts of social freedom. Strategic interests, productive efficiency, systemic mechanisms, economic hierarchies, financial capital, and so on are taken into account by the normative reconstruction but remain untouched as a critical theme. In fact, unlike personal relationships, in which Honneth dealt with certain types of relationships and the rules within them that subjects must be able to master to live social freedom, as far as the market is concerned, the relationships considered are not economic, but of solidarity or esteem within certain groups.[161] But then one could wonder: in what sense would the normative criteria and the norms of recognition be inherent to *the* market? One could say that they are external to the market in the strict sense, but internal to a broad conception of it or, as Honneth himself says in a later interview, to the market society.[162] In this way, Honneth's position would have the advantage of questioning the abstract view according to which the market is a sphere without agents,[163] thus de-naturalizing and de-reifying its so-called laws.[164] Moreover, showing the market's embeddedness to a (phenomenological) priority of moral interactions between subjects would avoid proposing a miniature proceduralism, according to which the criteria of justification and criticism should be elaborat-

---

160 See Honneth 2014b, p. 247.
161 See Pedersen 2015, pp. 258–59.
162 See Laitinen 2016, p. 277; Honneth and Raffnsøe-Møller 2015, p. 278.
163 See Busen, Herzog, and Sörensen 2012, p. 250.
164 See Arentshorst 2015, p. 142.

ed outside of the market and subsequently applied to it. That would impede an internal critique.

However, the institutionalization of the market would not represent a solution per se. That the possibilities of social critique coincide, according to Honneth, with a re-inclusion of the market in social institutions reveals a further shortcoming, namely, the lack of understanding of the fact that today the market is already strongly institutionalized,[165] both from the legislative and political point of view, and in terms of its pervasive influence in daily practices, models of life, etc.: in other words, due to its constitutive power.[166] Faced with this criticism, Honneth would probably answer that it is not the dynamics of institutionalization itself that enables critical theory, but rather *certain* institutionalizations—those related to social freedom—would provide necessary anchors to emancipatory interests and thus to intramundane transcendence. The decisive issue, then, is that of the position of social freedom within the market.

This further problem would not concern normative integration or the fact that the market owes—to some extent—its existence to norms and values. The point is: can we talk about the market as a sphere of social freedom? Even if Honneth takes the market as a model of moral economism, Hegel considers civil society as sphere of particular interests, where ethical life is essentially being removed.[167] Moreover, corporations and the administration of justice represent forms of ethical life outside the market itself, whose purpose is precisely to limit the disintegration that would otherwise be inevitable. Following Honneth's terminology, the market would be a sphere of negative and moral freedoms, while social freedom could be attested only in subsystems that somehow interact with (or against) the economy. This description would fit perfectly with Honneth's analysis of consumer associations or trade unions: even if they belong to the market, their attempts are to limit its own mechanisms.[168] However, Honneth seems to tell us, the demands raised by such groups would reveal a certain understanding of the market on the part of its participants, which would have no reason to be if the market itself did not somehow reveal a normative promise of social freedom. The very fact that protests about bread pricing and collective demonstrations about fair work take place would therefore reveal how the market should be, that is, its normative embeddedness. If there were no such (implicit) self-understanding, the emerging of these expectations would not be explainable. In order to consider the protests of those who have called for more social freedom within the market justified, one must consider the market, even to a minimal extent, as a possible source of social freedom. Otherwise, to give a rather trivial example, one could compare these normative demands to complaining that a goldfish does not speak three languages correctly, that is to say, attributing to it

---

[165] See Foster 2017, p. 460.
[166] See Thompson 2015, p. 154.
[167] See Hegel, *Philosophy of Right*, § 184.
[168] See Jütten 2015, pp. 194–96.

a deficit with respect to a standard that it is not in its potential to satisfy. If market is intrinsically unjust, it would make no sense to expect justice from it.

With respect to this position, two further problems arise. On the one hand, protests could be interpreted as a symptom of the injustice of the economic system, and not of its fundamental capability to respond to normative demands, that is, to be a sphere of social freedom.[169] The protests would therefore be motivated by the intrinsic defect of the market, which—in addition to generating systematic exclusion—would be essentially a sphere of instrumental reason alone. Moreover, if the contents of the demands are all but economic, then it seems more plausible that they represent a limitation from outside rather than an attempt to actualize the inner nature of the market.[170] On the other hand, the fact that social actors are persuaded that the market can represent a sphere of social freedom could be the result of ideological patterns.[171] And because of that the related normative self-understanding should not represent a starting point for the social critical theory, but rather its object. In fact, how could the participants disagree with the basic norms of the market if they are socialized through them?[172]

These two questions, therefore, concern how social freedom can be considered inherent to the market (and not a reaction to it) and whether the first premise of normative reconstruction can be taken into consideration. To make the problem even sharper, Honneth states in one passage that "in modern Western European societies there has always been a confrontation between two views of the market, whose differences can be measured in terms of whether they grasp the market as a social institution that enables either the mutual satisfaction of interests or individual advantage" (Honneth 2014b, p. 249). One could therefore wonder what instruments Honneth possesses to read the current neoliberal market as a misdeveloped sphere of social freedom and not as a full-fledged sphere of negative freedom and productive efficiency:[173] apart from an anthropological justification that poses the centrality of social freedom because of its capacity, through relations of recognition, to meet individuals' need for complementarity, or an action-theoretical justification, according to which social freedom should be preferred over other forms due to its capability of actualizing autonomy, *Freedom's Right* does not seem to provide other justifying elements. The problem, as we will see at the end of the chapter, is that Honneth rejects both these possibilities, embracing a sociological justification.

---

169 See Borman 2019, p. 116.
170 See Jütten 2015, pp. 197–98.
171 See Borman 2019, p. 115.
172 See Gregory R. Smulewicz-Zucker 2019, pp. 130–31.
173 See Jütten 2015; and Busen, Herzog, and Sörensen 2012, p. 261.

4.3.2.3 Democratic Public and Constitutional Democracy

In the last section of *Freedom's Right* Honneth elaborates a theory of democracy that deviates both from Hegel's view on state and from those that are predominant in the contemporary scenario. Thus, Honneth rejects a model that subsumes the subject into universality through the transition from horizontal to vertical relations, and the various proceduralist models centered on a liberal and deliberative paradigm. We could say that Honneth's third way is instantiated through the theory's social proximity: the analysis of democracy is primarily an analysis of democratic *society*, which represents the first fundamental element of the third sphere. The second element appears, in Honneth's view, as normatively subordinate to the first, that is, the constitutional democratic state should be dependent on democratic society. Such dependency of the state on society is also shown as a dialectical relationship of this last sphere with the previous ones:

> If the conditions of social freedom are not realized in personal relationships and on the market, then the social relations that enable citizens to take part in the process of democratic will-formation in an unforced and unrestricted manner will be absent. Therefore, in contrast to most contemporary theories of democracy, we should not view the political public sphere as a kind of supreme court, regulated by the rule of law, which freely determines the conditions to be established in the other two spheres. The relationship between these three spheres is far more complex, because the realization of social freedom in the democratic public sphere depends at the very least on the partial realization of the principles of social freedom in the spheres of personal relationships and the market. From the very beginning, therefore, deliberative will-formation in the many different forums of the public sphere is bounded; the latter can only live up to its principles of legitimacy if it learns, in a process of continuous debate over the conditions of social inclusion, the necessity of supporting struggles for social freedom in the two other spheres (Honneth 2014b, pp. 254–55).

Honneth's aim is thus to outline a theory of democracy that could be sufficiently abstract but not without adherence to social life, suitable with respect to issues of pluralism but not proceduralist, pre-institutional (according to the daily understanding of the term) but not unpolitical. In other words, a conception of democracy whose essential fabric is constituted by recognition and communicative relations. The dialectical relationship between the three ethical spheres is perhaps more immediately comprehensible regarding the state's initiative concerning economy and personal relationships—especially the family—via legislative measures. But if one tries to understand the other direction of these dialectical process—from intimate relationships and economy to the state—the matter becomes more complex. On the one hand, it seems counterintuitive to think that the exclusive relationships characterized by affection can influence a democratic ethical life.[174] On the other hand, Honneth is well

---

174 See van den Brink 2013, pp. 23–24.

aware of the correlation between economics and politics.[175] In fact, besides the pivotal role played by Dewey, the misdevelopments highlighted within the third sphere could be summarized under the common denominator of an interference of undemocratic structures in the sphere of peer debate. Both these relations—personal relations-democracy and economy-democracy—are issues that have engaged Honneth since *The Struggle for Recognition*.

Personal relationships enable a self-relation—self-confidence or inner freedom—that is perceived by Honneth as a necessary condition for the development of an undamaged practical identity. This would also reverberate in the public dimension, where persons could unfold freely and responsibly only to the extent that they live a certain security with regard to their own consistency, of which they can experience only thanks recognition relationships.[176] In a nutshell, the relationship between individual and public life would not differ—with due proportion—from the experience of the child who can try her hand at playing only when she is aware of a caregiver's approving presence. It goes without saying that self-confidence is not the only condition at stake for public participation, but this role played by personal relationships also sheds light on the more general view of democracy Honneth describes: the person is always conceived as multidimensional, whereby the private level cannot be detached from the legal-political and the social ones.[177]

Concerning the relationship between economy and democracy, in "Democracy as Reflexive Cooperation," Honneth identifies social division of labor as indispensable basis for formulating a model of democracy that is equally distant from republicanism and proceduralism. Perhaps more evidently than in *Freedom's Right*, the ideal democracy proposed here principally represents a critique of liberal models, that is, of their conception of autonomy and social deficiency. First, in this text, Honneth also believes that the flaw of liberal perspectives consists mainly in the failure to realize that "it is only in the medium of an interaction free from domination that each individual's freedom is to be attained and protected" (Honneth 1998, p. 766), that is, in social freedom. The second problem with liberalism consists in its purely political description of democracy, which is read as an institutional set of procedural practices. The unavoidable issue that such theories face is then their inability to take into account the collapse of democratic participation, which is due to the increased social

---

175 See Smulewicz-Zucker 2019, pp. 125–26. One could certainly discuss the alleged insufficiency of Honneth's view regarding the economic structures and power systems that are at work in them. And one could also argue that the truly problematic element is the disregard of the formative power of such structures in relation to subjectivity. While I admit that such objections could be discussed in turn, I believe that the analysis of the democratic sphere is the one in which Honneth gives more space to power systems of non-democratic matrix. The problem then becomes, if anything, how such systems can be included in his critical theory without re-proposing a Habermasian dualism. As I see it, this is the main problem that arises in *Freedom's Right*, also regarding the sphere of market.
176 See Honneth 1995c, pp. 38 and 107; Honneth 2009a; and Honneth 2009c.
177 See Lysaker 2017, pp. 3–5.

differentiation, ethical pluralism, and, more generally, the lack of aim-oriented coordination among subjects within wide cooperation contexts; thus, the role of the state seems confined to that of a bureaucratic administrator:[178] "under the conditions of complex industrialized societies, the revival of democratic publics presupposes a reintegration of society that can only consist in the development of a common consciousness for the prepolitical association of all citizens" (Honneth 1998, p. 776). Following Dewey, Honneth's attempt is to define a model of democratic state as a reflexive body through which society faces collective problems, thus deriving the political from the social. The starting point of such a perspective is a just division of labor, which obviously does not coincide with a reduction of social reality to production cycles, but rather with the consideration of those areas of social recognition related to individual contribution to the aims of all interaction partners. Through an operation that could seem a reduction of the society (*Gesellschaft*) to the community (*Gemeinschaft*), Honneth intends to unearth the formal dynamics that could establish a formal and democratic (indeed social) ethical life, that is, a theory of justice. However, one could say that cooperation and the division of labor, in order to be *just*, need a certain idea of justice, which cannot be the result of the division itself.[179] For this very reason, I believe, Honneth emphasizes the dialectical relationship between the spheres and between the principles of justice and the relations of recognition: one could say that the link between theory and analysis of society prevents thinking of a first element that grounds everything else. Again, drawing from Dewey, Honneth argues that the fact of cooperation represents a paradigm of joint problem-solving that, once extended, generalized, and formalized, can outline a socially informed model of democracy. Conversely, such problem solving is not conceivable if it is not always already embedded in large societies.

By considering democracy as reflexive moment through which public issues are addressed, three distinct needs are met: entailing the participation of citizens, outlining a third way between republicanism and proceduralism, and disclosing the possibilities of critical theory. With regard to the first issue, and besides the personal integrity conditions provided by recognition relations, the central matter is represented by what could be called an 'all-affected principle':[180]

> Social action unfolds in forms of interaction whose consequences in the simple case affect only those immediately involved; but as soon as those not involved see themselves affected by the consequences of such interaction, there emerges from their perspective the need for joint control of the corresponding actions either by their cessation or by their promotion. This articulation of the demand for joint problem-solving already constitutes for Dewey that which he will henceforth call "public": ... a "public" consists of the circle of citizens who, on the basis of a jointly experienced concern, share the conviction that they have to turn to the rest of society for the purposes of administratively controlling the relevant interaction (Honneth 1998, p. 774).

---

178 See Zurn 2005, pp. 94–95.
179 See Ferrara 1998, pp. 33–34.
180 See Honneth 1998; and Honneth 2014b, pp. 104–13.

4.3 Being with Oneself in the Other: Social Freedom in Modern Societies — 189

In order to shape a meaningful connection between social cooperation and democratic self-determination, Dewey postulates the need for cognitive elements such that social actors are aware of their being affected by the consequences of decisions taken at the political level, even if they are not directly involved. In this way, he outlines the motivational prerequisite for democratic participation. All potentially affected subjects would be encouraged to participate in democratic discussion, to the extent that it would be perceived as a collective problem-solving process.

If the difference between Honneth's argument and proceduralism is clear—since the criteria for justice can already be found in social reality—what distinguishes such a view from republicanism is more subtle. What Honneth criticizes about such theories is that they at least implicitly prioritize *a certain* identity before others. But, at first impression, the same issue arises from Honneth's depiction of the cooperation of communities: he would prefer a certain idea of the good and then widen it to the level of society. However, we should stress that Dewey's idea considers the plurality of ethical points of view as enriching collective problem-solving: the matter at issue is not a determinate conception of good life, but rather social coordination.

Although perhaps too strongly characterized by cognitivist views, the democratic form of life described in "Democracy as Reflexive Cooperation" primarily has the aim of showing the emergence of the political from the social, from the interaction, from the mutual relations of recognition, confirmation, and esteem. Thus, to describe democracy as a solution to collective problems does not coincide with the simple expansion of an epistemic model. Rather, Honneth's aim is to outline a model of democracy in which the person can know herself as already included member, involved with respect to her responsibility and her capability to contribute to joint will-formation. Moreover, as Honneth aims to demonstrate by his normative reconstruction, such collective will-formation processes would not be mere speculation, but possess historical grip, at least as normative promise entailed in the very concept of democracy.

And it is precisely by means of such a conception of democratic public sphere that Honneth depicts the third ethical sphere of social freedom in *Freedom's Right*. As such, he distils and analyzes six conditions for being with oneself in the other of the social totality of citizens, the We of democracy.

The first condition is represented by the legal measures that have been guaranteed for the formation of the bourgeois public sphere since the eighteenth century. Indeed, Honneth considers rights of association, assembly, and freedom of opinion and speech as propaedeutic and inherent to the political exercise. They outline the domain of exchange and discursive confrontation with others within which persons can recognize each other as endowed with equal rights and dignity. Thus, the central issue is represented by the complementary roles of speaker and listener, who, recognizing themselves as such, together formulate opinions and judgments on what concerns them as citizens: democracy would then not be—at least in the first instance—a legislative-institutional structure, but lifeworld practice. Thus, the joint solution of collective problems would not represent the stylization of a technical problem-solving, but properly a judging and debating arena.

The second condition hence coincides with the democratization of this arena, which historically entailed the increased role of media and the widening of political rights to collective self-determination:

> Dewey uses the term 'democratic public' to describe the totality of all the communicative processes that enable the members of 'large societies' with the help of the news media to take up the perspective of such a 'We' while judging the consequences of their actions. It constitutes a form of social freedom by enabling the individuals, in communication with all the other members of society, to improve their own living conditions (Honneth 2014b, p. 274).

In the course of historical evolution, Honneth observes, the extension of the scope of affected persons was immediately disclosed by the idea of nation, which, despite its *ambiguity* due to its exclusionary asset, represented an undeniable "source of the sentiments of solidarity required to commit otherwise different citizens to the common task of public deliberation" (Honneth 2014b, p. 266). Such ambiguity of the *demos* would appear in the 1894 Dreyfus affair: the idea of *Volk*, often fixed also in biological and not only cultural terms, constituted and offered polarized bonds of belonging such as to allow the perception of and the identification with a general and homogeneous We, which in turn entails the determination of an other. Nevertheless, Honneth does commit himself to taking this ambiguity of the national conception into account because not considering it would oversee its (controversial) contribution to the democratization of politics and abandon certain issues to their "nationalist instrumentalizations" (Honneth 2014b, p. 283). I think that the main issue Honneth faces in *Freedom's Right* is precisely the need to formulate an alternative basis for joint commitment. That is, one that could avoid the misdevelopmental elements that are seemingly equiprimordial to the concept of nation or *Volk*.

The third condition of social freedom is identified in "a highly differentiated system of mass media," which "enables its audience to take part in informed processes of will-formation by providing enlightening information on the emergence, causes and possible interpretations of social problems" (Honneth 2014b, p. 291). Honneth's concerns originate on the basis of what has been noted by, among others, Dewey, Adorno and Horkheimer, Habermas, and Arendt:[181] arguably, major information media, such as the press, radio, television, and, more recently, the internet, have historically undermined, rather than contributed to, the expression of democratic freedom. Therefore, even if commercialized and politically oriented media have proven themselves as homologizing functions and domination apparatuses, social freedom instantiated within large societies cannot help but being informed through generalized media. For the latter represent a fundamental level on which the joint will-formation can unfold because of their role by the all-affected principle.

---

181 See Honneth 2014b, pp. 270–77 and 281–86.

The fourth condition emphasizes the need to re-materialize the concept of the public sphere from the point of view of the subjects actively involved in it. What Honneth intends to highlight is the concrete dimension that symbolic communication within the democratic public sphere presupposes, if lively and capable of responding to its own promise of social freedom. Such collective will-formation is too often considered by the theory, Honneth claims, according to the opposite poles of face-to-face verbal exchange or generalized media. Between these two extremes, however, there is the time, commitment, and participation of those who contribute to actual discussions of general interest through pamphlets, flyers, posters, and so on. In the course of the normative reconstruction, the explicit reference is to the student and feminist movements of the 1960s and 1970s, whose fundamental task has been to question the conformation of the public sphere, precisely through the means provided by it, although reformulated according to the modalities to which Honneth dedicates this fourth condition.[182]

The fifth condition follows from the last and regards the perceived necessity of a background consensus among the persons involved in democratic processes. Throughout the normative reconstruction, besides the centrality of the nation-determined social bonds as historically unavoidable viaticum of such solidarity-based relations, another term that constantly occurs is apathy:[183] contrary to the spheres of personal relations and the market, participation in the third sphere is not simply due to socialization: one cannot be a passive member of the democratic public, at least not in the manner that could be conceivable for, say, family and the exchange of goods. We are not compelled by any natural drives to participate in social will-formation debates, and that would result in the increasing lack of involvement. Thus, the willingness to take part itself would need to be motivated:

> Therefore, the existence of a political culture that nourishes and permanently enriches such feelings of solidarity is an elementary precondition for revitalizing the democratic public and even for bringing it about in the first place. If this sphere is not to remain an empty space, constitutionally guaranteed but left hollow by its members and unused for the purpose of expressing opinions, then the civil commitment of citizens is needed who, despite their unfamiliarity with each other, are certain of their political commonalities (Honneth 2014b, p. 292).

---

182 I therefore find it problematic to argue, as Jansen does, that Honneth aims to depict a concept of undifferentiated *demos* and that this would consequently lead him to lose sight of the role played by excluded subjects (groups or individuals) in the democratic integration. If this second point is clearly addressed by Honneth through the mention of civil disobedience and social rights movements, as far as the first point is concerned, I believe that the misunderstanding is due to a misreading regarding the centrality that, in fact, the concept of nation carries out during the course of the normative reconstruction. Honneth does not intend to re-propose an undifferentiated *demos:* as the quick reference to Dewey has shown, even more so in *Freedom's Right*, the central issue is that of unearthing those social drives that can take charge of generalizing the solidarity bonds and social cooperation, without thereby depending on cultural belonging. See Yolande Jansen 2013, p. 34.
183 See Honneth 2014b, pp. 272–82.

Partaking represents the alternative to the trend of privatization and de-politicization of public life, which is highly interwoven with the widespread individualization of workers.

The sixth element of the normatively understood democratic public sphere represents, more evidently than the previous ones, both a condition and an outcome of its very existence. That is, the participants in the democratic public "must feel that the products of their will-formation are effective enough to be practised in social reality" (Honneth 2014b, p. 304). The possibility of seeing the results of the problem-solving collectively undertaken certainly represents a further motivational push. Then, this effectiveness represents above all the incidence of a democratic public aligned with the normative promises that characterize it, where the political dimension emerges from social cooperation.

The fundamental trait of the sixth condition is therefore the permeability of society and state, so that the latter be a functioning and responsive constitutional democracy.[184] However, historical circumstances are shown to be a progressive detachment of these two dimensions from each other: the analysis of the constitutional state is therefore the second object of Honneth's normative reconstruction. The ineffectiveness of the opinions of individuals and of their contribution to the state can be considered the key through which Honneth interprets the contradictory evolution of the rule of law. Honneth here provides some valuable insights into the method and motivations of his normative reconstruction. In fact, it is clear that for Dewey or Habermas, as for Honneth, the description of the democratic public does not correspond to "the actual behaviour of state authorities" (Honneth 2014b, p. 306). This view is not a mere idealization, but the expression of a certain understanding of both society and social theory. However, one might ask whether it would not be more appropriate to take a more realistic view, analyzing the contemporary state for what it has turned out to be: a more or less administrative organism of (explicit and implicit) power, domination, and violence. Honneth maintains two reservations with respect to this perspective, which finds its clearest reference in Foucault. First, in a later interview,[185] Honneth expresses some perplexities regarding the possibility of conceiving the phenomenon of power as primary with respect to that of freedom: the perception of power (understood here more as domination than as constitutive power) is in fact subordinate to an experience of freedom that must have already been given so that the former manifests itself as coercion. This rather simple observation shows the origin of the criticism according to which Honneth does not adequately consider the formative role of power, the fact that its mechanisms and structures shape subjectivity also on psychological and emotional levels.[186] The second element for which Honneth rejects a Foucauldian perspective also sheds light on the first point. In fact,

---

184 See Zurn 2015, p. 187.
185 See Honneth and Raffnsøe-Møller 2015, p. 262.
186 See, among others, Petherbridge 2013; Foster 2017; Thompson 2015; and Thompson 2019a.

to consider the power of the state as the result of a coherent evolution with respect to the mechanisms and logics intrinsic to it (and not as a misdevelopment) would prevent having the necessary normative criteria to criticize it. In other words, assuming power as starting point would allow a factual examination of the forms of domination, but would not disclose any critical possibility, since such power structures and authorities would not be confronted, "at least counterfactually" (Honneth 2014b, p. 307), with any claim of legitimacy: there would be no point of view from which domination could be defined as unjust. In this case, what appears as problematic is the very concept of misdevelopment that is implied by the idea of a primal legitimacy expectation: it would overlook the fundamental level of power, which would not represent a mere deviation, but, so to speak, the path itself.[187] If I correctly interpret the spirit of Honneth's argument, such power-centered theories, in order to criticize forms of domination regarding the constitution of subjects, would require a thick account on human nature or psychology, such as to allow the identification of their harmful distortion. If so, then there is no substantial difference with Honneth's account except for the fact that he seeks a greater formality: in any case, a normative criterion would be implicitly at work. Otherwise, they could be considered simply as factual elements of social integration. In general, therefore, Honneth believes that criticism can only unfold when certain factors of social life present themselves as not corresponding (or damaging) to previous claims of legitimacy in some way intrinsic to those same factors. It is in this sense, I believe, that negativity cannot be primary or total, for, if so, it would be impossible to identify structural elements as unjust(ified). This appears quite clearly concerning the normative reconstruction of the state:

> If we take up the opposing, normative perspective and emphasize the modern state's obligation to legitimate itself, then we cannot simply ignore the already mentioned characteristics of the one-sided exercise of force and control, but they do take on a different historical role and significance, because we no longer view these characteristics as indicators of an intrinsic tendency toward increasing power, but of an illegitimate, often interest-bound use of merely borrowed authority (Honneth 2014b, p. 307).

By identifying the realization of social freedom as legitimate task of the state in the eyes of citizens, the theory holds that implicit and formal idea of healthiness that allows us to consider misdevelopments and identify counterfactual gaps.

The elements that have disappointed legitimizing expectations, that have stifled the state's potential to achieve social freedom are, together, historical phenomena and conceptual elements—according to the very nature of the normative reconstruction. And Honneth identifies three phases that could summarize the relation between state and public sphere: the authoritarian, elitist, and exclusionary conduct of the nation-states and related social conflicts to widen democratic arenas; the crisis of

---

[187] See Smulewicz-Zucker 2019, p. 127.

the social bonds founded on the latter together with the very idea of *nation*-state after WWII, due to the establishment of supranational institutions and the end of colonialism; and the crisis of political participation, as interpreted by Honneth—besides the elements already highlighted by the analysis on the democratic public—as caused by the failure of political corporatism, the professionalism within political parties (and thereby their distance from the social in the direction of a more acute bureaucratization), and the individualization and privatization of citizens. Thus, the two major issues on which Honneth focuses his attention are the capitalist market interfering with governments, and the disputes about the role that the concept of nation should play by conceiving the state—whereby the two positions confronting each other are nationalism and constitutional patriotism. Due the subsumption of democratic structures to normative values, it therefore seems unlikely to say that Honneth reduces politics to ethics.[188] But also concerning the state, such properly systemic elements that prevent the actualization of social freedom do not find a real justification and seem introduced from a poorly investigated outside-of-recognition, giving the impression that certain similarities with the Habermasian colonization thesis are at play.[189]

The picture that emerges from the normative reconstruction is therefore rather discouraging. In fact, it does not seem that a form of state has become effective in modern society that would even for a single moment enable citizens to experience social freedom in the full sense. To that must be added the many shadows and few lights that arise in the current achievements of the sphere of consumption, the labor market, and the democratic public sphere.

Given such situations, Honneth tries to identify germinating realities that may perhaps lead to progress in new forms of inclusive freedom, trying to de-nationalize the idea of community and solidarity relations. Despite its ambiguity and all its contradictions, the concept of the nation had allowed citizens to feel more united than alien in a cohesive democratic public sphere: however, the processes of delegitimization of the nation-state model, transnational markets, and growing pluralism seem to have definitely undermined such a way of belonging to the social We. The viable alternative seems to be that of transferring the public to a transnational level, in search of new foundations for a renewed patriotism. However, the failure of the European Union in this sense seems rather clear, for its inability to generate actual political integration and, to date, does not leave much room for Honneth's investigation.[190] Honneth then turns to consider the example provided by transnational non-governmental organizations, which already exert an operating influence in the present, in the direction of curbing the deregulation of the market economy and affirming social freedom on a global scale.[191] Consequently, as the nation-

---

188 See Arentshorst 2016, p. 45.
189 See Arentshorst 2015, pp. 145–47.
190 See Honneth 2014b, pp. 327–28.
191 See Honneth 2014b, p. 300.

based public were informed by press, radio, and television, such transnational organizations could not have had the success they have without internet. The internet is certainly capable of overcoming national barriers, as it shows itself to be exponentially capable of structurally reconfiguring the characteristics of information exchange. However, Honneth does not fail to emphasize the radical fluidity and the deep unpredictability that is inherent to the size of the network and its uses. In the anonymity and distance that the use of the internet allows, the presumptions of rationality that continue to characterize the mutual exchange of arguments with another concrete or traditional medium are often lacking. Moreover, the total absence of barriers that characterizes the internet often does not contribute to a constructive transnationality, but rather to the generation of "delocalized" communities (Honneth 2014b, p. 301): the world wide web represents a non-world that does not promote the overcoming of particularisms, but rather the homologation to a model of communication that remains within the medium. Nevertheless, transnational organizations and their medium are seemingly unable to provide a renewed and transformed background consensus that would be necessary for the establishment of a new transnational public sphere. And it is only at this point that an element that has almost remained in the background of *Freedom's Right* emerges, though representing its *file rouge:* conflict.[192] Under present circumstances, Honneth places his (feeble) hopes on the background consensus that can be provided in acknowledging a commonality in the struggles for freedom that have characterized European modernity. One could perhaps say that normative reconstruction is, in last instance, not a reconstruction of the achievements of social freedom, but of the uninterrupted conflict in order to experience oneself as such in the other. Despite its disappearing from present outcomes, or its never fulfilled promises, social freedom could be defined through the aspirations of subjects involved in conflicts aimed at progress:

> Whereas the idea of constitutional patriotism remains too closely attached to the medium of law alone, the patriotism inherent in the European archive of collective struggles for freedom aims to realize all the promises of freedom institutionalized in the various social spheres. At a time in which the defence of freedoms that have already been won and the struggle for those that have not yet been fulfilled need a transnational, committed public more than anything else, there remains little more than the hope that on the basis of this historical consciousness, we will see the development of a European culture of shared attentiveness and broadened solidarity (Honneth 2014b, p. 335).

This final passage recalls that of *The Struggle for Recognition*, where Honneth expressed the need for the theory to take a step back from the formulations of the concept of solidarity that only social struggles could achieve. Here, on my reading, we are also told something else, which concerns precisely the method of normative reconstruction, and especially the much discussed first premise. The fact that social reproduction is bound to always-renewed legitimation implies the conflict as re-

---

[192] See Honneth and Raffnsøe-Møller 2015, p. 280.

sponse to the perceived institutional illegitimacy, that is, to the institutions' unfulfilled capability to instantiate norms and values. If, therefore, the first premise is interpreted above all as a "status quo bias" (Jörg Schaub 2015, p. 125), it also represents, according to Honneth, the motive of critical theory and social conflicts.

4.3.3 Some Open Issues: Immanent Critique, Recognition, and the Third

Although I do not have the space to do justice to the full scope of issues covered in *Freedom's Right*, two are most salient for our purposes. The first, widely discussed by critics, is the methodological one concerning normative reconstruction and its suitability for a critical theory of society. The second, which has been rather overlooked, concerns a certain redefinition of the gestures of recognition, as well as their relationship with social freedom, and the ethical spheres.

Scholars address different yet intertwined criticisms to Honneth's account of normative reconstruction. For the sake of clarity, they can be summarized in five problem areas, some of which we have already mentioned at the end of our analysis of the market.

First, by basing his critique on norms and values that are already institutionalized, Honneth takes an excessively affirmative and retrospective attitude, thus somehow endorsing the present in a way that is ill suited to the tradition of the Frankfurt School and that leads him to fail to consider utopian and more radical tendencies,[193] as well as the global scope of the matter.[194] Moreover, the motives of this retrospective view also seem to lack justification. Besides the reference to Hegel's *Philosophy of Right*, it is difficult to understand why Honneth identifies *certain* institutions—and not *others*—as areas in which social freedom should be instantiated. More specifically, the very idea of elaborating a critical theory from socially consolidated elements would weaken the project itself into a reformist point of view.[195]

Second, this would also affect the related concept of progress Honneth defends, which would precisely exclude transformative logics in favor of a more gradual perspective of changing institutions from within. Even without considering the distinction Honneth later proposes between institutional and normative revolutions[196]—that is, the possibility of a radical institutional change in the name of normative principles that they are no longer able to accomplish—I do not believe that this point can be shown to manifest a shift within Honneth's thinking. Indeed, Schaub argues that, in *The Struggle for Recognition* and *Redistribution or Recognition?*, for example, the shift to modernity would represent a normative revolution or even a misdevelopment because the transition from class models centered on honor to greater social

---

193 See Shafer 2008.
194 See René Gabriëls 2013.
195 See Schaub 2015; Freyenhagen 2015, p. 107.
196 See Honneth 2015b; and Honneth 2017.

4.3 Being with Oneself in the Other: Social Freedom in Modern Societies — 197

differentiation would coincide with a deviation from dominating values.[197] However, on closer inspection, we see that Honneth explains this reversal through the idea of an institutional and normative reformulation of the principle of honor (and equity) through the guidelines of inclusion, generalization, individualization, and so on. Also in that case, therefore, Honneth interprets drastic paradigm changes as necessarily based on actual normative elements that were perceived as no longer adequate to the needs that they themselves had generated by socializing individuals. What within Honneth's thought allows the re-elaboration of fundamental values—without having to adapt to those that are simply affirmed by the majority—is the concept of surplus of validity and the consequent almost unbridgeable distance between normative promises and institutional realizations. This leads to the paradox—intrinsic in the very concept of intramundane transcendence—according to which the emancipatory interest should not justify its own existence according to criteria of shared establishment. In this regard, I argue, *Freedom's Right* does not present any particular difference.

A third problematic point is the relationship between the principles underlying social integration and the participants. The fact that Honneth considers normative integration as *the* fundamental level would leave a certain social-theoretical idealism to be detected:[198] on the one hand, the role played by micro and macro systems in social integration is lost in sight and, on the other hand, Honneth would fail to consider that precisely these values and norms are the results of social integration, not the basis for it. This oversight would, in turn, have two consequences. Honneth overlooks the fact that behind the legitimizing assent of the participants hidden moralities and moral suffering could be at stake, themes on which he focused in his early writings, at least up to *Reification*.[199] Moreover, that the subjects legitimize institutions (especially if such assent is to be considered not as active involvement) could be more easily read as the result of individuals being socialized in them, rather than of the justice of those institutions. By being socialized according to certain principles, subjects would in turn be objects of ideological integration, that is, embedded from the outset in a context capable of shaping needs, directions, horizons, and identities. Assuming the ethical dimension as the basis of social integration would be then problematic both on the level of social ontology and on that of a subjectivity theory: on the one hand, a model would be proposed that considers almost exclusively the superstructure and not the structure, to put it in Marx's terms, or ideal actualities rather than actual institutions,[200] and, on the other hand, such ethical values and norms would be placed as at the disposal of the subjects, and not rather as having a shaping role in the ideological sense. The idea of a certain independence of the ethical spheres of recognition follows from this, which would coincide with a sort

---

197 See Schaub 2015.
198 See Zurn 2015, pp. 202–5.
199 See Borman 2019, p. 102.
200 See Ng 2015.

of oasis of freedom, while capitalist imperatives, commercialization of the media, and the authority of the state would originate outside of such mutual and free relations.[201] What the normative reconstruction highlights, especially in the market, are only the moral constraints tentatively imposed by cooperative and solidarity realities, but the relationship between the two realities (the narrow market and the broad market society) seems to be posterior to their being structured.

A fourth problematic issue concerns the identification of social freedom as the principle proper to the institutions considered. Considering above all the pessimism concerning the analysis of the market and the democratic state, one might ask what empirical relevance this idea might have, given that these institutional spheres have historically evolved almost as the opposite of social freedom actualizations. The question could be summarized according to the issue that Zurn calls alternative teleologies.[202] Even if one grants the centrality of normative principles in social integration, could one not say that the evolution of the market and of the state are presided over by other principles or by different principles at the same time—for example, in the market, competitiveness, negative freedom, and merit? What is the need to characterize the current institutional configurations as misdevelopments of an unrealized principle, rather than the full actualization of other principles?

The last and most fundamental point regards the identification of social freedom as hyper-value of modernity. The reconstruction Honneth proposes is unable to provide any justifying argument in this regard, according to three orders of questions. To begin with, it is not clear how the assumption according to which contemporary institutions represent the most advanced ones is justified, an idea that moreover exempts Honneth's theory from the necessity of a constructivist approach, that is, of outlining its principles of justice theoretically and then applying them to social reality.[203] But, on closer inspection, Honneth disseminates the analysis of the democratic public with statements that provide some kind of immanent justification for the idea that such institutional structure represent—*to date*—the most evolved one. Without dwelling on each case, these passages concern the greater degree cooperation, communication, discursive exchanges, and reflexivity that democratic institutional relations imply in their own concept.[204] That is, their greatest degree of social freedom, which also represents the criterion for the criticism of the nationalistic reduction of the state, for only by showing "the dependence of" the democratic sphere "on communicative practices reveals its current deficits" (Honneth 2014b, p. 255). A second problem is that Honneth's reconstruction, considering the perspectives of social actors and the values inherent to actual institutions almost exclusively, would not possess any general justification criterion, thus condemning the whole theory to a contextualism of certain degree. Even from within a reconstructive approach, the issue

---

201 See Thompson 2015, p. 147.
202 See Zurn 2016.
203 See Claassen 2014.
204 See, above all, Honneth 2014b, pp. 260, 263, and 268–74.

4.3 Being with Oneself in the Other: Social Freedom in Modern Societies — 199

emerges to the extent that Honneth—for obvious reasons—rules out the logic of the spirit at the basis of institutional evolution. In this way, he can no longer justify the identity between freedom, self-actualization, and justice that Hegel grounds ontologically,[205] and cannot rely on norm of truth provided by the rationality and dialectical reflexivity of spirit.[206] The problem would then be to find an extra-context reference that allows the theory to evaluate the intra-context elements, thus enabling the distinction between misdevelopments and developments. As Honneth already proposed before *Freedom's Right*, this kind of justification could be provided, for example, by anthropology or at least by a certain conception of human flourishing.[207] This view is abandoned in *Freedom's Right* as justificatory means, but it is not completely absent. Indeed, one could say that the primacy of social freedom is due to its capacity to correspond to the need for complementarity proper to (historically understood) human beings and inherent to the very idea of freedom—for only if freedom includes otherness within its concept could it then be actualized. Finally, as Classen claims, Honneth's approach in *Freedom's Right* would represent a concealed constructivism: rather than identifying social freedom's centrality in social reality, Honneth would have elaborated this principle philosophically and then applied it to social reality.[208] Otherwise, without an argumentative criterion prior to social analysis, misdevelopments could not be qualified as such, but should be considered as intrinsic progressive dynamics or coherent evolutions.

Regarding these criticisms, which go to the heart of Honneth's approach, I propose two possible answers, which do not claim to close the debate, but to clarify some elements that Honneth himself proposes as possible answers.

First, the characterization of state and market as spheres of social freedom responds to the need to elaborate an immanent critique and, together with the first premise of the normative reconstruction, to pose normative promises at the base of the spheres of interaction themselves, so that the expectations of the participants would also be inherent to them. This solution would make it possible to avoid a proceduralist approach and thus overcome a Habermasian dualism. But if that offers considerable advantages from a conceptual point of view, it seems ineffective for the results of the reconstruction: above all, it does not seem that cooperative associations and the democratic public can include in their concept *the* market and state power, both understood in the strict sense. The risk, therefore, is to re-propose a mitigated dualism, whereby the opposites are not system and lifeworld, but cooperative sub-spheres of social freedom that act in their respective macro-spheres. In such a distinction, the conception of institutions that characterizes Honneth's thought—namely, concretions of practices—plays a significant role. Such a perspective based on an action-theoretical account seems to be able to grasp only the normative dimen-

---

205 See David N. McNeill 2015, pp. 156–58.
206 See Buchwalter 2016, pp. 63–64.
207 See Zurn 2015, p. 195.
208 See Claassen 2013.

sion of the institutions, and not what Strydom calls the "cognitive dimension" (Strydom 2013, p. 541). If I correctly grasp what he means by this, this dimension would coincide with the socio-ontological elements of institutions, with the related structures, mechanisms, and apparatuses that are de facto independent from criteria of legitimacy and that represent an essential dimension of their reproduction and consistency—an aspect that, despite all criticism, Honneth addresses more deeply in *Freedom's Right* than in any of the previous major works. Clearly, Honneth's aim is to deny such independence from normative horizons and expectations, for the reasons mentioned above. The impression is that only a more in-depth discussion of the onto-normative status of institutions can settle the issue.

The second element concerns the identification of the principle of freedom as the arch-value of modernity and the suspicion of a silent constructivism. With respect to this objection, Honneth himself claims to have grounded his argument on sociological sources, finding in the documents of self-understanding produced by the participants the conviction that spheres themselves should realize the principle of freedom above all else. Therefore, *Freedom's Right* can be thought as a "hermeneutics of the ethical self-conception of modern societies" (Honneth 2013, p. 40), whereby Honneth provides a normatively oriented sociological justification. Also in this case, the theoretical motive behind this methodological approach is quite clear: ultimately, the need is to legitimize conflict, which, on closer inspection, constitutes the leitmotif of *Freedom's Right*. If the normative claims were not immanent to the spheres they pertain to, the reasons for conflict would be external to the latter and, so to speak, proceduralist themselves: if that were the case, then even if critical theory were immanent to social reality, emancipatory interests would not. Honneth himself admits that such an approach may not convince, but it seems that the only way to contradict the theory on this fundamental core would be to elaborate an alternative normative reconstruction that is able to show the centrality of other principles or to entail a multiplicity of them.[209]

The issue concerning institutions leads us to the second general aspect, which is mostly not addressed by critics: in *Freedom's Right*, Honneth reformulates the relationship between recognition gestures, principles, and spheres in a rather significant way, as well as, to a certain extent, their very concept.

First, the continuity outlined in *The Struggle for Recognition* between modes of recognition and ethical spheres is definitively abandoned. *Freedom's Right* outlines, respectively, three modes of recognition, five spheres of recognition, and three ethical spheres,[210] which intertwine with each other in ways that are summarized in the following table:

---

209 See Zurn 2015, p. 193; and Honneth 2013, p. 40.
210 See Honneth 2014c, p. 126; and Honneth and Raffnsøe-Møller 2015, pp. 276–77.

4.3 Being with Oneself in the Other: Social Freedom in Modern Societies — 201

Table 2: Spheres of freedom and modes of recognition

Modes of Individual Autonomy				
Negative/Legal Freedom	Reflexive/Moral Freedom	Social Freedom		
		Spheres of Ethical Life		
		Personal Relations	Market	Democratic Public
Depend on Modes of Recognition				
		Love		
		Respect		
				Esteem

From this reformulation it follows the non-identity of recognition and social freedom. On the one hand, not all relationships of recognition can generate social freedom. Those that underlie negative and moral freedom—based on the logic of respect—constitute reciprocal normative obligations that are too weak to lead to the experience of being with oneself in another. On the other hand, saying that not all cases of social freedom are bound to recognition relationships is more problematic. To understand why this is the case, it is necessary to return briefly to the definitions of recognition and social freedom. In *Freedom's Right*, Honneth defines recognition for the first time as mutual ascription/perception of normative statuses,[211] which lead to or coincide with complementary role obligations. Social freedom is represented by a commonality of aims that allows the fulfilment of the need for complementarity—need proper to individuals and to the very concept of freedom. Clearly, the two concepts are closely related to them, so much so that it can reasonably be said that recognition and social freedom represent, for each other, condition, equivalent, and consequence, whereby the central element of both concepts is represented by the idea of complementarity. However, when dealing with the concrete matter of social freedom, a greater gap between the two concepts is to be noted: the rather evident cases are those of play—a fundamental practice of social freedom as far as the family is concerned—of work and of the democratic public sphere. As far as the latter two are concerned, Honneth's emphasis is on the possibility of co-determination and collective self-regulation, which would presuppose the recognition of the other as an appropriate partner for this purpose. However, the realization of social freedom itself is not such a mutual ascription/perception of normative statuses, but the joint action of collective self-determination. It seems that an idea of joint commitment emerges

---

[211] See Honneth 2014b, pp. 96 and 107. Honneth later says also that recognition can be conceived as "reciprocal acknowledgment of normative statuses which entitle individuals to specific sets of actions" (Honneth 2013, p. 41).

from Honneth's account, which in turn *presupposes* recognizing the other as partner but, although such recognition must span the unfolding of co-determination, the latter and the former cannot be considered in the same way, since they have different objects and purposes.[212] As far as the case of play is concerned, instead, the intersubjective practice that allows one to overcome one's own finiteness is hardly conceivable in terms of recognition, even though playing entails interactivity and the assignment of roles: what remains unexplained by Honneth is which normative statuses are reciprocally ascribed in this case. Including playing in the definition of recognition would, in principle, seemingly lead to entailing any intersubjective interaction in the concept that provides for the assignment or interpretation of reciprocal roles. This possibility, which could be detected perhaps in the Hegelian master-slave dialectic, is not, however, compatible with Honneth's paradigm, in which recognition relations should represent the bundle of practices that enclose a certain normative perfection. Equating reciprocal ascriptions of normative statuses to the interactive polarity of social roles would therefore greatly weaken the critical potential of the concept.

Finally, and in continuity with *The Pathologies of Individual Freedom* and *Redistribution or Recognition?*, in *Freedom's Right*, the spheres of recognition play an indispensable role by the conceptualization of recognition gestures. It is the fact that subjects are socialized within second nature and through *certain* principles to constitute the horizon of recognitional norms, with their respective expectations, needs, and modalities. One could say, therefore, that the need for complementarity at the basis of social freedom finds its grounding in spheres where social freedom is already realized, as well as, say, the gestures of mutual recognition between friends can only be such because the subjects involved have been socialized in a normative horizon where friendship essentially entails certain complementary obligations, which the subjects must be able to master. As we have seen, Honneth maintains that the task of institutions is to favor a smooth interlocking by social action, *relieving* the actors from having to coordinate their aims again each time: rather, they find themselves sharing certain social contexts according to certain roles that allow them to complement each other (quasi-)automatically.[213] It is therefore clear that the relations of recognition—which for Honneth remain exclusively intersubjective—are not conceivable as decontextualized I-Thou polarity. Rather, the social analysis outlined in *Freedom's Right* offers a concept of second nature that informs the relationships and normative obligations that individuals must be able to comply with: a recognition order at the basis of potential progressive changes. Without a contextualizing third, recognition relationships would be devoid of the *why* and the *what-for* that de-

---

212 Here the expression 'joint commitment' is to be understood in general terms, but well expresses the complementarity of aims proper to social freedom. In this case, I relate mutual recognition and joint commitment in a slightly different way from Gilbert. Clearly, mutual recognition coincides with a joint commitment on the part of the partners, but in turn, co-determination implies a further undertaking of shared responsibility. See Margaret Gilbert 2011, p. 276.
213 See Honneth 2014b, pp. 53 and 125.

fine them. However, such a third seems to be in turn dispersed in the relations themselves, precisely because institutional reality is dealt with almost exclusively from a normative point of view, which falls within the relations of recognition.

Chapter 5
Recognition: from Affirmation to Mutual Authorization

As we have seen in the previous chapter, in *Freedom's Right* Honneth defines recognition as a differentiated intersubjective praxis that takes place within pre-defined relationship horizons, which in turn are crystallizations of those relations: this would entail in the very concept related role obligations, adding a greater emphasis on the normativity of the mutual dimension to the previous inquiries. However, it has also become clear that not all forms of recognition coincide (derive from or are at the basis of) the spheres of ethical life; rather, this second element is tied to and requires a thick conception of complementary aims, so that the intersubjective acts-coordination can lead to being with oneself in the other.

In *Recognition: A Chapter in the History of European Ideas* (original German: 2018), Honneth further addresses the issue of recognition, this time from a more theoretical perspective, thus providing a more in-depth depiction than the ones proposed so far. The purpose of this chapter is to address Honneth's latest reflections on the concept of recognition, which, however, have their roots in a debate left open since 2002, when *Inquiry* published an issue focused on the Honnethian concept of recognition. The first section will therefore focus both on the issues that are raised there and on Honneth's response in "Grounding Recognition," which was subsequently inserted as an afterword to *The Struggle for Recognition.* The issue at stake is to define what recognition is and how it is configured with respect to the traits of the person it affirms (or accepts and expresses). There, Honneth and his interlocutors face the alternative of conceiving recognition either as attribution or as reception (section 5.1). Section two focuses instead on "Recognition as Ideology." This article, subsequently added in *The I in We*, represents one of the few cases in which Honneth directly addresses the issue of power within recognition relationships and the risk contained in entrusting such practices with an exhaustive outline of normative horizons (section 5.2). The third section will focus specifically on *Recognition:* here, Honneth takes up precisely the problems raised in "Grounding Recognition" and "Recognition as Ideology," contextualizing them in a history of ideas that tries to place the different meanings that recognition assumes in three traditions of European thought: French, English, and German. Without dwelling too much on the many historical inquiries and comparisons Honneth carries out, our aim here will be to distil the image of recognition that emerges therein (section 5.3). After emphasizing the principal steps Honneth's concept of recognition undergoes in *Recognition* (section 5.4), we will finally provide an overview on the reconstruction of Honneth's thought we carried out so far, laying the theoretical ground for the discussion of the next, and final, chapter (section 5.5).

5.1 "Grounding Recognition": Response, Actualization, and Progress

In order to better understand the issues dealt with in *Recognition*, it is useful to take a step back to "Grounding Recognition." Prompted by the observations by Carl-Göran Heidegren, Heikki Ikäheimo, Arto Laitinen, and Antti Kauppinen,[1] Honneth in this article lays important foundations for his later developments of the concept of recognition. So it is important for us to emphasize the value of this work, which often has not been aptly considered by the scholars. Its relevance can be traced back to three main points. First, Honneth expresses the reasons that led him to move away from Mead more clearly than in his later work *Reification*, as well as from an anthropological justification of the normativity of recognition practices. Second, he provides, as never before, a formal definition of recognition, tentatively able to entail the multiple tensions that we have seen characterize the concept. Third, he clarifies the relationship between such recognition practices, their normative character, and the concept of progress; in this sense, the link between the I-Thou relations and the concept of second nature becomes clearer.

In this section we shall focus on these three issues, leaving aside what Kauppinen addresses in the same 2002 issue of *Inquiry*, that is, the position of the concept of recognition within the broader aims of social criticism. In fact, Honneth's responses to this issue are significantly consistent with the accounts we focused on in the previous chapter. That is, the aim of developing a social-critical theory that is not trapped by cultural relativism has to be developed through the reference to implicit norms of interaction (i.e. of recognition) that are unearthed via reconstruction. The non-relativistic character of a theory so conceived would hinge on a sufficiently strong conception of progress that has its roots in the idea of surplus of validity (*Geltungsüberhang*): the internal character that the critique must possess in order to fulfill its aims relies not only on the (manifest or counterfactual) contradictions between norms and their instantiations, but on an internal logic of refinement of recognition practices due to their intrinsic moral character.[2] We will gain a better understanding of this last point once we consider Honneth's further analysis of the concept of recognition, which he develops in response to proposals from Ikäheimo and Laitinen's.

Briefly stated, Heikki Ikäheimo proposes some further developments for recognition that themselves fall within Honneth's own paradigm. He then concentrates his efforts on clarifying the concept of recognition and reformulating the relationship between it and the respective dimensions of personhood.

Ikäheimo begins by observing that the term recognition is itself unclear because of a certain polysemanticity. His efforts are therefore oriented to distilling a general definition of the genus of recognition, that is, the basic practical logic of different in-

---

[1] See Heidegren 2002; Ikäheimo 2002; Laitinen 2002; and Kauppinen 2002.
[2] See Honneth 2002, p. 513.

tersubjective attitudes that can be traced back to the specific categories of love, respect, and esteem. The claim is that recognition could be conceived as complex of practical gestures, whereby one finds her own intentionality mediated by another. Such an encounter would be able to shape a space of reasons within which the intentions of both partners are habituated and informed by reciprocal mediations. Here, the underlying practical logic, that is, the genus of recognition, is defined as "a case of *A taking B as C in the dimension of D, and B taking A as a relevant judge*" (Ikäheimo 2002, p. 450). According to this definition, A would be the recognizer, B the recognizee, "C the attribute attributed to B in A's attitude" (Ikäheimo 2002, p. 451), and D the dimensions of the recognizee's personhood that are at issue.

Ikäheimo then reformulates C and D, using different terms than those used in *The Struggle for Recognition*. With regard to the dimension of love, the attribute attributed to B would be that of being someone whose happiness or well-being is important to A ($C1$); the second species of recognitional attitude concerns having rights or being entitled to x ($C2$); and, finally, $C3$ coincides with B's being worthy of esteem. Conversely, the dimensions of personhood taken into consideration by those recognitional attitude are re-termed as singularity ($D1$), autonomy ($D2$), and particularity ($D3$).[3] Once he has adopted and clarified this terminology, Ikäheimo's major efforts are aimed at questioning the close correlation between C and D postulated in *The Struggle for Recognition*, that is, between the modes of recognition (and their instantiations) and the personal dimensions affirmed through them.[4] But, since we have already seen that, quite evidently in *Freedom's Right*, Honneth himself shows a certain discrepancy by the interplay of C, D, and institutional (ethical) spheres, we will briefly focus on three further points.

First, Ikäheimo emphasizes that recognition can be fruitfully analyzed only for what concerns intersubjective relations: the risk at stake by considering such normative attitudes as concerning groups or institutions would be, according to him, that of reifying them; in other words, a more in-depth social-ontological inquiry would be needed in order to comprehend how or to what extent an institution, as such, could be comprehended as recognizer,[5] that is, as an intentionally mediated actor.

Second, if recognition is constituted by attitudes and judgments—that is, by one's attitude toward another, who in turn either accepts or denies that such an attitude is suitable[6]—then the naturalistic vocabulary inherited from Mead would not be appropriate.[7] The normative horizon entailed by the genus of recognition would

---

3 See Ikäheimo 2002, pp. 451–52.
4 See Ikäheimo 2002, pp. 452–58.
5 See Ikäheimo 2002, p. 451.
6 "[R]ecognition is a process where a person attributes in her attitudes certain relevant attributes to another person—whether in explicit speech acts, or implicitly in her overall orientation in the shared world—and the other person has a positively evaluative attitude towards the attribution, or 'accepts' it" (Ikäheimo 2002, p. 456).
7 See Ikäheimo 2002, pp. 456–57.

not be explicable through terms like 'urges' or by the concept of I, or through a narrative that hinges on the internalization of external demands because such accounts provide too thin of a background to place recognitional relations within a space of reasons.

Finally, Ikäheimo distinguishes 'recognitional attitude' and recognition.[8] On the one hand, recognitional attitudes can be defined as that class of gestures through which A attributes some features to B. In this sense, Ikäheimo thus describes recognition in exclusively attributive terms, as Honneth himself subsequently points out. On the other hand, recognitional attitudes alone do not constitute a sufficient condition: recognition indeed happens in the second practical movement, when B takes A as a relevant judge, thus accepting the related recognitional attitudes (C). Without such a judgment toward A, one cannot speak of recognition and, on closer inspection, the fact that the recognizee considers the recognizer as an adequate judge represents the most fundamental—perhaps even transcendental—level of mutuality that a normative concept of recognition must entail.

Similarly, Arto Laitinen intends his article to be a possible contribution or refinement to a theory of recognition inspired by Honneth's account. Contrary to other conceptions of recognition, Laitinen describes Honneth's as multidimensional (a), practical (b), and strict (c).

First (a), it is clear that Honneth's account entails multiple recognitional attitudes and various related dimensions of personhood. Even if they are in turn oriented to the overarching concepts of self-realization or freedom, the specificity of love, respect, or esteem is not to be confused or overlapped.

Second (b), it is also clear that for Honneth recognition represents a practical attitude. Maintaining Ikäheimo's literation, one could say that recognition happens when A treats B as C in the dimension of D, and B treats A as a relevant judge. Such a view does not coincide, for example, with Fraser's, where practical gestures do not necessarily accompany symbolic recognition—and thus the accent is posed on cultural patterns and not on the normative relevance of recognition.[9]

Finally (c), Laitinen defines Honneth's paradigm of recognition as strict and identifies four conditions to distinguish strict and broad conceptions of recognition. The first two conditions characterize recognition as an interpersonal matter. First, only persons can be recognizers. Laitinen justifies this assumption by referring to experiences of misrecognition. Misrecognition happens only when a certain degree of insult is felt. Not every kind of injustice or misfortune can be characterized in such social terms, and as such the term 'recognizer' could be determined only as equal and countervailing to a misrecognizer, that is, as a human being. However, this argument exposes itself to the rather simple observation that one can feel insulted (and therefore misrecognized) by institutions or even cultural models. In this case, it

---

8 See Ikäheimo 2002, p. 450.
9 See Laitinen 2002, p. 465.

seems more successful to take Ikäheimo's argument that the lack of clarity about *how* institutions can be considered recognizers suggests the necessity to avoid reifying formulations or excessive simplifications. In any case, it is true that *certain* normative demands to be recognized are suited to obligations that only human actors can meaningfully fulfill. Consequently, the second condition is that only persons can be recognizees. Recognition does not coincide with any consideration, statement, or expression of value: there are considerable differences between affirming the value of an object or the value of another person. The type of recognition that Honneth considers clearly involves human recognizees. Third, recognition requires a (public) *expression* of the other's cognized traits, and, fourth, those traits have to be *evaluative:* recognition does not concern, for example, the physiological traits of a person, unless they historically assume a certain cultural-qualitative dimension. Quite trivially, how tall a person is is not a matter of recognition,[10] but rather which qualities she expresses that manifest her status as a person, generically conceived. Honneth's (and Laitinen's) idea of recognition is thus multiple, practical, and strict, which in turn means interpersonal, expressivist, and evaluative/normative.

Laitinen's article is particularly noteworthy for the meta-ethical distinction he proposes between two models of recognition, which addresses the ambiguity of the concept: that is, its oscillation between knowing, that is, the mere attestation of personal characters, and making, which would coincide with the social constitution of the latter.[11] Laitinen names these two alternative models the generational-model and the responsive-model.[12]

According to the first one, gestures of recognition would represent the area of formation and emergence or, better, the acts that generate a persons' new characters, moral obligations, and so on. For example, granting rights to another person provides her with a disclosed set of possibilities that could not have been approachable before that specific act of recognition. In other words, the generation-model would emphasize the constitutive contribution of recognition in the formation of normative and social statuses, to the extent that Ikäheimo's lexical choices suggest: recognition would be a matter of attributing attributes to another. In contrast, the response-model argues that recognition is characterized as response to evaluative features that (somehow) precede it. To this extent, the fundamental dimension of recognitional gestures would be that of knowing, that is, of unveiling those value-based characters that *ought* to be recognized as worthy of public affirmation and expression.

Both these models, when exaggerated in their polarity, possess inherent problems. On the one hand, the constructivist approach of the generative model leads to a certain arbitrariness and contextual relativism: for example, on a conventionalist basis, one could agree to accord human features to inanimate objects, since recogniz-

---

[10] See Laitinen 2002, pp. 465–67.
[11] See Markell 2000, p. 496.
[12] See Laitinen 2002, p. 467.

ing the latter as persons would not require any effective reference to the characteristics of the recognizee—or, more problematically, to label human beings as inhuman. On the other hand, the response-model provides more criteria to determine the adequacy of recognitional acts from a normative point of view—where 'adequate' would refer to those gestures that are consistent with the evaluative features of another. However, such a value-based perspective, if excessively flattened on the pre-existence of what is to be recognized, would annul the role of recognition by the shaping an undamaged self-relation, as well as its contribution to the unfolding of individual autonomy.

Precisely for these reasons, Laitinen embraces a middle path: the evaluative features to which recognition bends, as in the responsive-model, and from which it receives its normative orientation would establish themselves on a *potential* level, whose *actualization* would be set in motion by recognitional attitudes. Terms such as autonomy or moral responsibility would be proper to the person as such only potentially, while they would find full expression only if recognized and, consequently, interpersonally or socially oriented. Thus, recognition would be both a response to evaluative features and a precondition of the personhood of a person.[13]

Honneth's proposals in "Grounding Recognition" mainly focus on the alternative proposed by Laitinen, but they also address the relationship between anthropology, social theory, and critical theory, which is precisely why this paper might represent *the* transition from the model presented in *The Struggle for Recognition* to the writings addressed in the previous chapter above.[14]

Honneth's starting point is once again the diverse meanings that the concept of recognition assumes in different traditions of thought, which thus also depends on nuances that the term possesses in different languages. In fact, in English, recognition has a certain closeness to the idea of repetition of a cognition. But this idea is excluded from the German *Anerkennung*, while *Wiedererkennung* better tracks the sense usually associated with the English term recognition. In any case, Honneth outlines four points, also shared by Laitinen and Ikäheimo, which can represent a basis for the formulation of a "*systematic* meaning" of the concept (Honneth 2002, p. 505). First, recognizing coincides with affirming qualities of human beings or groups, although it still has strong interpersonal features, according to Honneth. Second, recognition is a certain *attitude*, whereby symbolic or verbal expressions play only a complementary role: recognition is a matter of acts, and it hinges on how qualities are practically *treated*, rather than merely *affirmed*. Third, recognitional acts cannot be thought of as consequences or side-effects of other attitudes: they can be determined only as explicitly aimed at recognizing the other person so that

---

13 See Laitinen 2002, pp. 473–75.
14 Heidegren provides a quite detailed depiction of Honneth's thought up to 2002, and of the relation of the connections between these three areas of inquiry, proposing to conceive them as a (more or less) coherent constellation. See Heidegren 2002. What is at stake in "Grounding Recognition" is precisely the reformulation of Honneth's conceptual constellation.

they are transparent with their purpose. Thus, recognition cannot be confused with those positive attitudes that, for example, accompany almost every sort of cooperative action: if our aim is to undertake any activity together, a certain degree of esteem or respect could be implied. But that is not the case of recognition, where the only aim that defines our actions is recognizing each other. The fourth premise is that recognition is a genus that possesses different species. Love, respect, and esteem would represent different facets of treating the other as person, that is, affirming her qualities. Thus, given these first premises, Honneth says that "recognition is to be conceived of as the genus comprised of three forms of practical attitudes, each reflecting the primary aim of a certain affirmation of the other" (Honneth 2002, p. 506).

Honneth then tries to determine the generic case of recognition, that is, as independent of any specific kind of practical engagement with the other, but more generally concerning the "cognitive relation to those with whom we interact" (Honneth 2002, p. 506). Here, he not only reformulates Laitinen's distinctions, but he also interacts with Ikäheimo. On the one hand, there is the attributive or generative model, which emphasizes the constitutional role that recognition possesses regarding personhood—that is, the attribution of attributes. On the other hand, if recognition is conceived as a responsive attitude, then its role with respect to the qualities it perceives is to be thought as that of an interpersonal means of their unfolding or actualization. In other words, recognition can be conceived either as forming new normative statuses or as accepting and making explicit preexisting ones, even though such alternatives, as Laitinen points out, do not rule out each other completely. In fact, it seems difficult, even from within Honneth's theory, that is, from within a plural concept of recognition, to adopt only one of these alternatives.

Honneth believes that in order to obtain a normative concept of recognition, only the receptive model provides criteria both to assess the correctness or adequacy of recognitional gestures and also to distinguish them from misrecognition. The attributive model, on the contrary, would neither be able to provide any element that can respond to demands for recognition nor could it determine recognitional gestures as answer to moral injuries. In this sense, the attributive model would lend itself more easily to a translation of the recognition lexicon into domination and power terms, because if it is true that recognitional acts alone determine the recognizee's features—so as by attributive gestures—then there could be no point of reference that could be appealed to for an eventual emancipation from such sorts of labelling. In Honneth's words, "if the recognitional attitude were merely to attribute positive qualities to the other subject, we would no longer have an internal criterion for judging the rightness or appropriateness of such ascriptions" (Honneth 2002, p. 507). In such depiction, however, Honneth does not consider the second part of Ikäheimo's claim, that is, that an attribution can be considered recognition only if the recognizee considers the recognizer relevant judge. Even if that does not completely rule out the possibility of power relations, it implies that both interaction partners are able to transparently refer to the object of recognition: only if the recognizee can somehow consider, within her own self-relation, the recognized traits, can she judge the recognizer's acts as adequate.

The risk of adopting the receptive model is that of excessively flattening normativity to ontological assumptions about human nature. In other words, what nature would such features have, if they somehow exist before interpersonal interaction? The issue at stake, if we consider *The Struggle for Recognition* and the relationship between infant and caregiver, lies in the possibility of conceiving at least a nuclear self that precedes sociality or not—so moving toward a strong anthropology, rather than the weak one Honneth pursued. Even if such traits of personhood were, as Laitinen claims, evaluative and not ontological, their pre-existence would lead to a value realism that seems highly incompatible with many aspects of Honneth's theory:

> This unfortunate situation changes, however, once we admit the possibility that these values represent lifeworld certitudes whose character can undergo historical change; then the evaluative qualities that we would have to be able to perceive in order to respond 'correctly' to them in recognizing a person or group would no longer be immutable and objective but rather historically alterable. To be halfway plausible, however, the picture just outlined would have to be supplemented with a further element: the social lifeworld would have to be conceived of as a kind of 'second nature' into which subjects are socialized by gradually learning to experience the evaluative qualities of persons (Honneth 2002, p. 508).

In this way, the concept of second nature would allow us to outline a moderate value realism, that is, a mutable pre-existing horizon, but sufficiently consistent to allow the recognizer to welcome and express the traits of the other according to a shared understanding of values.[15] This leads Honneth to further define recognition as that intersubjective means through which some features of personhood—mainly, self-relation, and autonomy—that are per se conceivable in their potentiality can unfold into their actuality: "in our recognitional attitudes, we respond appropriately to evaluative qualities that, by the standards of our lifeworld, human subjects already possess but are actually available to them only once they can identify with them as a result of experiencing the recognition of these qualities" (Honneth 2002, p. 510). So, again using Ikäheimo's formulations, recognizing would be a matter of A treating B as C letting the dimension D actualize, where treating C represents a correct attitude if it aligns with the shared determination of D that takes place in the lifeworld of second nature. Two problems emerge. First, Honneth does not consider B's taking A as relevant judge, thus ruling out what Ikäheimo labeled as the most fundamental level of the mutuality of recognitional relationships. Second, if recognitional attitudes are determined for what concerns their normativity by the lifeworld, then the arbitrariness proper to the attributive model seems to appear again. In fact, the problem with the attributive model was that it did not possess any normative cri-

---

[15] Thus, Honneth here draws a very similar idea of recognition as that depicted one year earlier in "Invisibility."

teria useful for the distinction between recognition, misrecognition, and domination. But if the values that precede recognition do not have a self-standing status but instead represent the outcome of the ethical bargaining proper to the lifeworld, then once again such criteria seem to be confined within the limits of a cultural relativism. This can be avoided, according to Honneth, with a sufficiently strong conception of progress. It would represent a "directional index" (Honneth 2002, p. 509), whose developments are, on the one hand, always lifeworld-situated, but, on the other hand, (quasi-)transcendentally determinable. Honneth here makes two points, which coincide with the depiction provided in *Redistribution or Recognition?* First, progress within recognition relations could be indicated through a development in individualization and social inclusion, that is—always keeping Ikäheimo's literation—by a broadening of *D*'s scope in social terms and concerning *B*'s self-perception. Second, progress would be made explicit not only by the fact that "*de facto* practices and social order contradict their implicitly practised ideals" (Honneth 2002, p. 517)—which eventually lead to struggles for recognition. Rather, the surplus of validity of recognitional norms would call for their always better instantiation, even if the gap between facts and norms would not be so evident as to trigger social conflicts.[16] To this extent, the surplus of validity would represent an internal criterion of development and, simultaneously, the means of an internal critique of society. Thus, progress no longer represents a criterion to judge rightful claims of recognition, but becomes an essential component of the concept of recognition itself because second nature in turn hinges on it.

Such account on the correlation between recognition and the norms and values of second nature brings with it two main consequences. First, Honneth addresses questions concerning the extent to which recognitional acts can be considered moral. A first step concerns the mediation of recognition by evaluative reasons, but the moral connotation of such interactions can be understood as tied to Kant's definition of respect: "Respect is properly the representation of a worth that infringes upon my self-love" (Immanuel Kant 1997, p. 14). Thus, the morality of recognition is due not only to its being determined by (generical) values, but by those values or worthiness that can we recognize in the other, which are not determined by our own aims.[17] In other words, Honneth makes it clearer that the moral dimension of recognitional gestures hinges not only on outlining conditions for an undistorted practical identity, but above all that recognition itself represents, on the part of the recognizers, an "*attitude that goes beyond an immediate concern with their self-interest in being responsive to the needs of others*"(van den Brink and Owen 2007, p. 6).

Defining the morality of recognition in such terms also allows Honneth to avoid its functionalist understanding, that is, conceiving its role in actualizing human potentialities as mere means for the other to gain a full-fledged practical identity. Hon-

---

16 See Honneth 2002, p. 517.
17 Honneth had already made this point clear in "Recognition and Moral Obligation."

neth's starting point does not coincide with an analysis of the "functional demands of human nature," but rather is determined by "aspects of the value of human persons, aspects that have become differentiated as the result of a historical learning process" (Honneth 2002, p. 513), that is, as results of a progress-oriented lifeworld. To recognize is therefore not only to instrumentally allow the other to develop an undamaged self-relation, a condition or a precondition of autonomy; but it coincides with treating her morally according to those values that emerge as worthy according to a shared normative understanding. So, treating another morally is what allows her autonomy to unfold. Moreover, it is only thanks to the presence of the other, when our aims are somehow disrupted in their autonomous projections, that we become aware of those socially instantiated norms, thus mastering them,[18] and thus also becoming proper recognizers and recognizees capable of being committed to the related role obligations. Even at this point, it is clear that "Grounding Recognition" represents the very transition from *The Struggle of Recognition* and *Freedom's Right*. In fact, recognitional practices are no longer defined—even concerning their moral dimension—*directly* by human demands for self-realization. Rather, recognition receives its connotations *indirectly* from norms and principles, which in turn preside over human demands for self-realization via the socialization of persons. Phenomenologically speaking, demands for self-realization emerge always as first matter, but Honneth deepens the role of their being constituted within second nature.

Such transition concerns mainly Mead and the related account on progress. In "Grounding Recognition," progress finds its dynamical logics neither in the I-me polarity, nor, consequently, in the continuous tension between internalized norms—that is, the behavioral patterns of the generalized other—and the singularity of the self—that is, the I, with its drive-related indeterminacy and indeterminability. Rather, progress is conceived as learning process that takes place within the lifeworld. But above all, Mead's account now seems inadequate to develop the close connection that Honneth intends to propose between recognition practices and second nature. If progress has to be conceived as internal to recognitional attitudes for what concerns the twofold criterion of individualization and social inclusion, then the fact that Mead disregards the modes of the "reactive behaviour of the two participants" (Honneth 2002, p. 502), and only focuses on the cognitive processes of assuming the other's point of view, appears incompatible with a normative account of social integration. Moreover, Mead's cognitivist perspective about the I brings with it several problems, which could lead to confusing a normative account of the person and her social integration via values and principles and a depiction of unconsciousness and drives. In other words, because progress is founded on the "inner negation of internalized norms, rather than by means of judgments regarding 'objectively' given standards of action" (Honneth 2002, p. 503), Mead's account of second nature and progress appears now unsuited for a normative paradigm of recognition.

---

[18] See Honneth 2002, p. 515.

But what about conflict? The abandonment of Mead pushes Honneth to rule out the justification of social conflicts rooted in the I-me polarity. The risk contained in such a move is that of losing the instance of singularity of the self, who, socialized through the values and principles of second nature, might not possess the resources to overcome them, if not those provided by the context itself in the form of surplus of validity. Honneth is therefore led, with reference to Daniel Stern, to envisage a nuclear self whose anti-social drives of control over otherness could lead to the tendency to defy established settings. However, even this solution seems to bring with it the irreconcilability between normative arguments concerning moral injuries and a more psychoanalytically oriented drive-theory mentioned above, a risk that Honneth is aware of. Moreover, this solution has the disadvantage, compared to the model sketched from Mead, of allowing an almost exclusively negative, contrastive connotation of the conflict: it would represent a negation of intersubjectivity, rather than a creative reformulation of it.[19]

In "Grounding Recognition," Honneth thus states that recognition has to be conceived as an adequate-responding attitude that contributes by the unfolding of the evaluative features of the other that are perceived as worthy of consideration within the context of second nature. Such conclusions—whose consequences were already dealt with from "Invisibility" onward—are to be explained, in my view, with a peculiar emphasis Honneth proposes: what is at stake is not the experience of being recognized, as emphasized in *The Struggle for Recognition*, or the experience of being with oneself in the other, as described in *Freedom's Right*. Rather, the focus is shifted to better understanding what recognizing properly is. And precisely this theoretical need for clarification will lead us in the following sections.

5.2 "Recognition as Ideology": Is there a Way Out?

But what if the horizon of second nature by, through, and within which the person's evaluative features are shaped is ideological? Or, more precisely: what if, through relations of recognition, the addressee is—without coercion or repression—subjugated rather than set free? This is the question posed in "Recognition as Ideology."

The theorical interlocutor in this case is Althusser, who affirms—following the triad interpellation, recognition, and guarantee—that individuals are subjected by being confirmed in their subjectivity.[20] The case made by Althusser is quite simple, but poses different issues for recognitional theory in general, but specifically for a critically-oriented one. Whenever an individual is (re-)cognized on the street and interpellated by an acquaintance or a friend, their ritual gestures of greeting and shaking hands represents their mutual confirming and guaranteeing each other as sub-

---

19 See Honneth 2002, pp. 504 and 518; and Honneth 2012b.
20 See Althusser 2014.

jects—that is, they recognize one another. Now, their being subjects is considered—mostly drawing on Lacan and Foucault—as an ambivalent status, it represents individuals being determined in their possibilities: 'subject' is always already subjected, because practices and systems of subjectivation are those through which it is subjugated. One becomes subject only to the extent one becomes subjected to a system of rules that was determined behind one's back, that of social identity. If so, mutual recognition would coincide with mutual confirmation of a subjection-status—confirmation that happens, moreover, following modes and rituals that are predetermined themselves. And therefore, the reciprocal guarantee that instantiates in gestures of recognition would produce nothing but the reproduction of unjust production relations through what Althusser calls the mirror-structures of ideology.[21] In short, recognition would represent a means for conformation, homologation, and domination.

Confronted with such challenges, Honneth a) tries to show how difficult it could be to determine ideological forms of recognition; b) attempts to define what characters they should possess; and c) sketches a criterion thanks to which they could be identified, that is, distinguished from genuine recognition.

Dealing with the first issue, Honneth considers the matters at stake by once again trying to identify with the subjective experience of those who are supposedly affected by ideological forms of recognition. If, in fact, such intersubjective practices are repression-free, they cannot be merely equated with acts of misrecognition or non-recognition.[22] Thus, the complexity of the matter consists precisely in identifying a pathological social pattern without pathological outcomes on the part of the affected. The examples Honneth proposes highlight such difficulties. How will it be possible for the good slave and servant Uncle Tom, or a good housewife, or a heroic soldier, to discover that those very relations that affirm, esteem and confirm them are in truth merely reproducing their subjection?

> The choice of examples itself, indeed the very way they are described, is the result of a moral judgement that can be made only from the perspective of our morally advanced present. Because we live in an epoch that regards itself as being morally superior to past ages, we are certain that the esteem enjoyed by the virtuous slave, the good housewife and the heroic soldier was purely ideological. Yet if we put ourselves in the past, it becomes much more difficult to distinguish between a false, 'ideological' form of recognition and one that is correct and morally imperative, because the criteria of which we were so convinced suddenly become uncertain (Honneth 2012f, p. 77).

---

21 See Althusser 2014, pp. 268–70.
22 The identification of ideological forms of recognition poses a difficult task to critical thinking because they are systems of domination that remove their repression-appearance. It is therefore wrong, as Worsdale does, to connect ideological recognition with misrecognition or psychological suffering; see Worsdale 2017, pp. 619–21. The matter here is if it is to deal with repression-free, (supposedly) symptoms-free relations, but claiming that they are profoundly unjust.

The step Honneth takes clarifies the point that ideological forms of recognition can be identified only to the extent that we possess a different moral perspective from that of the second nature in which they take place. But even not considering the historical distance to such relations, other examples show us that it is properly a moral distance that allows us to consider a form of recognition as ideological. Think of the teenager making his way into the neighborhood gang, or the members of a radical sect. Both enjoy esteem within a certain environment, letting themselves into a context without an apparent way out. Thus, to assume, as Althusser does, that "intrinsically positive and affirmative practices in fact bear the negative features of an act of willing subjections" (Honneth 2012f, p. 78) would require to demonstrate—without any form of paternalism or universalism—that the context in which such acts of subjection are instantiated is structurally unjust, even if asymptomatical. In fact, that being confirmed as subject would coincide per se as being subjected would imply that social reproduction itself is unjust or wrong. Here, the burden of proof lies on which moral criteria we let into play, because we have to show that *that* kind of reproduction is detrimental, otherwise we could not use the term ideological with full justification. In other words, one cannot simply decouple moral validity and social validity.[23]

Honneth therefore claims that such normative-historical perspectivism is necessary to unveil the other side of the coin, also because the idea of recognitional gestures he proposes is the same as that developed in "Grounding Recognition": recognitional stances are to be conceived as a "bundle of habits linked to the revisable reasons for the value of other persons" that hinge on the horizon of second nature (Honneth 2012f, pp. 82–83). Thus, they depend—for their objects and their modalities of expression—on the context they inhabit. Nevertheless, their general moral character would not be extinguished by their being situated, on their being receptive, but rather on the fact that they let themselves "be determined by the value of other persons" (Honneth 2012f, p. 85). However, this general level as such is not to be found, and that is why Honneth specifies that what is at stake is not generic interpersonal recognition, but rather institutional recognition. Using this concept, Honneth does not intend to describe institutions as recognizers and recognizees, but only to make a step explicit, which he has already taken in *Freedom's Right*. Recognition becomes at best conceivable as taking place within institutional spheres, which in turn "can be understood as embodiments of the specific form of recognition that subjects accord each other on the basis of specific evaluative qualities." In this sense, by conveying certain principles about the evaluative features of individuals, institutions "do not intentionally accord recognition," yet "can be understood as crystallizations of patterns of recognition" (Honneth 2012f, p. 84). This specification has considerable weight. For, according to this view, one can say only in an indirect sense that the state, for example, recognizes rights of citizens. Mark Alznauer speaks

---

23 See Honneth, Allen, and Maeve Cooke 2010, p. 166.

in a similar way when he describes how Kant conceives of property rights: one can say that the state recognizes my right of ownership only because it compels my associates to recognize me as owner.[24] The state is therefore not the recognizer, but is so only indirectly: it grants me features that bind others to recognize me according to those features. Therefore, the character of second nature proper to institutional recognition outlines the individual's immanence to a context in which certain personal features emerge (more or less formally and rigidly) as potential recognitive object. Honneth defines what appears valuable in such ethical horizon as principles of recognition, namely, love, equality, and merit. And since ideological recognition does not present itself as misrecognition or non-recognition, it would seem that it is with respect to their relation with such principles and the consequent modes of self-relation that it is possible to exercise criticism.

If this is the case, given the decisive historical-normative distance mentioned above, a further difficulty emerges, namely, the role of the concept of progress. Already in *The Struggle for Recognition*, Honneth had stated that this concept represents a fundamental criterion for evaluating different forms of recognition or, better, of the principles on which they hinge. However, this idea also seems to yield here:

> the more we become aware of the fact that relations of recognition have been transformed, expanded and improved historically by means of new accentuations of general principles, the more difficult it becomes to identify merely ideological forms of recognition. Who can tell us for sure that an apparently functional, ideological evaluation is not just one of those shifts in accentuation by means of which the struggle for recognition unfolds historically? The issue is simple only in cases where the concerned parties actually resist new forms of evaluative distinction. Here we have at least an initial reason to question changed forms of recognition and to suspect that a mere ideology could be at work. But in the absence of such protest, where individuals seem to attain a stronger sense of self-respect through a new form of recognition, we initially lack all criteria for distinguishing between ideological and justified shifts in accentuation (Honneth 2012f, p. 89).

Take the case of the good housewife. Given such historical malleability of the forms through which the principles of recognition instantiate, the identification of that situation as an ideological horizon of beliefs becomes evident only when such status is disputed through social conflicts, which in turn revolve on a better application of the same grounding principles by which the first could have been supported in the first place. But such a centrality of the historical modifiability of the instantiations of principles makes the question even more problematic: what *today* seems *to us* to be a form that functionalizes subjects to the reproduction of the dominant order could instead represent a decisive step for a refinement of the institutional concretions of recognition. It is not a question of justifying the possible subjection of today in view of tomorrow teleologically: rather, if progress is conceived as an open-ended learning

---

24 See Mark Alznauer 2015, p. 90.

progress, we do not dispose, now, elements that could tell us definitively what forms the tension between institutionalized forms and surplus of validity will take.

Precisely this point helps us in understanding the second step in the inquiry, that is, describing the features ideological recognition must possess according to its own concept.[25] First, the principles affirmed in such patterns of recognition must give public expression to the value of a subject or a group; thus, for example, discrimination does not fall into the concepts we are dealing with. Otherwise, ideological recognition would coincide with misrecognition, thus triggering social conflict, or at minimum resistance. Second, the affirmation thereby conveyed must be credible in the eyes of the addressees. And third, such kind of recognition must be "contrastive," that is, not simply normalizing. These conditions are meant to express that "ideological forms of recognition operate within an historical 'space of reasons'" (Honneth 2012f, p. 88): they must be rationally credible for the people who experience them—and pass them on—otherwise they could not crystallize into institutional forms; instead, they would simply be refused. And they must be positive and contrastive, that is, putting the addressee somewhat in the foreground—and not simply normalizing (like Althusser's case)—so that subjects *feel* effectively recognized. These passages contain all the difficulties that Honneth's paradigm is compelled to deal with when faced with such issues, since this connection between institutions, principles, and social actors brings out precisely what will be criticized in the later concept of normative reconstruction. Moreover, the concept of progress does not seem to be able to provide external support in its evaluation: the lack of an explicit emancipatory interest on the part of social actors prevents a simple recourse to it, unless one calls on thick teleological implications.

Honneth is therefore faced with the need to find an *internal* criterion that can help us distinguish ideological forms from genuine ones—and that is his third step. The example Honneth analyzes is that of the "entreployees (*Arbeitskraftunternehmer*)": such labelling "asserts that every qualified member of the labour force is capable of planning his or her career path as a risk-filled enterprise, requiring the autonomous application of all of his or her skills and abilities" (Honneth 2012f, p. 91). As we have already seen (see section 3.1 above), this idea is revealed in its pathological consequences according to the elements already highlighted by Honneth in "Organized Self-Realization": under the promise of greater freedom and possibilities for self-realization, the regulatory conditions are increasingly thinned, under further pressure to develop identities capable of adapting elastically. What would constitute the ideological element derives precisely from the fact that recognition cannot be reduced to a merely symbolic form. Rather, it coincides with a certain way of *treating* another: going back again to the example, the public esteem entailed in the very term entreployee should be accompanied by regulatory and redistributive measures. Simply put, the praise of the worker who embraces his or her

---

25 See Honneth 2012f, pp. 86–88.

career as a risk-filled challenge is not supported by the sharing of the material consequences that would be conceivable if the role of the employee were really considered to be comparable to that of the entrepreneur: "the deficiency by which we might recognize such ideologies could consist in their structural inability to ensure the material prerequisites for realizing new evaluative qualities"(Honneth 2012f, p. 93). Such an internal criterion comes very close to a straightforward idea of immanent criticism, where the terms of comparison are the content of the promise and its fulfilment. Some evaluative features are affirmed, but the conditions for living them out are not assured.

However, as Amy Allen argues, not all cases of ideological recognition can be identified with a failure to increase the material conditions of the addressees. Through an example now well known in the debate, Allen argues that recognition and domination are closely intertwined. Elizabeth, a child educated according to traditional perspectives on femininity and women's role in society, in order to be addressed with affection and recognition, behaves at least passively toward the models of subordination proposed by her parents.[26] The case described by Allen is such that it becomes very difficult to speak of familial love as a mutual recognition. Quite the opposite, caregiver-child relations could be described as mutual in a very thin sense, which would not add very much to the mere concept of relation. Once again, the tensions between mutuality, reciprocity, and symmetry emerge. According to Allen, the parent-child relationship would be so asymmetric that the child's attachment would not convey a greater equality within the relations—as Honneth claims regarding the principle of love. Instead, attachment would open the doors to forms of subordination about which the child has no say because of her physical dependence on her parents. Therefore, vulnerable and exposed, Elizabeth would be socialized according to cultural patterns that undermine her possibilities for emancipation even as an adult, thus reproducing the ideological element, that is the concealment of domination itself.[27] And finally, in a case like Elizabeth's, the material criterion would be of no use, because it is precisely through her being subjected that she is addressed with family care—or rather, the two things would collapse on each other.[28] In other words, Honneth's claim according to which ideological recognition operate within an historical space of reasons would imply a degree of autonomy and transparency on the part of the subject that is always already undermined by its being socialized.

These issues seem to exacerbate the difficult position in which the recognition paradigm finds itself when confronted with a productive and not repressive idea of power. And it is precisely on such questions that many of the efforts of the last text that we are addressing in our historical reconstruction are concentrated. Before moving on to *Recognition*, however, it seems useful to clarify the material criterion

---

[26] See Allen 2010, pp. 25–26.
[27] See Allen 2010, p. 28.
[28] See Allen 2010, p. 30.

Honneth mentions at the end of "Recognition as Ideology." Such a criterion does not merely refer to equity and distributive justice: what is *materially* lacking in the case of the entreployee concerns the *imbalance* between risks and sharing of consequences. She is promised, and must take over, flexibility and responsibility in the elaboration of her work biography, but, then, her actual situation coincides with a greater exposure, in which such idea of authorship fades away and plays very little role. Here too, in my view, Honneth thinks of criticism as unfolding from the counterfactual gap between principles and practical concretions: if this were not the case—and we reduce the material criterion to distributional issues—the example of the heroic soldier would cease to be ideological if he were generously rewarded, which, evidently, is not a satisfying solution.

In any case, the question for a critical theory based on the concept of recognition is: is there a way out? On the one hand, the use of moral criteria that go beyond social validity would coincide with a universalism that seems reasonable to reject. But, on the other hand, linking recognition practices to the concept of second nature appears to give us a static image according to which the individual is bound to merely repeat the rules according to which he or she has been socialized. And if these rules are ideological, then she will be forced to live in ideology, thus subjected. The normative perspectivism Honneth suggests seems, once again, to give priority to the concept of progress and suggest that philosophy can only come into play after history. But the impression one gets is that the very potential of criticism is sharply diminished.

5.3 *Recognition:* from Affirmation to Authorization

The two previous sections provided the necessary preconditions to aptly approach the issues Honneth discusses in his last monograph: *Recognition: A Chapter in the History of European Ideas*. Indeed, the book discusses two fundamental questions that have arisen in previous sections. First, the book itself faces the complexity of meanings that the term recognition takes on in various philosophical and socio-political discourses. As we have seen, In "Grounding Recognition," Honneth had already traced this polysemy back to different nuances that the terms *Recognition*, *reconnaissance* and, indeed, recognition possess, even in their everyday use. The attempt in *Recognition* is thus to reconstruct, through a history of ideas (*Ideengeschichte*), in quasi-Weberian tones, the elective affinities between certain thinkers and the historical-cultural context they inhabit, which dialectically (i.e. in a process that cannot be interpreted as unilaterally oriented) would constitute different strands or traditions of thought. Rather than reconstructing different *Volksgeister*, Honneth measures himself with such different philosophical outcomes regarding the concept of recognition and tries to illuminate the red threads of their origins—in France, England, and Germany, respectively.[29] Our first aim is to retrace the essential features of such a reconstruction, focusing mainly on the conceptual nodes that are decisive for Honneth's discourse itself. I will neither focus on the historical-exegetical correctness of Honneth's readings of the respective authors he discusses, nor on the connection he alludes to between their elaborations and their social context. In both cases, Honneth himself does not raise the claim of an exhaustive investigation: what is at stake —for him as for us—is to engage in dialogue with the different ideas of recognition (section 5.3.1). Subsequently, our principal aim is to analyze the developments of Honneth's account of recognition, also considering what emerged in our analysis of "Grounding Recognition" and "Recognition as Ideology," which show the necessity and the risk that the concept of second nature represents for the very idea of recognition. On the one hand, recognition practices always have a *where*—namely, the institutionalized spheres—and a *for-what*, that is, the evaluative features at stake in the affirmation of the other, and which can only emerge by virtue of a broader framework than a single practical interaction. On the other hand, the suspicion that arises is that the potential of such practices is exhausted into the context to which they belong and that, indeed, their only potential is that of reproducing it, thus renewing structures of domination. Honneth's aim in *Recognition* is to harmonize (if and where possible) those different traditions, so that a greater clarity to the concept of recognition could be gained. Our aim in this case will be, above all, to see how Honneth himself significantly reformulates his theory of recognition, while not changing the foundations of his own paradigm (section 5.3.2).

5.3.1 One Word, Different Concepts

Honneth begins his analysis of the history of the concept of recognition in France by way of a confrontation with Rousseau and Sartre. Despite the many differences between these two authors, the following passage from Rousseau's *Discourse on the Origin of Inequality* (henceforth, *Second Discourse*) neatly captures Honneth's view on the idea of recognition they propose: "the savage lives in himself; the man accustomed to the ways of society is always outside himself and knows how to live only in the opinion of others. And it is, as it were, from their judgment alone that he draws the sentiment of his own existence" (Jean-Jacques Rousseau 1992, p. 70). Such view on sociality would find its fulcrum in the concept of *amour propre*, that is, the somewhat artificial (in the sense of pertaining to our second nature) need that pushes individuals to an almost compulsive search for social consideration, in an attempt to be, or simply to appear, above others. This desire, which emerges in the *social* nature of every man, would thus imply a felt need to consider one's own characters according to the judgment that others might have of them. In

---

29 On the methodological premises of Honneth's inquiry, see Honneth 2021, pp. 1–9.

other words, social beings would not simply *act*—as the non-social do—but always do so with concern for the effects or repercussions that their actions might have on the social consideration they eventually enjoy.[30] Thus, Honneth writes: "the perspective of society and the craving for recognition share a common origin" (Honneth 2021, p. 25). So, entering society, humans stop behaving and start to *behave (!)* because of the need to be not only socially appreciated but, more importantly, preferred. By projecting out into social milieus the (moral) observer of one's actions, and being motivated by the *amour propre*, the individual shows a certain plasticity in order to adapt to the socio-cultural conditions that surround her—precisely because in them resides the criterion of judgment. This dynamic would imply, according to Honneth's reading of Rousseau, the "danger of losing one's self" (*Selbstverlust*) (Honneth 2021, p. 27). But such loss is not only moral or political, it also does not regard what one might call a certain (compelled) inauthenticity of our actions alone. Not only is *what* I do affected by outsourcing my perspective, but also *who* I might be and am. As Honneth points out, there is a "cognitive difficulty," an "epistemic problem of self-recognition" (*Selbsterkenntniss*) (Honneth 2021, p. 33): the individual would be robbed of the "sentiment of his own existence," as the *Second Discourse* reads (Rousseau, p. 70), since social recognition would impose a heterogeneous perspective on him. In other words, having to constantly tailor my actions and my person to social criteria that could guarantee me recognition, I would fall into the impossibility of knowing who I really am, either because I would not be able to know if the characters exposed publicly are actually mine—or only the standardized outcome of emulations and fictions—or because my attitudes are always considered having the other out of the corner of my eye as my authoritative judge: an inner access to my inner dimension would therefore be precluded.[31]

Such cleavage of self and self-perception is also central to Sartre's account. While there are certainly many points of difference between Rousseau's and Sartre's accounts, Sartre's *Being and Nothingness* shares with Rousseau the idea that the presence of others does not represent the original nature of human beings. Indeed, the phenomenological-subjectivist approach Sartre implements compels him to justify the existence of others, as something that—at a *certain* moment— begins to influence

---

30 "I say that in our primitive state, in the veritable state of nature, egocentrism [i.e. *amour propre*] does not exist; for since each particular man regards himself as the only spectator who observes him, as the only being in the universe that takes an interest in him, as the only judge of his own merit, it is impossible that a sentiment which has its source in comparisons that he is not in a position to make could germinate in his soul" (Rousseau 1992, p. 90; see Honneth 2021, p. 22).

31 "because subjects are driven by their 'amour propre' to prove their feigned or real characteristics, they will eventually fail to recognize themselves. With every attempt to prove their worth they will become increasingly uncertain about who in fact has the authority to define their attributes and abilities – public opinion or themselves, to whom they likewise feel accountable? On the basis of this epistemic confusion, Rousseau develops the inner drama …: Individual subjects, torn between their own judgment of their personal identity and that of others, ultimately fail to know who they really are" (Honneth 2021, p. 38).

the consciousness' field of experience.³² As the well-known example of the keyhole shows, the appearing of the Other in the horizon marks the passage through which the subject, through being-for-Other, can know his being as his own object. Peeping through a keyhole, suddenly, I am lost in the world, my "consciousness sticks to my acts, it is my acts," living the "free project of my possibilities," an *unreflective consciousness* (Jean-Paul Sartre 1993, p. 259). But as one sees me, I am frozen, the Other's gaze fixes me to certain traits, crystallizing me as object; and indeed by reflecting this gaze, consciousness would cease to be *un*reflective; thus, "the person is presented to consciousness *in so far as the person is an object for the Other*" (Sartre 1993, p. 260). The existence of the Other alone, and his gaze, allows that objectification that makes it possible for me not only to *be* myself, but to *have* myself; but, conversely, such gaze would represent the *solidification* and the *alienation* of my possibilities, which were not constrained until that encounter.³³ So it is clear why Honneth describes such a moment as a recognition (*Anerkennung*) that is simultaneously misrecognition (*Verkennung*), recognition that is reification.³⁴ So, by directing his gaze at my physical being and acting—so that I can become aware of it—the Other would fix my possibilities by tracing them back to my concrete (petrified) shape: "If I am to be able to conceive of even one of my properties in the objective mode, then the Other is already given" (Sartre 1993, p. 270). Perhaps playing with the suggestions that the identified link between Rousseau and Sartre evokes, one could even say that it is no coincidence that such upsurge of the Other causes shame and pride as primary reactions.³⁵ But Honneth emphasizes that the heart of the matter is represented

---

32 See Manfred Frank 2004.
33 It is worth quoting the following passages from *Being and Nothingness* in order to better understand how Sartre conceives recognition as *coinciding* with reification. "When I am alone, I can not realize my 'being-seated;' at most it can be said that I simultaneously both am it and am not it. But in order for me to be what I am, it suffices merely that the Other look at me . . . For the Other *I am seated* as this inkwell *is on* the table; for the Other, *I am leaning* over the keyhole as this tree *is bent* by the wind. Thus for the Other I have stripped myself of my transcendence. This is because my transcendence becomes for whoever makes himself a witness of it ... a purely established transcendence, a given-transcendence; that is, it acquires a nature by. The sole fact that the *Other* confers on it an outside. This is accomplished, not by any distortion or by a refraction which the Other would impose on my transcendence through his categories, but by his very being. If there is an Other, whatever or whoever he may be; whatever may be his relations with me, and without his acting upon me in any way except by the pure upsurge of his being—then I have an outside, I have a *nature*. My original fall is the existence of the Other. Shame—like pride—is the apprehension of myself as a nature although that very nature escapes me and is unknowable as such. Strictly speaking, it is not that I perceive myself losing my freedom in order to become a *thing*, but my nature is—over there, outside my lived freedom—as a given attribute of this being which I am for the Other.
  I grasp the Other's look at the very center of my *act* as the solidification and alienation of my own possibilities" (Sartre 1993, pp. 262–63).
34 See Honneth 2018, pp. 68; and Honneth 2021, p. 44. See also Honneth 2003b.
35 "In short there are two authentic attitudes: that by which I recognize the Other as the subject through whom I get my object-ness—this is shame; and that by which I apprehend myself as the

by *becoming addressees* of another intentional being, thus going to characterize the matter at the level of a "purely ontological occurrence" (Honneth 2021, p. 46).

In any case, it is important to emphasize that both Rousseau and Sartre conceive of recognition as "a kind of propositional cognition or factual claim" (Honneth 2021, p. 45) aimed at personal (external) features. Be it that these features are explicitly attributed or perceived by others (but the latter always show a certain generative power on the first), be it that they actually belong or are simply pretended by the addressee, the latter would find himself in a situation of unbridgeable discontinuity between what he *is* and what he *sees* whether he looks himself being. He is therefore thrown either in an insecurity about his true nature (Rousseau), or in a limitation of his freedom as ontological dimension, a limitation of his being free from any conditioning (Sartre). Briefly, the fact that the other knows me, unveils me, coincides with my being veiled.

But also in the philosophical developments that took place in France as reaction to the centrality of the subject as structuring factor—i.e. Poststructuralism—a negative accent is maintained with regard to the concept of recognition. Clearly in this case, recognition is not and cannot be conceived as an encounter between two concrete subjects, but precisely as "an effect [*Wirkmechanismus*] of whole systems" and "a bundle of systematically organized practices through which certain attributes are "ascribed" (*zuerkannt*) to subjects (Honneth 2021, p. 48).[36]

Taking first Althusser and then Lacan briefly into consideration, Honneth shows their rejection of the being-for-itself of the subject described by Sartre: the upsurging of the other and his gaze would not reify or destabilize an already-given subjective core; rather, it is only the call of the other that generates the subject in its functions. As we have already seen with respect to Althusser, recognition would have no moral character, it would not concern the conscious experience of being recognized, and would not coincide with an epistemic act of (un)veiling personal features. That of recognition is a dynamic "ascription of demanded characteristics for the purpose of stabilizing a system of domination" (Honneth 2021, p. 50). The mutual confirmation that is realized through gestures of recognition would concern participants' being subject(ed) to social identities that are (pre)defined and (pre)determined by the over-individual Subject. The reciprocity of the subjects would coincide, therefore, with an equal submission to a systemic order that is imposed on them, which interpersonal mutuality instrumentally and non-coercively reproduces. For Honneth's purposes, it is important to emphasize that such mutual recognition is an act of at-

---

free object by which the Other gets his being-other—this is arrogance or the affirmation of my freedom confronting the Other-as-object. But pride—or vanity—is a feeling without equilibrium, and it is in bad faith. In vanity I attempt in my capacity as Object to act upon the Other. I take this beauty or this strength or this intelligence which he confers on me—in so far as he constitutes me as an object—and I attempt to make use of it in a return shock so as to affect him passively with a feeling of admiration or of love" (Sartre 1993, p. 290).
36 See Honneth 2018, p. 73.

tribution of personal features, whose definition is over-individual and over-practical, and has to be found elsewhere, scattered in the domination system's reproduction. On the part of the subject, one can only expect to adapt to such features, passively constituting its identity through being integrated by and within institutional models (the school, for example).

With Lacan, the matter gets even more acute. Put briefly, by analyzing the process of the constitution of subjectivity, Lacan highlights the centrality of submission of the child's impulses. Our drives are shaped by and through a foreign element, namely, the "system of language" (Honneth 2021, p. 50), that is introduced by the caregiver in the attempt of interpret and respond to them. The child is then henceforth bound to articulate her urges according to a verbalization that was imposed on her. Thus, language would simultaneously reveal and hide her drives: it would constitute subjectivity itself by granting it shape—as Sartre puts the point: "I *am* language" (Sartre 1993, p. 372)—but can never coincide with the impulses themselves. Such "division" (*Spaltung*) opened by the impossible meeting between verbalization and drives would emerge particularly in the psychoanalytical process, in the labor of analysis, as Lacan calls it (Honneth 2021, p. 51; see Honneth 2018, p. 77):

> Does the subject not become engaged in an ever-growing dispossession of that being of his, concerning which ... he ends up by recognizing that this being has never been anything more than his construct in the imaginary and that this construct disappoints all his certainties? For in this labour which he undertakes to reconstruct *for another*, he rediscovers the fundamental alienation that made him construct it *like another*, and which has always destined it to be taken from him *by another*.
> This ego, whose strength our theorists now define by its capacity to bear frustration, is frustration in its essence (Jacques Lacan 2001, p. 32).

The subject *is* frustration, not because its desires are prevented from coming true, but because, as the mirror stage shows, the ego can never coincide with the representation it constructed of itself by the help of another who linguistically bridged the hiatus between *me* and my reflected *image.*

Be it that my search for social consideration makes me a stranger to my own attitudes (per Rousseau), or that the Other's gaze binds me to my object-ness by the free unfolding of my possibilities; be it that the other greeting me does nothing but confirming the reproduction of my (being subjected to a) social identity, or that the Other—language—constitutes a pervasive order that leaves in shadow the most original dimension of the self, in all these cases "recognition and self-loss have a common origin" (Honneth 2021, p. 51). Honneth therefore argues that recognition is therefore be conceived in the French tradition primarily as acknowledgment (*Zurkenntnisnahme*) of (authentic or fictitious) characteristics that subjects possess or finds themselves possessing. That this perspective is more epistemological than normative in character would be apparent from a lack of "gradation" (*Graduierung*) that pertains the act of recognizing. Recognition can be an effective or failed knowledge; the other's gaze sheds light (or not) on "'objective' facts" (Honneth 2021, p. 135): it either sees me peeping through the keyhole or does not. Thus, recognition "hopelessly exposes" the person to the other, that is, to society (Honneth 2021, p. 137). But, driven by the desire to participate in it, she would be forced to adapt to typified standards that would not be hers in the first place. Then, one could say, the epistemic character of recognition would not to be conceived in contemplative terms; rather, it concerns "the social act of ascribing [*Zuschreibung*] personal characteristics through which the subject can expect to find social acceptance and even admiration" (Honneth 2021, p. 137)—causing a hiatus within the person. Intersubjectivity is always "associated with the threat of self-loss or self-alienation":[37] recognition would be the moment when the self loses the authority of the "first-person perspective" (Honneth 2021, p. 139). This is because—it is good to repeat it—either the subject finds herself in the vortex of social consideration or precisely because the first-person perspective itself dissolves, as origin, into the otherness of the other.[38]

Honneth next considers recognition in the context of English-speaking treatments, arguing that the terms at stake are similar to those used by the French thinkers we have just discussed, while also showing how the evaluation of these terms changes significantly. Now considering Hume, Adam Smith, and John Stuart Mill, Honneth opens a new direction of research as far as the recognition studies are concerned, focusing on a domain that tended to be overlooked, but that reveals itself as having great significance both for the influence exerted on Kant and for the closeness between how recognition is conceived by those English thinkers and the daily use of the term: in fact, it is understood first and foremost as praise, opposed to blame. We can summarize Honneth's reconstruction according to four main conceptual steps.

First, both Hume and Smith give a central role to sympathy, conceived as that naturally delivered, affectively loaded capability to access another's mental states and to co-experience them, thus sharing their unfolding.[39] Such capability to "sympathize" (Honneth 2021, p. 74), to jointly feel (*Mitempfinden*), would not represent an anthropological, invariant character alone, but would provide us with certain implicit normative criteria to evaluate the actions of our associates. In other words, "we generally tend to morally approve or commend characteristics that manifest themselves in actions" that provoke sympathy in us (Honneth 2021, p. 60). It is useful to highlight two aspects already. Clearly, we have not yet defined an act of recognition because, Honneth claims, "we still need to add the ascription of a certain amount of authority to the other"; however, such an "emotional co-vibration" seems to be a necessary precondition for any recognitional act (Honneth 2021, p. 61). Interestingly, Honneth here refers to *Reification*.[40] It seems, then, that the conceptualizations outlined there did not properly define recognition, but a dimension

---

[37] In German, Honneth speaks of division or splitting of the subject, "Spaltung des Subjekts" (Honneth 2018, p. 188).
[38] See Honneth 2018, pp. 183–88.
[39] See Honneth 2021, p. 60.
[40] See Honneth 2021, p. 61, n. 14.

5.3 *Recognition:* from Affirmation to Authorization — 227

of *Erkennen* that every *Anerkennen* must entail, which is to be conceived in holistic and participatory terms and not purely cognitive ones, as stated by certain instances of of the French tradition. So, to say that sympathy is a necessary presupposition for every act of recognition seems to implicitly affirm that at least one flaw of the French tradition was to think of recognition as taking a subjectivist-cognitivist perspective as starting point, which would rule out this basic sympathy that characterizes (certain) human interactions. The second aspect concerns the *object* of such sympathy, that is, the attention has shifted from (attributed) personal characters to the actions of others or, better, the other, by revealing its personality through its own acts, is the evaluated object.

However, and this is the second step, it would be wrong to make moral judgment and sympathy coincide, both because we do not in fact feel the same degree of sympathy toward all our associates, and because it would seem unjustifiable to leave moral evaluations in general prey to our inclinations. The solution proposed by Hume and Smith is that of a cognitive operation, through which the adequacy of our moral criteria would be entrusted to "the correcting role of a 'spectator'" (Honneth 2021, p. 64), which, provided with normative authority, would free our judgment-formation from inconsistencies and personal preferences. Such objectivation-via-externalization of the normative criteria would then make it possible to judge our moral reactions depending on the possible agreement (or disagreement) of an external observer. This normative judge would result through a rational process of generalization of the multiple perspectives that could eventually come into play by observing an interaction: thus, guaranteeing normative authority to such observer would coincide with granting it potentially to any member of the social community.[41] According to Hume, generalizing our perspective would inform our moral sense, thus enabling us to distinguish sympathy and respect. The issue would be slightly different for Adam Smith, who actually identifies two forms of recognition. The first form is sympathy, which is no longer regarded as presupposition alone, while the second involves the search for a more general normative criterion for our moral evaluations. Smith understands the rational process of the generalization of perspectives as effective to the extent that such a generalized observer is then internalized in the figure of an inner judge. Once internalized, such an observer/judge would be able to inform us about the adequacy of our moral reactions, thus harmonizing it with the whole community. It is in this sense that Honneth speaks of "a gradual shift of perspective from the second person to one's own self" (Honneth 2021, p. 155).

> Smith therefore sees the need for a second stage of recognition ... This new form of recognition consists in internalizing as many perspectives as possible in order to produce the voice of an impartial and knowledgeable judge to whom we grant the authority to harmonize our emotions with those of others by means of approval and disapproval. Whereas the first, emotional form of recognition is directly related to others, whom we assume to have the same need for communi-

---

41 See Honneth 2021, pp. 62–64, 76–79.

cative sympathy, the second form of recognition depends on a generalized other, and is thus indirect and aimed at others (Honneth 2021, pp. 80–81).

If, therefore, sympathy directly addresses the interaction partner in the form of a reaction, this (properly normative) second form of recognition would require the inner judge as instance of moral mediation, thus considering the other person only indirectly. The inner judge would directly address our moral reactions, which are in turn directed by the behavior of others. We would praise another if the judge informs us about the adequacy or the value of that person's behavior we are reacting to.

The third step concerns the motivation for recognition, which would essentially coincide with the desire to be considered as members of the community we are in. But contrary to Rousseau, being a member of society would not make us hostages (*Geisel*) of its moral judgment; rather, for these English thinkers this coincides with being players (*Mitspieler*) in a community: "'Recognition' in this case is a social act of moral praise that a subject must be able to imagine for itself in order to be confident of being respected as a legitimate member of the social community" (Honneth 2021, p. 137). The generalization and internalization of normative criteria would make recognition multidirectional, avoiding the unilaterality proper of the French authors we considered, who mainly focused on being recognized, whereby the addressee had no say about the aptness of the recognition she was addressed. In the English paradigm, to be recognized coincides with being regarded as actors, that is, one who is able to morally judge—and possibly control—one's actions according to the criteria provided by the generalized other. If one does so, if one listens to the inner judge, then one's acts would be in accordance with a community-shared perspective, and thus worthy of praise. This normative authority would also be at work by recognizing, sifting through our moral reactions before the other. What motivates being recognized and recognizing would then be the desire for praise and the fear of blame, or, as John Stuart Mill says, of "disapproval" (Honneth 2021, pp. 88–89). But even in this case, Adam Smith adds one more element: what would motivate us to recognize and be recognized is not only the desire to be addressees of praise or affection, but rather to be "praise-worthy" (Honneth 2021, p. 78). It would not be enough for *any* personal features to be attributed to us or for us to be addressed by *any* attitudes: they must be perceived as *pertinent* to our person.

An individual whose desire for social membership can only be satisfied if its moral behavior and judgments are judged to be in line with the internalized norms of its community will feel compelled to subject its own social practices to constant moral inspection. In this tradition, therefore, intersubjective encounters are nearly automatically linked to the positive effect of learning to conform to the standards of the social community. The kind of recognition the subject receives from its "internal" observer, which in turn represents society as a whole, will reinforce its willingness to exercise moral self-control (Honneth 2021, p. 139).

Then, to the extent that we depend on other people and that we desire to be appreciated by them, we would feel driven to evaluate our actions from the perspective of the other (be it concrete or ideal), and to harmonize the first—and not just to fictitiously tailor them, as in Rousseau—to the criteria of the other, so that we are enabled to consider ourselves part of the game, full-fledged members of the social context we inhabit. Recognition would therefore result in the individual willingness to self-control, motivated by the desire to consider oneself a *legitimate* member of the community.

The fourth and last aspect Honneth mentions is that it is precisely this idea of recognition that is actually the one closest to the daily use of the term: it responds to what could be defined as a reward-logic, according to which the one worthy of appreciation and praise is a person able to meet the evaluative standards of the social context within she acts. Although it is true that a certain multi-directionality is at stake in the English tradition, even in this case the recognitional gesture itself is conceived unilaterally. *A* praises *B* and *B* accepts such praise as pertinent to her acts. What changes from the French tradition is that *B* would now be (reasonably) sure of the pertinence or adequacy of *A*'s judgement—thus not undermined in her self-certainty—and, above all, that *B* can also judge *A*'s attitudes. But such evaluations are at best temporally discrete and alternative, there is no real mutuality; and this is why Honneth argues that in such cases one should simply speak of recognitional reactions and not of recognition (Honneth 2021, p. 144). It is not difficult to see—having just read the debate that Honneth responds to in "Grounding Recognition"—a certain similarity between such recognizing reactions and Ikäheimo's perspective, whereby *B*'s role was identified only in recognizing *A* as a proper judge, thus outlining a de-powered mutuality.

According to Honneth, it is only the German tradition that affirms that mutuality necessarily pertains to the very concept of recognition.

The analysis starts with Kant and with the role the concept of interpersonal respect (*Achtung*) plays in solving the difficulties of grounding moral action. In short, once the categorical character of moral law (*Sittengesetzt*) has been codified, Kant finds himself at the impasse of having to explain what would push subjects to submit to it without recurring to heteronomous motives, that is, motives that are not determined by reason alone. As Honneth illustrates,[42] the solution Kant proposes in the *Groundwork of the Metaphysics of Moral* reconciles a twofold necessity. On the one hand, an epistemological issue, that is the need for a certain kind of objectivity that can be discovered by our cognitive faculty (*Anschauung*) as the embodiment of the moral law. On the other hand, a practical issue, namely, how such an object of knowledge would be able to elicit a motivation for moral action.[43] As is well known, the encounter with another person—that is, the object embodying moral law—would spark *Achtung* as motivating emotional reaction. It is worth reading some passages from the footnote on which Honneth's reconstruction focuses:

---

42 See Honneth 2021, p. 104, n. 11.
43 See Honneth 2021, pp. 98–104.

It could be objected that I only seek refuge, behind the word *respect*, in an obscure feeling, instead of distinctly resolving the question by means of a concept of reason. But though respect is a feeling, it is not one *received* by means of influence; it is, instead, a feeling *self-wrought* by means of a rational concept.... What I cognize immediately as a law for me I cognize with respect, which signifies merely consciousness of the *subordination* of my will to a law without the mediation of other influences on my sense. Immediate determination of the will by means of the law and consciousness of this is called *respect*, so that this is regarded as the *effect* of the law on the subject, and not as the cause of the law. Respect is properly the representation of a worth that infringes upon my self-love.... The *object* of respect is therefore simply the *law*, and indeed the law that we impose upon *ourselves* and yet as necessary in itself. As a law we are subject to it without consulting self-love; as imposed upon us by ourselves it is nevertheless a result of our will.... Any respect for a person is properly only respect for the law ... of which he gives us an example. Because we also regard enlarging our talents as a duty, we represent a person of talents also as, so to speak, an *example of the law* (to become like him in this by practice), and this is what constitutes our respect (Kant 1997, p. 14).

Thus, respect for others would represent, first, a "epistemic act" (*Erkenntnisleistung*):[44] we discover the other as a moral worth in herself; she is an example of the moral law, i.e. she has dignity. Second, this knowledge has "an effect on our empirical system of motivations" (Honneth 2021, p. 106), precisely because the perceived worth would depend on the submission of the other to moral law. What would infringe upon our self-love would be acknowledging the worth that consists in submitting to the moral law. And, in turn, such a perception would motivate us to give priority to the moral law over our self-centered interests.

In this way, according to Honneth, the concept of respect would decisively lay the foundations for how recognition is conceived both by Fichte and Hegel, who will explicitly use the term: at the center, there is not the demand or craving to be recognized, but the recognition that "we pay or owe to others". At the same time, the spectrum of motivations does not concern a psychological necessity experienced by the person, but rather the "spiritual," that is, rational dimension of the subject (Honneth 2021, p. 108). Two central elements of the concept recognition in the German tradition follow from these observations: "reciprocity" (*Wechselseitigkeit*) and "individual freedom" (Honneth 2021, p. 109).[45] Again, respect coincides with that emotional attitude that accompanies the acknowledgment of the other as the personification of the moral law. Now, given that every human being represents such an embodiment of the moral law and that every human being, by means of her rational capabilities, is compelled to perceive another as such embodiment, it would follow that everyone must consider each other in her being an exemplification of the *Sittengesetzt*, thus forming an interpersonal net of mutual respect. Second, since such recognition would concern the intimate connection between the individual person and moral law, it follows that the true object of respect is other's freedom, which would

---

[44] See Honneth 2018, p. 146.
[45] See Honneth 2018, p. 150.

coincide with his or her capability to self-determination by submitting to the moral law.

However, this view would entail an intrinsic ambiguity. On the one hand, *Achtung* involves an *empirical* event, the perception of an object with human features; on the other hand, it also enjoins a rational moral obligation. Thus, it possesses an obvious dynamic, characterized by a certain automatism,[46] because it supposedly accompanies every interpersonal encounter. But conversely the other person can be comprehended as a moral being only by virtue of a "particular form of his power of judgment" (Honneth 2021, pp. 110–11),[47] which exceeds the mere empirical realm. Thus, according to Honneth, such an act of knowledge would bridge the gap between the two *Critiques*, the division between the empirical and the intelligible dimensions.[48]

Faced with such an alternative between these two realms, both Fichte and Hegel opt to ground recognition within a rational domain. However, Honneth points out, the "rational motive" underlying the moral dimension of interpersonal relations must be repositioned in the broader persuasion regarding the "rationality of the real": recognition would then concern our nature, not according to Rousseau's or Adam Smith's use of the term, but to the extent that our nature expresses itself in our "spiritual activity." Even in a detranscendentalized framework such as Hegel's, our motives to moral (inter-)action could not be conceived other than flowing from our rational nature (Honneth 2021, p. 112).

Fichte's considerations take their move precisely from the interpersonal encounter between two rational subjects, which would open with a "summons" (*Aufforderung*) or exhortation from one to another (Honneth 2021, p. 115). Contrary to Althusser's concept of interpellation, according to which being approached would fix the addressee to her own social identity, such a summons has to be characterized as "invitation" (*Einladung*) "to undertake something": it would therefore constitute neither an order nor a demand. In his second step, Fichte follows the Kantian model, taking into account the outcomes of such an encounter. If by Kant the recognition of the other as an example of moral law causes respect, "Fichte's analysis of this communicative situation focused primarily on the interpretive acts the addressee must perform." In fact, Fichte points out that the "imperatives" (*Veranlassung*) here at stake do not follow the same rules as "natural causality," which responds to cause-effect binomials. So, respect cannot be merely *caused*. Rather, the invitation outlines the framework for a "second kind of causality," which is based on "reason," that is, our capability to understand (*Verstand*).[49] The invitation reveals the other as a rational being, able to understand the communicative content addressed to her, and therefore to respond. Approaching the other could not then coincide with a mechanistic

---

46 See, e.g. Timothy L. Brownlee 2015.
47 See Honneth 2018, pp. 151–52.
48 See Honneth 2021, p. 106.
49 See Honneth 2018, p. 158.

attribution of some features: it "demands a free reaction" (Honneth 2021, p. 116), it asks for an answer *from freedom* (*aus Freiheit*), precisely because the answer—both for what regards its modes and its contents—cannot be conceived as a reflexive mechanism.[50] But if the invitation awaits a response from freedom, then the respondent, in responding, is aware that the other has already limited his or her own freedom. By exhorting *B*, *A* leaves room for her freedom, limiting her own; and *B* knows that:

> Thus the relation of free beings to one another is necessarily determined in the following way, and is posited as thus determined: one individual's knowledge of the other is conditioned by the fact that the other treats the first as a free being (i.e. limits its freedom through the concept of the freedom of the first). But this manner of treatment is conditioned by the first's treatment of the other; and the first's treatment of the other is conditioned by the other's treatment and knowledge of the first, and so on *ad infinitum*. Thus the relation of free beings to one another is a relation of reciprocal interaction through intelligence and freedom. One cannot recognize the other if both do not mutually recognize each other; and one cannot treat the other as a free being, if both do not mutually treat each other as free (Johann G. Fichte 2000, p. 42).

The step Fichte takes here is decisive. The mutuality of recognition would not be realized in *B*'s response, in the consideration of *A* as an adequate judge of *B*'s traits (as it would on Ikäheimo's reading). Rather, *Wechselseitigkeit* would consist in the mutual self-restriction (*Selbstbeschränkung*) that underlies, as condition of possibility and necessary presupposition, any communicative interaction between rational, that is, free beings. One could say, however, that *Aufforderung* constitutes an igniting gesture and that *B*'s eventual response realizes mutuality only at a second moment, *after* the summons. If so, however, one should ask why *A* does not invite, say, a stone or a chair in the same way as he summons another person. Fichte is telling us that, for *A* to treat *B* in *C*, mutual recognition is already necessary: the summons itself results from a self-limitation that implies a *prior* recognition of the other as being able to respond freely. Thus, recognition is implicit in any linguistically mediated interaction because it coincides with a mutual self-limitation that leaves room for the other to invite and respond. Communication partners mutually recognizing each other would therefore coincide with their mutual recognizing as capable of understanding and (possibly) of responding, that is, as *rational*, that is, *free* beings. And precisely such communicative interaction would mark the passage from the spontaneous freedom to structure one's own world rationally to the *realization* of freedom: my capacity for self-determination would gain consistency and reality through its mutual confirmation.[51]

However, Fichte's scheme is limited by a serious worldlessness and he has find himself with the difficulty "to render such idealizing determinations of recognition more plausible in terms of our actions in the lifeworld" (Honneth 2021, p. 123).

---

50 See Honneth 2018, p. 159.
51 See Honneth 2021, pp. 118–123.

That is why Honneth identifies Hegel's merit with having carried out a detrascendentalization (*Detranzendentalisierung*) of the Fichtean model.[52] Hegel would not be interested in identifying invariant structures of social interaction such as those conditioned by the anthropological constant of *amour propre* or the Fichte's transcendental encounter. Rather, he intends to identify historical configurations of intersubjectivity in which the dynamics Fichte describes can actualize and instantiate themselves. Speaking of *Anerkennung*, then, he would mean *institutionally coagulated* forms of communication in which the involved subjects a) complementarily limit themselves with regard to their aims and freedom, b) act expressively toward each other, thus manifesting a certain attitude, and c), by fulfilling these first two points, mutually recognize each other in their self-being or self-determination.[53] "These configurations must be institutionalized, and thus 'real' or 'objective,' forms of human communication in which subjects restrict their respective self-interest by 'expressively' showing their respect for each other as equals in their being-for-itself" (Honneth 2021, p. 127).

These three conditions—complementary self-limitation, the centrality of expressive gestures, and mutuality in being confirmed regarding one's own worth as rational/free being—are found, according to the young Hegel, in love relations, which then constitute a form of being by oneself in the other. On the one hand, being recognized (*Anerkanntsein*) would coincide with a confirmation of one's self-being, since the self-limitation of the other would let the normative validity (*Geltung*) of one's capability to self-determination emerge. Only to this extent freedom is not mere arbitrariness, but gains objectivity: because, within the relationship, it has received a social space, its *right to exist*. On the other hand, recognizing (*Anerkennen*) would not mean attributing any features to the addressee, but first and foremost limiting oneself, thus granting the other that space-for-freedom in which she can determine herself without coercion.

Such an account reaches its full-fledged dimension only with the elaboration of theory of objective spirit. Thus, first, the worth that the other embodies would not depend on "individual preference" as by love but would express the historically situated "social order of preferences." Those facets of subjectivity that are worthy of recognition and of which one demands recognition would emerge only through and within "the particular set of institutions that have become 'second nature'" (Honneth 2021, p. 128). Second, because they are socially and institutionally embodied, such acts of recognition also constitute the spark for social conflict. The demand intrinsic to any recognition relationship is not a generic desire of the other,[54] any an-

---

52 See Honneth 2018, p. 168. The passage I am referring to is absent in the English edition.
53 Honneth literally speaks of "institutionell geronnene" forms, an effective expression which is lost in the English edition: see Honneth 2018, p. 173.
54 Here Honneth criticizes Kojève's reading; see Honneth 2021, pp. 128–131. So far as I know, these are the only passages in which Honneth considers directly the *Phenomenology of Spirit* exept for an other text, focused precisely on the demand for recognition. See Honneth 2012c, pp. 3–18.

thropological craving, or a psychological drive. Rather, demanding recognition coincides with demanding the possibilities of realizing one's own rationality, namely, one's freedom: Hegel "grasped the 'need' for recognition as the desire to realize our ability for a kind of rational self-determination that desires to be free and undisturbed" (Honneth 2021, p. 131). As we have seen, such realization can only be articulated through the mutual outlining of a detrascendentalized space-for-freedom. Thus, if freedom can actualize itself only socially, the absence or narrowness of such a space, if perceived as unjustified given the social order of preferences, would give rise to social conflict. Here Honneth provides us with the best overview of his own account:

> When two subjects encounter each other in institutionally organized relations of recognition formed as a result of the historical process of "progress in the consciousness of freedom", each offers the other a particular form of "respect", because, as a result of their socialization, they have learned to adhere to the norms underlying the respective sphere. If these subjects come to view relations of recognition as being too narrow, too constricting or too unequal, Hegel is convinced that the constant force of our rational will for self-determination will necessarily lead to struggles for new, expanded forms of recognition (Honneth 2021, p. 132).[55]

Before going any further, it is essential to highlight two nuances of the concept of freedom we are discussing. First, Kant's influence is manifest in the idea that freedom is deeply linked to norms of action, and to the authorship that subjects possess in bringing them about. Fundamentally, to be free means to act according to rational norms. Second, it follows from this that both Fichte and Hegel conceive the demand to be free that inhabits recognitional relations as a demand to express one's own nature of being rational. In the German tradition, recognition is hence conceived of as the way through which individuals grant each other the "capacity to follow autonomous norms" (Honneth 2021, p. 136). Only because recognition is "both a restriction and an expansion of freedom at the same time" (Honneth 2021, p. 140), it allows the realization of one's own possibilities to self-determination, namely, to rationality. This, in Hegel's view, would coincide with (inter-)acting according to norms provided by social context, which however have to be justified with regard to their being actual condition of one's rationality's unfolding.

5.3.2 An Attempt at Harmonization

The three traditions Honneth has dealt with provide us with a contrasting scenario. In the French paradigm, the constitutive dependence on recognition coincides with a "threat to our 'authentic' relationship-to-self." The British authors share the idea that

---

[55] I have modified the translation slightly to include the reference to recognition "spheres," which is not to be found in the English edition. See Honneth 2018, p. 179.

intersubjective recognition represents a "chance for moral self-control" and for the communal refinement of moral practices. Finally, the German tradition considers intersubjective recognition as "the condition of the possibility of individual self-determination" (Honneth 2021, p. 134).

These three approaches present us with such a diversity of meanings that one can legitimately wonder whether they refer to the same phenomenon. Even the distinction between positive (as with Taylor and Honneth) and negative (as in Sartre, Althusser, and Butler) theories of recognition, now in use in the literature, would seem to ignore an acute difference. On the one hand, the French tradition considers recognition as "the social ascription of certain (typifying) properties without any normative" connotation. On the other hand, the paradigm of Fichte and Hegel thinks of recognition—and here is Honneth's first decisive step to the reformulation of the concept—as a praxis of "moral authorization" (Honneth 2021, p. 142). The alternative, as Honneth now perceives, is therefore no longer between the attribution or perception-expression of evaluative features, as it was in "Grounding Recognition," but between (quasi-ontological) attribution of traits and mutual, normative authorization.

However, Honneth continues, an attempt at harmonization is not to be ruled out though. His purpose is not to dissolve the differences of the three traditions of thought in order to derive a homogeneous (and blurred) concept: rather, the account proposed in the last chapter of *Recognition* consists of two steps. First, Honneth argues that it is necessary to bracket out the different methodological approaches and the historical distances at play to identify which of the three paradigms could represent an apt starting point. Second, he claims that the other two approaches can be integrated in the attempt to overcome the possible shortcomings of the remaining model. In this attempt, Honneth intends to be guided by the question as to "which of the three models makes the strongest claim in terms of explaining our social form of life as a whole" (Honneth 2021, p. 146), since, in one way or another, this is the common object of every single idea of recognition we have encountered so far.

It is hardly surprising that Honneth's choice falls on Hegel, but the reasons for justifying such a decision allow us to understand a further evolution in his thought. Keeping in mind that we are pursuing a better comprehension and representation of our social form of life, Hegel's paradigm appears to be the most appropriate starting point—that can integrate the others, but not vice versa—basically for three reasons.

First, only Fichte and Hegel explain what it means for us human beings to live in a "spiritual world," that is, a world in which we orient ourselves according to "shared norms" or, as "Recognition as Ideology" reads, in a space of reasons (Honneth 2021, p. 147). This perspective further accentuates the normative character of the recognition Honneth has always defended, in a direction where the deontological influence of Brandom, Pinkard, and Pippin—explicitly mentioned in a footnote[56]—is hardly

---

56 See Honneth 2018, p. 199, n. 5. Such an explicit reference is omitted in the English edition; see Honneth 2021, p. 147, n. 5.

negligible. According to these authors, the shift, by Hegel, from first to second nature coincides precisely with the entry into a normatively characterized world.[57] That the German tradition takes such normative dimension into account would not play an indifferent role if the aim is to understand recognition in the wider horizon of our form of life. In fact, we can properly explain our living together (*Zusammenleben*),[58] Honneth says, if we conceive of "a practice in which subjects mutually recognize each other as co-authors" of the "shared norms" that regulate their (inter-)practices (Honneth 2021, p. 150)—echoing the concept of complementary role obligations outlined in *Freedom's Right*.

Second, Fichte's and Hegel's "intersubjectivist reinterpretation of Kant's notion of respect" illuminates the "communicative conditions" that all other traditions also presuppose (Honneth 2021, p. 147), both on an ontological and, above all, on a normative level. That the other is present to me communicatively is quite evident, but it is significant that he or she is always seen as "a person who is authorized to co-determine our common life" (Honneth 2021, p. 148).[59] Arguing that such a normative-communicative condition is valid even in Rousseau's thought seems to imply that, even if we understood sociality in a negative way, that is, as power or domination, the subjected person recognizes the other's authoritative faculty on the norms of *our*—hers and mine—acting. Honneth seems to maintain that even in such a case we are always communicative *co-authors* of the norms that regulate our (inter-)acting, perhaps with differences of potential. Also in this sense, I think, Honneth speaks of a gradation that pertains to the concept of recognition: not every recognitional concretion realizes such co-authorship in equal terms, as the idea of mutuality would suggest. Anyway, Fichte and Hegel show that what would constitute our societies *as* spiritual world is a practice in which subjects mutually recognize each other as co-authors of the norms they follow.

Finally, Hegel—more than Fichte—is the author to take into consideration because he understands such mutual authorization to authorship not only as a condition for the existence of social norms, but also "as a set of practices rooted in the lifeworld and structured by institutions—practices engaged in by living subjects driven by moral concerns" (Honneth 2021, p. 151). The detranscendentalization allows us to understand the spiritual world not in an idealistic way, but, again, as a historic space of reasons, as a second nature. Therefore, Hegel's theory of recognition represents the most appropriate model because it includes the communicative conditions that

---

57 "[R]ecognition is a *normative* attitude. To recognize someone is to take her to be the subject of normative statuses, that is, of commitments and entitlements, as capable of undertaking responsibilities and exercising authority. This is what it means to say that as reciprocally recognized and recognizing, the creatures in question are *geistig*, spiritual, beings, and no longer merely natural ones" (Brandom 2007, p. 35).
58 See Honneth 2018, p. 199.
59 Honneth speaks of a "right to have a say" (*Mitspracherecht*) that the subjects recognize each other. See Honneth 2018, p. 200.

allow us to shed light on our shared world in accordance with its peculiarity: to be inhabited by actors endowed with statuses, responsibilities, and commitments. Hegel is the only one to historically consider our (inter-)acting according to norms, and consequently to conceive recognitional practices as mutual self-limitation that authorizes the emergence of a space-for-freedom for questioning such norms.

Now, the confrontation with some aspects of the other two traditions allows Honneth to refine this definition and to recall (or specify) the place of recognition with respect to most of the different issues we have encountered during our reconstruction—from social reproduction to social pathologies, from social conflict to interpersonal and systemic power dynamics.

The major contribution provided by the English tradition consists in a more refined explanation of the "belief that our moral customs represent a kind of second nature" (Honneth 2021, p. 152).[60] As we have seen, Hume, Smith, and Mill outline a certain harmonization between interactional norms and social habits, by means of which we are enabled to express blame or praise; and that would represent a pattern of how institutional standards are took on by subjects in the process of socialization. Hegel's shortcoming in this case is that he fails to explain such a second nature exclusively through the Aristotelian concept of *habitus*, thus through mechanistic terms, while the "psychological aspects of this process remain relatively obscure" (Honneth 2021, p. 153).[61]

The English paradigm offers a decisive contribution precisely in conceiving of the socialization process with a certain degree of complexity—and in proper normative terms. The starting point is set regarding the motives that would drive us to recognize and being recognized. Honneth is not persuaded by Fichte's and Hegel's idea that the demand for recognition is be grounded in a drive to unfold one's rationality. This overly idealistic depiction has its lifeworldly side in the account according to which our motives to act morally must be rooted in our "striving for membership in the social community." What motivates us to act in accordance with the norms of a community is the "subjective expectation of receiving the approval of the other members of society" (Honneth 2021, p. 153). A clear risk of a conformist or conventionalist explanation of socialization must be immediately mitigated in two ways. First, Honneth is not denying that the element at stake in recognition relationships is

---

[60] Honneth here speaks of the 'second-naturality' *Zweitenaturhaftigkeit* of our customs; see Honneth 2018, p. 205.

[61] Clearly, Honneth here refers to the paragraphs of the *Encyclopaedia* on habits, where Hegel explicitly talks of second nature in mechanistic terms. See Hegel, *Philosophy of Mind* §§ 409–410. However, connecting these passages with other Heglian accounts on *Bildung* and culture could do a better justice to Hegel, thus providing us with a dialectical account of the integration of individuals within the horizons of our second nature. See Hegel, *Philosophy of Right*, specially §§ 187 and 270. See also Hegel, *Phenomenology of Spirit*, above all §§ 616–631. However, it is true that when Hegel has to tell us precisely *how*, pragmatically, our spiritual dimension would assume features of second nature, the mechanistic accent of habit plays a major role. However, I argue, Honneth's disregarding the *Phenomenology* here shows its shortcomings.

individual autonomy: he is objecting to the idealism that characterizes the Hegelian view. Let us take a step back. Faced with the ambiguity intrinsic to the idea of *Achtung*—half empirical act of knowledge, half moral obligation—both Fichte and Hegel gave priority to our rational nature, grounding moral action in general and recognition on human beings' drive to unfold their rationality. By opting for an English solution, Honneth is trying to bring the motivational horizon back to an empirical level. The desire to be considered legitimate members of a community motivates gestures of recognition, which in turn do not simply represent the means of persons' being *assimilated* into society. Rather, by virtue of recognition, people who strive to take part in the space of reasons are *included* in it. Being a member of our spiritual world means being endowed with those statuses and commitments that make us co-authors of the norms we ourselves instantiate in acting, that is, it means exercising freedom. This brings us to the second point, that is, the continuity that one must acknowledge with *Freedom's Right*:[62] freedom, according to Honneth, is such only if it is *social*. So, being with another in a community is a necessary precondition for being with oneself in it, that is to be free. I can be with myself in the other only if there are reasons for me to share with others the norms that guide our action, only if I participate in spheres of social action. Entering the spheres of freedom means entering social, historically given spheres.

But how does one enter these spheres of freedom? Generally speaking, the matter is that of the individual's integration into society, that is, into the horizon whereby moral actions coagulate into configurations of the second nature. Here, the main advantage provided by the English tradition is the concept of the "inner spectator" (Honneth 2021, p. 153), which is grounded on our striving to adopt moral norms in order to be considered legitimate players, and, more importantly, mediates our acting with social standards, constantly informing us about the latter. Contrary to the Hegelian concept of moral conscience (*Gewissen*), which remains (intentionally) bound to a certain fixity, the inner observer should be conceived "as the psychological representation of the moral reactions of a gradually 'generalized' other" (Honneth 2021, p. 155). To this extent, our inner life could be represented as a concert of different voices, as a dialogue between different instances that internally reproduce the communicative structure of our lifeworld.[63] The brief reference Honneth

---

[62] Honneth offers some important clarifications about the connection between social freedom and joint norms-authorship in *The Idea of Socialism*. The fundamental dimensions of social freedom, being together (*miteinander*) and for each other (*füreinander*), are expressed at the social level in economic experimentalism and the structures of public opinion. See Honneth 2017, esp. chs. 3 and 4.
[63] Although Honneth believes that Plessner's thought is flawed by a marked solipsism (see Honneth and Hans Joas 1988, p. 84), and given that their theoretical interests are certainly directed elsewhere, it is difficult not to find here a certain legacy from the German anthropological philosophy, which certainly shaped Honneth's first elaborations. The perspective according to which inner life can be represented in the form of a *dialogue between instances* is here reformulated rather clearly according to the idea that (moral) persons represent triadic structures, which reproduce the triadic structure of our spiritual world or shared world. See Honneth, 1999. If in the case of the lifeworld there is me, the

makes to Freud's Super-Ego as the inner concretion of social normative standards further clarifies what is at stake.[64] In *The Struggle for Recognition*, the appeal to Winnicott and especially Mead was to justify the emergence of the *intra*-psychic processes starting from *inter*-psychic interactions: play, game, and vocal gestures were conceived there as the third element mediating I and me. But, as we have seen in "Grounding Recognition," Honneth rejected Mead's view for its psychologist approach, namely, a functionalistic reduction of self-relational instances, as well as of the individual socialization.

The elements at stake in this new explanation of socialization, however, are similar: the inner observer emerges as the "gradual shift of perspective from the second person to one's own self" (Honneth 2021, p. 155), as the concretion of social norms, the generalized other, the capacity to consider myself reflectively. Or better, the moral person rises as the capacity to consider myself according to a second-order reflectivity, because I relate to myself according to what I expect the others to expect (*Erwartungs-Erwartungen*).[65] And even more so, such an inner dialogue reproduces the structure of an intersubjective relationship, which will always be articulated through the mediation of the generalized other. The extra step that Honneth seems to take in appealing to the inner-observer account is that of trying to translate what he inherited from Mead into normative terms: the I-me polarity outlined in *The Struggle for Recognition* is proposed anew but with regard to motives and reasons to actions, not psychological functions or anthropological structures. However, as the reference to Freud shows, that does not mean that Honneth completely abandons psychological or anthropological explanations.

The integration of the two paradigms therefore leads to the following depiction:

> According to the conception I have outlined, the relation between these two understandings is that Hegel's notion defines the elementary conditions of mutual recognition under which a constantly changing life-world can be regarded as being normatively regulated at all, whereas Hume and Smith's conception names the practices of social approval and affirmation by which cooperatively constructed norms become anchored in individuals' own systems of motivation. In the first case, the term "recognition" indicates the practice of mutual authorization to create and examine norms; in the second case, it merely refers to the affirmative reaction of an already normatively constituted community to the moral behavior of individual members of society (Honneth 2021, p. 156).

On the one hand, Hegel, with his model of mutual recognition and the related conflictuality, allows us to conceive our lifeworld in normative terms, since it outlines

---

other, and the generalized other, in the case of the person it is easy to distinguish the mediation operated by the third, the inner observer, between me and my moral reactions. Both the shared world and the person would then constitute We-forms that cannot be reduced to I-Thou polarities. See Helmuth Plessner 2019, p. 280. On the triadic structures of our *Mitwelt* and our persons, see Hans-Peter Krüger 2006; and Krüger 2019, p. 86.

64 See Honneth 2021, p. 154.
65 See Gesa Lindemann 2006.

the social contexts of articulation and questioning of norms. On the other hand, Hume and Smith provide the means to anchor such interactions in the systems of motivation: the desire to be free and to be co-author of the norms that guide my actions cannot be thought of as disarticulated from my desire to be part of a social context. However, Honneth points out, the role of social approval boils down exclusively to this motivational scheme, since mutual recognition and recognizing reactions cannot coincide: they remain too one-sided and too dependent on the lifeworld in its current configuration to be a satisfactory model. In other words, recognizing reactions are useful to the extent that a complex—namely, mediated, triadic—understanding of them would provide us with a more refined account on the normative socialization of the individual, the process through which we become legitimate members of a given second nature. But they would fall short when it comes to explain what it would mean to be legitimate members, which entails the capability to reformulate the rules.

As far as French tradition is concerned, Honneth's operation is twofold, because Rousseau and Althusser illuminate two different aspects that can interact with the Hegelian theory. Regarding Rousseau, the theme of social pathologies can represent a point of contact. As we have seen, Rousseau believes that striving for social affirmation pushes individuals to display certain (real or fictitious) characters or qualities, the recognition of which then jeopardizes their possibilities to access their true self. One could also say that, since public space is dominated by the recognition of simulated attitudes, thus representing a "masquerade" (Honneth 2021, p. 158), the subject is prevented to get access to who he or she actually is. Honneth maintains that such are the pathological "reactions" (*Reaktionsbildungen*) Hegel describes regarding those who are excluded from corporations (Honneth 2021, p. 161),[66] who would "accordingly try to gain *recognition* through the external manifestations of success" (Hegel, *Philosophy of Right*, § 253). Such individuals, not being recognized as members of a social context, not being included within the ethical fabric of a cooperative "space-for-freedom" (*Freiheitsspielraum*) (Honneth 2021, p. 162, my translation),[67] react by developing eye-catching attitudes oriented at stimulating approval. Rousseau's and Hegel's descriptions of, respectively, recognition and reactions to non-recognition appear alike. The outward self-displaying and the consequent inward estrangement are therefore caused by a still unripe broadening of the norms inherent to recognition that are instantiated only in *some* institutional concretions. The lack of democratization, of co-authorship, and co-authority pushes—Honneth seems to tell us—those who are excluded to a distorted adaptation, and they will remain so inasmuch as they never really participate in the communicative, norm-elaborating processes that regulate the relations in which they find themselves. Thus,

---

[66] See Honneth 2018, p. 216.
[67] While Joseph Ganahl translates *Freiheitsspielraum* with the term "freedom," from now on I will use the expression 'space-for-freedom,' as it is more adequate to render Honneth's idea. See Honneth 2018, p. 217.

Rousseau's description does not concern recognition but precisely the social consequences of non-recognition, which depend on political, economic, and institutional settings. Earlier in *Recognition*, Honneth interprets Hegel's well-known master-slave dialectic in the same way: in this figure of the *Phenomenology*, the failure of recognition is due to the social norms the participants inhabit, to the structures of second nature in which the relationship is implemented, which prevent an effective sharing of normative tasks.[68] Only changing the frame of authorization through conflict and renewed norms of recognition will allow a wider and more inclusive recognition between persons.

The relationship between recognitional interactions and socio-cultural background is at the center of Honneth's confrontation with Althusser and Butler, whereby the former attempts to clarify further his position before the ideological dimension that recognition can take on. The position of the so-called negative theories of recognition can be summed up with this main idea: interpersonal confirmation of roles and social identities convey, through a positive self-perception gained within and thanks to the relationship, forms of domination and submission without repression. Butler's focus on family and gender roles highlights the idea that the very affection that characterizes such contexts, as well as the natural dependence of children on caregivers, opens the door to a subordination through recognition that is voluntarily embraced. One adapts to or gets inscribed in a state of affairs that is thus imposed. Clearly, some elements are similar to Rousseau, but it seems useful to highlight the properly ideological component taken into consideration by this second account, which operates behind the back of all the actors involved: here, the issue at stake is not the desire to belong to certain groups and the consequent modulation of one's own features or skills. Rather, social relationships themselves (perceived positively by the actors) inevitably do nothing but reproduce patterns that pre-outline, thus determine, the possibilities of those who are socialized into them.[69] In this case, recognition means little more than that (more or less state-related) institutions provide individual or collective actors with socially typified features, which induce them to unforcefully fulfil pre-assigned roles.[70]

Honneth shows that not every relationship Hegel describes as a "relationship of mutual recognition is in fact free of domination, dependence and oppression" (Honneth 2021, p. 170). The example Honneth considers is the condition of women as it is

---

[68] See Honneth 2021, pp. 128–129.
[69] "How is it that the subject is the kind of being who can be exploited, who is, by virtue of its own formation, vulnerable to subjugation? Bound to seek recognition of its own existence in categories, terms, and names that are not of its own making, the subject seeks the sign of its own existence outside itself, in a discourse that is at once dominant and indifferent. Social categories signify subordination and existence at once. In other words, within subjection the price of existence is subordination" (Butler 1997, p. 20). See also Kristina Lepold 2014.
[70] This passage is absent in the English edition. Honneth says "auf gewaltlose Weise zur Erfüllung der ihnen zugewiesenen Rollen". See Honneth 2018, p. 218; and Honneth 2021, pp. 162–163.

the described in the *Philosophy of Right*. According to Hegel, marriage represents a *"free surrender"* of one's own atomistic individuality, hence an ethical sphere of being with oneself by the other oriented by the recognitional norms of "mutual love and support," as well as the satisfaction of sexual needs (Hegel, *Philosophy of Right*, §§ 168 and 164). According to the definition of recognition, both partners should be endowed with the possibility of questioning their (inter-)practices by resorting to motives and reasons that appear legitimate within the normative horizon of those very practices. In other words, both partners can always resort to the norm of mutual care, reformulating it and adapting it to needs experienced from time to time. However, that Hegel argues that a "girl's vocation [*Bestimmung*] consists essentially only in the marital relationship" and his general conception *the* feminine and *the* role of women in the household raises, euphemistically, serious doubts about the *parity* of such relation, that is, the actual possibility in recurring freely to those norms (Hegel, *Philosophy of Right*, § 164Z).[71] How is it possible that women freely (*aus freien Stücken*) accept such subordination?[72] One could simply reply that that idea of marriage per se, for its institutional configuration, does not support any form of equality; on the contrary, it is pure domination conveyed by ideological recognition. But Honneth once again decides to start from the point of view of the involved actors, who actually live and experience equality in affection and freedom in being with each other. He again proposes the methodological historical-hermeneutical perspective defended in "Recognition as Ideology": even with all the criticism that *we* can *now* address to the idea of marriage that Hegel describes, it would be almost undeniable that precisely this relational form is experienced as an ethical good by the subjects involved, as a condition to good life. And if this experience of those involved is not taken seriously into consideration, the risk is to lose grip on social reality, which is so decisive for critical theory. It is important here to briefly repeat what the problems of a perspective that is disengaged with the participants' experience would be. Using Habermas's terms, the problem with third-person perspectives is that they "get at the meaning of behavior through the functional role that it plays in a system of modes of behavior" (Habermas 1987, p. 7), without supposing in the involved beings the same access to meaning. Now, radically implementing such an approach with regard to *human* beings entails either universalism or ethical paternalism, because it would disregard or dissolve the normative status, agency, and capabilities of the participants for getting access to the meaning (good life) of their living. Then, instead of the third-person perspective, Habermas and Honneth—not without differences—opt for a second-person approach, one that takes the participants' own view of their normative experience into account. Such an approach increases the burden of opacity that the theory is supposed to bear, due to its historical and experiential setting—

---

[71] See also Hegel, *Philosophy of Right* §§ 166–167.
[72] See Honneth 2021, pp. 163–165.

thus making it more difficult to distil a concept of ideological recognition without reducing critical thinking to contextualism.

The first step to untangling these difficulties is that Hegel describes the subordination of women as grounded *outside* the norms of care and the space for interpreting them. This "outside" (*Außerhalb*) is represented by a certain idea of "nature" that influences and unbalances the whole recognition relationship (Honneth 2021, p. 165). It is the feminine nature itself that determines certain roles and social collocations and that defines the *Bestimmung* of women. Clearly, Honneth's interest is not to emphasize the conservative side of Hegel's depiction, or his being a son of his own time: rather, it is noteworthy for him that, by describing ethical forms of a spiritual world, nature in this case appears as a completely unmediated element. Within second nature, the first nature rises again—but, *for us*, clearly as product of the second. Marriage *is* a kind of mutual authorization, but some personal features of the participants do not derive from the outlined ethical space-for-freedom. Rather, they appear as unchangeable matters, coming from outside our spiritual world. That implies that "mutual authorization to examine the implementation of shared norms"—love and support—cannot give any clue about what "reasons" are actually "at the disposal of those involved" (Honneth 2021, p. 166). For, evidently, what can be challenged by the participants in order to reformulate their intersubjective practices must be considered *changeable* from their point of view. For example, a different division of domestic work can be discussed by virtue of the mutual authorization of the partners if they consider it as matter that falls within the space of reasons they disclose for each other, thus not determined by nature.

> The size of the space of the reasons upon which objections to the prevailing interpretation of a shared norm can be based within a given order of recognition is not determined solely by the fact that the participants mutually grant each other the equal right to judge and criticize their shared practices. What determines the number of legitimate reasons that can be brought forth, and thus what can be criticized, objected to or called into question, are instead *worldviews* and *systems of interpretation* that intrude into the relation of recognition *from the outside* by distinguishing between the unchangeable and the changeable, between nature and culture (Honneth 2021, p. 166, my emphasis).

Such worldviews therefore operate a breach between what is *geistig* and what has no normative value—nature—thus subtracting it from possible discussions and reformulations. And "the larger the domain of given facts" (*Bereich von Gegebenheiten*), "the smaller the scope of reasons" (*Umfang der Gründe*) (Honneth 2018, p. 223, my translation).

This blind spot in Hegel's theory of recognition allows a dialogue with Althusser. If certain institutional arrangements prevent some elements from being objects of mutual authorization, then the recognitional relation, that is "intended to prevent relations of domination, would in fact perpetuate that relation of subordination." For, "from above," another type of recognition forces the participants to perceive their own features as "unchangeable elements of their own nature" (Honneth

2021, p. 168). However, if Honneth argues that, given that the issue regards either what elements are taken away or not available for the recognition relations itself in the first place, it is misleading to describe such ascriptions using the term recognition. Clearly, such ascriptions—which, again, come from *above* or from *outside* the interpersonal dimension—to a large extent shape and condition the relationships of recognition, the ethical contexts in which they happen, their modalities, and their contents. But the acts of ascription still do not coincide with the mutual acts of recognition, that is, with the self-limitation that gives space to other's freedom to express normative considerations. To consider some features as one's own and as immutable, that is, features that are therefore not available to normative evaluation, can instead be conceived as "the looping effect of a politically defined and relatively stable classification," or "as the subjective effect of a socially hegemonial way of speaking," aimed at "preserving social and economic privileges" (Honneth 2021, pp. 168–169).

The example of Uncle Tom given in "Recognition as Ideology" perhaps makes us better understand what Honneth's proposal is. While it is possible to grant—not undoubtedly—that the master's esteem for his good servant is sincere, it is clear that such an attribution does not coincide with recognition, according the new emphasis placed on the concept. An attribution of esteem, a confirmation of socially and publicly displayed qualities, the reception of certain evaluative features—which, for example, can help a slave trader to distinguish a 'good' slave from a 'bad' one—are not sufficient to define recognition. Such an evaluation could very well coincide with a reification—in a literal sense—of the other. At most, one could speak of the esteem for the good slave as a really thin recognizing reaction, which, in fact, unfolds as one-sided attribution. That does not coincide with recognition because the space-for-freedom to which Tom is authorized is non-existent and, above all, one can well imagine that he does not exercise any kind of demand about a widening of that space. His answer to the master's *Aufforderung* is be confined to mere acceptance and how he is being addressed is not be mediated by his own freedom. Accordingly, that the slave accepts such a state of affairs is not derived from recognitional relations themselves. Rather, it is due to the ideological influence that certain classification and linguistic practices have in shaping those features, for which an actor perceives herself as a *non-actor*, that is, as not being legitimated to be a player (*Mitspieler*) of the social space endowed with capabilities of co-authorship. Since gestures of recognition concern the cooperative delineation of spaces-for-freedom, confusing such interactions with the attribution of characteristics that effectively exclude individuals from such spaces would bring no major advantages. The only one—a minimal one, according to Honneth—is to clarify to a certain extent the "simultaneity of enticement and subordination, attraction and constriction" (Honneth 2021, p. 169). One can make a rather trivial example. Certainly, short-sightedness considerably affects the ability to see, it shapes the conditions of possibility of sight. The scope of my vision is then determined by my short-sightedness, but myopia and sight are not the same thing. Similarly, Honneth claims, the space of reasons for recognition is shaped by conditions that are different from it, and he argues that it is good to keep this distinction clear. The issue can be further clarified in terms of possibilities (of self-realization) gained by the participants within the relationship: both in the marriage and in the master-slave examples, it is clear that the imbalance between the poles of the relationship consists in the potential difference that concerns the *actual* use of freedom that is mutually granted. One could almost say that Honneth here renews the material criterion of "Recognition as Ideology" in normative terms: the genuineness of recognition can be detected if its expressive acts are accompanied by the effective authorization to reshape the relationship itself by authoring its governing norms—and even then, only after the fact.

The two branches of the French tradition therefore do not deal with recognition, but with non-recognition or dysfunctional recognition, thus outlining two faces of *exclusion*. On the one hand, social pathologies that are instantiated in mystifications of one's own traits and qualities are the result of "social closure" (Honneth 2021, p. 170). On the other hand, the potential of mutual recognition is eroded by an "argumentative closure" (Honneth 2021, p. 172): the space of reasons is subtracted from under the feet of the participants through the naturalization of certain traits by means of classification and linguistic practices. Such reified personal features can therefore no longer be resorted to as arguments for questioning the norms governing the relationships.

In this context, two aspects are fundamental. First, the concept of gradation (*Graduierung*) that Honneth used in some passages, especially at the beginning of the comparison between the three paradigms.[73] Given the porous correlation between systems of interpretation and relationships of recognition, the connection between the space of reasons and areas of facts cannot be conceived except as dialectical and always open to discussion. To this extent, norms are never completely disjointed from facts. It is precisely Hegel's merit, namely, detrascendentalization, that supposedly leads him to describe relational configurations as contaminated by non-recognition, by fixations of personal features. From this point of view, then, the spaces-for-freedom delineated by mutual authorization are always *gradual*, since they are never free from unfinished discussions on the margins of such spaces, on their inclusiveness, and on correlation that conflicting norms should assume before each other —for example, legal forms and emotional ties in the family.

This brings us, second, to the concept of conflict.[74] In fact, Honneth claims that such relationships of recognition cannot be conceived as always already institutionalized, as accomplished in themselves, and not in need of reformulations. Surely,

---

[73] See Honneth 2021, pp. 135–136.
[74] I think Honneth here draws from Bertram and Celikates, who endow a conflictual character to normative relations of recognition, and define recognition as mutual granting of "leeway," namely, a space-for-freedom. Anyway, Honneth emphasizes that proper conflict concerns precisely the *scope* of the space-for-freedom and its participants more than the interpretation of single norms. See Bertram and Celikates 2015.

"their respective normative contents must consist of routine practices that have evolved into individual habits that have become second nature." However, both the recognitional spheres and their normative content "must be conceived as being constantly controversial" and conflictual (Honneth 2021, p. 173).

> It is easy to see that the susceptibility of relationships of recognition to the most diverse forms of conflicts results from the fragility of the material making up these relationships. If the bonds of recognition consist merely in socially institutionalized norms among subjects who authorize each other to co-determine how these norms are interpreted and put into practice, then conflicts can constantly arise over the extent of their application as well as the circle of individuals to whom they apply (Honneth 2021, p. 173).

In this sense, conflict allows us to conceive of the process of institutionalization of norms as an open horizon and not as an already closed one.

5.4 Some Open Issues: A Spatial Account of Recognition

This chapter has provided an overview of three main issues that have accompanied us since the beginning of our reconstruction of Honneth's paradigm of recognition: the nature of gestures of recognition, their mutual character, and the tension between recognition and power—issues that also appear as Honneth is criticized of psychologizing and culturalizing justice (see section 1.3 above).

In "Grounding Recognition," Honneth outlines four general features that a general definition of recognition should entail. First, recognizing has to do with affirming or confirming certain qualities of human beings or groups. Second, recognition is a certain *attitude*, whereby symbolic or verbal expressions come down to a certain point: recognition is a matter of acts and it hinges on how those qualities are practically treated, rather than merely affirmed. Third, recognitional acts cannot be thought of as consequences or side-effects of other attitudes. Fourth, recognition is conceived of as a genus that entails different species, namely, love, respect, and esteem.

Taking these characters into account, Honneth opts for a second step for a receptive model, according to which recognition represents a moral stance that adapts itself to the evaluative features of the other, which in turn emerge as such thanks to the standards proper to our second nature. Thus, recognition, by expressing them publicly, allows their actualization. Precisely such letting oneself be determined by the other with regard to one's features, namely, the adequateness of my stance and acts to them, represents the moral element of recognition. One could then add that only once affirmed in the public space would these characters have such a consistency as to enable the recognizee to relate to herself according to them.

However, taking *Recognition* into account, such a definition per se could end up coinciding with recognizing reactions. But the rather evident developments Honneth implements in his latest monograph do not go in the opposite direction. The remarkable gain for the concept of recognition is that of a clear, and indeed necessary, mutual framework. If, in fact, the receptive model proposed in "Grounding Recognition" is conceived in truly bilateral and reciprocal terms—that is, not relegating mutuality to *B*'s judgement on the correctness of *A*'s recognition—one obtains nothing but the mutual authorization to the normative tasks described in *Recognition*. Thanks to the idea of authorization, Honneth can fully conciliate the two emphases we have encountered so far: recognition as an affirming reception and as a chance for freedom and joint commitments. One can further clarify such continuity by merging the respective terminologies. Authorization means that recognition is a mutual self-limitation of freedom that *coincides* with the reception of the evaluative features of others, because—as we have seen with Fichte—I limit myself only before a free being. The features of others are hence not to be thought of as mere attributes (according to the Aristotelian idea of the term), but properly as an actor's possibilities, capabilities, and entitlements: as a normative status, whose granting accompanies any self-limitation. And such normative capabilities, which in theory are proper to each actor as such, can only be expressed, that is, actualized, by means of a previous co-authorization to co-authorship.

The advantage of the strong mutual implications that the idea of authorization possesses is that of being able to more sharply distinguish the lexicon of recognition from that of power. Three aspects mark recognition before subjecting gestures, that is before the ascriptions of features, whose dominating consequences are not completely alien to one-sided recognizing reactions.

The first point is a more pre-Hegelian description of being with oneself in the other. Freedom that pertains to recognition relations does not merely coincide with complying with the many role obligations, with being the member of an ethical sphere. Honneth here emphasizes that social freedom is realized *only* if the ethical-social norms to which we submit can be traced back to our own authority, that is, to our being their (co-)authors. If not, that would be a sign of us not being considered full-fledged actors.

The second aspect is related to what we may call the Habermasian tones through which Honneth nuances his account. The mutual authorization to be full-fledged actors is reciprocally granting each other the right to have a say: recognition opens— and coincides with—those *communicative* spaces of negotiation of the norms that guide our action. The spheres of recognition do not merely represent contexts in which the person is able to develop an undamaged self-relation, or domains in which she can be free by experiencing a satisfaction of her need for complementarity alone. These two dimensions find their fulfilment and actualization in communicative practices that regard joint commitments to (co-)authorship among the participants: "Each person participates in the role of co-legislator in a *cooperative* enterprise" (Habermas 1998, p. 31). This is a decisive element, useful for distinguishing between practices of power and practices of recognition, as it provides a criterion for evaluations after the fact with regard to a person's normative performance: from our historical point of view, one could assess the genuineness of certain institutionalizations of recognition from the quality of the normative powers granted to participants. But from a general point of view, what determines recognition as recognition is not the species it assumes, but precisely an unimpaired access to normative formulations, accorded intersubjectively.[75]

The third aspect hence concerns the space of reasons or, better, its unclear relationship with recognition interactions. On the one hand, the first coincides with the horizon of second nature that, in turn, does not coincide with recognition relations: rather, the latter inhabit it and are informed by it. On the other hand, the mutual gestures of recognition themselves outline the space-for-freedom, that is, the space of reasons. Recognition draws spaces-for-freedom, and it is drawn by them. This apparent overlapping does not regard a mere chicken-egg problem, but precisely concerns the difficult relationship between sociality and society that we have seen throughout the whole reconstruction, which can be translated into the terms of intersubjectivity and system we have already encountered. It is, one might say, the problem of the beginning that every account of society that is inspired by Hegel has to face.

I believe that this spatial concept of recognition can be deciphered by considering three issues, which in turn are problematic to a certain degree. The first is related to the very concept of second nature. The latter should be conceived as intrinsically dialectical, that is, at the same time a condition and the outcome of recognitional gestures, and to this extent always susceptible of modification and (mis-)developments. In this sense, not only is society a condition for the existence of sociality,[76] since our interpersonal relationships are always informed by contexts that precede and go beyond them. But sociality is, in turn, also a condition of society, since our form of life, normatively understood, can only express itself in a space of reasons that is articulated intersubjectively.

However, second, this conception implies outlining two spaces: the space of reasons and its outside. Such a perspective, elaborated to describe the reciprocal intertwining and mutual distinguishing of domination practices and gestures of recognition, seems almost a re-proposal of the Habermasian colonization thesis. This, besides exposing Honneth's theory to solutions that certainly do not fall within his intentions, exacerbates the hiatus already perceived in *Freedom's Right*, for example in the difference between market society and market—more generally, between cooperative spheres of freedom and the context they inhabit, between *Gemeinschaft* and

---

75 "Since communicative processes and forms of life have certain structural feature in common, [the participants] could ask themselves whether these features harbor normative contents that could provide a basis for shared orientations. Taking this as a clue, theories in the tradition of Hegel, Humboldt, and G. H. Mead have shown that communicative actions involve shared presuppositions and that communicative forms of life are interwoven with relations of reciprocal recognition, and to this extent, both have a normative content. These analyses demonstrate that morality derives a genuine meaning, independent of the various conceptions of the good, from the form and perspectival structure of unimpaired, intersubjective socialization" (Habermas 1998, p. 40).
76 See Volker Schürmann 2010, pp. 73–89.

Gesellschaft. I do not think that this impression is only due to unfortunate consequences of the spatial lexicon, which in *Recognition* takes on a greater specific weight than the previous idea of recognitional spheres. The difficulty consists precisely in having to identify through a moral-theoretical monism, within one practical form of (inter-)action, two matrices of acts (inside and outside), that at the same time are informed by the context and also shape it. Honneth's theory, considered in its social-ontological elements, does not seem to possess the tools to address such an outside, if not as entering, colonizing element.

This leads us to the last point, namely, conflict. In *Recognition*, it is conceived by Honneth as the means of broadening of the space of reasons before the domain of facts—in the terms of *Redistribution or Recognition?*, social inclusion and individualization. Besides the concept of surplus validity—which we must consider in the background—it is noteworthy that the greater weight given to the dialogical-communicative dimension, to the idea that recognition does not concern the affirmation of traits, but the mutual willingness to include the other in the reformulation of the respective roles, is accompanied by the identification of a fragility of the related normative arrangements. The vulnerability and indeterminacy of individuals is therefore not solved and resolved by and within ethical life, filled with content and therefore immobilized. Rather, the spheres of recognition delineate those spaces in which the burden of being free can be shared by being freed. In this sense, recognition and conflict do not represent alternative, mutually exclusive moments: rather, simultaneously, they continuously outline our lifeworld, that is, its very reformulation. The co-legislation disclosed by and coinciding with mutual recognition would be conflictual to the extent that it draws argumentative practices carried out in the historical opacity of institutionalized contexts.

5.5 Sediments of Reconstruction

The reconstruction of Honneth's thought I proposed throughout the book opened with some perplexities and criticisms from different angles toward him. First, the fact that Honneth assumes as his starting point the subjective experience of moral injury, as well as the role of the pathology/health simile in dealing with misdevelopments of society raises some doubts with regard to a certain psychologizing attitude. To this first issue, we should add that Honneth identifies several features of self-realization in mainly psychological terms.[77] Such a psychological approach turns out to be deficient to the extent that it fails to address the dynamics of injustice that fall outside the horizon of reflexive personal experience. Thus, critical theory, on the one hand, lends itself to an inability to unmask the ideological forms of recognition and, on the other hand, confuses injustice with what is simply felt as such.

---

[77] See, above all, Honneth 1999; Honneth 2008; and Honneth 2009d.

The same lack of objectivity is claimed by those who charge Honneth of an excessive culturalization of (in)justice. The clearest example of this criticism is carried out by Nancy Fraser, who argues that Honneth's monism reduces the scope of critical theory. All in all, a recognition paradigm is allegedly well suited for addressing pluralism, identity conflicts, the balance or agonism between ethnic-cultural groups and their social standings, as well as hierarchical cultural structures. This implies that Honneth does not adequately take the material-systemic factors of injustice (even if they emerge in the experiential-reflexive horizon) into account, while Fraser's bifocal approach does so.

These two criticisms are articulated with reference to Honneth's anthropological phase, but find greater resonance in what could be considered their reformulations that in turn emerge with the shift to the historic-normative phase—namely, regarding *Freedom's Right*. This is the direction of the criticism, carried out mainly by Thompson, according to which Honneth's proposals represent an idealistic drift of critical theory. Here, rather than subjectivism, the problem is intersubjectivism, which would make Honneth's theory rely on an a-contextual dynamic, untying critical social theory from social reality's being-product and constituted by relations and systems that cannot be reduced neither to the I-Thou polarity, nor to normative integration.[78] This issue could to a certain extent be translated with the classical distinction between base and superstructure. What is read critically, that is, is not simply that intersubjectivity represents a starting point—also because, in Honneth's own theory, recognitional relations are always conceived as situated within second nature. Rather, the problem lies in not adequately implying systemic factors (not only productive, but mediatic, bureaucratic, juridical, institutional etc.) that form and contribute to the crystallization of the normative principles whose instantiations and evolutions constitute, according to Honneth, the fabric of the social. Honneth's position is therefore idealistic in that it confuses a product with the actual given, in the same way as "*the* Fruit" elaborated by speculation replaces the individual material apples, pears, strawberries, and almonds, as outlined by Marx and Engels in *The Holy Family*.[79]

The criticism of idealism is therefore not unrelated to that of constructivism (addressed here in section 4.3.3 together with its correlates). In fact, the retrospective approach Honneth adopts, especially in *Freedom's Right*, would be warped by an a priori assumption, that is freedom's central role, which is an operation that enables one reconstruction among the many possible, among the alternative teleologies of which Zurn speaks.

The last criticism concerns precisely an overly pronounced teleologism. On the one hand, as mentioned in section 1.3, this issue concerns Honneth's prioritizing

---

[78] The same criticism is levied against Searle's theory of institutions. If their constitution cannot be reduced to cognitive-linguistic processes, this also applies for recognitional relations and principles. See Thompson 2017, p. 225.
[79] See Karl Marx and Friedrich Engels 2010, p. 57.

the good (and its achievement) over the right (and its procedures). But this charge possesses another, deeper facet. In this second case, the problem does not concern Honneth's reconstructive approach, the identification of certain trends or tendencies, or describing the instantiations-conflicts dialectic as a learning progress. Rather, what appears problematic is that developments and misdevelopments are identifiable, according to Honneth, only to the extent that we dispose of a contrast material, that is, the idea of healthiness. Nonetheless, this contrast material does not seem to be subjected to the same becoming as the social facts it allows to evaluate. To be sure, both the concept of self-realization and the normative principles of recognition go through reformulations and refinements: they historically become. But the structures of weak anthropology, as well as the integrative function and surplus of validity of principles do not yield their quasi-transcendental position with respect to social reality. In this sense, Honneth's teleologism instantiates in not fully detrascendentalizing the theoretical perspective itself with respect to the surpluses of validity identified as the immanent root of emancipatory transcendence.

From this brief overview of the major criticisms that emerged during the reconstruction of Honneth's thought, it is quite clear that the bone of contention is not the concept of recognition itself, but rather the role attributed to it by interpreting social reality and positing the possibilities and aims of critical theory. More specifically, the greatest perplexities concern the presumed self-sufficiency of the recognition principles, that is, the moral-theoretical monism Honneth proposes. While Fraser argues that it cannot be the only criterion for assessing the hindrances to parity of participation, and Thompson believes that such a monism cannot take into account social facts as products of complex dynamics, the perplexities Siep voices are quite insightful.[80] For they come from an author who contributed greatly to bringing recognition back into the limelight, and because they stress the necessary situatedness (and therefore partiality) of recognition and its principles. Indeed, while Siep stresses the relevance of mutual recognition as a practical modality of interactions, he detects its inability to determine its own contents and contexts.

The first issue regards distributive justice. On the one hand, here mutual recognition—even understood in immediate terms as oriented by equality and generalized respect—can play a fundamental role by the modes of distribution, shaping their fairness. But, Siep argues, it is the goods themselves that to a certain extent frame their own distribution, rendering the related demands or struggles justifiable, or not—according to Walzer's distinction of different spheres of justice. For example, struggles for civil and political rights, for access to education and so on are also justified by the generalizability of the respective cases. While more particularistic goods, such as citizenship or access to social welfare and assistance or scholarships, would more hardly justify claims by groups and individuals outside their spectrum—which of course can be expanded, and reformulated, but hardly universalized. For sure, access to

---

80 See Siep 2011, pp. 136–39.

health care seems to be a universal right in principle, but treatment depends on the respective diagnoses. Clearly—and this is a second indeterminacy of recognition—to say that the goods themselves can frame their own distribution coincides to say that the goodness and distribution of goods are matter addressed through and within a shared evaluative horizon that can hardly be enclosed by the modes of mutual recognition. The second limit Siep identifies concerns pluralism, with respect to whose challenges it does not seem sufficient to outline a model in which the different perspectives on the good or the different groups recognize each other. Or rather, this would only become possible in the name of a shared perspective on a well-ordered society—drawing from Rawls's model. Certainly, one could say that a well-ordered society is one where everyone recognizes each other. But in order to gain greater concreteness—thus avoiding purely proceduralist perspectives—such a dynamic must each time enter into the merits of the proposals made to the social community by individuals and groups. And actually, Honneth's paradigm of recognition finds its anchorage and unfolding point in a more general idea of ethical life, oriented by the principle of self-realization or by the plurality of principles of recognition that do not coincide with the logic of reciprocal recognition. The paradigm requires a certain idea of progress and material criteria to distinct progressive and regressive, genuine and ideological struggles and modes of recognition. Siep seems to tell us that, for example, freedom can be considered the pivotal principle of western societies, even if its instantiations involve struggles for recognition and relational institutionalizations, does not derive from reciprocal recognition alone, but requires other factors too. The third shortcoming is then that recognition provides few elements regarding the relationship between man and nature—understood in general terms as a dimension not completely produced by and not completely available to the purposiveness of human beings. Siep mainly mentions bioethical issues (self- and social relations to bodies), and the relationship with animals. However, the main problem seems to me to be that mutual recognition offers few possibilities to outline ecological accounts without anthropomorphizing nature itself. To be sure, Honneth addresses the relation with one's own and others' body mainly in *The Struggle for Recognition* with the binomial violence-love. And *Reification* provides some elements regarding natural objectuality, but care and mimetic reasoning do not fully coincide with the idea of mutual recognition that he defends more clearly in other works. Even in this case, therefore, recognition seems to offer many cues to outline an ethical way of dealing with the other, but it is lacking in content to understand what the other is.

Honneth's rejoinder would likely concern the *whence* of the normative criteria involved in each of these criticisms. Where do they come from? What immanence do they possess with respect to social reality and action? How can they avoid universalistic implications? For the division between issues of distribution and issues of recognition, as well as the delineation of a well-ordered society or consensus about values and goods, fall within normative criteria that cannot be disjointed from social (inter-)action—where Honneth's paradigm has its core. In the same way, the relationship with nature (under its different guises) can hardly be disconnected from that kind of 'knowing-treating' that we can call recognizing. And finally, as far as the being-product of social relations and recognition themselves are concerned, the issue is not foreign to Honneth, who indeed includes genealogical methodologies among the necessary tools of critical theory.[81] Returning to *The Struggle for Recognition*, it is easy to see how Honneth derives the access point for the spheres of social action, but above all for the readiness to overcome and reformulate them, from historically situated anthropological forms.[82] Equally, the surplus of validity of principles represents nothing but the theoretical formalization of what comes to the surface through the upheavals of institutional concretions as desideratum, as projection of emancipatory interests. The focus on recognition relations does not represent for Honneth an all-encompassing hypothesis that explores the formation and reproduction of social reality, but rather a theoretically necessity that is useful to delineate the normative structure, the moral grammar, and the innovative reproductions of social reality.

Since, after all, the aforementioned criticisms aim at Honneth's monism, it seems necessary to go back and try to illuminate its all too often misunderstood porosity and comprehensiveness. How, in fact, can a monism be reconciled with the fact that self-realization and the principles of recognition, as well as the material criteria and those of progress, do not coincide with the relationships of recognition themselves? It might seem that recognition relationships and ethical life do not coincide. Saying this is both true and false.

It is true to the extent that the concept of ethical life represents the framework of instantiation and source of criteria for recognition relations: thus, the former performs quasi-transcendentally with respect to the latter. Moreover, ethical life, namely, second nature inhabited and delineated by normative principles, differs from mutual recognition to the extent that theory itself derives from the former the criteria for evaluating the latter (in order to say whether recognitional forms are progressive or regressive, ideological or realizations of freedom)—which, incidentally, shows that Honneth also has regressive or harmful forms of recognition in mind. Because if recognition were considered positive per se, it would not be necessary to adopt these external criteria for justifying or criticizing it. And, finally, the lack of coincidence between modes and spheres of recognition that was quite evident in *Freedom's Right* makes it clear that not every form of freedom and every form of recognition is ethical; moreover, not every concretion of ethical life (family, market society, public sphere) fully actualizes freedom and recognition.

It is false to the extent that recognition relationships are the tangible structure of the formal concept of ethical life: thus, the first is the *reality* of the second. Moreover,

---

81 In addition to *The Struggle for Recognition* and *Freedom's Right*, see Honneth 1991; and Honneth 2009f.
82 See Heidegren 2002, p. 437.

inclusion and individualization (i. e. the trajectories of progress Honneth identifies) and the material criterion represent nothing but the actualizations, the refinements, and broadenings of mutuality. Therefore, Honneth considers the external criteria to evaluate recognition as the distillate of the norms that flow through relationships of recognition. And, finally, the lack of coincidence between modes and spheres of recognition, the actual non-adherence of forms of freedom and recognition to the actual spheres of social action precisely shows the very immanence of the norms, which can be evoked by the participants to criticize their insufficient or detrimental institutionalizations.

This scenario of coincidence and non-coincidence shows a dialectical monism, which articulates itself in practices and norms, which in turn, while co-implicating each other, can to a certain extent be disjointed. In this sense, Honneth speaks of progress as a learning process, since the concretions of recognition practices allow the thematization of their own norms on the part of the participants, representing a starting point for new forms. That this monism is dialectical also implies a distinction between interpersonal interaction in general and recognition—which is too often overlooked. Within Honneth's monism, the principles of recognition are not the only ones underlying normative integration or interactions among persons. If this were the case, one could not understand social pathologies and forms of misrecognition, the structure of reifying attitudes and organized self-realization, the actual narrowness of social freedom despite institutional normative promises, and the 'outside' at play in any recognition relationships. Mutual recognition is to interpersonal interaction and social spheres as grammar is to the speech acts and language: the logic underlying the articulation of symbolic contents cannot replace them and does not coincide with a self-standing rationale that allows the expression of meaning. But it is fundamental in order to judge the correctness of a sentence, to justify it, to criticize it.

In my view, therefore, the fundamental question is not about determining the self-sufficiency or the insufficiency of mutual recognition—since, evidently, the monism itself, the normative grammar Honneth proposes, cannot make all-encompassing and explanatory claims. Indeed, it is not without ambiguities that Honneth develops his theory and describes the social as articulating itself on a dialectical game between relationships, principles, and second nature that lets the non-self-sufficiency of recognitional interactions emerge, if under the last concept we understand a purely I-Thou affirming exchange of treatments. In order to fully grasp and further develop the pivotal role that the concept of recognition already possesses in social, political, and practical philosophy, the fundamental question regards the necessity to delineate a concept of recognition that can be enough porous and non-exclusive with respect to other logics of action and non-normative dimensions that characterize our lifeform and lifeworld. Only in this way will it be possible to understand the moral and critical specificity of mutual recognition, and, consequently, its role for social reality and theory. But at this juncture, a number of other problems arise, precisely because most of the issues we have encountered in the course of the reconstruction of Honneth's thinking and of the confrontation with his critics stem from a substantial confusion about what recognition is.[83] The following table—subject to due simplifications—already shows that, even within Honneth's paradigm, it is difficult to distil *one* concept of recognition.

Table 3: Honneth's paradigms of recognition

Work	Core Idea of Recognition	Modes of Recognition	What is Recognized	For What is Condition
The Struggle for Recognition (1992)	Reciprocal affirmation	Emotional support, cognitive respect, social esteem	Needs and emotions, moral responsibility, traits, and abilities	Undamaged self-relation, self-realization
"Invisibility" (2001) & *Reification* (2005)	Meta-actional stance, expression of underlying relationality	Identification, imitation, attunement	Human features	Non-reification
Redistribution or Recognition? (2003)	Reciprocal affirmation	Love, respect, esteem	Needs; responsibility; contributions	Refined instantiations of surpluses of validity
Freedom's Right (2011)	Instantiation of complementary role obligations	Love, respect, esteem	Normative statuses within the relational contexts we inhabit	Social freedom (both as ego-boundaries dissolution and as cooperative self-determination)
"Grounding Recognition" (2002)	Actualization of evaluative features	Non-epistemic reception and public expression	Evaluative features	Actualization of individual potentials
Recognition (2018)	Mutual authorization	Granting of possibilities; joint outlining a space-for-freedom	Normative capability to self-determination	Joint normative (re-)formulations

---

83 See Sobottka and Saavedra 2009; and Giovanni Giorgini and Elena Irrera 2017.

Chapter 6
Recognition between Actuality and Potentiality

The reconstruction of the concept of recognition in Honneth's works—and its multiple roles in delineating the possibilities of a critical theory of society—has revealed the need to acquire greater clarity on the notion of recognition in general, which is so central but so ambiguously interpreted in contemporary debate. Taking some decisive steps in this direction is the task of this concluding chapter. To do this, it is necessary to keep in mind that a paradigm of recognition inspired by Hegel must move between different levels, which characterize Honneth's thought in a decisive way. In fact, for both Hegel and Honneth, recognition represents an empirical-social fact, a practical-evaluating norm, and a hermeneutical-critical criterion.[1] Such polyvalence is implemented strongly in Honneth's approach to the extent that the normative dimension and the functional dimension of the social collide and coincide in recognitional practices.[2]

Maintaining this theoretical framework, the first step of our analysis is to recollect four ideas of recognition that Honneth puts in place—critically or positively—and to explain four major perplexities about his paradigm. In other words, we begin by giving voice to some unresolved knots, especially regarding the relationship between recognition and identity (section 6.1). Then, we distinguish between three macromeanings of recognition, which prove to be useful in throwing analytical clarity on the contemporary debate on recognition, which is too often inhabited by inexplicit positions. By distinguishing between re-cognition, acknowledgement, and mutual recognition, the aim is to spotlight a set of practical modes—linked together by a thin action-theoretic thread—that is complex and holistic, which hardly lends itself to unilateralizations (section 6.2). The following steps embrace Honneth's emphasis on detranscendentalization as Hegel's key operation, strengthening the bond of recognition with our lifeform, thus acquiring elements to delineate the specificity of interpersonal recognition (sections 6.3 and 6.4). The most important focus of this chapter consists in analyzing the confession-forgiveness dialectic depicted in the *Phenomenology of Spirit*. Through this analysis, it becomes possible to place the concept of mutual recognition in Hegel's broader action-theoretical account, which is articulated between the dialectical poles of expressive identity and necessity of the finite (section 6.5). From these elements, I outline a generative account of mutual recognition, which stands in contrast with the crystallizing role to which it is often confined. In conclusion, I argue that, as a fluidifying We-form, mutual recognition can represent a peculiar and specific critical criterion aimed at identifying emancipatory and reformulating interests (section 6.6).

---

1 See Siep 2011, p. 135.
2 See Deranty 2009, p. 274.

6.1 Interpersonal Recognition: Four Different Ideas

In the course of our reconstruction of Honneth's works, and especially in the preceding chapter, we encountered four main ideas of interpersonal recognition: they differ from each other not just in their respective objects, which can for the moment be generically summarized under the equally generic appellative of the other—but already here, it is difficult to find a unified view of *what* should be addressed by recognition. The greatest differences emerge as we begin to describe the nature and logic of recognition, which can be understood as an epistemological act or moral attitude, as primarily addressing deontological or axiological features, as unilateral or reciprocal, as asymmetrical or symmetrical, as morally characterized by equality or dissymmetry, and so on. In a word, it is not clear what recognition is or what we should understand, among all the forms of human interaction, as a species of this conceptual genus.

But, even more so, such a lack of clarity can be exacerbated when one agrees that a certain ethical-moral and political-social role is immanent within the concept itself. And a further set of questions opens as we attempt the difficult process of defining which are the principles of recognition—or at least the most significant ones. The purpose of this chapter is precisely to provide some additional elements in relation to these two sets of problems by clarifying the concept of recognition and the specificity of mutual recognition.

A first, preliminary step is therefore represented by outlining the main features of the four recognition ideas we encountered.

Recognition as attribution of personal features. To interpret recognition as an ascription carried out monologically by A toward B would entail three main implications. First, the elements at stake by, within, and through recognition relationships do not by themselves provide any (evident) criteria for assessing the *adequacy* of the recognitive acts. The latter have no evaluation counterweight, because their content would be determined exclusively by the recognizer. So, if recognition represents a pure attributive act, then recognizing, say, rights to someone does not in principle hinge on any view about her being a person, that is, a rights bearer entailing and expressing dignity. Second, it follows from this that the recognizee finds herself to a certain extent passive toward those features attributed by others, which represent, so to speak, an encumbrance around which she would have to carve out her own person—as we have seen, for example, in Rousseau and Sartre. Third, connected to this is the epistemological matrix Honneth focuses on in *Recognition:* the gaze of the other would shed light only *some* sides of me, inevitably leaving others in the shadows, giving space to an inevitable irreconcilability between self and public self. Both from a normative point of view and from a more ontological one, therefore, the recognizee would find herself described by the (to some extent) arbitrary recognizing gestures of another, but never fully coinciding with such description: A recognizes/discovers (C) the trait D, which determines/covers my (true/authentic) person (B):

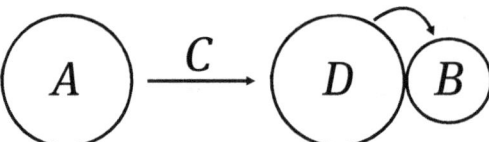

As we shall see, it is no coincidence that most criticisms concerning the relevance of the concept of recognition for a social-critical theory, as well as regarding the concept itself, derive from this perspective, or from a reversal of the following one.

Recognition as praise. This second account is closer to the daily use of the term, which gives a certain priority to those traits of the other that provoke moral reactions in me such as sympathy, respect, and esteem. Therefore, recognition does not coincide with me granting the other any attributes that somehow stand juxtaposed to her person, but rather it concerns the fact that some of her features publicly emerge as *worthy* of consideration. Setting aside the consequences that such a perspective would imply on the harmonization of social actions—which represent Honneth's focus in *Recognitionn*—it is clear that this model outlines a *receptive* account of recognition. B's trait (D) manifests itself to A, who reacts (C) by recognizing, expressing, and affirming it. Thereby, B's selfhood would be gain in consistency through the confirmation of her trait (D), the relation with which is not one-sided or arbitrary, rather represents a fundamental step for personal integrity:

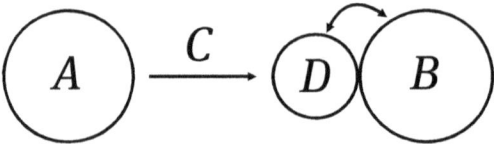

Both of these models do not require any reciprocity, symmetry, or even mutuality in the strict sense in order to define recognition, which we could therefore articulate as a monological phenomenon, carried out by one of the partners toward its addressee. What distinguishes them from another is the precedence that, alternatively, is given either to the gesture of recognition or to its object, that is, recognition is conceived either as a response or as a creative act. Thus, B's relationship with her recognized features is also read in a profoundly different way. In the first case, once discovered by A, they would cover B's more proper dimension, to the extent that those traits exert a certain power over the person. In the second case, the evaluative qualities that are the object of recognition would represent a non-problematic expression of B's own personhood, which can allegedly unfold only through such external confirmation.

We have seen also two slightly, but decisively, different accounts on mutuality that stem from the receptive account.

Recognition as appropriate judgement. We have met such view as synthesized by Ikäheimo's contributions,[3] whereby a *thin* mutuality is outlined. Proper recognition would necessarily entail *B*'s judgement (*E*) as to whether the recognizer (*A*) represents a competent judge of the first's features (*D*)—which obviously implies whether *A*'s judgment (recognition) is adequate or not:

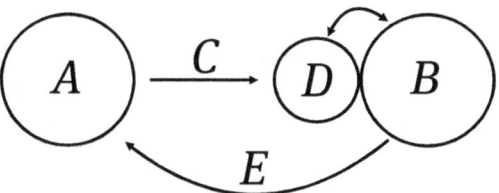

The adequacy-issue to be assessed by *B* is twofold: the judge's adequacy would be indeed expressed in the perceived adequacy of her judgment, but the first cannot be reduced to the latter, and vice versa. Let us say that I did an impeccable test. After observing it, a fellow student recognizes that, thus making a judgment appropriate to how the test looks. Then, after examination, the professor expresses the same judgment. Clearly, in the eyes of all the participants, the professor is a more competent judge, although he makes exactly the same judgment as my classmate and myself. It is therefore likely that the impact of the professor's recognition in terms of affirmation and confirmation will be greater than my classmate's one: the recognized competency of the judge matters for recognition. Considering the second side, that is, the adequacy of the judgement itself, there would be no recognition if *A* and *B* did not in some way agree on the *content* of or *object* addressed by recognition if the recognized traits were not perceived by the recognizee as expressive of her own person, or simply affirmed in a proper way. Thus, this form of mutuality would guarantee a further limitation of the possible arbitrariness of the recognizing expressions, implying a non-passive stance on the part of the recognizee, so as a certain transparency between the latter and her own traits. With regard to the first side—namely, a judge's adequacy—it would imply a certain parity among the participants. Taking both sides together, we have a thin mutuality, which instantiates diachronically and that can consequently entail a certain asymmetry. Even more, precisely such asymmetry could be constituent of the relationship itself, so as by student-professor, patient-doctor, customer-mechanic, and so on. But from these examples it emerges that a substantially asymmetrical relationship requires reciprocal and structurally symmetrical acts of recognition with regard to the acceptance by both of their respective roles. We therefore need to determine at what level (structural or normative) mutuality in the strict sense is established and what connection there is between *rela-*

---

[3] See Ikäheimo 2002; and Ikäheimo and Laitinen 2007.

tionships of recognition and *acts* of recognition. I believe that most of the ambiguities in the contemporary debate arise from the failure to detect this double distinction.

Recognition as mutual authorization. With *Recognition*, Honneth unties the concept of recognition from the lexicon of affirmation, both in its attributive and the receptive matrixes: at the center are not the personal (evaluative) features of the other, but rather her freedom, not her capacity for self-determination, but rather the context for its unfolding. In this sense, the recognition *relationship* would represent a We-structure characterized by the joint action of self-limiting one's freedom, which may be followed by the joint action in a strong sense of discussing the norms that regulate the relationship itself. That would imply a *thick* mutuality and symmetry of the normative status that the participants grant each other by means of the self-limitation—thus, not only the respective recognizing acts are structurally symmetrical, but also the relational poles themselves. Recognition would therefore coincide with a passive involvement (authorization) of the other, properly a letting-space into a sphere of co-authorship about the normative directions of *our* actions. Schematizing: A and B jointly outline a space-for-freedom (F) on the basis of and fostering the mutual consideration (E) of their status, thus disclosing possibilities (P) for the (re-)formulation of normative standards:

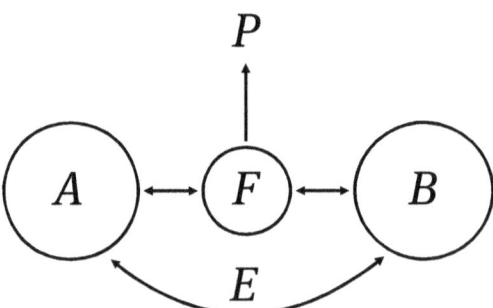

With respect to these four models, Honneth's attempt is to assign the title of mutual recognition exclusively to the fourth, on the basis of the normative specificity that a relationship outlined in this way would possess: to disclose intersubjective spaces-for-freedom. As we have seen, Honneth excludes the phenomena described by the first model from the concept of recognition: rather, they would be better described taking into consideration the linguistic-classifying practices carried out by and through hierarchical power mechanisms. The second model would instead revolve around (mis-)recognizing reactions as blame and praise, not mutual recognition. Limiting the virtual contribution of such accounts for a normative paradigm of recognition, Honneth considerably narrows the scope of his own concept, especially with regard to the role of recognition by individual socialization and social reproduction. For he rather clearly argues that not every interpersonal interaction should be considered as a recognitional interaction, but only that specific kind oriented by and to a certain equality among the participants, which results in the mutual delivery of a right to have a say. The other side of the coin is precisely an implicit denial of a totalizing view of his own moral-theoretical monism, since the outside of recognition would play a fundamental role by social integration and the instantiation of second nature.

Briefly, the main problem is that, by defending a strong concept of mutual recognition, Honneth does not grant other practical forms the legitimacy of being called recognition. But keeping the focus on defining recognition, it emerges that, by highlighting the respective incompatibility of these models, we miss an opportunity to address two fundamental questions.

First, why should we conceive of recognition as an exclusively interpersonal practice? Honneth's argumentative approach in support of the intersubjective character of recognition, both in "Grounding Recognition" and *Recognition*, revolves around the nuances of meanings that distinguish *anerkennen*, which would imply a strong intersubjective connotation, and the terms derived from Latin (recognize, *reconnaître, riconoscere*), which, etymologically speaking, would instead emphasize a kind of knowing-again. From this follows the distinction between the epistemological dimension underlying, above all, the French tradition and the purely normative character of the Hegelian paradigm.

However, one should not overlook that, in the common use, even a situation, an error, or an opinion can be correlated with *anerkennen*. Both the recognizee and the recognizer can be a non-human: *anerkennen* can also concern the relationship between states, institutions, and so on, without implying an overly reifying view of the structures and functions of these realities. This is exactly the point defended by Laitinen, who opts for an adequate regarding-insight against a mutuality-insight.[4] The latter stands for the idea that recognition can only concern recognizers who relate to each other: the relationship of recognition is either reciprocal or not. There is therefore an "objective character of the logic that imposes itself on those who are confronted" (Cortella 2016, p. 173), emerging primarily as underlying mediating middle, and eventually as explicit factor of the second-order experience of the practitioners.[5] The adequate regard-insight instead represents an unrestricted normative ac-

---

[4] See Laitinen 2010.

[5] The distinction between these two levels, between the logic of reciprocity and the experience of mutuality, is the focus of Ricoeur's analysis of the practices of giving and giving in exchange, and related aporias. On the one hand, the third party (either as medium or as context) imposes a logic of exchange on the interactions of donor and recipient. An example of such self-transcendent level, according to the well-known study by Mauss, is represented by the Maoris identifying the *hau*, that is, the power attributed to the gift itself to compel the recipient to give something back. According to Ricoeur, such perspectives, even once disenchanted and demystified, overlook the fact that, for the participants, the initial gift always represents a risky imbalance, a decentralization whose consequences are not existentially reducible to an economic equation, if not by an external observer at the end of the circle. See Ricoeur 2005, p. 225–263; Marcel Mauss 2002. For a throughout analysis of the relation between gift and recognition, see Bedorf 2010, sec. 2.6. For a synthetic and

count of recognition, which basically coincides with an active responsiveness to the normatively relevant features of the other. Therefore such adequately taking notice is usually considered as unveiling relevant reasons for acting accordingly, for *treating* the other accordingly. What is even more important, however, is that such a definition of recognition makes it possible to avoid falling into a loop so that if *A* recognizes *B*, but *B* does not respond in the *same* way, then *A*'s gesture would not count as recognition either. That is to say, we are not forced, trivially, to declassify the gestures of recognition of a person toward her pet, of a caregiver toward his or her newborn, or of a healthcare assistant toward an unconscious patient. To free recognition from a strict logic of mutuality and symmetry thus allows us to take into account all such cases, which are given in our social life, and in which *giving* and *getting* recognition implies and requires an imbalance between the participants.

Honneth approaches these issues in *Reification*, portraying a two-level account of recognition, the first normative and the other more epistemological, originary, related (or even coincident) to our openness to the world. Honneth there describes it as an attitude that precedes mere knowledge (*erkennen*) also with regard to object reality and one's inner contents: a mode of apprehension before any subject-object fixating polarization, thus a disobjectifying mode of objectification.[6] This hypothesis, however, besides being sidelined, does not fully account for the fact that every recognizing entails a cognizing, which stands for *how* the recognizee appears to me, whatever it may be. Keeping the matter on the interpersonal plane, in order to recognize the other (authorize her), I have to recognize (encounter) her as free being. Only when such (re-)cognition is given can I impose limitations on my own freedom and adapt my stance to the evaluative traits I discover as characterizing the other. This detail already illuminates the complexity of recognitional gestures, which cannot be reduced to a single logic of action.

I therefore intend to argue that the nuances of different languages do not follow different practices—against Honneth, who instead distinguishes between proper (mutual) recognition, recognizing reactions, and classification/attribution—but that such variety of meanings is due to stratifications of meaning that legitimately pertain to recognition, that co-belong to each other according to non-causal degrees of derivation: above all epistemological and normative dimensions, which Honneth has endeavored to distinguish, depend on one another. And, in fact, he himself has argued in favor of such a correlation, implying that the horizon of second nature grounds the *appearing* of certain traits as worthy of recognition.[7] In other words, Honneth's intention to distinguish recognition from power practices, to untie normatively loaded intersubjective *relations* from eventually asymmetrical interpersonal *acts*, should not lead us to overlook that recognition describes a certain kind of knowing: a way

---

accurate analysis of the gift as third domain between utilitarian and normativist approaches in sociology, see Frank Adloff 2006.

6 See Lucio Cortella 2005, p. 152.
7 See, above all, Honneth 2001; and Honneth 2002.

through which I am invited to assume a practical position before certain features of the other. This is the core of the receptive account Honneth himself embraces: according to it, recognition is a passively involved and not detached praxis, through which one leaves space for the other to appear. One cannot, in order to give precedence to recognitional relations over acts of recognition, and to prioritize *anerkennen* over *erkennen*, suppress that kind of *erkennen* inherent to every *anerkennen*. Taking this into account, it is clear that this type of knowledge cannot be limited to the interpersonal dimension.

The second, related question would thus be: Why should recognition be conceived exclusively as mutual practice? This question takes us back to the theoretical tensions that accompany us from *The Struggle for Recognition* between reciprocity, mutuality, symmetry, and asymmetry. Clearly, understanding recognition as a practice that is not exclusively interpersonal also allows us to widen the meshes of a symmetry that, especially in *Recognition*, is reinforced by Honneth as an antidote against the assimilation of recognition to power relations. Such a strictly normative connotation, motivated by socio-critical aims, cannot, however, completely erase the possibility of describing, to take a notorious example, the master-servant relationship Hegel describes in the *Phenomenology* as one where recognition plays a significative role, even though the latter does not bring the relationship itself to an emancipated equality. For precisely the existence of such a relationship itself presupposes a mutual recognition of the respective roles—playing with the terms, a *symmetrical recognition* of *asymmetrical roles*. But the same dynamic regards Honneth's taking the caregiver-child relation as a recognitive one, which has been sharply criticized. The fact that one emphasizes either only the asymmetrical status of the participants or solely their symmetrical reciprocally interacting seems to me grounded both in missing the distinction between acts and relationships of recognition, and in not detecting the two different planes reciprocity and mutuality necessarily refer to, whereby the latter does not necessarily accompany the first. In fact, the master and servant example shows that structurally identical subjective acts can occur in and lead to unequal relationships, and that this is *allowed* by both taking each other as one's alter. The whole issue revolves around the fact that the participants merely recognizing each other in a neutral way does not lead to what seems to deserve the title of recognition relationship in which Honneth identifies sources both for social emancipative interests and, consequently, for critical theory. Clearly, a certain autonomization of the normative dimension pursued for the sake of the equity of the participants implemented in *Recognition* leads Honneth to focus on mutual relations of recognition, rather than on recognitional acts, which, as Laitinen shows, can be carried out properly even without involving two full-fledged recognizers.

In view of these two fundamental questions and given Honneth's tendency to render his concept of recognition stricter and stricter,[8] it is now necessary to deal

---

[8] Here I am using the term "strict" according to the meaning given by Laitinen, mentioned in the

with two fundamental criticisms of the concept of recognition in general, not only as it is outlined by Honneth. Here, I have in mind two major issues raised by Patchen Markell and Thomas Bedorf, respectively. In different ways, both deal with the ambivalences that characterize recognition, emphasize its reifying potentialities, and take into account a certain degree of skepticism or lack of transparency regarding personal identity. What is particularly interesting is that all these issues are addressed from a standpoint similar to Honneth's to the extent that recognition qua epistemological act is either the aim of criticism (Markell) or bracketed (Bedorf).[9] However, both conceive of it as *addressing* the other, thus shaping its being *as* other,[10] and make recognition revolve around its strong connection with the concept of identity.

The first criticism, elaborated by Markell in *Bound by Recognition*, concerns the connection between recognition, identity, and agency. The most problematic aspect of identity politics is to conceive of identity as *fait accompli*, as the antecedent from which acting derives. In this sense, identity is conceived of as a "rule" because it determines the agents' courses of action (Markell 2003, p. 186), fixating the latter to the alleged fixity of identity itself. Recognition comes into play when such a monolithic identity collides with other interests, directions of action, and social actors: demanding recognition therefore derives from the impossibility of articulating our own sovereignty as actors monologically, because of our vulnerability. A second and decidedly fascinating aspect of Markell's critique is that the purpose of a politics of recognition does not seem to be a reformulation of the political taking such vulnerability seriously into account, but rather to merely restore the lost sovereignty. This would manifest itself in the fact that the demands for recognition virtually compel "that others recognize us as who we *already* really are" (Markell 2003, p. 14). The principal shortcoming of recognition therefore derives from a distorted depiction of

---

previous chapter. In his description, Honneth's concept of recognition is strict to the extent that only persons can be recognizers and recognizee, and recognition requires a public expression of the evaluative traits it addresses. See Laitinen 2002.

9 Even though this holds true, one can nonetheless notice similarities to the two forms of pessimism toward recognition identified by Smith. The first, "pessimism from certainty,"— points to the derived nature of personal identity, which makes it impossible to recognize the other because this other is, in essence, a product of its context and history. The second pessimism, pessimism "from uncertainty," instead revolves around the more classic skeptical argument about the inaccessibility of other minds. See Adam Smith 2017, p. 207.

10 Bedorf stresses that the concept of recognition implies that the "priority given to the initiative and demands" of the alter represents a "constitutive element of the experience" in general (Bedorf 2010, p. 137, my translation). With the removal of the Fichtean logic, according to which the *Aufforderung* is already conditioned by the other's being free and capable of understanding, it is not difficult to grasp the connection between the act of addressing and a gesture of power, understood primarily as a delimitation of the possibilities of the other. That is to say, "taking the floor" would be a power (meaning "I can") that is not available to those who have to respond. Whoever responds cannot speak herself, but is bound to a heteronomous situation from the beginning—generalized, we, as humans, are structurally in such a condition. See also Norbert Ricken 2013; and Lepold 2014.

identity as a (more or less) substantial unity from which action flows, rather than the other way around. This misunderstanding is further enhanced by conceiving of recognition as a cognitive act aimed at discovering the object (identity) that is supposed to be just out there. In this way, political measures are meant to reestablish sovereign agency, giving identities what they are due.

Clearly, the first target of such criticism is Charles Taylor, who raises certain perplexities in this regard when, for example, he describes identity as "the background against which our tastes and desires and opinions and aspirations make sense" (Charles Taylor 1994, pp. 33–34). Or when, more generally, he conceives of ethnic-cultural groups as an already formed whole that grounds political demands.[11] It is less obvious to connect Honneth with this objection. For, as Markell admits, Honneth describes the binomial identity-recognition in provisional terms,[12] stressing that conflict emerges precisely because of the need for a continuous reformulation of social reality and practical identities. However, as saw in the second chapter, Markell expresses reservations about Honneth's conception according to which recognition shapes identity by actualizing its potential features.[13] But even though it holds true that identity, for Honneth, does not stand for a static object—also because recognition is not a mere perception of it—this would not change Markell's main criticism, because the actualization of identity, the formation of an undamaged practical identity would in any case be prior to and the proper condition for authentic agency. We can perhaps add to this the fact that the concept of co-authorship outlined in *Recognition* reveals that Markell's criticism is well suited. In Honneth's view, the impression is that domination can be overcome only through a (intersubjectively gained and implemented) sovereignty of action.

Concerning Markell's alternative proposal, which consists of shifting the focus from recognition to *acknowledgment*, it seems to me necessary to retain three fundamental aspects. The first is drawn from Cavell's distinction between knowing and acknowledging in response to the skeptical objections that the mental states of the other are, in principle, inaccessible. The other person's suffering would remain unknown to me because I cannot suffer the same pain. I can possibly say: "I have been through the same," but that pain is not the same: it is at most similar, but according to the criteria of judgment (yours and mine) a true comparison is impossible. Briefly, the question that Cavell poses is this: are we sure that, when faced with the other's utterance, "I am in pain," the most appropriate response is a kind of knowledge? The demand involved in saying "I am in pain" is not that the other knows exactly what the pain feels like, but rather to be treated according to what is expressed through behavior: "your suffering makes a *claim* upon me. It is not enough that I *know* (am certain) that you suffer—I must do or reveal something (whatever can

---

[11] On this aspect, Bedorf also criticizes Taylor for a certain naivety with which the concept of culture is treated. See Bedorf 2010, pp. 41–42.
[12] See Markell 2003, pp. 15–16.
[13] See Markell 2007.

be done). In a word, I must *acknowledge* it" (Stanley Cavell 2015, p. 243). What matters in our relation to another is not, says Markell, "knowing him (his pain, pleasure, humanity, character, or very being)," as if we have to reach out through cognition to the other's identity "once and for all," but "*what we do* in the presence of the other, how we respond to or act in the light of what we do know" (Markell 2003, p. 34). The issue does not consist in perfecting a (impossible) knowledge of the other, but in embracing the practical finitude that characterizes us humans, that is, in exercising an *epoché* with respect to any claim to sovereign action. Two important elements derive from this.

First, acknowledgment is "self- rather than other- directed" (Markell 2003, p. 38). By acknowledging another, what counts is not primarily looking at her and discovering who she has already been, but orienting our way of acting with respect to what the other expresses to us: what matters is the *stance* we assume in relation to the other, not how the latter determines my action, not how *B*'s already-given identity compels *A* to re-act. This criticism of the receptive model should not be understood as a relapse into the arbitrariness of the attributive model: rather, it emphasizes that claiming that our action is to be entirely plotted by what we perceive is unfounded. Rather, given the derived, constructed, fluid, and multiple character of identity, it is necessary for us to address the latter in an appropriate way, whereby the appropriateness is instantiated in taking into account the intrinsic *partiality* of our doings. We acknowledge the other not by virtue of *knowing* her, but because we are *acquainted* with her.

The second decisive aspect is that acknowledgment is able to emancipate itself from a certain economic logic that can be found in recognition practices, whereby granting more recognition to subordinated groups does not differ so much from redistributing a certain good. And the problems emerge here in the many implications of conceiving of identity and agency as goods that can be distributed. But, according to Markell, establishing the matters at this level makes us overlook a more fundamental kind of (in-)justice, namely, one that is nondistributive. Again taking into account Cavell's case and Honneth's starting point in *The Struggle for Recognition*, namely, suffering, one can legitimately wonder whether recognition as giving back what is due is enough. Taking his cue from Hannah Arendt, Markell wonders, that is, whether the fundamental expectation that inhabits requests for recognition does not find a more genuine satisfaction in being welcomed than in being the recipients of the distribution of a certain good.[14]

While not exempt from possible criticism—especially for the unrefined concept of recognition he discusses—Markell's critique focuses on two elements that seem to me essential. First, it helps us recover the role of recognition in delineating non-legal forms morality, as Wildt suggested (see section 2.1 above). Second, the imbalance that follows, besides questioning whether reciprocity itself represents a

---

[14] See Markell 2003, pp. 179–81.

moral criterion that brings possible ambivalences with it, makes us focus again on the recognizer's act of recognizing, on its motivational ground, and on its moral structure. In fact, as Markell says, to "welcome someone says more about the welcomer than the welcomed" (Markell 2003, p. 180). Since the issue is not knowing an identity understood in objective and fixed terms and giving her what is due with respect to who she is, the primary plane of morality shifts accordingly from the correctness of recognition to the personal position I assume by interacting with the other. Consequently, the welcomer's stance would be characterized by an awareness of practical finitude deriving from the indeterminateness proper to the identity of both the participants, which emerges retrospectively in our (inter-)acting, not before it.

In *Verkennende Anerkennung*,[15] Thomas Bedorf goes one step further. While it is difficult to do justice to Bedorf's excellent inquiry, some essential elements of his analysis are particularly fruitful for our purposes here. First, while Markell's criticisms revolve around an epistemological conception of recognition, Bedorf makes it clear that recognizing is not a matter of knowing, but a way of treating, which, however, cannot be conceived of as unrelated to such knowing. Second, while the proposal to shift the focus from recognition to acknowledgment highlights the need to take our practical finitude into account, and the opacity of many terms that are often taken for granted in the current debate on recognition (and on identity politics in particular), Bedorf problematizes precisely the ambivalent relationship between what Markell calls recognition and acknowledgment, between *erkennen* and *anerkennen*: "it is obvious that cognizing [*Erkennen*] is not the same as recognizing [*Anerkennen*]. As in the examples mentioned, it is not a matter of knowing *who* someone or a group is, but *as whom* one *treats* him or her" (Bedorf 2010, p. 127).

But that recognizing does not coincide with knowing is not simply justified by a consideration of the value of the prefix 'an-' in *anerkennen*, but rather by a reflection on the "doubling of identity" (*Verdopplung der Identität*) that necessarily accompanies recognition. This doubling is due to the fact that recognition represents a *confirmation* of identity, not a creative act, nor an unveiling gaze. It is therefore necessary to imply two moments or degrees of personal identity. On the one hand, a minimum degree of identity expressing itself in the act of posing and expressing the demand for recognition—if we hold on to the receptive model, what presents itself as worthy of recognition. On the other hand, we have a second degree of identity resulting from and emerging with the confirmation, the public and symbolic expression of recognition. Accordingly, if we shift the focus from being recognized to recognize such doubling of the recognizee would prevent us from thinking of recognition according to dyadic structures that respond to the formula *A* recognizes *B*. Instead, it is necessary to think of recognition always in reference to a third term, meaning by that not solely context, content, or medium of recognition, but *also* its inner logic or

---

15 Bedorf 2010. Henceforth, all translations of the work are my own.

structure. Recognition means: *A* recognizes *B* as *C*, where *C* does not stand for the personal feature of *B* that is addressed and affirmed, but as the emerging identity of *B* by such affirmation, as *B*'s other ego.[16] Bedorf therefore finds an uncertainty similar to Rousseau's in this triadic structure of recognition with respect to the who of personal identity, defining it in more structural terms: neither the minimum nor the second degree of identity is I, I *cannot* be neither the addressee of recognition nor the recognizee—I am somewhat between these two poles. "The threefoldness [*Dreistelligkeit*] of recognition means that a rift in the self-relation always occurs, which cannot be closed. I am neither the one who can be recognized, nor the one who can be represented in the intersubjective relationship" (Bedorf 2010, p. 125). The issue is different from those Honneth deals with in *Recognition*. In fact, it is not about dealing with the individual's entry into society, as it was for Rousseau and Sartre, or about deconstructing the recognitional interactions in their socially constructed origin, as for Althusser and partly Butler. Rather, the heart of Bedorf's argument is to question the transparency of the concept of identity implied, as we have seen, by both thin and thick perspectives on mutuality. That identity does not stand for unity—which after all does not differ so much from the Meadian distinction of I and me—that the first emerges as concretion of unstabilizable processes of identification-with, that thus identity is non-identical with itself leads Bedorf to the structural notion of *unconciliated recognition* (*Unversöhnte Anerkennung*). That is, one could say that recognition comes too late with respect to who I already am, and too early with respect to who I emerge as being by virtue of it, thus unable to come full circle.

But the provisional character of identity is to be read as intrinsically related to the dependence on the context from which and in which recognition is articulated —a connection made evident by Honneth too, for the evaluative features of a person emerge only by virtue of their situatedness in framework of second nature. One could therefore say that the triadic structure Bedorf stresses is mediated by a threefold third party. In fact, "*A* recognizes *B* as *C*" implies that the *C* of identity is in fact brought to light by the two elements that qualify its related *as:* the instantiating context, which functions as situated a priori through which I can see the other, and our interaction medium, that is, symbolic expressions—understood at this level indifferently both as spoken word and as gesture.[17] The structural impossibility of "*A* recognizes *B*," that

---

16 See Bedorf 2010, pp. 118–26.
17 This perspective clashes with three of the six distinctions put forward by Ikäheimo in defining the concept of mutual recognition. The first, posed by Siep, is that between vertical and horizontal forms of recognition; with the second, purely intersubjective recognition, on the one hand, and institutionally mediated recognition, on the other, are distinguished; the third distinction concerns the norms of recognition, finding its poles in the non-institutionalized norms that regulate the intersubjective dyad, and in the norm-systems of proper institutions that regulate institutionally mediated recognition, which implies a third instance, autonomous from the actors. Bedorf's perspective differs to the extent that it considers the recognition relationship, being it always contextualized, as always entail-

is, the non-unmediateness of every act of recognition leads to an equally structural conclusion: every recognition is a misrecognizing recognition:

> This means that every recognition necessarily misrecognizes the other *as* other, because it can "merely" integrate him as this or that other into the medium of recognition. The "mere" here has no normative sense and does not indicate any unwillingness that could be corrected by dealing with the other "correctly," but underlines that misrecognition is inevitable. The *misrecognizing recognition* is neither pure misrecognition, because one could not relate to the completely misrecognized; nor is it pure recognition, because without the difference it could not be motivated to a recognizing behavior (Bedorf 2010, p. 145).

Thus, according to Bedorf, in the pre-normative level of opacity related to the situatedness of our form of life, recognition is structurally impossible.

It is helpful to clarify the path I have proposed in this section. After collecting and explicating four ideas of recognition (*attribution, praise, judgment, mutual authorization*), I outlined four related issues. The first two problems concern interpersonality and the mutuality of recognition, and both of these issues call into question different evolutions of Honneth's thinking. The shift from the anthropological justification based on vulnerability to the historical-normative one based on principles of recognition and their institutionalizations coincides with a shift of emphasis from the motivational binomial misrecognition-conflict to the depiction of the recognition order that characterizes modern (western) societies. Connected to this is a gradual shift from the centrality of being recognized to the investigation of recognizing, from the import of the intersubjective conditions for an undamaged practical identity oriented toward self-realization to the complementary normative obligations of such relationships oriented by the surplus of validity of freedom. Both these shifts of emphasis—it would be incorrect to speak of phases in the strict sense—lead Honneth to ground the critical potential of recognition not so much on its outcomes with respect to personal integrity, but on its internal structure—conceived more and more in deontological terms, meaning the reflexive capability of participants to jointly orient their agency and actualizing their shared freedom. Therefore, if, for example, in *The Struggle for Recognition*, the plain asymmetry between caregiver and child does not hinder conceiving such relation as effective condition by the self-realization of the latter, in *Recognition*, the same asymmetry is subtracted from the concept of mutual recognition. The only example made regarding the parent-child relationship is meant as an explanation of the nature of conflict. In the particularity of the example—which can be quite easily generalized in political terms—the struggle for recognition concerns the parents' eventual discussions about whether or not the children should be involved in the active decision-making processes regarding the family's

---

ing a vertical dimension, thus not being purely intersubjective, rather mediated, i.e. always referred to, shaped and informed by a third instance. Clearly—especially with respect to the first and third distinctions—Bedorf and Ikäheimo's accounts are articulated on slightly different levels. See Ikäheimo 2014.

orientations, about the aptness of authorizing co-authorship: that is, a removal of the asymmetry, indeed.[18] On this view, that the other becomes a partner or a player coincides with a substantial equality (with regard to principles and norms prevailing in each sphere of recognition).

However, the now evident polysemy of recognition requires us to explore its different variants, while also searching for an identification of the specificity of the interpersonal dimension. Connected to this is the multiplicity of levels on which asymmetry and symmetry and reciprocity and mutuality are intertwined, which must be followed by an identification of the normative specificity of the relationships of recognition. For, as we shall see, reciprocal recognition and reciprocity in general cannot be confused.

Moreover, outlining a normative concept of recognition cannot fail to take the issues raised by Markell and Bedorf into account. That is, we must consider the inconclusiveness of the identity-agency relationship and problematize the self- and other-directed character of the meta-attitude of recognizing, as well as delineating its ambivalent and aporetic character without expiring into a skepticism that would jeopardize a normative conceptualization of (inter-)acting that would deprive critical thinking of its pre-theoretical sources.

Before attempting this, however, it is necessary to step back and gain some clarity about the multivalent meanings of recognition.

6.2 What is Recognition?

Before we expound the meaning of recognition it is necessary to address (quasi-phenomenologically) the use of the word, with the aim of letting such praxis emerge from *our* complex form of life. Taking this as a starting point, the meaning of recognition emerges as being irreducible to symmetrical interpersonal relationships. Rather, in different western languages, recognition involves a broad scope of human (inter-)actions. Recognition shows itself as complex and holistic, characterized by different levels that are analytically distinguishable, but practically connected to each other according to non-causal logics. For the sake of clarity, we can discern three species of practical attitude that refer to the term recognition.[19]

---

[18] See Honneth 2021, pp. 173–74.
[19] Ricoeur offers the finest analysis of the vast diversity of meanings of recognition in the Introduction to his *The Course of Recognition*, through the recourse of several etymological dictionaries of the French language. Clearly, the same spectrum of meanings has not been established in every language. Besides the peculiarity already highlighted by Honneth in *Recognition*, the most peculiar case of discrepancy seems to me that of the Italian and French participle adjectives *riconoscente* and *reconnaissant*, which stand for being thankful and showing gratitude—in other words, recognizing that "I owe you one." Because of such polysemy, philosophical inquiry has, on the one hand, the difficult task of working its way through nuances that are possibly undetected even for native speakers themselves,

Re-cognition. The first species of recognition I propose is the normatively most neutral meaning, which indicates a certain cognitive attitude: it is about identifying something for what it is. As identification already makes clear, this attitude does not coincide with an attributive act, since the qualities of the other that I encounter are supposedly not ascribed, but rather received by the knower.

I choose re-cognition for two main reasons. First, both Ricoeur and Ikäheimo and Laitinen define this level of recognition with the term identification. While there is clearly a link between the two terms, avoiding reducing the former to the latter can prevent us from falling into some risks (made explicit by Markell and Bedorf) entailed by the relation with the concept of identity—recognizing X as *that X* does not merely mean identifying it: there is something more. The second reason concerns the prefix re-, as opposed to the prefix an- of *anerkennen*. Honneth correctly understands that the former implies a repetition, so that recognizing can be considered as equivalent to knowing again. But it is apt to recall that in Latin the prefix re- denotes, first, a backward movement, second, a return to an anterior state, and, third, a repetition.[20] A particularly well suited example is that of *respicio*, which shares its root with *respectus* (respect). *Respicio* does not mean looking again, but refers to what we do when we turn or take a step back in order to look—meanings maintained in regard, *regard*, *riguardo*, and *Rücksicht*. The one who is respected, regarded, or considered is not merely looked at again: rather, given that she is a distinct person, others would turn to look at her, or keep a certain distance to better watch—this second meaning is rendered by the ambivalence of the German *Achtung*.[21]

Re-cognizing therefore does not just mean knowing again, that is, recalling something already known: rather, it more deeply indicates that moment of discontinuity in which we become aware of *what* something is, it being something that was already present in our sphere of experience, albeit somehow undetectably or anonymously. Such becoming aware is certainly enabled by certain traits or elements that favor the identification of X, such as the physiognomy of the supermarket customer, whom I recognize as my primary school friend, the scar that reveals the identity of Ulysses on his return to Ithaca,[22] the peculiar style that allows me to guess the author of a painting, or the melody that distinguishes the song broadcast in a waiting room. These traits, one might say, allow us to relate the singular quality with the whole of X's identity—an identical scar on another person would not reveal Ulysses's identity,

---

and, on the other, of not depending totally on lexical analysis. A good example of this kind of analysis is provided by Ikäheimo and Laitinen with the distinction between identification, acknowledgment, and recognition. See the introduction to Ricoeur 2005; and Ikäheimo and Laitinen 2007.
20 See Alfred Ernout and Alfred Meillet 2011, s.v. re-, red-.
21 By reversing the dynamic of re-garding—that is, giving more emphasis to being-recognized than to recognizing—it becomes possible to describe recognition as a form of passive power, that is, as the ability to attract recognition. It seemingly represents a fruitful alternative to think of the connection between recognition and power out of a domination-determination framework. See Testa 2016.
22 See Ricoeur 2005, pp. 72–75.

but another's. And that this relating can be fallacious—a misrecognizing re-cognition—derives primarily from the dialectic relation between *X*'s identity and its features: Patroclus who is recognized by all as Achilles because of his armor, or the passer-by who, because of her backpack and her hair, is mistaken for a friend, but is in the end a stranger.

So far, however, the meaning of re-cognizing does not differ much from that of identifying, and, in fact, in many of these cases we are still within the domain of *erkennen*. The slight and at times elusive difference is that a certain normative dimension—even if minimal—cannot be ruled out, since appercepting something for what it is somehow entails an invitation to assume certain (and not other) attitudes toward it. The daily use of the term can help us again here. I recognize myself in the mirror and I can fix my hair or, recognizing someone on the street, I can decide whether to greet them or lower my gaze: both these possibilities are *enabled* by recognizing. The same holds true even if neither the recognizee nor recognizer are persons. For example, I recognize the situation of being late and therefore I speed up the pace;[23] two states recognize each other and either do or do not cross the respective borders; I recognize the no entry sign and change my route; or I recognize that what I have in my hand is a pen (and not a pencil), so I do not underline the book I borrowed, as I was about to do. As I see it, this level of recognition comes very close to the antecedent recognition Honneth depicts in *Reification*, even if his interpersonal approach was still stronger than the matters at hand. Taking into account the most borderline case addressed in the debate following Honneth's Tanner Lectures, namely, slavery, our survey of the meaning of re-cognition arguably allows us to say that even this case implies minimal, but decisive, normative dimensions. Reifying a slave implies recognizing them as human being. For in order to have a reification process we need a non-thing that is objectified: one cannot reify a stone, if not in a very poetical sense. So, the atrocity of slavery derives precisely from this minimal level of recognizing. Here we can also grasp the usefulness of distinguishing this first form of recognition, which shows itself as underlying even moral wrongs.[24] And this hinges on what Bedorf emphasizes: one cannot misrecognize what is already fully misrecognized, thus not appearing in our field of experience as the *X* it is.

From the variety of these examples, we can sketch five fundamental elements. First, re-cognizing corresponds to an attitude of becoming aware of what stands before oneself for what it is. Second, of course, such what it is is always contextualized,

---

[23] "It isn't as if being in a position to acknowledge something is *weaker* than being in a position to know it. On the contrary: from my acknowledging that I am late it follows that I know I'm late (which is what my words say); but from my knowing I am late, it does not follow that I acknowledge I'm late" (Cavell 2015, p. 237). Although the term acknowledging brings with it several implications, it seems to me useful to point out that already at the level of re-cognizing there is a difference with bare knowing and, therefore, with identifying—a difference in which re-cognizing seems in many cases to have a genetic and categorical priority.

[24] See Butler 2008; and Geuss 2008.

eventual, and therefore potentially problematic and questionable. Third, from such becoming aware it would be reasonable to expect one to act accordingly: saying this does not imply that the content of recognition causes certain *re*actions, but that it informs our actions. It is important to emphasize that by recognizing we are invited to take on a certain stance: not every cognitive performance or identification implies that we must take a stance, while re-cognition apparently does. Fourth, re-cognizee and re-cognizer can be non-human. Finally, such stance, if interpersonal, can, but not necessarily, be reciprocal, according to different degrees. Two acquaintances who meet on the street re-cognize each other as human beings, but it may be that only one of them recalls (knows-again) who the other is. In any case, the minimal normative indication already consists in re-cognizing the other as a human being, which prevents me, for example, from trying to find a door handle on her shoulder, but it does not prevent me—indeed it *enables* me—to insult her or treat her badly, for instance.

Acknowledgment. This second nuance of the meaning of recognition alludes to the stance one assumes when one accepts the other for what it is, expressing a confirmation of such acceptance. The subtle distinction with re-cognizing consists in the greater degree of active, voluntary involvement on the part of the acknowledger,[25] who not only adapts her acting to the features of the other, but who also *performs* gestures that show that she is doing so. That this can coincide with attributive utterances or gestures, however, is not to be understood as something arbitrarily at the disposal of the acknowledger, since those expressions are mostly experienced by the participants as an (adequate) response to the other as it presents itself: acknowledgment is a matter of accepting and expressing, confirming the other with regard to what is perceived *to be due* to it. A more normative horizon is therefore embedded in these kinds of (inter-)actions, for they represent a responsive process of evaluation. For example, a judge acknowledges a certain petition submitted to her as conforming to the legal code, or a poet is considered as unjustly unacknowledged by his contemporaries. On the first page of a text, acknowledgments are made public to those who contributed to its drafting. The acquaintance I meet on the street is sad or upset, and I acknowledge it by asking her how she is doing. In this case, the dynamic is also not limited to the interpersonal sphere. One can say that the law acknowledges the validity of a claim, the government acknowledges an emergency, and that the court acknowledges the constitutionality (or otherwise) of a bill. Indeed, acknowledgment is rarely understood as directly addressed to *X*, but rather, and above all, to *certain traits* of *X*, her efforts, status, role, truthfulness, validity, or performances. For instance, acknowledging what has been said is not primarily assessing its being pronounced, but it regards its being true or false, appropriate or not, and insightful or misleading. Returning to the example of the no entry sign can help us to further understand this factor with respect to the difference emerging with re-cognition: I *re-*

---

25 See Wildt 2010, p. 191.

cognize the no entry sign, I *acknowledge* that norm's validity and that crossing, given the circumstances, is wrong, so I walk away. So, as Markell stresses, what matters in acknowledging is not so much knowing, but what we do given and in front of what we experience.

These examples also inform us with regard to five elements. First, acknowledging coincides with accepting something *as* something, giving public expression to the content at stake, thus confirming and admitting it. Second, also in this case, the correctness of the acknowledgments is all but obvious. Third, such adequacy must be evaluated on two sides. For both apperception and response can fail because accepting and admitting have a twofold nature insofar as they allude to a holistic fashion of gestures that are both passive and active in principle. I can truly appreciate my coworker's contributions (thus acknowledging them), but do not express it during a meeting (thus not acknowledging them). Fourth, acknowledger and acknowledged can be nonhuman. Finally, I think, within an interpersonal relationship, acknowledgment in most cases outlines precisely the thin, diachronic mutuality we have seen in recognition as appropriate judgment: the master can acknowledge that the servant has done a good job, and the latter can acknowledge the former as his master, that is, an appropriate judge expressing an appropriate judgment. But that would be the case even of school grades: the teacher evaluates the students' performances as expressing some of their traits and efforts, expressing such evaluation through the grade she attributes to their tests. The evaluation is considered an acknowledgment if it respects two conditions: first, if the students in turn acknowledge the teacher's role, for a note written on the same test by a classmate would only be a number; second, if it is perceived as fitting to one's performance, thus accepting the grade. This set of practices is therefore strictly normative in so far as it consists of evaluative (inter-)actions. But we cannot necessarily derive a particular moral standard for the gestures that the participants address each other from this, that is, the instantiation of personifying practices such as those in the case of master-servant.[26]

Mutual recognition. It is the third meaning we will consider, which Honneth describes as exclusively interpersonal, mutual, and symmetrical. It is crucial to notice that the focus shifts to recognition *relations*, whose characterizing *gestures/acts* possess a certain specificity. For they do not simply address other's features or her performances. Rather, Honneth argues, the heart of mutual recognition is the mutual authorization of participants to take part in a space-for-freedom, which is accompanied by both taking on a co-authoritative status. This status is neither granted to nor apperceived in the other, but emerges as a side-effect of authorization. The fundamental step, therefore, is for Honneth to untie recognition from the lexicon of identity: the matter at stake is not who or what the other *is*, but rather our being a We by drawing together our freedom.

---

26 See Ikäheimo 2014; and Ikäheimo and Laitinen 2010.

It is important to stress here that recognition relationships do not depend on exchanges of different recognition gestures. Let us say, for example, that I have a rather strict routine for going to university: on the train, I always prefer to get in the same carriage and try to sit in the same place. Then, when I am about to take the subway, I head to the point of the platform that is most functional for getting out quickly from the arrival station, and so on. After a while, I notice that another person has similar habits: after all, having similar habits is quite common for commuters. With time, we re-cognize each other more and more readily, sometimes we even chat and are so used to seeing each other that it becomes easy for both to acknowledge when the other is tired, relaxed, stressed, and so on. Do we share, for this reason, a relationship of mutual recognition? Not necessarily: the experience of mutuality that this concept seems to presuppose does not seem to derive from the sum of individual gestures of reciprocity that we can exchange. And in this experience of mutuality, *continuity*—which certainly represents one of the elements of the institutionality of recognitional spheres Honneth describes—plays a decisive role. One element determining this discontinuity between gestures and relationships is therefore represented by the fact that a relationship of mutual recognition certainly depends on the acts of recognition that the participants exchange with each other, but at a more fundamental level on the second-order awareness with which they experience such interactions: only at this level can one speak of a relationship.

Clearly, re-cognition, acknowledgment, and mutual recognition overlap semantically and practically, making any rigid separation almost impossible. However, I believe it is possible to identify non-causal derivative connections, that is, modes of co-implication between these practical forms, which can also be described respectively as apperception, acceptance/admission, and authorization. First, mutual authorization implies that participants apperceive each other as human beings and accept each other as free beings. Mutual recognition cannot be seen as disconnected from these first two steps, but it also represents the condition of new forms of acknowledgment, since only from within and starting from the mutual authorization can the participants acknowledge each other as players of the cooperative (re-)formulations of the norms governing their acting. Second, these three levels do not necessarily have to proceed in agreement. Let us consider Honneth's reading of Hegel's account on marriage, where equal access to the space-for-freedom is prevented by the pervasive images on *the* female nature. In this case, one could say, the two participants re-cognize each other as human beings, and as those specific individuals who are, respectively, each other's spouse. Given this fact, they should in principle mutually recognize each other as members of the sphere that they share as equals, that is, their own marriage. However, the husband does not *acknowledge* the wife as capable of acting normatively like himself—and the wife, having internalized this judgement, acknowledges herself as moral person. Leaving aside the historical-cultural causes of this situation and how the participants could become aware of it, we are for the moment interested in highlighting the fact that certain modes of acknowledgment undermine the quality of mutual recognition, or even prevent it. If sharing such second-order We of recognition—as in the case of marriage—does not guarantee an emancipatory relationship because of the ways of acknowledgment, it is clear that recognition relationships can provide a normative resource if they meet certain, further, conditions. They do share a We, but they do not acknowledge each other as equals. Plainly, the concept of mutual recognition needs to be clarified further.

6.3 A Detrascendentalized Account: Limitation and We-Structures

This brief overview of the meanings of recognition, which can be divided into the three connotations of apperception, acceptance/admission, and authorization, has, if possible, made the picture even more intricate. However, we have gained three key insights.

The first concerns the specificity of recognition as practical form. Although they differ in terms of objects, modes of execution, logics of action, actors at stake, all the examples mentioned above concern a particular practical form in which the agent allows herself to be informed by the features of otherness, marking a practical discontinuity with the previous state of affairs. In recognizing, in any of its forms, a certain awareness arises, whereby the priority of the other somewhat guides our actions. This also applies to views that conceive recognition more in terms of rewarding, as in Amy Allen's example of Elizabeth (see section 5.2 above).

Second, shifting the focus to mutual recognition, we have seen how it moves (at times ambiguously) between two levels, which Ricoeur distinguishes as logic of reciprocity and experience of mutuality. The pervasiveness of the logic of reciprocity, which essentially concerns every interaction, is what leads, in my view, to the confusion of recognition and intersubjectivity. Clearly, according to Honneth, the intersubjective formation of the person also plays a fundamental role. For it justifies human vulnerability as a normative starting point and helps in outlining the basic elements of the coordination of social action. But this cannot lead us to superimpose a normative concept of mutual recognition on any socially contextualized interaction. Or, better, all interactions imply a fundamental level of reciprocity, normative to the extent that their participants know their acting as bound by (even the thinnest) role obligations. But, first, this can be almost devoid of ethical-moral connotations. For even revenge responds to such a logic of reciprocity, trading deed for deed.[27] Second—and above all—the division of role obligations represents a side-effect with reference to a third instance, the cause or purpose for which we find ourselves in relation. At this level, reciprocal recognition and social integration can be superimposed, since, precisely, every social interaction requires this level of reciprocity. Things are different as far as the experience of mutuality is concerned, which represents a spe-

---

27 See Ricoeur 2005, pp. 227–28; and Bernstein 1996, p. 59.

cific second-order awareness on the part of the participants, so that the distance between the complementary obligations and the third instance to which they refer is narrowed almost to the point of disappearing: as Honneth says, we cannot understand recognition as a side-effect, as the non-thematized acceptance/admission of my chess opponent's skills that accompany our playing.[28] It follows from this that mutual recognition requires extremely specific standards, summarized by Hegel with his definition of the pure concept of recognition: "They *recognize* themselves as *mutually recognizing each other*" (Hegel, The Phenomenology of Spirit, § 184). It is not enough for me to recognize you as my partner for the purpose X. Nor would it be enough for both of us to recognize ourselves as fundamental for the joint realization of our we-intention. The relationship of mutual recognition is a relation in which actors are primarily aware of their reflexive comprehending themselves as a We. I will return to this in the following sections.

Third, since, as Honneth stresses in *Recognition*, mutual recognition represents a detranscendentalized interaction, that is, proper to our lifeworld, it emerges as not decouplable, among other practical forms, from re-cognition and acknowledgment. But precisely in *Recognition*—in contrast with *Reification* and "Grounding Recognition"— Honneth fails to emphasize that a full-fledged mutual authorization can only occur if it relies on appropriate forms of apperception and acceptance/admission. The normative interpersonal dimension cannot be separated from the first two (broadly understood) epistemological ones. If one does not want to discard the term recognition in its specificity, one has to address the difficult matter of how—in both meanings of under what conditions and with what features—the other appears to me. Without at least some hints in this direction, the risks are to de-detranscendentalize the discourse on recognition, to empty the term of its semantic content, and to fail to justify why the morality proper to recognition is only to be grasped in interpersonal terms— thereby depowering its critical potential. Using Laitinen's terms, in order to defend a paradigm oriented by the mutuality insight it is necessary that specific elements come into play at the level of adequate regarding among persons.

If the concept of recognition refers to different practices, but these share a priority given to the other that informs our consequent acting, a first way to distinguish mutual recognition without decoupling it from re-cognition and acknowledgment is to take the peculiarity of the recognizee as a starting point. To this extent, it does not seem enough to argue that recognition among humans is related only to our second nature. For our being human has to do also with our first nature.[29] Ob-

---

[28] See Honneth 2002, p. 506.
[29] It is no coincidence that Hegel, in describing mutual recognition, starts from a reflection on life, and on that peculiar lifeform that the human being is. With respect to this issue, which I must leave open, see Testa 2005; Testa 2010; Testa 2012; Hegel, *The Phenomenology of Spirit*, §§ 166–173; Hegel, *Philosophy of Mind*, §§ 424–437; and Ikäheimo 2014, p. 13. In this sense, it seems reductive to describe the spiritual dimension as exclusively normative, that is, as a mere departure from the natural. In the same way, to disqualify certain Hegelian perspectives (e.g. on the relationship between states) as

serving this, of course, does not coincide with the intent to propose a physiologist or biologist reductionism, since the access to our first nature we are endowed with can be found from within the second.[30] In the same way, it is not intended to make the discourse on mutual recognition coincide with a paradigm of onto- and phylogenetic processes, since, as we have seen, the former and social integration, although intertwined, differ.

In trying to take a step forward in understanding what is specific to recognition among human beings, I believe that a fundamental element is identified by Wildt through the distinction between "propositional" and "personal" recognition.[31] With propositional recognition, Wildt indicates what we referred to using re-cognition and acknowledgment, that is, a more or less affirmative attitude through which one takes notice and accepts the most varied phenomena for what they are, be it a situation or a problem, practical norms or state laws, down to one's own faults. What distinguishes such forms from personal recognition is a different experience of limitation that encountering another person implies. Recognizing the other person represents a discontinuity that I cannot come to terms with as easily as when I stumble upon an object: the other is alter. To say this does not coincide with re-proposing an atomistic perspective on the individual, so that we would fall back into the modern idea of a subject already formed before entering the world, regarding identity as a *fait accompli*. Instead, I argue that such limitation is to be understood in phenomenological terms similar to Heidegger's, as a 'disruption of reference': the other appears as always posing to me a *certain*—in some cases merely potential—unhandiness and unusefulness, which to a certain extent puzzles me.[32] Think Hegel's account of the transition from *Begierde* to Self-Consciousness, which he describes precisely in terms of the inability to nullify the self that appears before me;[33] or of the caregiver's obstinacy before the aggressive gestures of the child described by Winnicott and taken up by Honneth in *The Struggle for Recognition*—which plays a decisive role by developing the ability to stay by oneself without fear.[34] Or, again of what has been said about *respicio* and *Achtung*. Briefly, the other is a limit for me in a way that an object cannot be, and vice versa. Focusing on these modes of manifestation avoids the assumption of an undisputed image of human nature but

---

characterized by the presence of too much nature somewhat misses the target (See Patrice Canivez 2011). The process of mediation of natural immediacy—in *this* consists its sublation—does not fall into a transcendentalism, in fact, only if, even considering the fundamental role of *Bildung* and habits, this process is always to be reformulated. In other words, the objective spirit keeps on being bound to human needs and natural resources. See Siep 2011, p. 127. For a different view on the relation between nature and spirit, and more precisely on subject's animality, see Luca Illetterati 2016.
30 See Krüger 2019, pp. 90–95.
31 See Wildt 2010.
32 See Martin Heidegger 1996, pp. 69–71. Incidentally, most of Heidegger's examples are very similar to the basic form we described as re-cognition.
33 See Hegel, *The Phenomenology of Spirit*, § 175.
34 See Honneth 1995c, p. 101.

allows us to access to some basic peculiarities of the human living being, which are well reconciled with Honneth's perspective taken as a whole, especially with his early writings. In fact, in presenting itself as a limitation, the other appears first as body and voice, but, above all, as intentionally projecting itself, as an acting being, that is, as fundamentally decentering itself.[35] In this way, the other invites me to attitudes of self-restriction—that must not be morally loaded—in which reside minimal normative indications.[36] It follows from this that the threshold of such modes of the manifestation of the other should not be thought of as a transcendental framework, if one equates transcendental with ahistorical. Rather, it is transcendental to the extent that it provides legalities, but it is historical to the extent that the a priori is already a posteriori qua social, cultural, and historical context: a *detrascendentalized* second nature, an enabled enabling condition.

Emphasizing that the other appears as limitation does not mean that we are heading toward a kind of atomism, whereby the aim of human interaction is to bridge an unbridgeable gap between ego and alter. In this sense, if we take, as Honneth does, forms of interaction and spheres of social action as a starting point, such limitations instantiate not just in an interruption of multi-personal forms, that is, as it is by misrecognition or nonrecognition. Rather, it means taking seriously the opposing tendencies,[37] the ambivalences that characterize human interaction and recognition among persons—an aspect to be re-evaluated of the negative theories of recognition. Thus, we can avoid a mimetic misinterpretation of "being with oneself in the other," hence we do not forget the first leg of the expression, and we emphasize that every *inter*-relation is a *tension* between ego-boundaries and ego-dissolution, a *balance* between determinacy and indeterminacy. That such mutual boundaries are not liquefied is also decisive in order to avoid equating our dependence on recognition with the compulsion to live in the eyes of others.[38] In other words, a distinction between recognition and empathy has to be drawn, which consists precisely in the fact that our need for complementarity (*Ergänzungsbedürftigkeit*) is fulfilled via acts of self-limitation toward the other, thus outlining a more complex image of unity. A unity—that of mutual recognition—that is not homogeneous indeterminacy, but the determinacy of you and me disclosing to *us*.

---

35 See Schürmann 2006; and Honneth 1995a. While Honneth's theory certainly derives a number of advantages from taking as its point of departure the negative of misrecognition and, more generally, the unbalance of the individual on otherness—vulnerability, moral injury, decentered and social freedom—this element is almost always framed from a first-person perspective. The other is rarely described as vulnerable or decentered. I believe that it is useful—also to illuminate the motivational horizon of recognition—to emphasize that these are structural elements that also pertain to the other I meet, whom I am invited to recognize.
36 These elements—insightfully highlighted by Berendzen—are particularly evident in Honneth's only analysis of Hegel's *Phenomenology*. See Honneth 2012c; and Joseph C. Berendzen 2019.
37 See Wildt 2010, p. 195.
38 See Wildt 2010, p. 205; and Neuhouser 2010.

If it is true, then, that mutual recognition requires re-cognizing and acknowledging as its moments, re-cognition and acknowledgment alone are not sufficient to have mutual recognition. Keeping that the dimension of re-cognizing is seemingly not under question, some issues emerge if one sticks to the moment of acknowledgment alone. In particular, we have already encountered four risks during our reconstruction.

First, the fact that I acknowledge the other does not in any way prevent me from subjugating her. On the contrary, taking notice of the other as limit can be precisely the motivational and social ground for an asymmetrical relationship. Moreover, even if I knew the other in an unquestionably positive way, there would be no inner logic that could guarantee the relationship from being ideological—in the sense of Honneth's account on ideological recognition.[39] Second, the very fact of encountering the other could be correctly perceived as a determination of her possibilities, just as she is of mine. From here to a (constitutive) power relation the step would be short.[40] For emerging under the other's gaze assumes the traits of a structurally misrecognizing over-determination, since we are already posed in certain (and not other) conditions by the other. Third, if such evaluative knowledge widens to the point of coinciding with individual socialization—meaning recognition as subject(ificat)ion—then it is difficult to overlook the homologating and levelling power of such acts, at least as viaticum of pre-formed ethical-cultural patterns: the "subjection of desire," once internalized, would lead to the "desire *for* subjection" in terms similar to Allen's example of Elizabeth (Butler 1997, p. 19).[41] The fourth and last risk coincides with an extreme generic idea of recognition, characteristic of a certain automatism that pertains to the Kantian account of respect.[42] In that context, recognition concerns *any* interaction among humans merely because the participants are aware that they are dealing with persons, and the specificity of the concept risks to be lost in a misleading coincidence with reciprocity in general.

The shortcoming of such a perspective would then not be, as Honneth maintains, that they confuse recognition with pathologies of recognition or with classifying linguistic practices, but that they make mutual recognition coincide with acknowledgment, namely, with that practice, at most thinly reciprocal, symbolically expressing

---

[39] This helps to consolidate the persuasion that a recognition paradigm is not self-sufficient if it is understood to be relevant to the intersubjective dyad alone. See Siep 2011, p. 135. As we have already seen, however, Honneth (more or less explicitly) refers to triadic forms, both to justify the forms of recognition and to explain their formation.
[40] See Lepold 2014.
[41] "What is it, then, that is desired in subjection? Is it a simple love of the shackles, or is there a more complex scenario at work? How is survival to be maintained if the terms by which existence is guaranteed are precisely those that demand and institute subordination? On this understanding, subjection is the paradoxical effect of a regime of power in which the very 'conditions of existence,' the possibility of continuing as a recognizable social being, requires the formation and maintenance of the subject in subordination" (Butler 1997, p. 27).
[42] See Brownlee 2015.

and confirming personal traits by means of taking notice of their doings, achievements, and performances. In other words, they cannot account for the specificity of the experience of mutuality, since they basically disregard the second-order We-forms implied in the very concept of mutual recognition.

In order to better grasp the two levels at stake—and their inevitable practical interweaving—it is useful to have recourse to Michael Quante's reading of the opening sentence of section A. of the chapter on Self-Consciousness in the *Phenomenology of Spirit*:[43]

> Das Selbstbewußtsein ist *an* und *für sich*, indem und dadurch, daß es für ein Anderes an und für sich ist; d. h. es ist nur als ein Anerkanntes.
>
> Self-consciousness is *in* and *for itself* while and as a result of its being in and for itself for an other; i.e., it is only as a recognized being (Hegel, *The Phenomenology of Spirit*, § 178).

According to Quante, the fact that Hegel specifies that recognition takes place according to an *indem* and to a *dadurch, daß* would make it possible to identify two different logics at stake: those of a when-relation and a by-relation (in Pinkard's translation we just referred to: "while" and "as a result"). The latter would insist on the *causal* character of recognition gestures, in which the self-consciousness *B* would be structured *as a result* of *A*'s recognizing it. This dimension would in turn be divided into two subclasses, which Hegel inherits from Fichte. The first is *diachronic* and *asymmetric*, that is, it coincides with the one-sided *Aufforderung* of a temporally prior self-consciousness that puts into play the elements necessary for a (more or less active) *individual-genetic* process on the part of *B*. The second, instead, would shed light on the *motivational* side of recognition relations. Here, both *A*'s invitation and *B*'s eventual response are conceived as being mutually *conditioning* each other: *A* treats *B* having already recognized her as free being, having already experienced her being a limit for him—and vice versa as far as *B*'s answer is concerned. Even if that happens in discreet moments between them, both the invitation and the answer imply a prior recognition of the other that conditions the modalities and motivations of the reciprocal approach, according to a hypothetical game of mutual conditioning that could continue ad infinitum.[44] Although synchronic and symmetrical, this dynamic is still characterized by a certain dichotomy of first- and second-person perspective: the relationship does not overcome the singularities of the intentions at stake. If we take a closer look, both the four risks mentioned above and the criticisms made by Markell and Bedorf move within this perspective, thus still tied to an analysis of individual *acts* of recognizing.

This singularity would instead be overcome in an when-relation, with which we can see a shift from the first and second person to the first person plural: "*I* that is *we* and the *we* that is *I*" (Hegel, *The Phenomenology of Spirit*, § 177). Here, more than on

---

[43] See Michael Quante 2010.
[44] See Fichte 2000, p. 42.

individual acts of recognition, the emphasis is on the *qualitative* difference that structures the relationship. The relationships of mutual recognition would shape and, at the same time, be instantiated in and through We-structures in which "the contemporaneity of two actions" is comprehended by the participants as "constitutive for one another in the sense that being moments of an overall structure is part of their identity conditions as individual doings" (Quante 2010 p. 102). Thus, the key to understanding the distinction between acknowledgment and mutual recognition is not identifiable just in the diachronicity or simultaneity of *A* or *B*'s gestures. Nor can we understand the issue taking symmetry as our guiding star, since it also instantiates in the bad reciprocity of revenge or in patterns of purposive functionalization of the other into logics à la *do ut des*. Rather, the specificity of mutual recognition emerges by the becoming shared of the first-person perspective, so that there are no discreet I and you, but *us*. My acting can instantiate only through *our* acting, whereby the coordination of our doings does not merely represent an aim or an achievement, but the condition of possibility of our being actors.

6.4 A Demanding Concept: Sketches for a Generative Account

With this further clarification, we have brought the last element of the demanding concept of mutual recognition that we are looking for into play. In sum, it has to meet six conditions.

First, it must embed the complexity of its own moments—identifiable, but essentially holistic in their actualization: re-cognition, acknowledgment, and mutual recognition. What we are looking for is a complex practical bundle that is articulated on several levels, all dialectically concurring and occurring in shaping recognition. That is to say, we have to take into account both the when- and the by-relation in their mutual intertwining, still being able to distinguish them, thus not making them collapse on each other.

Second, we are in search of a paradigm that outlines the movement of mutual recognition as non-automatic, that is, as not resulting from the mere fact that two human beings encounter each other. It also follows from this that recognition cannot draw its features exclusively from the context in which it takes place—it is not enough to say that, for example, two coworkers recognize each other by merely taking each other as coworkers. Consequently, but maintaining the differentiation between by-relation and when-relation, it will be useful to emphasize the necessity of such automatism that pertains to the logic of reciprocity, but which does not allow to overcome interactional forms oriented by and to legal-economic logic of exchange. In this context, the peculiarity of mutual recognition, as Wildt argues is precisely that of instantiating non-legal forms of morality and modes of relation, which disclose thicker modes of respect than the Kantian one.[45]

Recognition must therefore, third, be distinguishable, by virtue of its specificity, from individual socialization and reciprocity in general, without abandoning its constitutive connection with sociality and social reproduction. Recognition is not simply matter of being humanized, even if it certainly possesses a humanizing role, with regard to all the nuanced levels that the word human entails. The usefulness of pursuing a diversified paradigm of recognition consists in showing its irreducibility to an act of imprinting—be it biologically, psychologically, or culturally conceived. In this sense, one can say that recognition represents an inclusion in personhood,[46] but not every inclusion in personhood is recognition.

In the same way, the following account on mutual recognition distances itself from the lexicon of identity. Besides rejecting a one-sided idea of attribution, what we must distance ourselves from is the idea that recognition coincides with a heteronomous constitution of personhood. If that were the case, recognition would almost coincide with reifying or labelling gestures—and what distinguishes Honneth's view from, say, Althusser's seems to be a mere prior choice about whether it is positive or negative that humans are social animals. However, it is necessary to avoid the opposite direction as well, that is, to describe an intersubjective practice that is unrelated to the structuring of the practical identity of an individual, which would then be, so to speak, abandoned to a fluid indeterminacy without anchorage points to unfold a biographical path. The distinction between acknowledgment and mutual recognition as moments of recognition allows us to distance ourselves equally from the risks of indeterminacy and over-determinacy regarding the person. With Hegel, we will see that "the most profound form of recognition has little to do with the problematic of identity," rather its "true meaning" is reconciliation (Canivez 2011, pp. 867–68).

Fifth, it is necessary to shed light on mutual recognition as *inner* logic of progress, one able to avoid the bad infinity involved in the succession of fixation and unfixation.[47] Honneth's theory attracts the most criticism, after all, because it attributes the emancipatory tasks to conflict, not to recognition. Despite Honneth's attempt in *Recognition* to stress the fragility and provisional character of the recognitional forms, the basic idea seems to remain that the latter play a crystallizing role. The institutional contexts in which such (inter-)actions take place are indeed nothing but coagulations of the (inter-)actions themselves. If, on the one hand, there is coagulation, the task of fluidification, on the other hand, is assigned to conflict. But then, if structurally one cannot reach a state of peace (as Ricoeur would like) because this would coincide with theoretically implying an annulment of both surplus of validity and progress, it follows that every form of recognition *is* a misrecognizing recogni-

---

[45] See Laitinen 2017.
[46] See Ikäheimo 2009.
[47] See Markell 2003, p. 183.

tion. Otherwise, what would be the motivations for the rising of social conflicts? Only the insufficiency and the perceived narrowness of the actual forms of recognition can justify struggle. Then, one would almost find oneself, accepting Honneth's social-normative theory, in the paradoxical situation of rejecting his concept of recognition; for it, as a crystallized step in the learning process of social history, has to be structurally fluidified by struggle. It is possible to come out of this impasse if recognition and conflict are not conceived as two alternative moments,[48] that is, if we re-evaluate the generative capability of mutual recognition, in terms of its capability to release forms of discontinuity.

Finally, it is necessary to consider the specificity of our lifeform. This becomes possible, thanks to Hegel, by thinking mutual recognition in relation to a broader theory of action and the medium of language.

6.5 Back to Hegel: Recognition and Forgiveness

It will not come as a surprise that this generative account will be outlined with the help of Hegel. But it may raise eyebrows that this reference is articulated in an analysis of *The Phenomenology of Spirit* and, more specifically, of the narrative on confession and forgiveness placed at the end of the section entitled Spirit.

Indeed, two criticisms can already be directed at this choice. The first, which is shared by both Habermas and Honneth, is that, in the *Phenomenology*, Hegel abandons his previous intersubjective and social-ontological approach in favor of a philosophy of consciousness, a "monological concept of spirit" that would be little suited to contributing for a post-metaphysical social philosophy (Honneth 2012d, p. viii). It follows from this that the shadow cast over the whole narrative by the last section —Absolute Knowing—would seem to thwart any attempt to mediate the cumbersomeness of a metaphysical end of history, even more than in the *Philosophy of Right* and in the *Philosophy of History* themselves. In other words, this repressed intersubjectivity not only undermines the role of reciprocal recognition, but it also teleologically functionalizes it, unbalancing the dialectic between particular and universal.[49] Second, even if one wanted to refer to the *Phenomenology* in order to investigate recognition, the best place from which to draw elements would be the section on Self-Consciousness—the pure concept of recognition, the struggle for life and death, and the master-servant dialectic. These elements are not equally available in the parable on forgiveness, which, after all, merely concerns the reintegration of the individual into the ethical community, the first adjusting to the latter. For it is difficult to overlook that this whole narrative can stand for nothing but the integra-

---

48 See Bertram and Celikates 2015.
49 Besides what Siep has already said with respect to this issue (see section 2.1 above), see also Habermas 1999; and Michael Theunissen 1991.

tion of the "outsiders" into the community (Siep 2014b, p. 200)[50]—thus not differing so much from what is addressed in *Recognition* with the idea of classifying linguistic hierarchical practices.

Clearly, these two objections pose very broad issues about Hegel's thinking in general and its relevance to contemporary debates. And this difficulty is compounded by the multiplicity of starting perspectives with which we approach both the concept of recognition and Hegel himself: ethical-moral, social-ontological, political, critical-normative, and so on. It is therefore equally clear that this is not the place to definitively settle these interpretative issues on the *Phenomenology*. However, being that our aim is to develop a deeper understanding of recognition, I believe that some elements may provide a framework in which it becomes possible that the two objections mentioned above will not undermine our attempt.

The first question concerns the choice to refer to the *Phenomenology* rather than to the *Philosophy of Right*, which is usually preferred in the contemporary debate on recognition. The decisive element in the first text consists in its narrative structure, which provides for the coexistence and distinction of two perspectives: the *experience* of consciousness and the *for us* of the philosophical gaze. If we do not want to reduce this for us to an ahistorical eye, it is easy to find one of the classical themes of critical theory in this doubled view, one that is so decisive for Honneth: critical theory's attempt to identify with social actors, to let the emancipatory interests set the theoretical agenda. Certainly, identifying this nexus requires not only not reducing the *for us* to an ahistorical eye, but to grant a certain autonomy to the various figures of the *Phenomenology*, without dissolving their peculiarity in their supposed end point. In other words, it is a question of taking seriously the concept of experience (*Erfahrüng*), the gestation and the work of the negative that characterize this text in a peculiar way. It is a matter of conceiving the *for us* as a hermeneutical vanishing point—i.e. as the emerging of a third dimension—not as an element that functionalizes to itself its self-generated moments. As far as the question of recognition is concerned, the advantage offered by taking this twofold perspective into account is to have leeway in order to place Ricoeur's distinction of logic of reciprocity and experience of mutuality. That is, to outline the contours and the meaning of the *between* of the relationship between *A* and *B*, to better understand the role of symmetry and asymmetry in the relationships of recognition. Thus, moving between these two levels makes it possible to avoid getting totally unbalanced either on what the participants experience or on what happens behind them. For, after all, this twofold perspective draws our attention on those moments of the *Phenomenology* in which it is no longer twofold, but the for us of theory becomes the for us of experience.

---

[50] Siep obviously sketches a more Hegelian scenario to the extent that such integration cannot be one-sided and un-dialectical—but the impression persists that forgiveness is nothing more than a subjection of the confessing conscience.

The second issue regards the choice of the Spirit section, rather than the seemingly more natural option offered by that on Self-Consciousness. This focus is motivated by the fact that, in this section, Hegel brings many of the experiential steps of consciousness previously outlined into the historicity and sociality proper to our lifeform and lifeworld. In particular, a significant relevance is covered by the detrascendentalization of action-theoretical elements depicted in the subsections B and C of Reason (especially paragraphs b. Law-Giving Reason and c. Reason as Testing Laws). In the same way, many questions left open by the evident gap between the pure concept of recognition and the struggle for life and death, on the one hand, and master-servant dialectic, on the other, find their place in the context of our being-in-recognition, rather than in the struggle for it. Put into more Honnethian terms, the discussion of recognition is dealt with here starting from our second nature, which is already inhabited by normative orientations and promises instantiated within relational and institutional frameworks. Evidently, Hegel does not here distinguish the spheres of recognition, but outlines a properly objective phase of spirit. In this sense, starting from Spirit rather than from Self-Consciousness makes it possible to remove the *Phenomenology*'s account of recognition from the misunderstanding that usually affects it, being it often "misconstrued as a dialogical interaction between subjects rather than as the dialectical development of a social world through the interaction of subjects with their natural, cultural, institutional and political environments" (Tobias 2007, p. 115).

Third, the choice to focus on paragraph Conscience; the Beautiful Soul, Evil, and its Forgiveness in the Morality section is mainly motivated by two elements. First, by the fact that, given the thrift with which Hegel uses the term *Anerkennung* in the *Phenomenology*, it is not difficult to notice that its recurrences are concentrated in section B Self-Consciousness and in the paragraph previously mentioned.[51] The difference between the two episodes is, however, abysmal if we consider that the first, a proto-historical narration, in fact, does not lead to a relationship of recognition in the strict sense, while the second, which bears all the historical-social evolution that precedes it, represents a point of light in the succession of failures, self-deceptions and denials of which *Phenomenology* is interwoven: it *can* lead to a relationship of mutual recognition—in a way and in a sense yet to be seen. What has been outlined in the pure concept of recognition is not fully realized nor in the antagonistic relation between desiring self-consciousnesses, nor in the master-servant relationship,[52] but has to wait for its actualization until the experience of mutual forgive-

---

[51] See Siep 2010, pp. 108–9.
[52] This statement may be questionable, especially if one considers the description Hegel proposes in the *Encyclopaedia*, where the master also exercises duties of care toward the servant, thus in some way reciprocating the work of the latter. See Hegel, *Philosophy of Mind*, §§ 424–37; Ikäheimo 2014. The whole question is how to conceive of the *quality* of the necessary and sufficient conditions for a mutual recognition relationship—what we have tried to clarify by distinguishing between acknowledgment and mutual recognition, and between by- and when-relation. If it is certainly true that the

ness.⁵³ Second, there is literally a world that separates the struggle for life and death and forgiveness. However, it is easy to see that it is the second episode that helps us most in delineating a normative (demanding) concept of mutual recognition. First, the starting point of the two consciousnesses at stake is oriented by their moral acting, rather than by *Begierde:* conflict is therefore not engaged with sword or spear, but is a verbal conflict, a struggle of arguments. The poles are in fact mediated by language, speech (*Rede*) rather than by the desire to assert oneself against the other. The emergence of unity, not only for us, but also for the participants, from the "aporetic experience of conflict" instantiates in the fact that consciousness "learns to *relativize* its worldview, to see it as *one of many* perspectives" (Cortella 2005, p. 153, my translation).⁵⁴ It learns that is to include the other in its view, to distance oneself from a coincidence with one's own acts. What Hegel describes through the binomial confession-forgiveness is the actualization of a relationship in which the participants conceive themselves as such, recognize themselves as mutually recognizing each other—which cannot be implied as second-order awareness neither by the struggle, nor by the master-servant relation.⁵⁵

6.5.1 Guilt as Finitude and Being-For-Others

In order to frame the complexity of issues Hegel addresses in the section Spirit and how these lead to Morality, a good starting point seems to me to be a quotation from Habermas in which he describes the relationship between normativity and social reality in a way that also distinguishes Honneth's theory:

> every moral system provides a solution to the problem of coordinating actions among beings who are dependent on social interaction. Moral consciousness is the expression of the legitimate demands that members of a cooperative social group make on one another. Moral feelings regulate the observance of the underlying norms (Habermas 1998, pp. 16 – 17).⁵⁶

In this sentence, even with all the precautions of the case, one can find Honneth's persuasion that experiencing moral injury reveals the misdevelopments of social co-

---

master is such only *when* with the servant (and vice versa), one may wonder if here there is a We at all.
53 See Sinnerbrink 2009, p. 276.
54 Here Cortella is not talking explicitly about the experience of forgiveness but is describing the emergence of self-consciousness by replacing the medium of the struggle with that of the word. The result of this modified description, however, is very similar to the closing of the Morality section, further evidence of the close link between the two passages.
55 In what follows, I refer to Bertram's and Brandom's interpretations because they seem to me well suited to illuminate how Hegel can offer a contribution to the issues that have arisen. See Bertram 2017, ch. 7; Bertram 2008; and Brandom 2019, ch. 16.
56 Here, Habermas engages in dialogue with Allan Gibbard and Ernst Tugendhat.

ordination. In this moral grammar, then, reside the motives for struggle, which in backlight would unveil the ethical fabric of social reproduction and integration, the normative structure underlying the interactions among persons. The latter are in turn articulated through and within spheres of recognition via the participants taking on complementary role obligations that instantiate surpluses of validity.

Hegel puts these conceptualities into play in the Spirit section, which presents itself as the reconstruction of the historical and dialectical tensions between different normative horizons, acting directions, and modes of knowing whereby the self increasingly considers herself as opposed against the ethical life she lives within, thus being actually reliant on it. Overcoming the obstacle that the apparent subjectivist approach may represent, one can realize that Hegel continuously puts forward failures and self-deceptions by the coordination of social action, which is always questioned again and again by its own, inevitable, emerging historical fragility. For the rupture of the ethical community and the progressive self-consciousness's individualization would dialectically lead to an ongoing co-dependence between acting and its descriptions. Thus, Hegel exposes some fundamental elements of a theory of action, investigating historical-conceptual figures in which the unstable balance between rule-following and the singularity of actors, between freedom and its process of externalization (*Entäußerung*), between self-reflexivity (being-for-itself) and heteroriflexivity (being-for-others) by justifying and criticizing norms of actions and worldviews, resides and emerges. In other words, Hegel faces the restlessness of the acting consciousness that finds itself being conditioned *and* unconditioned, who strives to *break* free, but cannot help realizing its being *here and now*.

In this complex scenario, recognition shows different facets that can be dealt with through the different meanings hinted above and posits itself as hosting elements sketched both by the positive and negative theories that characterize the contemporary debate. Nonetheless, the major role is played by *mutual* recognition, which appears in its specificity as elusive reconciliation by means of which the reflexivity aimed at justifying (and therefore criticizing) action is widened and shared. On the slippery ground Hegel deals with, between individual and social action, norms, laws, and historical trends, an important role is given to the concept of guilt, which, significantly, is placed at the beginning and at the end of the narrative on Spirit. In this term, all the levels mentioned are condensed. Guilt indicates that, by acting, self-consciousness actualizes its completeness and incompleteness, that is, its independence and insufficiency, its untying itself from the determinacy of context to find itself again entangled in it:

> Through the deed, [self-consciousness] abandons the determinateness of ethical life, of being the simple certainty of immediate truth, and it posits a separation of itself within itself as that between what is active and what is for it the negative actuality confronting it. Through the deed, it thus becomes *guilt*, since the *deed* is its own doing, and its own doing is its ownmost essence.... *Guilt* is not the indifferent, ambiguous essence; it is not as if the deed, as it *actually* lies open to the light of day, might or might not be the guilty self's *own doing*, as if something external and accidental could be attached to the doing which did not belong to it and according

to which the doing would therefore be innocent. Rather, the doing is itself this estrangement; it is this positing of itself for itself and this positing of an alien external actuality confronting itself. It belongs to the doing itself that such an actuality is, and it only is through the act. Hence, innocence amounts to non-action, like the being of a stone, not even that of a child (Hegel, *The Phenomenology of Spirit*, § 467).

It is essential to emphasize two aspects. First, acting, by instantiating a discontinuity with respect to the world "as it is," is distinguished from the latter's immediate determinateness, that is, from the ethical community's irreflexive homogeneity. As opposed to it, it is *un*determined. But, being acted, actualized, the act turns out to be determined, that is to say, reasons, norms, aims, and effects pertain to it. This discrepancy between what the agent thinks of her doing and what this turns out to be is the starting point of the confession-forgiveness binomial. Second, Hegel does not exclude that guilt may coincide with crime or moral wrong, namely, with acts that explicitly disrupt moral evaluative coordination. But he does not reduce it to them. Rather, guilty is the acting consciousness to the extent that it acts. I do not think that the matter at stake should be considered as "sin of existing,"[57] although finitude plays certainly a role in Hegel's considerations. That acting and guilt are considered as coextensive means that guilt and responsibility are coextensive.[58] In the Spirit section, we witness the *reflexive* emergence of such guiltiness, the becoming self-aware of acting's referability to the agent, that is, that agency and imputability come to coincide.[59] Through this essential connection, Hegel implies that every acting embeds a claim to justifiability, which can only find proper satisfaction via mutual recognition, thus abandoning one-sided approaches.

Before moving on to analyze the last part of the section, it is useful to sketch some features of the theory of action Hegel proposes, which is usually dealt with by the secondary literature with respect to the *Philosophy of Right*, but, as we shall see, plays a fundamental role also in the following passages of the *Phenomenology*.

---

57 See Jacques Derrida 2015, pp. 171–72.
58 See Alznauer 2015, ch. 2.
59 There are, I think, no better words than Ricoeur's for describing such coincidence: "The experience of fault offers itself as a given to reflection. It gives rise to thought. What is first offered to reflection is the designation of the fundamental structure in which this experience comes to be inscribed. This is the structure of the imputability of our actions. . . . [I]mputability is that capacity, that aptitude, by virtue of which actions can be held to someone's account. This metaphor of an account constitutes an excellent framework for the concept of imputability, one that finds another fitting expression in the syntax common to languages that employ the modal verb 'can': I can speak, act, recount, hold myself accountable for my actions—they can be imputed to me. Imputability constitutes in this respect an integral dimension of what I am calling the capable human being. It is in the region of imputability that fault, guilt, is to be sought. This is the region of articulation between the act and the agent, between the 'what' of the actions and the 'who' of the power to act—of agency" (Ricoeur 2004, p. 460).

The fundamental issue is represented by Hegel's distinction between action (*Handlung*) and deed (*Tat*) highlighted by Quante.[60] With this conceptual distinction, Hegel intends to bring three elements into play. In fact, both action and deed refer to an act-event, that is, an individual and identifiable event that can be described as flowing from a will in a narrow sense. An act-event implies by its essence an act-description that consists in the imputability of the first to an agent. That a stone, to take Hegel's example, does not act becomes evident primarily because the individual events that concern it—its being distinct, in itself, its rolling down the hill—cannot be described in terms of intentionality. But act-descriptions in general are not unitary: not everyone evaluates, or can evaluate, the same gesture in the same way. In this sense, Hegel distinguishes with deed that act-event referring to an act-description that does not involve the perspective of the agent, while with action he means the act as it is described by the latter. In a different manner, Pippin talks of this distinction between *Handlung* and *Tat* as the first being "a deed that can be attributed to me," and the second "something that happened because of me" but "which cannot be attributed to me as something for which I bear responsibility or Schuld" (Pippin 2008, p. 166).

Leaving open the possible interpretative debates, it is nevertheless important to maintain that Hegel has in mind a much more complex relationship between identity and agency than the one Markell imputes as implied by a politics of recognition. And this issue, as Pippin emphasizes,[61] concerns both the *Philosophy of Right* and chapter V of the *Phenomenology*, Reason. We can delineate it as follows. First, Hegel's critical objective is exactly to conceive of will as a causal medium between acting identity and acted act. And this is because, second, the outcome of my acting, that is, the act that I perform, is not simply the result of an encounter between the (active) will, my intention, and the (passive) matter that I shape or resist. So that if I attempt something, but do not accomplish it, my intention keeps on being intact as my inner content. Rather, the act-event that I put into the medium of being, as action and deed, as being-for-me and for-others is able to shed light on the truth of my purposes, as well as on their abstractness, emptiness, one-sidedness, and so on. So it can be that the unintended consequences of my doings reveal who I am and was, what my purpose was: "I did not want to hurt you, but I did: I see it now." One cannot therefore speak of identity as preceding agency, precisely because the externalization that action represents constitutes a fundamental element for the self-acknowledgement of identity with respect to its own intentions: the *process* of acting unveils identity. But settling the issue here would be just as one-sided as thinking that identity determines agency. And in fact, third, Hegel says that Oedipus "cannot be accused of parricide" (Hegel, *Philosophy of Right*, § 117Z). That is, he should not be held responsible for a deed that is not his own action. Yes, his action was a murder, but a murder in

---

60 See Michael Quante 2004.
61 See Pippin 2008, ch. 6.

which the victim was an unknown bystander. The distinction between these two act-descriptions means a dialectical relationship between my right of knowledge, that is, the fact that I can be held responsible for the foreseeable consequences with respect to the knowledge available to me, and the unpredictable or unknown consequences of my deeds. For, actually, Laius was killed.

On the one hand, therefore, Hegel rejects a concept of will that does not consider the consequences of action, thus the very process of acting, but, on the other hand, is aware of the risks involved in extending the concept of responsibility ad infinitum.[62] How do we get out of this (apparent) contradiction? Hegel, once again, starts from our lifeform, characterized by the *"necessity of the finite"* (Hegel, *Philosophy of Right*, § 118): "It is true that I cannot foresee those consequences which might be prevented, but I must be familiar with the universal nature of the individual deed" (Hegel, *Philosophy of Right*, § 118Z). In other words, acting—and in particular acting responsibly—cannot be based on an exact knowledge of all the possible consequences that may arise from it. But, being a finite action, it is placed in a world and in a context in which what the act itself is not exclusively dependent on what was intended of it: it is not only action, but deed as being and being-for-others, as exposed to the (normative and causal) legalities that pertain to the environment in which it is performed. Acting responsibly has to embed an acquaintance with that, namely, with the very nature of acting itself.

Given these action-theoretical elements, we are ready to deal with the last paragraph of the Morality section, which concerns the dialectical relation between action and deed. As often happens in the *Phenomenology*, Hegel opens the paragraph with a formal picture of the episode that will unfold. And as is well known, in the case of Conscience the critical objects are the Kantian concept of duty and the related idea of moral subject, split between "arbitrary free choice" and "the contingency of his unconscious natural being" (Hegel, *The Phenomenology of Spirit*, § 643). Moral conscience, in its capacity to rationally refer to the universal of duty, is absolutely free, that is, unconditioned by any heteronomy, capable of acting normatively, that is consciously. As Brandom says, conscience means a "metanormative conception" according to which my attitude of acting under a norm ought to "be authoritative for" those "who *assess* the correctness of what" I do (Brandom 2019, p. 588). Since my action flows from the universality of duty, the others should also acknowledge its falling under the norm. However, Hegel observes, such pure referentiality to the norm is, *in fact*, conditioned in four senses. First, conscience is a natural being.

---

[62] "The maxim [*Grundsatz*] which enjoins us to disregard the consequences of our actions, and the other which enjoins us to judge actions by their consequences and make the latter the yardstick of what is right and good, are in equal measure [products of the] abstract understanding. In so far as the consequences are the proper and *immanent* shape of the action, they manifest only its nature and are nothing other than the action itself; for this reason, the action cannot repudiate or disregard them. But conversely, the consequences also include external interventions and contingent additions which have nothing to do with the nature of the action itself" (Hegel, *Philosophy of Right*, § 118).

This implies that its acting cannot be oriented solely by reference to norms: rather, by its agency comes into play the satisfaction of needs useful for survival and reproduction, as well as motives, attitudes, stances and aims. Second, even if one were to consider the form of action that flows directly from duty, conscience would find itself having to deal with contents of duty, namely, with one's ends: it is therefore clear that "each content bears the *flaw of determinateness* in itself" (Hegel, *The Phenomenology of Spirit*, § 645). Duty is always *my* duty, and always *this* duty. Third, this is due to the fact that consciousness moves in a lifeworld, whereby "what counts is not *universal knowing* but rather *conscience's acquaintance* with the circumstances" (Hegel, *The Phenomenology of Spirit*, § 646). Our way of acting is bound to a way of being in the world that does not unfold according to intellectual knowledge, but rather according to the proximity to multifaceted and complex circumstances, from which we derive elements for a determined action. So far, Hegel's objections relate to the necessity of the finite, that is, the determinacy of our agency with regard to our first and second nature. It is with the fourth objection that the difference between action and deed, so as their dialectical relation with individual identity, come into play:

> That this right, what conscience does, is at the same time a being for others means that an inequality seems to have been introduced into conscience. The duty which it fulfills is a *determinate* content, and that content is indeed the *self* of consciousness, and in that respect, that content is its *knowing* of itself, its *equality* with itself. But when it is fulfilled, when it is placed into the universal medium *of being*, this equality is no longer *knowing*, is no longer this differentiating which just as immediately sublates its own differences. Rather, in being placed into [the sphere of] *being*, the difference is posited as stably existing, and the action is a *determinate* action, unequal to the element of everyone's self-consciousness and thus is not necessarily recognized (Hegel, *The Phenomenology of Spirit*, §648).

Indeed, agency cannot be understood simply through the coincidence of conscience with duty, it cannot be thought of as an immediate expression of self's identity, because, being in the world, one's deeds acquire consistency only in a *shared* world: they are not for me alone, but being-*for-others*.

6.5.2 Confession and Forgiveness, Acknowledgment, and Mutual Recognition

Being the deeds in the public eye, imputability emerges: this is why Hegel imagines the splitting of this figure of the *Phenomenology* into two consciousnesses. On the one hand, the acting conscience, persuaded to act according to duty; on the other, the universal or judging conscience, who, having avoided all action, witnesses the deeds of the other. The dynamic that takes place in the encounter between these two consciences can be read as a conflict for the *validity* of action, a conflict of arguments. By putting itself in the field in this linguistic confrontation, the acting consciousness offers the validity that it acknowledges as pertaining to its doings to the evaluation of the other. At the center of the encounter between the two consciences is thus a claim to validity exercised in two opposite ways, which are intertwined on the different planes implied by the distinction between action and deed, and between self-acknowledgment and being acknowledged. On the one hand, the acting conscience knows itself as recognized conscience, being it exposed through its deeds to the judgement of others—but considers the acts themselves (and therefore, by virtue of imputability, their contribution to its identity) as inessential with respect to its reference to duty. It does not acknowledge its actions as an independent source for self-acknowledgment. On the other hand, the judging conscience, refusing to enter the medium of being through its acts, does not expose itself to recognition and to the necessity of the finite, considering itself self-sufficient, beautiful soul:

> language emerges as the mediating middle between self-sufficient and recognized self-consciousnesses, and the *existing self* is immediately universal, multifaceted, and, within this multifacetedness, it is simple recognition [*Anerkanntsein*]. The content of conscience's language is the *self knowing itself as essence*. This alone is that to which it gives voice, and this giving voice is the true actuality of the doing, is the validity of the action. Consciousness gives voice to its *conviction*, and this conviction is that solely within which the action is a duty. It also solely *counts as* duty as a result of its having *given voice* to the conviction, for universal self-consciousness is free from action that is only existent determinate action. To itself, the *action* as *existence* counts for nothing. Rather, what counts is the *conviction* that the action is a duty, and this is actual in language (Hegel, *The Phenomenology of Spirit*, § 653).

It may be puzzling, after what has been said, that Hegel argues that in language conscience knows itself as essence by pronouncing the true actuality of action, which is not the innerworldly deed itself, but its normative validity. This is because the four objections, as well as the difference between action and deed, begin to emerge *for us* and *for others*, but not for consciousness itself. These discrepancies open Hegel's reflections on hypocrisy. For hypocrisy does not merely stand for the incontinency of conscience's claims but represents precisely the divergence of how she and others describe her doings. The judging conscience, confronted with other's deeds, cannot help but notice its hypocrisy, its inability—an almost structural impossibility—to actualize its duty, imputing the action to motives other than duty: it "spins" the other's "action off into the inward realm, and explains the action according to an intention and a self-serving motive which is different from the action itself." The judging conscience is such precisely because it traces the deed back to its supposed and inferred motives and ends, along the imputability track and with reference to gains and consequences: "If the action is accompanied by fame, then it knows this inwardness to be a *craving* for fame" (Hegel, *The Phenomenology of Spirit*, § 665). Thus, it explains the other's "actions in terms of nonnormatively characterized motives (attitudes)" (Brandom 2019, p. 591), showing in any case the other side of the coin of human agency, since it is impossible for us humans to always act in agreement with norms. But this entails two flaws. The first is to reduce the doings and motives of the other in a way that coincides with accusing Oedipus of parricide: if the access point provided by the deed represents the last word on one's doings, our imputing judgment takes on the features of an alienating assertion. Second, the beautiful soul does not realize that in so doing it is actualizing a position structurally identical to the one it criticizes, hypocritical to the extent that true duty is *its* duty: actually, an inner law of action *acknowledged* as duty. Moreover, by criticizing the validity of the other's deed, it implicitly acknowledges the existence of several norms of action, thus revealing that "what it called true duty and which is supposed to be *universally* recognized, is *what is not universally recognized*" (Hegel, The Phenomenology of Spirit, § 663). Here, in addition to the many possible planes, there is the double level of acknowledgment, which corresponds to nothing but the ambivalence of affirmation: to criticize, to misrecognize, or to not affirm something presupposes affirming it at least not only as being, but as *that* particular being with *those* characteristics. In order to misrecognize a norm of action, I must have already recognized it as a norm of action.

The hypocrisy of both consciences is due to the profound dissimilarities that occur between act-events and act-descriptions—the difference between actuality and speech—as well as between the different act-descriptions—the different claims to validity: "In both of them, the aspect of actuality is equally distinguished from that of speech; in one, through the *self-interested ends* of action, and in the other, through the *lack of action* at all, action of which the necessity lies in talking about duty itself, for duty without deeds has no meaning at all" (Hegel, The Phenomenology of Spirit, § 664). Being the one exposed to its being-for-others, it is the acting consciousness that first takes a step beyond hypocrisy. With its confession (*Eingeständnis*, and not *Beichte*, the religious confession), with its *admission* and *avowal*, the acting consciousness *acknowledges*. What? We can identify two subsequent contents. First, the conscience admits its hypocrisy, seeing that its doings belong to the necessity of the finite, exposed to other act-descriptions and unintended consequences, moved by particular ends and motives: to this extent, acknowledgment is self-directed. But, most important is the second object of this acknowledgment, namely, its equality with the other, who is hypocritical and subjected to finitude, too: only by virtue of the first, self-directed acknowledgment, the acting consciousness can glimpse in the other the same, structural human condition. And, in turn, dialectically, the first self-directed acknowledgement is allowed only by seeing the other as similar to me: only through the other can I become aware of my condition, of the fragility and intrinsic inconsistency of my claims. In this sense, one can say that admission *realizes recognition*, because judging the standpoint of consciousness is recognized as structurally shared by the acting conscience and, in these particular standpoints, they *reflect* the conditions of recognition in their equality,[63] to the extent that they recognize themselves as mutually recognizing each other, each considering the other's acting, being posed one before the other:

---

63 See Bertram 2017, p. 244.

Intuiting this equality and *giving voice* to it, he *confesses* this to the other, and he equally expects that the other, just as he has in fact placed himself on an equal plane to him, will reciprocate his *speech* and in that speech will pronounce their equality so that recognitional existence will make its appearance. His confession is not an abasement, nor a humiliation, nor is it a matter of his casting himself aside in his relationship with the other, for this declaration is not something one-sided through which he would posit his *inequality* with the other, but rather it is solely on account of the intuition of *his equality* with the other that he gives voice to himself, that in his confessions he gives voice on his own part to *their equality*, and he does this because language is the existence of spirit as the immediate self. He thus expects that the other will contribute his own part to this *existence*.

But following on the admission of the one who is evil—*I am he*—there is no reciprocation of an equal confession (Hegel, *The Phenomenology of Spirit*, §§ 666–67).

I do not think that Pinkard's translation does justice to the content of the admission: *Ich bin's*. For sure "It's me" may stand for "it's me, at the door," thus not differing from "*I am he*, the evil one." But in this case the ambivalence of the German *es* can indicate a more profound "*I am it, this* is me": the acting conscience indeed admits its being conditioned, its determinacy, its being evil, namely, its guilt, its responsibility, its being an *actor*. He identifies with its own doing comprehending it as action and deed. And, in fact, for the first time its deed (confession) and its speech *reflexively* coincide: by admitting hypocrisy, it sublates it. Paradoxically or, better, dialectically admitting one's determinacy would free one from being tangled by it. Thus, conscience knows itself in its essence, namely, that of being agent. Recognizing the determinacy of the deed as one's own means that it does not take place behind the back of conscience but becomes itself reflexive content.

It is essential to emphasize that the act of confession has three elements, in order to better understand the recognitional existence that emerges here. First, and surprisingly, if we consider the terms we have used previously, this expression of acknowledgment is articulated neither as an attribution, nor as an affirmative gesture addressed to the other. Rather, *A* communicates *herself*, she communicates her reflexively gained status as an actor. The acting conscience does not assert itself posing again an inequality but gives voice to the intuited equality: the language of confession means revealing "what is shared *as* shared," thus replacing the "language of conviction" (Bernstein 1996, p. 44).[64] This stands in a dialectical, non-causal relation with the second acknowledgment, whereby *A* recognizes its equality with *B*. The content of speech does not directly refer to the other, but rather to *A*'s own being reflexively aware of its condition, enabled by encountering the other as other, as limit: "the speech is the assurance of spirit's certainty in its inward turn" (Hegel, *The Phenomenology of Spirit*, § 671). Third, by communicating herself, she expects, invites the other to do the same, as if to say: confession is a by-relation that requires, that asks for a when-relation. Recognition here is realized only as *Aufforderung*: recipro-

---

[64] With respect to the fact that not every language is the language of and for mutual recognition, see Francesca Menegoni 2016.

cal on a first level and *for us*, but not mutual on the second-order one, that is, for the participant. The acting conscience can only hope for mutuality—that *its* equality with the other becomes *their* equality.

Though such admission, which relies on the acknowledgment of the equal guiltiness, that is, agency, of mine and an other's, would represent a first step out of duty and deed being opposed to each other, this very deed is still being for others, exposed to their questioning. That it represents a form of acting consciously can be criticized, thus not reciprocated by the judging consciousness, which therefore does not sublate the limitation that each represents for the other. Admission may not be reciprocated, it may be followed by the hard heart of the judging conscience, who "rejects any continuity" with the other (Hegel, *The Phenomenology of Spirit*, § 667). Freedom is not only the outcome or the very existence of mutual recognition: the latter flows from freedom,[65] and consequently it may not even take place: "What is posited here is the highest indignation of the spirit certain of itself, for, as this *simple knowing of the self*, this spirit intuits itself in others, namely, it does so in such a way that the external shape of this other is not ... the essenceless itself, not a thing" (Hegel, *The Phenomenology of Spirit*, § 667). Re-cognizing and acknowledging the other as not a thing, as the same as myself, *should* be enough to affirm my continuity with her, that is, the discontinuity with respect to our being limit for each other. But this may not be the case, since the specificity of mutual recognition is attested in its being *contrastive* with respect to the relational or social concretions that precede it, even with the related modes of acknowledgment.[66] Re-cognition and acknowledgment are not sufficient conditions to reach the We-form the acting conscience asked for by confessing, because they do not provide sufficient elements to treat the other as value, to significantly change my hard heart, my stance in front of her, that is, treating her as equal to me. This does not coincide with saying that re-cognition and acknowledgment are not necessary conditions, as it is clear that they provide normative indications to the extent that the "moment of apperception in each, each being bound to enter ethical life through their individuality, itself becomes the source of what is shared or common or universal between them" (Bernstein 1996, p. 43). The point is that the logic of reciprocity involved in any human interaction (which requires acts of re-cognition and acknowledgment in order to articulate itself) does not necessarily lead to the experience of mutuality. According to Hegel it *should*, but it *must* not: mutual recognition proceeds from freedom, it is not an outcome of a given knowledge—and this is why it happens so rarely, while re-cognition and acknowledgment are always at stake in our lifeworld. The issue becomes even more problematic when one considers that, in the face of guilt, not granting forgiveness can be considered a form of acting accordingly to the other's

---

65 See Bertram and Celikates 2015.
66 Being contrastive pertains to the features of recognition Honneth identifies in "Recognition as Ideology." See Honneth 2012f.

features: in fact, forgiveness can be asked for, but not demanded. Indeed, we are here in front of an "*a*symmetrical *re*cognitive relation" (Brandom 2019, p. 592), which makes us grasp though that in face of the fragility of our actions and our vulnerability, the expectation of being truly recognized is not satisfied by a pre-existing logic of exchange, by a payment in kind, by the binomial action-*re*action.[67] "It is not just a prize to be won, but a gift that grows each time it is offered" (Lauer 2012, p. 37). Here lies the difference between forgiveness, pardon, and amnesty: the first is unsuitable to institutionalizations.

It follows from this that forgiveness possesses an enigmatic nature, which is shown by the following quotations. Here Hegel describes the shift from the hard heart to forgiveness, that is, the emergence of spirit as dimension of reconciliation, as mutual recognition:

> In that way, the hard heart shows itself to be the consciousness forsaken by spirit, the consciousness denying spirit, for it does not recognize that in its absolute certainty of itself, spirit has a mastery over every deed and over all actuality, and that spirit can discard them and make them into something that never happened (Hegel, *The Phenomenology of Spirit*, § 667).

> The breaking of the hard heart and its elevation to universality is the same movement which was expressed in the consciousness that confessed. The wounds of the spirit heal and leave no scars behind; it is not the deed which is imperishable, but rather the deed is repossessed by spirit into itself; the aspect of singular individuality, whether present in the deed as intention or as existing negativity and limitation to the deed is what immediately vanishes (Hegel, *The Phenomenology of Spirit*, § 669).

> The word of reconciliation is the *existing* spirit which immediately intuits in its opposite the pure knowing of itself as the *universal* essence, intuits it in the pure knowing of itself as *singular individuality* existing absolutely inwardly—a reciprocal recognition which is *absolute* spirit (Hegel, *The Phenomenology of Spirit*, § 670).

Spirit, which has its existence in language, has the capacity to discard the act in its particularity, in its obstinate opposing itself as individuality, to include it again in itself through that kind of reconciliation that we call forgiveness. According to Brandom, such capacity is to be understood as a work of recollection, as interpretative practice carried out via speech acts, through which the single deed is included in a cooperative and open-ended learning process, in which every attempt, in its finiteness, finds its place.[68] Forgiveness therefore coincides with fully embracing the imputability-relation between agent and deed, showing the latter by its contextual validity, thus overcoming the moral consciousness's sclerotization between being conditioned and unconditioned: they both can become familiar with the universal nature of the individual deed, can intuit that acting normatively has to be contextual in order to be moral. Besides, the act of forgiveness, as well as confession, is not to be conceived primarily as one-sided act of granting or bestowing something to

---

67 See Bernstein 1996, pp. 46–49.
68 See Brandom 2019, p. 600.

the other. Instead, it "is the renunciation of itself, of its *non-actual* essence" on the part of the judging consciousness, who "lets go of" the "difference between determinate thought and its determining judgment" (Hegel, *The Phenomenology of Spirit*, § 670). Forgiveness structurally coincides with confession as a linguistic act in which, so to speak, form and content no longer differ from each other and in which the self abandons the absoluteness of duty in order to be able to reflexively embrace its true essence, that of responsible agent. By forgiving, the forgiver can finally be who she is, sublating hypocrisy: "this self has no other content than this, its own determinateness, a determinateness which neither goes beyond the self nor is more restricted than it" (Hegel, *The Phenomenology of Spirit*, p. § 671).

At this point, Hegel bewilders us by saying that *A* and *B* "are still different," not only for us, but also for them themselves, who acknowledge themselves to be opposed in their concepts and perspectives. And shortly afterwards he concludes: "The reconciling *yes*, in which both I's let go of their opposed *existence*, is the existence of the *I* extended into two-ness, which therein remains the same as itself and which has the certainty of itself in its complete self-relinquishing and in its opposite" (Hegel, *The Phenomenology of Spirit*, p. § 671). This is only an apparent contradiction. The two-ness of ego (We) is not realized as immediate integration, and therefore dissolution of the self, which would supposedly be encompassed in a somewhat ontological meta-subject. Instead, it is the mediated permanence of both participants in mutual recognition. What was formally posed with the pure concept of recognition, it is now clear not only for us, but for both consciousnesses:

> What will later come to be for consciousness will be the experience of what spirit is, this absolute substance which constitutes the unity of its oppositions in their complete freedom and self-sufficiency, namely, in the oppositions of the various self-consciousnesses existing for themselves: The *I* that is *we* and the *we* that is *I* (Hegel, *The Phenomenology of Spirit*, § 177).

Confession-forgiveness represents a complex intersubjective practice that is articulated on several levels. First, respectively, *A* and *B* are not just their determinacy, but they acknowledge it: it is accepted as a dimension of one's self-relation, and to this extent sublated. If I acknowledge something, then it is *other* to me. This *can* enable *A* to acknowledge itself as equal to *B* and vice versa, that is, as agents. Both these acknowledgments are made explicit through the medium of language, which, as conditioned unconditionality, universal that is spoken here and now, discloses a further reflexive possibility, that of mutual recognition. The latter, however, is a possibility that *can* happen, which has no necessity derived from the given context or nature of the participants. This coming-from-freedom means that even meeting the conditions of both acknowledgements by both subjects may not be sufficient—as the hard heart shows. The We that emerges instead with forgiveness is the becoming shared of the first-person perspective that leaves its poles intact, in an enigmatic way—as Hegel's quotations testify.

6.6 Conclusion: Generativity as Critical Criterion

We can now see how Hegel's proposal helps us with the issues we laid out at the beginning of the chapter.

The first question was, why should recognition be conceived as an exclusively interpersonal practice? The point that Hegel himself helps us understand is that recognition *can*, but *must not*, be interpersonal. Or, better, interpersonality is always at stake only at a very general level, because all our actions are, to a certain extent, also interactions. Thus, the fact that the acting consciousness acknowledges its own determinacy or the fallibility of its normative acting cannot be realized except within its being-for-others, besides its being already immersed in otherness, that is, in a shared world. This does not preclude the possibility that specific objects of re-cognition and acknowledgment can be non-human—as the uses in the different languages considered here suggest. In the relationship between these various forms of recognizing and those of knowing, the peculiarities of the former do not simply consist in the more active involvement on the part of the recognizer than of the knower: rather, the emphasis should be placed on the normative indications that, in different degrees, the respective givens offer us, similar to an invitation to act in a certain way—a summon, which raises a certain awareness. By re-cognizing and acknowledging we become aware of (and possibly must beware of) something that was already there, but somewhat veiled or concealed. Thus, the specificity of interpersonal recognition hinges on the peculiarity of the object that presents itself to me, which has the qualities of a non-object, and which therefore always—albeit in minimal terms—invites me to act taking its non-objective features into account, to assume a dis-objectifying attitude toward my non-objectual object. Even moral wrong, reification, and power all necessarily fall within modes of inter*human* action.

The second question was, why should interpersonal recognition be conceived in terms of mutual recognition? Why can it not be thought of as adequate regard? The answer to this question is twofold. First, it is also good to emphasize here that recognition *can*, but *must not*, be mutual. On a first level, certainly, it must be reciprocal, since it concerns *inter*personal *inter*action. By necessity, therefore, any gesture of A's cannot be conceived as unilateral but must be thought of as already conditioned by B's personhood. However, this first level of reciprocity does not give us many indications with respect to the various normative-moral criteria we have encountered in our path, that is, the binomials symmetry-asymmetry, equality-inequality, and so on. A profoundly reciprocal relation, such as between master and servant, can be profoundly asymmetrical and unequal. On the one hand, a greater substantialization of the reciprocity-criterion—which therefore ceases to be mere *logic* of interaction—seems to be a good antidote against relational-agonic forms of power. On the other hand, such substantialization risks not giving many indications about the goodness or morality of the interactions at stake, since the risk of economizing the exchange of gestures is always just around the corner. A higher degree of equality-symmetry does not provide us, per se, with a significant normative concept. The second leg of the answer, instead, starts from the fact that, certainly, recognition *can* be —above the logic of reciprocity—one-sided: Hegel's depiction of confession-forgiveness is filled with examples. Then are we inclined to conceive recognition as an adequate regard? Without wiping out the value of such recognizing forms—which constantly instantiate in our lifeworld—with the confession-forgiveness binomial Hegel clearly tells us that to be treated properly, for what is *due* to us, is not enough: he describes a form of mutual recognition that escapes from the logic of merit that has imposed itself with the struggle for life and death. Forgiveness, that is, requires us to think of an answer to the demand for recognition that exceeds the scope of the demand itself: it is not a distributive practice, but a restorative one, which concerns reconciliation. In this sense, Hegel refuses to describe "adequate" in the terms of "due" proper to exchange. To think about recognition outside of mutuality-insight seems to make us slip back into the logic of due and that may lead us to a dead end.

The way out is offered by the fact that the We-form Hegel outlines in the when-relation of mutual recognition is not characterized by a plain symmetry. Rather, the core of mutual recognition is the "self-reflexivity of recognition" (Bertram 2008, p. 887, my translation). Indeed, the pure concept of recognition does not suggest that mutual recognition coincides with two subjects that merely recognize each other. Instead, the criterion Hegel provides us with at the beginning of the Self-Consciousness section is to look for, during the experience of consciousness, moments, or figures where two subjects recognize themselves as mutually recognizing each other. This self-reflexivity coincides with what Ricoeur calls the experience of mutuality, which does not simply coincide with identical doings on the part of the participants, but with the fact that they recognize their acting as emerging from and finding place in a reflexive We-ness.

It follows from this that the Hegelian account that we are outlining is more sensitive to the third issue, that is, the criticism levelled by Markell. Indeed, Hegel's account at the end of the Morality section is principally aimed at deconstructing the "modern fantasies of self-sufficiency" (Pippin 2007, p. 76), sovereign, purely normative agency. With this in mind, Hegel conceptualizes a dialectical relationship between identity and agency, which cannot be thought of as following one another, but which co-imply and refer to each other within the complex lifeworldly condition of the human being, between will, responsibility, and the necessity of the finite. If there can be a purely normative orientation of action, there can be no purely normative action. In this sense, recognizing cannot clearly be thought of as knowing an object out there precisely because identity is ambivalent with respect to every acting, it is both its source and its outcome. What matters, in front of the other, is what we do, and that the "recognitional existence" is both, at the same time, self- and other-directed (Hegel, *The Phenomenology of Spirit*, § 666). I, thanks to the other, can acknowledge my finitude and my non-mastery over my deeds, and only by virtue of this acknowledgment can see that the other is the same as me. By bringing these three steps together, it will become clear that mutual recognition does not consist of a sum of different acts carried out by identities toward each other. The reconciliation that mutual recognition enables and is does not represent just a mode of "setting the other free" (Canivez 2011, p. 855), but a way of setting ourselves so that *we* can be free. Being with oneself by the other emerges through and as a "reconciliation by mutual renunciation" (Siep 2010, p. 114), whereby what is renounced, the first-person authority over my act-descriptions, is not merely abandoned, but *shared*. Retrieving Honneth's conceptualities, one can say that the authorship over the norms that regulate our (inter-)acting must be a co-authorship—since a proper act-description cannot be carried out monologically—and has to take into account the fragility and vulnerability entailed in our being exposed to the non-mastery that characterize our individual condition.

The last, and most challenging issue is the one posed by Bedorf, which can be broadened in the terms used by Allen. That recognizing always entails misrecognizing can, in fact, mean both a structural dynamic that establishes itself in the complex intertwining of identity and interaction, and the possibility of ideological recognition, which also embeds the constitutive role of power. On two different levels, both accounts aim at undermining recognition as critical concept to the extent that they show its determining power, which binds individuality to identity, possibility to subjectivity. On the pre-normative level Bedorf outlines, this determination is to be understood as structurally missing its aim, since identity is actually a more fluid and lively being than the fixation of it that recognition represents: the non-identity of identity undermines the possibility of recognition. On the normative level dealt with by Butler, Allen, Lepold, and, to a certain extent, Markell, recognition shows itself in its deceptive features to the extent that, somewhat in empowering and rewarding disguise, it binds human life to possibilities that narrow individual self-determination from the outset. In these terms, then, the main criticism levelled at recognition coincides with its being a heteronomous source of individuation, which, by virtue of internalization, shapes identity.

This issue arises in problematic terms for Honneth's theory, which in fact reveals three different approaches. First, Honneth's thinking lays itself open to such criticisms when he, to mention two pivotal examples, describes the recognitional gestures and spheres as antidote to the modern and post-modern suffering from indeterminacy (*The Pathologies of Individual Freedom*) and as ensuring a smooth interlocking of the respective activities of participants (*Freedom's Right*). The general problem is namely that of the role assigned to recognition by society's normative integration. But taking this as unilateral depiction, second, would overlook that Honneth himself employs a more refined idea of the relation between determinacy and indeterminacy —a legacy due to his Hegelianism—that also allows him to oscillate, on a justice-theoretical level, between liberalism and communitarianism. This not naive image is to be found above all in the description of interpersonal relationships as tension and balance between ego-boundaries and ego-dissolution, which, translated in terms of personal freedom, finds its seminal depiction in Hegel's *Philosophy of Right:* "In this determinacy, the human being should not feel determined; on the contrary, he attains his self-awareness only by regarding the other as other. Thus, freedom lies neither in indeterminacy nor in determinacy, but is both at once" (Hegel, *Philosophy of Right*, § 7Z). The whole issue, Hegel seems to tell us, is not opting for indeterminacy or for determinacy. Since the human condition (and our brief excursus on Hegel's theory of action has given us a good picture of it) is articulated in having to deal with the co-existence and co-extensiveness of these two dimensions, and with the related consequences in terms of personal responsibility. The key to understanding freedom—and recognition, in which the first manifests itself—consists in those forms of determinacy in which the individual should not feel over-determined, bound to its determinacy: being with oneself by the other. Concrete freedom is to inhabit a world in which we can reflexively acknowledge ourselves as being home, familiar with the universal nature of the individual deed. But what is imputed to the concept of recognition and to Honneth's theory is precisely the shortcoming of not considering the ambiguity of not feeling determined. Honneth himself admits the difficulty of assessing, from within the recognition relationship, the justifiability or otherwise of the relational form itself, for example when dealing with Hegel's description of woman's role in marriage.[69] As we have seen, this problem has always posed itself for Honneth, who since *The Struggle for Recognition* states between the lines that interpersonal self-realization cannot be the unique criterion of critical evaluation. In fact, how can the quality of a relationship be evaluated if it itself forms evaluation criteria? The solution is to refer to a third criterion, that is, not immediately coinciding, even if not irrelated, with the relationships of recognition. This is the case of the material criterion and of the means provided by the concept of progress to discern progressive or reactionary forms of conflict,[70] so as of the surplus of validity. The solution Honneth presents—the concept of progress as open-ended learning progress—leads to a further, major problem on which the viability of mutual recognition as critical concept depends. The problem is that Honneth more or less implicitly decouples recognition and conflict for what concerns their roles by social integration and differentiation.[71] Recognition in fact appears as a dynamic that instantiates its own principles, according to the self-generating dialectic of second nature. The role of conflict is instead that of fluidification and reformulation of such relationships and contexts of second nature, it represents the means of a situated overcoming, which broadens and refines its own premises. This division of labor between fixation and unfixation, which is persuasive and successful from many points of view, however, fails to deliver a progressive logic inherent the relationships of recognition themselves, which are thus left with their determining role, while an indetermining and creative role is assigned to conflict.

So we are apparently back to the starting point, where the major perplexities about the concept of recognition revolve around its over-determining power. As

---

69 See Honneth 2021, pp. 162–67.
70 See Honneth 2012f, p. 93; and Honneth 1995c, pp. 168–69.
71 See Bertram and Celikates 2015, pp. 4–6.

I see it, a solution to these concerns lies in the threefold operation carried out in this chapter, which makes it possible to identify progressive and unfixing tasks entailed in mutual recognition relationships, understood as generative movement.

First, the identification of the different meanings of recognition makes it possible to accommodate different concepts and practical levels involved in human (inter-)action without having to opt unilaterally for one perspective rather than another—i.e. for a positive or a negative account on recognition. This allows a first analytical understanding of a holistic phenomenon—that of recognition—that clearly presents an ambivalent normative logics within it. This also means embracing and radicalizing Honneth's pluralistic approach, subdividing not just three modes of interpersonal-mutual recognition, but a complex variety of recognition that precede such subdivision itself.

The second fundamental step coincides with the distinction, within interpersonal recognition, between by-relation and when-relation. The first concept allows us to highlight the reciprocal conditioning that every human interaction seems to imply, which, even when conceived outside diachronic and asymmetric patterns, does not seem able to escape from the economic logic of exchange. The delineation of this first fundamental level—meaning both its being basilar and significance—which can and in most cases happens behind its participants, sheds light on the oscillation between pre-normative, normative, and moral planes. Going back to the notorious example of master and servant, one can say that such a relation is certainly normative—for both implement role obligations—reciprocal, but amoral. But identifying this level of reciprocity helps us to understand the different degrees involved in Hegel's defining the mutuality-rule of the pure concept of recognition. In fact, explicitly in the *Encyclopaedia*, even the master is described as carrying out duties of care toward the servant, aimed at ensuring the continuity of latter's services.[72] Service and care, as acts respectively implemented by each, are to a certain extent symmetrical and complementary. But such symmetry is asymmetrical and abstract—it is not part of the second-order horizon embedded by the participants' reflexive understanding of the relationship itself. Or, if so, solely to the minimal degree implied by the functionalization of the other in one's own purposive projections. That is why it is so difficult for us to speak of the interactions between lord and bondsman as emerging from and within a recognitional relationship, since they consist, at most, in reciprocal exchanges of recognitional acts. Conversely, the practical forms described under the title *of when-relation* indicate a mode of experiencing a relationship that reflects the participants' mutual recognizing each other. They instantiate the reflexive awareness that their acts do not simply represent complementary intertwining I-mode expressions, or a collective intentionality aimed at a common purpose. As is already clear, the coordination of social action in recognition relationships cannot be thought of as a mere sum and harmonization of particular

---

72 See Hegel, *Philosophy of Mind*, § 434.

intentions expressed with the first person singular. There is indeed an "irreducibility of we-mode states" that cannot be misunderstood as outcome of mine and your intentions or efforts (Raimo Tuomela 2006, p. 50): the when-relation is not the result of (even only logically) subsequent by-relations. For the first keeps a *qualitative* difference with respect to the latter. However, mutual recognition and "plural subjecthood are not coextensive" (Laitinen 2001, p. 320). Equating the We-forms of mutual recognition to "forgroupness" (Tuomela 2006, p. 46)—the second-order awareness of being an indivisible group—or to plural subjects in general entails, among other eventual unclarities, the twofold risk of making the concept of mutual recognition slip back onto a one-dimensional concept of group-identity and of losing the tracks for what concerns the reciprocity-rule, bringing into play a vertical notion of recognition between the group and its members. The issue is not belonging to any groups, since the We-form of mutual recognition concern a dialectical concept of unity, reconciliation as described by Hegel through the confession-forgiveness binomial—where the I is "extended into two-ness" and the two poles are still different from each other.

The third passage, the analysis of Hegelian narration in the *Phenomenology*, has provided us with fundamental elements to clarify the normative and critical specificity of mutual recognition. To fully understand it—thus concluding our account—it is useful to divide this last step into three moments.

First, it is necessary to clarify the meaning of forgiveness. In Hegel's account, forgiveness constitutes the moment where a recognitional existence emerges—a recognitional existence that entails the multiple levels that have been indicated with the different meanings of recognition and with the distinction between by-relation and when-relation. In a nutshell, the moment of the hard heart shows the insufficiency of relational forms that do not go beyond the intertwining of distinct I-modes as reciprocal conditioning. That is to say, the *under*lying unity and equality intuited and admitted by the acting conscience—and already *under*way in the We-structure of speech—must become explicit, that is, self-reflexive for both of them. But what is this unity and continuity that the beautiful soul rejects and that forgiveness should reconcile? On a first level, it is the unity that they share because both are not a thing: they, as humans, do not merely are, but act. This shows that the emergence of mutual recognition is deeply intertwined with the human lifeform as normative agency in a shared world. It follows from this that the particularity of meaningful action is guilt in two overlapping meanings. On the one hand, since it is exposed to the world, namely, subject to the necessity of the finite, incapable of entailing in planning and decision making the totality of the possible consequences. On the other hand, since it is exposed to the shared world as being-for-others, from which emerges the argumentative conflict regarding the possible configurations of conscientious acting. From these two partly overlapping meanings of guilt it is possible to derive two similarly partly overlapping meanings of forgiveness. The latter coincides with that interpersonal movement that does not make action collapse on deed but allows to comprehend the two act-descriptions as complementary: to this extent, as recollection, namely, as discursive tracing-back of motives and reasons, it first liberates agency from the burden of mechanistic causality and of the inevitable non-coincidence between what one can and duty. And, second, it discloses the relativization of both I-mode act-descriptions, which was already abandoned on the part of the acting conscience by admitting the finitude of its doings. Thus, forgiveness coincides with the participants' "constant mutual release from what they do can" by means of which "men remain free agents" (Arendt 1998, p. 240). To this extent, it would have, according to Hannah Arendt, a productive potential for social coordination on an equal footing with promises, that is role obligations—so decisive for Honneth's paradigm of recognition. Overcoming the finitude of actions, forgiveness can namely, disclose a creative potential that allows us to move on, showing its social-political relevance. Such potential coincides with forgiving's capacity to alter the normative situations that come with guilt, the obligations under which the wrongdoer falls, as, for instance, showing a will-to-change and repentance.[73] This dynamic concerns the most disparate cases, from two people apologizing to each other because they got in the way at the entrance to the subway, to the deepest wounds that can affect public spaces. Here, forgiveness reveals itself as the mediated interruption of the immediate bad reciprocity of revenge. Being a self-directed stance in the first place, it implies and requires a change of heart that cannot be demanded, and in most cases not even asked for: there are, in most cases, no sufficient external reasons for forgiving, which brings with it that, conversely, we may well forgive, but then realize that we had not. This is why it seems so difficult to explain good reasons and institutional settings for forgiving.

This brings us to the second moment, which concerns mutual recognition—and its representing a discontinuity from what precedes it. Forgiveness releases from what persons *can*, and this means that it alters the situation emerging with the admission. As we have seen, the admission-hard heart binomial is inhabited by a double level of acknowledgement. On the one hand, the acting conscience acknowledges the imputability of its deeds, admitting its finitude and to this extent acknowledging the equality with the other. On the other hand, the judging conscience paradoxically acknowledges that the other shares humanity with him, since both can trace any what of deed back to an acting who, but rejects such equality, thus *mis*acknowledging it. If we were to linger at this (diversified) level of acknowledgment there would be no relationship of mutual recognition, no We-form, but only asymmetrical acts of conditioning, which exhaust their dynamics in the respective reciprocity and fixity of roles. The alteration brought about by forgiveness is to be explained as "an unconditioned moment" (Bertram 2008, p. 883, my translation), for forgiveness itself cannot find its sources in the forms of (mis-)acknowledging interactions that fix the imputability-nexus, that tend to make action collapse on deed, that hinge on a bare exchange of gestures.

---

[73] See Christopher Bennett 2018.

The aporetic character of mutual recognition that Hegel depicts expresses itself in two facets. The first side of the issue concerns the reasons or motives to recognize —which is actually an issue in Honneth's paradigm. Why should we recognize another, or vice versa? Why, in other words, should humanity intuited also by the judging conscience lead him to a change of heart, to embrace the continuity with the other? Honneth's theory finds an answer in the reference to the spheres and principles of recognition, which would shape relationships according to the different matters respectively at stake: in love, right, or cooperation, we find ourselves together before a third instance that informs and shapes our joint and complementary acting—the why and what-for of recognition. This reference to a third instance is fundamental to understand any interaction, but represents a far too general level, thus proving incapable of providing good reasons for mutual recognition—it indeed describes the fundamental form of (inter-)action. The answer that Hegel proposes with the emerging recognitional existence via confession-forgiveness is that adequate reasons for recognition always come too late,[74] because the sole reasons for recognizing and being recognized are to be found in an already shared recognition, in the already continuous We made explicit at a second-order level.[75] It would seem that the conditioned, rather than the unconditioned, character of mutual recognition prevails. However, such conditioning would not fall under the succession of by-relations, and under the circle of misrecognizing recognition in its two meanings. On the contrary, the picture is reversed: in order to acknowledge each other, we must already inhabit a relation of mutual recognition. Indeed, the judging conscience's rejection consists precisely in the following: it fails to acknowledge the other's admission because it has already refused the We-form that would enable such acknowledgment. It is not aware that the other's being not a thing represents a ground for continuity. The moment of forgiveness—as moment where mutual recognition reaches existence—makes explicit the second facet of its aporetic character, which hinges on the quality of the We-form we inhabit together. As we have already seen, the first level of reciprocity that any interaction entails "imposes itself as an objective logic" (Cortella 2016, p. 173), which can even disregard the participants embracing it or not. It happens for and by inter-acting. Such first level of interaction both presupposes and shapes a reciprocal taking on of roles on the part of the practitioners that acknowledge each other in their respectively acquired statuses, capacities, and obligations. The unconditional moment of forgiveness is realized when both lift the "metonymic shift" (Bernstein 1996, p. 60) of admission: *Ich bin's*, where agent and deed come to coincide in the awareness of the partiality of action—a metonymic shift that the hard heart does not intend to move. Such acknowledgment—*Ich bin's*—which fixes the agent to the deed, is altered by forgiveness, to the extent that it unfixes the identity

---

74 See Bernstein 1996, pp. 48–49 and 54.
75 This being-constituted of the constituting-being is a peculiarity that a Hegel-inspired thought of social forms must maintain and emphasize, also at the general level of institutions. See Vincent Descombes 2011.

acquired by the identification with the act. So if, on the one hand, Bedorf showed us that recognition always comes too early or too late with respect to identity, we can also say that identity comes too early or too late with respect to mutual recognition. Put another way, the identity acquired and expressed through action, the awareness of finitude, and the speech act of admission is fluidified, recollected, and relativized. From the *I am it* of admission we shift to the *I's two-ness* of mutual recognition, that is, to the moment in which the other's perspective is authorized to enter the reflexive understanding of my condition: still distinct, we are continuous. Just as the intuited equality dialectically (not mechanically) enables the admission, the sublation of hypocrisy, so forgiveness allows one to understand the argumentative conflict in different terms: in terms of reconciliation. Reconciliation is the becoming shared of the first-person perspective, through which we can remain agents and judges arguing about what deserves to be considered acting consciously. But we have meanwhile become familiar with the universal nature of individual action, mediating between action and deed, between necessity and autonomy, taking into account all these elements. The authoritative point of view on the act-descriptions is not mine or yours, but ours. Such a reconciliation is not an outcome of my self-acknowledging or your acknowledging me: rather, it is the condition for the formulation of new forms of acknowledgment, for more qualitatively demanding forms of interaction, in which the relativization of my perspective does not simply derive from a logic that imposes itself on the subjects, but can be object of gratitude, since the widening and inclusion of more points of view enriches my familiarity with our world. In this sense, it becomes clear that ego's coming into the We of mutual recognition does not coincide with an annulment of the former in a subordinating homogeneity, or with flattening all differences in the name of a legal-economic reciprocity. Rather, Hegel invites us to think of the We as plurality of I's which are in themselves plural, as they embed We in their individuality.[76]

In a nutshell, mutual recognition can be explained as a generative movement because the We-form that instantiates in, through, and by it cannot be considered a consequential outcome of the interactive forms that precede it. Rather, the latter represent fundamental but not sufficient steps, since mutual recognition proceeds from freedom, like a change of heart that gives voice to the underlying continuity between you and me, which allows us to treat each other differently from reciprocal conditioning and exchange. The conclusion I come to in encountering, or better, clashing with the shared world, the realization that my deed has something to say about my action, is de-absolutized and overturned by forgiveness, by the fact that these two descriptions become interdependent, thus disclosing the possibility of being with oneself by the other—not only intersubjectively understood, but as a way of inhabiting the

---

[76] As Samonà shows, such a perspective makes it possible not to sharply disjoin an intersubjectivistic perspective and the Hegelian concept of Spirit. Namely, it makes it possible to not employ the Hegelian criticisms against the abstract universal to criticize his own concept of absolute. See Leonardo Samonà 2016.

world.[77] And this means that I can live by my being-for-others, decentered in it, but not overcome by it.

The third and concluding moment of our analysis coincides with the explanation of the critical import of such account on mutual recognition. If forgiveness coincides with the mutual release from the metonymic shift from deed to agent, of the expressive self-assertion and of the fixation of identity, this leads to decisive repercussions for the critical role of the concept, since it allows to think otherwise the relationship between recognition and conflict. In fact, that in the end Hegel tells us that, in reconciliation, the acting and the judging consciences are still different makes clear that the participants no longer experience the argumentative conflict at stake as "an *against* each other" (*ein Gegeneinander*) but as "a *with* each other" (*ein Miteinander*) (Bertram 2017, p. 252, my translation and emphasis). By inhabiting a space-for-freedom, we can welcome our perspective as authoritative with respect to my and your condition—that is, without the demand of homologating the other to my point of view. That mutual recognition discloses different modes of acknowledgment, not deriving them from the logical level of reciprocity, means, however, that recognition itself is set free from the fixing task to which the recognition-conflict pendulum seemed to have confined it. For Hegel invites us to conceive reconciliation and conflict not as two alternative phases, but as dialectically co-present moments. In this way, the critical-normative criterion provided by recognition coincides with its generativity, that is, its capability to mark discontinuity with the fixities of reciprocally interacting roles. Clearly, this criterion is always local, as it is always empirical and difficult to outline a priori. In this resides the cross and delight of a properly Hegelian social theory, which leaves the priority to the unfolding of the social, keeping the pace by trying to unearthing the eventual emancipative interests. This account represents a normative criterion for evaluating institutional and relational forms, since this definition of mutual recognition does not reject, but rather accentuates the detrascendentalization Honneth emphasizes in *Recognition*. Nor does it reject the possibility of a normative reconstruction oriented by centrality of freedom in modern western societies. However, a generative account of mutual recognition offers the possibility of focusing on the emancipatory role of recognition itself, rather than that of the struggle for recognition. For the role of mutual recognition is to indetermining, but not undermining, the determining by-relations of acknowledgment. That is to say, it certainly enables the actualization of personal potentialities, but most of all allows actuality's potentiality. In this way, the difference between the logic of reciprocity and the experience of mutuality itself becomes a possibility for de-reifying the institutionalizations of acknowledgment, since the happening of mutual recognition itself represents the latter's aporetic overcoming.

---

77 See Alford C. Fred 2017.

Bibliography

Works by Axel Honneth

Honneth, Axel (1979). " Zur "latenten Biographie" von Arbeiterjugentlinchen." In: Rainer Mackensen, and Felizitas Sagebiel (Eds.): *Soziologische Analysen. Referate aus den Veranstaltungen der Sektionen der Deutschen Gesellschaft für Soziologie und der ad-hoc-Gruppen bei 19. Deutschen Soziologentag.* Berlin: DGS, pp. 903–39.

Honneth, Axel, and Hans Joas (1988). *Social Action and Human Nature.* Translated by Raymond Meyer. Cambridge: Cambridge University Press.

Honneth, Axel (1991). *The Critique of Power. Reflective Stages in a Critical Social Theory.* Translated by Kenneth Baynes. Cambridge, London: The MIT Press.

Honneth, Axel (1992a). "Integrity and Disrespect: Principles of a Conception of Morality Based on the Theory of Recognition." In: *Political Theory* 20. No. 2, pp. 187–201.

Honneth, Axel (1992b). *Kampf um Anerkennung. Zur moralischen Grammatik sozialer Konflikte.* Frankfurt am Main: Suhrkamp.

Honneth, Axel (1995a). "Decentered Autonomy: The Subject after the Fall." In: Honneth, *Fragmented World*, pp. 261–71.

Honneth, Axel (1995b). *The Fragmented World of the Social. Essays in Social and Political Philosophy.* Edited by Charles C. Wright. Albany: SUNY Press.

Honneth, Axel (1995c), *The Struggle for Recognition. The Moral Grammar of Social Conflicts.* Translated by Joel Anderson. Cambridge: The MIT Press, 1995.

Honneth, Axel (1997). "Recognition and Moral Obligation." In: *Social Research* 64. No. 1, pp. 16–35.

Honneth, Axel (1998). "Democracy as Reflexive Cooperation. John Dewey and the Theory of Democracy Today." In: *Political Theory* 26. No. 6, pp. 763–83.

Honneth, Axel (1999). "Postmodern Identity and Object-Relations Theory: On the Seeming Obsolescence of Psychoanalysis." In: *Philosophical Explorations* 2. No. 3, pp. 225–42.

Honneth, Axel (2000). "Pathologien des Sozialen." In: Honneth, *Das Andere der Gerechtigkeit. Aufsätze zur praktischen Philosophie.* Frankfurt am Main: Suhrkamp, pp. 11–69.

Honneth, Axel (2001). "Invisibility: On the Epistemology of 'Recognition.'" In: *Aristotelian Society Supplementary Volume* 75, pp. 111–26.

Honneth, Axel (2002). "Grounding Recognition: A Rejoinder to Critical Questions." In: *Inquiry* 45. No. 4, pp. 499–519.

Honneth, Axel (2003a). "On the Destructive Power of the Third: Gadamer and Heidegger's Doctrine of Intersubjectivity." In: *Philosophy & Social Criticism* 29. No. 1, pp. 5–21.

Honneth, Axel (2003b). "Erkennen und Anerkennen. Zu Sartres Theorie der Intersubjektivität." In: Axel Honneth, *Unsichtbarkeit*, pp. 71–105.

Honneth, Axel (2003c). "The Point of Recognition: A Rejoinder to the Rejoinder." In: Honneth and Fraser, *Redistribution or Recognition?*, pp. 237–67.

Honneth, Axel (2003d). "Redistribution as Recognition: A Response to Nancy Fraser." In: Honneth and Fraser, *Redistribution or Recognition?*, pp. 110–97.

Honneth, Axel, and Nancy Fraser (2003). *Umverteilung oder Anerkennung? Eine politisch-philosophische Kontroverse.* Frankfurt am Main: Suhrkamp.

Honneth, Axel (2004a). "Considerations on Alessandro Ferrara's Reflective Authenticity." In: *Philosophy & Social Criticism* 30. No. 1, pp. 11–15.

Honneth, Axel (2004b). "Organized Self-Realization: Some Paradoxes of Individualization." In: *European Journal of Social Theory* 7. No. 4, pp. 463–78.

Honneth, Axel, and Gwynn Markle (2004). "From Struggles for Recognition to a Plural Concept of Justice: An Interview with Axel Honneth." In: *Acta Sociologica* 47. No. 4, pp. 383–91.
Honneth, Axel (2007a). "Between Justice and Affection: The Family as a Field of Moral Disputes." In: Honneth, *Disrespect*, pp. 144–62.
Honneth, Axel (2007b). "Pathologies of the Social: The Past and the Present of Social Philosophy." In: Honneth, *Disrespect*, pp. 3–48.
Honneth, Axel (2007c). "The Social Dynamics of Disrespect: On the Location of Critical Theory Today." In: Honneth, *Disrespect*, pp. 63–79.
Honneth, Axel (2008). *Reification. A New Look at an Old Idea*. Edited by Martin Jay. New York: Oxford University Press.
Honneth, Axel (2009a). "'Anxiety and Politics.' The Strengths and Weaknesses of Franz Neumann's Diagnosis of a Social Pathology." In: Honneth, *Pathologies of Reason*, pp. 146–56.
Honneth, Axel (2009b). "Appropriating Freedom. Freud's Conception of Individual Self-Relation." In: Honneth, *Pathologies of Reason*, pp. 126–45.
Honneth, Axel (2009c). "Democracy and Inner Freedom. Alexander Mitscherlich's Contribution to Critical Social Theory." In: Honneth, *Pathologies of Reason*, pp. 157–64.
Honneth, Axel (2009d). *Pathologies of Reason. On the Legacy of Critical Theory*. Translated by James Ingram. New York: Columbia University Press.
Honneth, Axel (2009e). "A Physiognomy of the Capitalist Form of Life. A Sketch of Adorno's Social Theory." In: Honneth, *Pathologies of Reason*, pp. 54–70.
Honneth, Axel (2009f). The whole title is: "Reconstructive Social Criticism with a Genealogical Proviso. On the Idea of 'Critique' in the Frankfurt School" In: Honneth, *Pathologies of Reason*, pp. 43–53.
Honneth, Axel (2009g). "A Social Pathology of Reason. On the Intellectual Legacy of Critical Theory." In: Honneth, *Pathologies of Reason*, pp. 19–42.
Honneth, Axel, Amy Allen, and Maeve Cooke (2010). "A Conversation Between Axel Honneth, Amy Allen and Maeve Cooke, Frankfurt Am Main, 12 April 2010." In: *Journal of Power* 3. No. 2, pp. 153–70.
Honneth, Axel, Jonas Jakobsen, and Odin Lysaker (2010). "Social Critique Between Anthropology and Reconstruction: An Interview with Axel Honneth." In: *Norsk Filosofisk Tidsskrift* 45. No. 3, pp. 162–74.
Honneth, Axel (2010). *The Pathologies of Individual Freedom. Hegel's Social Theory*. Princeton, Oxford: Princeton University Press.
Honneth, Axel (2011a). *Das Recht der Freiheit. Grundriß einer demokratischen Sittlichkeit*. Berlin: Suhrkamp.
Honneth, Axel (2011b). "Rejoinder." In: Danielle Petherbridge (Ed.): *Axel Honneth: Critical Essays. With a Reply by Axel Honneth*. Leiden, Boston: Brill, pp. 391–421.
Honneth, Axel (2012a). "The Fabric of Justice: On the Limits of Contemporary Proceduralism." In: Honneth, *The I in We*, pp. 35–55.
Honneth, Axel (2012b). "Facets of the Presocial Self: Rejoinder to Joel Whitebook." In: Honneth, *The I in We*, pp. 217–31.
Honneth, Axel (2012c). "From Desire to Recognition: Hegel's Grounding of Self-Consciousness." In: Honneth, *The I in We*, pp. 3–18.
Honneth, Axel (2012d). *The I in We. Studies in the Theory of Recognition*. Translated by Joseph Ganahl. Cambridge: Polity Press.
Honneth, Axel (2012e). "Labour and Recognition: A Redefinition." In: Honneth, *The I in We*, pp. 56–74.
Honneth, Axel (2012f). "Recognition as Ideology: The Connection between Morality and Power." In: Honneth, *The I in We*, pp. 75–97.

Honneth, Axel, Andreas Busen, and Lisa Herzog (2012). "Die Rekonstruktion der Freiheit." In: *Zeitschrift Für Politische Theorie* 3. No. 2, pp. 271–86.
Honneth, Axel, and Gonçalo Marcelo (2013). "Recognition and Critical Theory Today: An Interview with Axel Honneth." *Philosophy & Social Criticism* 39. No. 2, pp. 209–21.
Honneth, Axel (2013). "Replies." In: *Krisis. Journal for Contemporary Philosophy* 1, pp. 37–47.
Honneth, Axel (2014a). "The Diseases of Society: Approaching a Nearly Impossible Concept." In: *Social Research: An International Quarterly* 81. No. 3, pp. 683–703.
Honneth, Axel (2014b). *Freedom's Right. The Social Foundations of Democratic Life*. Translated by Joseph Ganahl. Cambridge: Polity Press.
Honneth, Axel (2014c). "Réponse." In: Mark Hunyadi (Ed.): *Axel Honneth. De La Reconnaissance à La Liberté*. Lormont: Le Bord de l'eau, pp. 109–29.
Honneth, Axel (2015a). "Education and the Democratic Public Sphere. A Neglected Chapter of Political Philosophy." In: Odin Lysaker and Jonas Jakobsen (Eds.): *Recognition and Freedom. Axel Honneth's Political Thought*. Leiden, Boston: Brill, pp. 17–32.
Honneth, Axel (2015b). "Rejoinder." In: *Critical Horizons* 16. No. 2, pp. 204–26.
Honneth, Axel, and Morten Raffnsøe-Møller (2015). "Freedom, Solidarity, and Democracy. An Interview with Axel Honneth." In: Odin Lysaker and Jonas Jakobsen (Eds.): *Recognition and Freedom. Axel Honneth's Political Thought*. Leiden, Boston: Brill, pp. 260–82.
Honneth, Axel (2016). "Of the Poverty of Our Liberty. The Greatness and Limits of Hegel's Doctrine of Ethical Life." In: Katia Genel and Jean-Philippe Deranty (Eds.): *Recognition or Disagreement. A Critical Encounter on the Politics of Freedom, Equality, and Identity*. New York: Columbia University Press, pp. 156–76.
Honneth, Axel, and Joel Whitebook (2016). "Omnipotence or Fusion? A Conversation between Axel Honneth and Joel Whitebook." In: *Constellations* 23. No. 2, pp. 170–79.
Honneth, Axel (2017). *The Idea of Socialism. Towards a Renewal*. Translated by Joseph Ganahl. Cambridge: Polity Press.
Honneth, Axel (2018). *Anerkennung: Eine Europäische Ideengeschichte*. Frankfurt am Main: Suhrkamp.
Honneth, Axel (2021). *Recognition: A Chapter in the History of European Ideas*. Cambridge: Cambridge University Press

Other works

Aboulafia, Mitchell (1991). "Self-Consciousness and the Quasi-Epic of the Master." In: Aboulafia (Ed.): *Philosophy, Social Theory, and the Thought of George Herbert Mead*. Albany: SUNY Press, pp. 223–34.
Adloff, Frank (2006). "Beyond Interests and Norms: Toward a Theory of Gift-Giving and Reciprocity in Modern Societies." In: *Constellations* 13. No. 3, pp. 407–27.
Adorno, Theodor W. (2005). *Minima Moralia. Reflections on a Damaged Life*. Translated by E. F. N. Jephcott. London, New York: Verso.
Adorno, Theodor W., and Max Horkheimer (2002). *Dialectic of Enlightenment. Philosophical Fragments*. Edited by Gunzelin Schmid Noerr and translated by Edmund Jephcott. Stanford: Stanford University Press.
Alexander, Jeffrey C., and Maria Pia Lara (1996). "Honneth's New Critical Theory of Recognition." In: *New Left Review* 1. No. 220, pp. 126–136.
Alford, C. Fred (2017). "Forgiveness and Transitional Space." In: Matthew H. Bowker and Amy Buzby (Eds.): *D. W. Winnicott and Political Theory. Recentering the Subject*. New York: Palgrave Macmillan, pp. 185–201.

Allen, Amy (2006). "Dependency, Subordination, and Recognition: On Judith Butler's Theory of Subjection." In: *Continental Philosophy Review* 38. No. 3, pp. 199–222.
Allen, Amy (2010). "Recognizing Domination: Recognition and Power in Honneth's Critical Theory." In: *Journal of Power* 3. No. 1, pp. 21–32.
Allen, Jonathan (1998). "Decency and the Struggle for Recognition." In: *Social Theory and Practice* 24. No. 3, pp. 449–69.
Althusser, Louis (2014). "Ideology and Ideological State Apparatuses." In: Althusser, *On the Reproduction of Capitalism. Ideology and Ideological State Apparatuses*. Translated by G. M. Goshgarian. London, New York: Verso, pp. 232–72.
Alznauer, Mark (2015). *Hegel's Theory of Responsibility*. Cambridge: Cambridge University Press.
Anderson, Joel (2013). "The Fragile Accomplishment of Social Freedom." In: *Krisis. Journal for Contemporary Philosophy* 1, pp. 18–22.
Arendt, Hannah (1998). *The Human Condition*. Chicago: University of Chicago Press.
Arentshorst, Hans (2015). "Social Freedom in Contemporary Capitalism: A Reconstruction of Axel Honneth's Normative Approach to the Economy." In: *Studies in Social and Political Thought* 25, pp. 132–51.
Arentshorst, Hans (2016). "Towards a Reconstructive Approach in Political Philosophy: Rosanvallon and Honneth on the Pathologies of Todays Democracy." In: *Thesis Eleven* 134. No. 1, pp. 42–55.
Aristotle (1887). *Politics*. In: W. L. Newman (Ed.): *The Politics of Aristotle. With an Introduction, Two Prefatory Essays and Notes Critical and Explanatory. Vol II*. Oxford: Clarendon Press.
Athens, Lonnie (2012). "Mead's Analysis of Social Conflict: A Radical Interactionist's Critique." In: *The American Sociologist* 43. No. 4, pp. 428–47.
Bankovsky, Miriam (2012). *Perfecting Justice in Rawls, Habermas and Honneth. A Deconstructive Perspective*. London: Continuum.
Basaure, Mauro (2011). "In the Epicenter of Politics: Axel Honneth's Theory of the Struggles for Recognition and Luc Boltanski and Laurent Thévenot's Moral and Political Sociology." In: *European Journal of Social Theory* 14. No. 3, pp. 263–81.
Bedorf, Thomas (2010). *Verkennende Anerkennung*. Berlin: Suhrkamp.
Bennett, Christopher (2018). "The Alteration Thesis: Forgiveness as a Normative Power." In: *Philosophy and Public Affairs* 46. No. 2, pp. 207–33.
Berendzen, Joseph C. (2019). "Reciprocity and Self-Restriction in Elementary Recognition." In: Volker Schmitz (Ed.): *Axel Honneth and the Critical Theory of Recognition*. Basingstoke, New York: Palgrave Macmillan, pp. 13–39.
Bernstein, J. M. (1996). "Confession and Forgiveness: Hegel's Poetics of Action." In: Richard Eldridge (Ed.): *Beyond Representation. Philosophy and Poetic Imagination*. Cambridge: Cambridge University Press, pp. 34–65.
Bernstein, J. M. (2005). "Suffering Injustice: Misrecognition as Moral Injury in Critical Theory." In: *International Journal of Philosophical Studies* 13. No. 3, pp. 303–24.
Bertram, Georg W. (2008). "Hegel und die Frage der Intersubjektivität. Die *Phänomenologie des Geistes* als Explikation der sozialen Strukturen der Rationalität." In: *Deutsche Zeitschrift für Philosophie* 56. No. 6, pp. 877–98.
Bertram, Georg W., and Robin Celikates (2015). "Towards a Conflict Theory of Recognition: On the Constitution of Relations of Recognition in Conflict." In: *European Journal of Philosophy* 23. No. 4, pp. 838–61.
Bertram, Georg W. (2017). *Hegels "Phänomenologie des Geistes". Ein systematischer Kommentar*. Stuttgart: Reclam.
Borman, David A. (2019). "Bourgeois Illusions: Honneth on the Ruling Ideas of Capitalist Societies." In: Volker Schmitz (Ed.): *Axel Honneth and the Critical Theory of Recognition*. Basingstoke, New York: Palgrave Macmillan, pp. 97–124.

Brandom, Robert B. (2007). "The Structure of Desire and Recognition: Self-Consciousness and Self-Constitution." In: *Philosophy and Social Criticism* 33. No. 1, pp. 127–50.
Brandom, Robert B. (2019). *A Spirit of Trust: A Reading of Hegel's Phenomenology*. Cambridge, London: Harvard University Press.
van den Brink, Bert, and David Owen (2007). "Introduction." In: Bert van den Brink and David Owen (Eds.): *Recognition and Power. Axel Honneth and the Tradition of Critical Social Theory*. Cambridge: Cambridge University Press, pp. 1–30.
van den Brink, Bert (2011). "Recognition, Pluralism and the Expectation of Harmony: Against the ideal of an Ethical life 'free from Pain.'" In: Danielle Petherbridge (Ed.): *Axel Honneth: Critical Essays. With a Reply by Axel Honneth*. Leiden, Boston: Brill, pp. 155–176.
van den Brink, Bert (2013). "From Personal Relations to the Rest of Society." In: *Krisis. Journal for Contemporary Philosophy* 1, pp. 23–27.
Brownlee, Timothy L. (2015) "Alienation and Recognition in Hegel's *Phenomenology of Spirit*." In: *Philosophical Forum* 46. No. 4, pp. 377–96
Buchwalter, Andrew (2016) "The Concept of Normative Reconstruction: Honneth, Hegel, and the Aims of Critical Social Theory." In: Harry F. Dahms and Eric R. Lybeck (Eds.): *Reconstructing Social Theory, History and Practice. Current Perspectives in Social Theory (Vol. 35)*. Bingley: Emerald Group, pp. 57–88.
Busen, Andreas, Lisa Herzog, and Paul Sörensen (2012). "Mit Hegel zu einer kritischen Theorie der Freiheit. Eine Heranführung an Honneths *Das Recht der Freiheit*." In: *Zeitschrift Für Politische Theorie* 3. No. 2, pp. 247–70.
Butler, Judith (1997). *The Psychic Life of Power. Theories in Subjection*. Stanford: Stanford University Press.
Butler, Judith (2008). "Taking Another's View: Ambivalent Implications." In: *Axel Honneth: Reification*. Edited by Martin Jay. New York: Oxford University Press, pp. 97–119.
Canivez, Patrice (2011). " ." In: *Philosophy and Social Criticism* 37. No. 8, pp. 851–87.
Cavell, Stanley (2015). "Knowing and Acknowledging." In: Stanley Cavell: *Must We Mean What We Say? A Book of Essays*. Cambridge: Cambridge University Press, pp. 220–45
Chari, Anita (2010). "Toward a Political Critique of Reification: Lukács, Honneth and the Aims of Critical Theory." In: *Philosophy and Social Criticism* 36. No. 5, pp. 587–606.
Claassen, Rutger (2013). "Justice: Constructive or Reconstructive?" In: *Krisis. Journal for Contemporary Philosophy* 1, pp. 28–31.
Claassen, Rutger (2014). "Social Freedom and the Demands of Justice: A Study of Honneth's *Recht Der Freiheit*." In: *Constellations* 21. No. 1, pp. 67–82.
Cobben, Paul (2012). *The Paradigm of Recognition. Freedom as Overcoming the Fear of Death*. Leiden, Boston: Brill.
Connolly, Julie (2010). "Love in the Private: Axel Honneth, Feminism and the Politics of Recognition." In: *Contemporary Political Theory* 9. No. 4, pp. 414–33.
Cortella, Lucio (2005). "Originarietà del riconoscere. La relazione di riconoscimento come condizione di conoscenza." In: *Giornale di metafisica* 27. No. 1, pp. 145–56.
Cortella, Lucio (2008). "Riconoscimento normativo. Da Honneth a Hegel e oltre." In: *Quaderni di teoria sociale* 8, pp. 15–32.
Cortella, Lucio (2016). "Freedom and Nature: The Point of View of a Theory of Recognition." In: Italo Testa and Luigi Ruggiu (Eds.): *"I That Is We, We That Is I." Perspectives on Contemporary Hegel. Social Ontology, Recognition, Naturalism, and the Critique of Kantian Constructivism*. Leiden, Boston: Brill, pp. 169–80.
Crespi, Franco (2008). "Riconoscimento e relativizzazione delle identità." In: *Quaderni di teoria sociale* 8, pp. 33–43.
Da Cunha De Souza, Luiz Gustavo (2016). "Recognition, Disrecognition and Legitimacy: On the Normativity of Politics." In: *Thesis Eleven* 134. No. 1, pp. 13–27.

Dejours, Christophe, Jean-Philippe Deranty, Emmanuel Renault, and Nicholas H. Smith (2018). *The Return of Work in Critical Theory. Self, Society, Politics*. New York: Columbia University Press.

Deranty, Jean-Philippe (2004). "Injustice, Violence and Social Struggle. The Critical Potential of Axel Honneth's Theory of Recognition." In: John Rundell, Danielle Petherbridge, Jan Bryant, John Hewitt, and Jeremy Smith (Eds.): *Contemporary Perspectives in Critical and Social Philosophy*. Leiden, Boston: Brill, pp. 297–322.

Deranty, Jean-Philippe, and Emmanuel Renault (2007). "Politicizing Honneth's Ethics of Recognition." In: *Thesis Eleven* 88. No. 1, pp. 92–111.

Deranty, Jean-Philippe (2009). *Beyond Communication. A Critical Study of Axel Honneth's Social Philosophy*. Leiden, Boston: Brill.

Deranty, Jean-Philippe (2011). "Reflective Critical Theory: A Systematic Reconstruction of Axel Honneth's Social Philosophy." In: Danielle Petherbridge (Ed.): *Axel Honneth: Critical Essays. With a Reply by Axel Honneth*. Leiden, Boston: Brill, pp. 59–88.

Derrida, Jacques (2015). "To Forgive. The Unforgivable and the Imprescriptible." In: Hent de Vries and Niels Schott (Eds.): *Love and Forgiveness for a More Just World*. New York: Columbia University Press, pp. 144–81.

Descombes, Vincent (2011) "The Problem of Collective Identity: The Instituting We and the Instituted We." In: Heikki Ikäheimo and Arto Laitinen (Eds.): *Recognition and Social Ontology*. Leiden, Boston: Brill, pp. 373–89.

Ernout, Alfred, and Alfred Meillet (2001). *Dictionnaire étymologique de la langue latine. Histoire des mots*. Paris: Klincksieck.

Feenberg, Andrew (2011). "Rethinking Reification." In: Timothy Bewes and Timothy Hall (Eds.): *Georg Lukács: The Fundamental Dissonance of Existence. Aesthetics, Politics, Literature*. London: Continuum, pp. 101–20.

Feenberg, Andrew (2013). "Heidegger and Marcuse: On Reification and Concrete Philosophy." In: Francois Raffoul and Eric S. Nelson (Eds.): *The Bloomsbury Companion to Heidegger*. New York: Boomsbury, pp. 171–76.

Feenberg, Andrew (2015). "Lukács's Theory of Reification and Contemporary Social Movements." In: *Rethinking Marxism* 27. No. 4, pp. 490–507.

Ferrara, Alessandro (1998). "Democrazia e teoria sociale: un ponte ancora da costruire. Riflessioni sul saggio di Axel Honneth "Democrazia come cooperazione riflessiva. John Dewey e l'odierna teoria della democrazia"." In: *Fenomenologia e Società* 21. No. 3, pp. 28–36.

Ferrara, Alessandro (2004). "The Relation of Authenticity to Normativity: A Response to Larmore and Honneth." In: *Philosophy & Social Criticism* 30. No. 1, pp. 17–24.

Ferrara, Alessandro (2011). "The Nugget and the Tailings. Reification Reinterpreted in the Light of Recognition." In: Danielle Petherbridge (Ed.): *Axel Honneth: Critical Essays. With a Reply by Axel Honneth*. Leiden, Boston: Brill, pp. 371–90.

Ferrara, Alessandro (2015). "Esemplarità e teoria critica. Quale normatività per una teoria critica come critica immanente?" In: *Politica & Società* 4. No. 3, pp. 355–70.

Fichte, Johann Gottlieb (2000). *Foundations of Natural Right according to the Principles of the Wissenschaftslehre*. Edited by Frederick Neuhouser and translated by Michael Baur. Cambridge: Cambridge University Press.

Foster, Roger (2017). "*Freedom's Right*: Critical Social Theory and the Challenge of Neoliberalism." In: *Capital and Class* 41. No. 3, pp. 455–73.

Foucault, Michel (2003). *"Society Must Be Defended." Lectures at the Collège de France 1975–76*. Edited by Mauro Bertani and Alessandro Fontana and translated by David Macey. New York: Picador.

Frank, Manfred (2004). "Against a Priori Intersubjectivism: An Alternative Inspired by Sartre." In: Dieter Freundlieb, Wayne Hudson, and John Rundell (Eds.): *Critical Theory after Habermas. Encounters and Departures*. Leiden, Boston: Brill, pp. 259–79.

Fraser, Nancy (2003a). "Distorted Beyond All Recognition: A Rejoinder to Axel Honneth." In: Axel Honneth and Nancy Fraser, *Redistribution or Recognition?*, pp. 198–236.
Fraser, Nancy (2003b). "Social Justice in the Age of Identity Politics: Redistribution, Recognition, and Participation." In: Axel Honneth and Nancy Fraser, *Redistribution or Recognition?*, pp. 7–109.
Freyenhagen, Fabian (2015). "Honneth on Social Pathologies: A Critique." In: *Critical Horizons* 16. No. 2, pp. 131–52.
Gabriëls, René (2013). "There Must Be Some Way out of Here. In Search of a Critical Theory of World Society." In: *Krisis. Journal for Contemporary Philosophy* 1, pp. 5–9.
Geuss, Raymond (2008). "Philosophical Anthropology and Social Criticism." In: *Axel Honneth: Reification*. Edited by Martin Jay. New York: Oxford University Press, pp. 120–30.
Gilbert, Margaret (2011). "Mutual Recognition and Some Related Phenomena." In: Heikki Ikäheimo and Arto Laitinen (Eds.): *Recognition and Social Ontology*. Leiden, Boston: Brill, pp. 271–86.
Giorgini, Giovanni, and Elena Irrera (2017). "Recognition: A Philosophical Problem." In: Giovanni Giorgini and Elena Irrera (Eds.): *The Roots of Respect*. Berlin: de Gruyter, pp. 17–38.
Greblo, Edoardo (2009). "Paradigmi di giustizia. Sulla controversia Fraser-Honneth." In: *Ragion pratica* 39. No. 1, pp. 337–53.
Habermas, Jürgen (1973). "Labor and Interaction: Remarks on Hegel's Jena Philosophy of Mind." In: Habermas, *Theory and Practice*. Translated by John Viertel. Boston: Beacon Press, pp. 142–69.
Habermas, Jürgen (1984). *The Theory of Communicative Action, Vol. 1, Reason and the Rationalization of Society*. Translated by Thomas McCarthy. Boston: Beacon Press.
Habermas, Jürgen (1987). *The Theory of Communicative Action, Vol. 2, Lifeworld and System: A Critique of Functionalist Reason*. Translated by Thomas McCarthy. Boston: Beacon Press.
Habermas, Jürgen (1991). *The Structural Transformation of the Public Sphere: An Inquiry into a Category of Bourgeois Society*. Translated by Thomas Burger and Frederick Lawrence. Cambridge: The MIT Press.
Habermas, Jürgen (1992). "Individuation through Socialization: On George Herbert Mead's Theory of Subjectivity." In: Habermas, *Postmetaphysical Thinking. Philosophical Essays*. Translated by William Mark Hohengarten. Boston: The MIT Press, pp. 149–204.
Habermas, Jürgen (1996). *Between Facts and Norms: Contributions to a Discourse Theory of Law and Democracy*. Translated by William Rehg. Cambridge: The MIT Press.
Habermas, Jürgen (1998). "A Genealogical Analysis of the Cognitive Content of Morality." In: Habermas, *The Inclusion of the Other. Studies in Political Theory*. Edited by Ciaran Cronin and Pablo De Greiff. Cambridge: The MIT Press, pp. 3–46.
Habermas, Jürgen (1999). "From Kant to Hegel and Back Again. The Move towards Detranscendentalization." In: *European Journal of Philosophy* 7, pp. 129–57
Habermas, Jürgen (2003). "The Debate on the Ethical Self-Understanding of the Species." In: Habermas, *The Future of Human Nature*. Cambridge: Polity Press, pp. 16–74.
Harris, Neal (2018). "Recovering the Critical Potential of Social Pathology Diagnosis." In: *European Journal of Social Theory* 22. No. 1, pp. 45–62.
Hedrick, Todd (2013). "Reification in and through Law: Elements of a Theory in Marx, Lukacs, and Honneth." In: *European Journal of Political Theory* 13. No. 2, pp. 178–98.
Hegel, Georg Wilhelm Friedrich (1970). *Phänomenologie des Geistes*. Frankfurt am Main: Suhrkamp.
Hegel, Georg Wilhelm Friedrich (1991). *Elements of the Philosophy of Right*. Edited by Allen W. Wood and translated by H. B. Nisbet. Cambridge: Cambridge University Press
Hegel, Georg Wilhelm Friedrich (2004). *Encyclopaedia of the Philosophical Sciences (1830). Vol. 2: Philosophy of Nature*. Translated by A. V. Miller. Oxford: Clarendon Press.

Hegel, Georg Wilhelm Friedrich (2007). *Encyclopaedia of the Philosophical Sciences (1830). Vol. 3: Philosophy of Mind*. Translated by W. Wallace and A. V. Miller. Oxford: Clarendon Press.

Hegel, Georg Wilhelm Friedrich (2018). *The Phenomenology of Spirit*. Translated by Terry Pinkard. Cambridge: Cambridge University Press.

Heidegger, Martin (1996). *Being and Time*. Translated by Joan Stambaugh. Albany: State University of New York Press.

Heidegren, Carl-Göran (2002). "Anthropology, Social Theory and Politics: Axel Honneth's Theory of Recognition." In: *Inquiry* 45. No. 4, pp. 433–46.

Heidegren, Carl-Göran (2004). "Recognition and Social Theory." In: *Acta Sociologica* 47. No. 4, pp. 365–73.

Held, Jacob (2008). "Axel Honneth and the Future of Critical Theory." In: *Radical Philosophy Review* 11. No. 2, pp. 175–86.

Herzog, Benno (2015). "Recognition in Multicultural Societies. Intergroup Relations as Second-Order Recognition." In: *Revista Internacional de Sociología* 73. No. 2, pp. 1–12.

Hirvonen, Onni (2018). "On the Ontology of Social Pathologies." In: *Studies in Social and Political Thought* 28, pp. 9–14.

Hirvonen, Onni (2019). "Grounding Social Criticism: From Understanding to Suffering and Back." In: *Digithum. A Relational Perspective on Culture and Society* 23, pp. 1–10.

Horn, Anita (2018). "Anerkennung und Freiheit: Subjekttheoretische Grundlagen einer Theorie demokratischer Sittlichkeit." In: *Archiv für Rechts- und Sozialphilosophie* 104, pp. 16–40.

Ikäheimo, Heikki (2002). "On the Genus and Species of Recognition." In: *Inquiry* 45. No. 4, pp. 447–62.

Ikäheimo, Heikki, and Arto Laitinen (2007). "Analyzing Recognition: Identification, Acknowledgement, and Recognitive Attitudes towards Persons." In: Bert van den Brink and David Owen (Eds.): *Recognition and Power. Axel Honneth and the Tradition of Critical Social Theory*. Cambridge: Cambridge University Press, pp. 33–56.

Ikäheimo, Heikki (2009). "A Vital Human Need: Recognition as Inclusion in Personhood." In: *European Journal of Political Theory* 8. No. 1, pp. 31–45.

Ikäheimo, Heikki, and Arto Laitinen (2010). "Esteem for Contributions to the Common Good: The Role of Personifying Attitudes and Instrumental Value." In: Michael Seymour (Ed.): *The Plural States of Recognition*. Basingstoke, New York: Palgrave Macmillan, pp. 98–121.

Ikäheimo, Heikki (2011). "Holism and Normative Essentialism in Hegel's Social Ontology." In: Heikki Ikäheimo and Arto Laitinen (Eds.): *Recognition and Social Ontology*. Leiden, Boston: Brill, pp. 145–209.

Ikäheimo, Heikki (2014). "Hegel's Concept of Recognition—What is It?." In: Christian Krijnen (Ed.): *Recognition—German Idealism as an Ongoing Challenge*. Leiden, Boston: Brill, pp. 11–38.

Illetterati, Luca (2016). "Nature, Subjectivity and Freedom: Moving from Hegel's Philosophy of Nature." In: Italo Testa and Luigi Ruggiu (Eds.): *"I That Is We, We That Is I." Perspectives on Contemporary Hegel. Social Ontology, Recognition, Naturalism, and the Critique of Kantian Constructivism*. Leiden, Boston: Brill, pp. 183–201.

Jaeggi, Rahel (2005). "'No Individual Can Resist': *Minima Moralia* as Critique of Forms of Life." In: *Constellations* 12. No. 1, pp. 65–82.

Jaeggi, Rahel (2006). "Anerkennung und Unterwerfung: Zum Verhältnis von negativen und positiven Theorien der Intersubjektivität." https://www.*philosophie.hu-berlin.de/de/lehrber eiche/jaeggi/mitarbeiter/jaeggi_rahel/anerkennungunterwerfung*, visited on 25 October 2019.

Jaeggi, Rahel (2018). *Critique of Forms of Life*. Translated by Ciaran Cronin. Cambridge, London: Harvard University Press.

Jansen, Yolande (2013). "The 'Us' of Democratic Will-Formation and Globalization." In: *Krisis. Journal for Contemporary Philosophy* 1, pp. 32–36.

Jütten, Timo (2010). "What Is Reification? A Critique of Axel Honneth." In: *Inquiry* 53. No. 3, pp. 235–56.
Jütten, Timo (2011). "The Colonization Thesis: Habermas on Reification." In: *International Journal of Philosophical Studies* 19. No. 5, pp. 701–27.
Jütten, Timo (2015). "Is the Market a Sphere of Social Freedom?" In: *Critical Horizons* 16. No. 2, pp. 187–203.
Kant, Immanuel (1997). *Groundwork of the Metaphysics of Morals.* Translated by Mary Gregor. Cambridge: Cambridge University Press.
Kauppinen, Antti (2002). "Reason, Recognition, and Internal Critique." In: *Inquiry* 45. No. 4, pp. 479–98.
Kauppinen, Antti (2011). "The Social Dimension of Autonomy." In: Danielle Petherbridge (Ed.): *Axel Honneth: Critical Essays. With a Reply by Axel Honneth.* Leiden, Boston: Brill, pp. 255–302.
Kavoulakos, Konstantinos (2017). "Lukács' Theory of Reification and the Tradition of Critical Theory." In: Michael J. Thompson (Ed.): *The Palgrave Handbook of Critical Theory.* New York: Palgrave Macmillan, pp. 67–85.
Kavoulakos, Konstantinos (2019). "Reifying Reification: A Critique of Axel Honneth's Theory of Reification:" In: Volker Schmitz (Ed.): *Axel Honneth and the Critical Theory of Recognition.* Basingstoke, New York: Palgrave Macmillan, pp. 41–68.
Koch, William (2015). "Phenomenology as Social Critique." In: Hans Pedersen and Megan Altman (Eds.): *Horizons of Authenticity in Phenomenology, Existentialism, and Moral Psychology. Essays in Honor of Charles Guignon.* Dordrecht, Heidelberg: Springer, pp. 311–28.
Kompridis, Nikolas (2004). "From Reason to Self-Realisation? Axel Honneth and the "Ethical Turn" in Critical Theory." In: John Rundell, Danielle Petherbridge, Jan Bryant, John Hewitt, and Jeremy Smith (Eds.): *Contemporary Perspectives in Critical and Social Philosophy.* Leiden, Boston: Brill, pp. 323–60.
Kompridis, Nikolas (2007). "Struggling over the Meaning of Recognition. A Matter of Identity, Justice, or Freedom?" In: *European Journal of Political Theory* 6. No. 3, pp. 277–89.
Krüger, Hans-Peter (2006). "Die Antwortlichkeit in der exzentrischen Positionalität. Die Drittheit, das Dritte und die Dritte Person als philosophische Minima." In: Hans-Peter Krüger and Gesa Lindemann (Eds.): *Philosophische Anthropologie im 21. Jahrhundert.* Berlin: Akademie, pp. 164–83.
Krüger, Hans-Peter (2019). *Homo Absconditus. Helmuth Plessners philosophische Anthropologie im Vergleich.* Berlin: de Gruyter.
Lacan, Jacques (2001). "The Function and Field of Speech and Language in Psychoanalysis." In: Lacan, *Écrits. A Selection.* Translated by Alan Sheridan. London, New York: Routledge, pp. 23–86.
Laitinen, Arto (2002). "Interpersonal Recognition: A Response to Value or a Precondition of Personhood?" In: *Inquiry* 45. No. 4, pp. 463–78.
Laitinen, Arto (2010). "On the Scope of 'Recognition': The Role of Adequate Regard and Mutuality." In: Hans-Christoph Schmidt am Busch and Christopher F. Zurn (Eds.): *The Philosophy of Recognition. Historical and Contemporary Perspectives.* Lanham: Lexington Books, pp. 319–42.
Laitinen, Arto (2011). "Recognition, Acknowledgement, and Acceptance." In: Heikki Ikäheimo and Arto Laitinen (Eds.): *Recognition and Social Ontology.* Leiden, Boston: Brill, pp. 310–47.
Laitinen, Arto (2015). "Social Pathologies, Reflexive Pathologies, and the Idea of Higher-Order Disorders." In: *Studies in Social and Political Thought* 25, pp. 44–65.
Laitinen, Arto (2016). "Freedom's Left? Market's Right? Morality's Wrong?" In: Giorgio Baruchello, Jacob Dahl Rendtorff, and Asger Sørensen (Eds.): *Ethics, Democracy, and Markets: Nordic Perspectives on World Problems.* Natchitoches: NSU Press, pp. 258–81.

Laitinen, Arto (2017). "Hegel and Respect for Persons." In: Giovanni Giorgini and Elena Irrera (Eds.): *Roots of Respect. A Historic-Philosophical Itinerary*. Berlin: de Gruyter, pp. 171–86.

Lauer, Christopher (2012). "Multivalent Recognition: The Place of Hegel in the Fraser-Honneth Debate." In: *Contemporary Political Theory* 11. No. 1, pp. 23–40.

Lear, Jonathan (2008). "The Slippery Middle." In: Axel Honneth: *Reification*. Edited by Martin Jay. New York: Oxford University Press, pp. 131–43.

van Leeuwen, Bart (2006). "Book Review: Axel Honneth, *Verdinglichung*." In: *Ethical Theory and Moral Practice* 9. No. 2, pp. 237–42.

Lepold, Kristina (2014). "Die Bedingungen der Anerkennung." In: *Deutsche Zeitschrift für Philosophie* 62. No. 2, pp. 297–317.

Lindemann, Gesa (2006). "Die dritte Person—Das konstitutive Minimum der Sozialtheorie." In: Hans-Peter Krüger and Gesa Lindemann (Eds.): *Philosophische Anthropologie im 21. Jahrhundert*. Berlin: Akademie, pp. 125–45.

Loick, Daniel (2015). "'Expression of Contempt': Hegel's Critique of Legal Freedom." In: *Law and Critique* 26. No. 2, pp. 189–206.

Loose, Donald (2014). "Kantian Version of Recognition. The Bottom-Line of Axel Honneth's Project." In: Christian Krijnen (Ed.): *Recognition—German Idealism as an Ongoing Challenge*. Leiden, Boston: Brill, pp. 165–89.

Lovell, Terry (2007). "Nancy Fraser's Integrated Theory of Justice: A 'Sociologically Rich' Model for a Global Capitalist Era?" In: Terry Lovell (Ed.): *(Mis)Recognition, Social Inequality and Social Justice: Nancy Fraser and Pierre Bourdieu*. New York: Routledge, pp. 66–87.

Lysaker, Odin, and Jonas Jakobsen (2015). "Introduction: Recognition and Freedom in Axel Honneth's Political Thought." In: Odin Lysaker, and Jonas Jakobsen (Ed.): *Recognition and Freedom. Axel Honneth's Political Thought*. Leiden, Boston: Brill, pp. 1–16

Lysaker, Odin (2017). "Institutional Agonism: Axel Honneth's Radical Democracy." In: *Critical Horizons* 18. No. 1, pp. 1–19.

Markell, Patchen (2000). "The Recognition of Politics: A Comment on Emcke and Tully." *Constellations* 7. No. 4, pp. 496–506.

Markell, Patchen (2003). *Bound by Recognition*. Princeton: Princeton University Press.

Markell, Patchen (2007). "The Potential and the Actual: Mead, Honneth, and the 'I.'" In: Bert van den Brink and David Owen (Eds.): *Recognition and Power. Axel Honneth and the Tradition of Critical Social Theory*. Cambridge: Cambridge University Press, pp. 100–132.

Martineau, Wendy, Nasar Meer, and Simon Thompson (2012). "Theory and Practice in the Politics of Recognition." In: *Res Publica* 18, pp. 1–9.

Marx, Karl, and Friedrich Engels (2010). *The Holy Family, or Critique of Critical Criticism: Against Bruno Bauerand Company*. Translated by Richard Dixon and Clemens Dutt. In: Marx and Engels, *Collected Works*. Vol. 4 (1844–45). London: Lawrence & Wishart, pp. 5–211.

Mauss, Marcel (2002). *The Gift. The Form and Reason for Exchange in Archaic Societies*. Translated by W. D. Halls. London, New York: Routledge.

McCarthy, Thomas (2005). "Review: *Redistribution or Recognition?*" In: *Ethics* 115. No. 2, pp. 397–402.

McNay, Lois (2008a). *Against Recognition*. Cambridge: Polity Press

McNay, Lois (2008b). "The Trouble with Recognition: Subjectivity, Suffering, and Agency." In: *Sociological Theory* 26. No. 3, pp. 271–96.

McNeill, David N. (2015). "Social Freedom and Self-Actualization: 'Normative Reconstruction' as a Theory of Justice." In: *Critical Horizons* 16. No. 2, pp. 153–69.

McPherson, Tristram (2018). "Authoritatively Normative Concepts." In: Russ Shafer-Landau (Ed.): *Oxford Studies in Metaethics*. Oxford: Oxford University Press, pp. 253–77.

Mead, George Herbert (1964). "The Social Self." In: George H. Mead, *Selected Writings*. Edited by Andrew Reck. Chicago: University of Chicago Press, pp. 142–49.

Mead, George Herbert (1972). *Mind, Self, and Society.* Edited by Charles W. Morris. Chicago: University of Chicago Press.

Meehan, Johanna (2011). "Recognition and the Dynamics of Intersubjectivity." In: Danielle Petherbridge (Ed.): *Axel Honneth: Critical Essays. With a Reply by Axel Honneth.* Leiden, Boston: Brill, pp. 89–123.

Menegoni, Francesca (2016). "Hegel's Theory of Action: Between Conviction and Recognition." In: Italo Testa and Luigi Ruggiu (Eds.): *"I That Is We, We That Is I." Perspectives on Contemporary Hegel. Social Ontology, Recognition, Naturalism, and the Critique of Kantian Constructivism.* Leiden, Boston: Brill, pp. 147–56.

Neuhouser, Frederick (2000). *Foundations of Hegel's Social Theory. Actualizing Freedom.* Cambridge, London: Harvard University Press.

Neuhouser, Frederick (2010). "Rousseau and the Human Drive for Recognition (*Amour Propre*)." In: Hans-Christoph Schmidt am Busch and Christopher F. Zurn (Eds.): *The Philosophy of Recognition. Historical and Contemporary Perspectives.* Lanham: Lexington Books, pp. 21–46.

Neuhouser, Frederick (2016). "Hegel on Social Ontology and the Possibility of Pathology." In: Italo Testa and Luigi Ruggiu (Eds.): *"I That Is We, We That Is I." Perspectives on Contemporary Hegel. Social Ontology, Recognition, Naturalism, and the Critique of Kantian Constructivism.* Leiden, Boston: Brill, pp. 31–48.

Ng, Karen (2015). "Ideology Critique from Hegel and Marx to Critical Theory." In: *Constellations* 22, pp. 393–404

Nozick, Robert (1999). *Anarchy, State, and Utopia.* Oxford: Blackwell Publishing.

Nys, Thomas (2013). "Which Justice, Whose Pathology?" In: *Krisis. Journal for Contemporary Philosophy* 1, pp. 10–13

O'Connor, Brian (2012). "The Neo-Hegelian Theory of Freedom and the Limits of Emancipation." In: *European Journal of Philosophy* 23. No. 2, pp. 171–94.

Owen, David (2010). "Reification, Ideology and Power: Expression and Agency in Honneth's Theory of Recognition." In: *Journal of Power*, 3, pp. 97–109.

Pedersen, Jørgen (2015). "Writing History from a Normative Point of View. The Reconstructive Method in Axel Honneth's *Das Recht der Freiheit*." In: Odin Lysaker and Jonas Jakobsen (Eds.): *Recognition and Freedom. Axel Honneth's Political Thought.* Leiden, Boston: Brill, pp. 237–59.

Pensky, Max (2011). "Social Solidarity and Intersubjective Recognition: On Axel Honneth's *Struggle for Recognition*." In: Danielle Petherbridge (Ed.): *Axel Honneth: Critical Essays. With a Reply by Axel Honneth.* Leiden, Boston: Brill, pp. 125–53.

Petherbridge, Danielle (2013). *The Critical Theory of Axel Honneth.* Lanham: Lexington Books.

Pilapil, Renante D. (2011). "Psychologization of Injustice? On Axel Honneth's Theory of Recognitive Justice." In: *Ethical Perspectives* 18. No. 1, pp. 79–106.

Pippin, Robert B. (2000). "What Is the Question for Which Hegel's Theory of Recognition Is the Answer?" In: *European Journal of Philosophy* 8. No. 2, pp. 155–72.

Pippin, Robert B. (2001). "Hegel and Institutional Reality." In: *Southern Journal of Philosophy* 39, pp. 1–25

Pippin, Robert B. (2007). "Recognition and Reconciliation: Actualized Agency in Hegel's Jena Phenomenology." In: Bert van den Brink and David Owen (Eds.): *Recognition and Power. Axel Honneth and the Tradition of Critical Social Theory.* Cambridge: Cambridge University Press, pp. 57–78.

Pippin, Robert B. (2008). *Hegel's Practical Philosophy. Rational Agency as Ethical Life.* Cambridge: Cambridge University Press.

Pippin, Robert B. (2014). "Reconstructivism: On Honneth's Hegelianism." In: *Philosophy and Social Criticism* 40, pp. 725–41.

Piromalli, Eleonora (2012). *Axel Honneth. Giustizia sociale come riconoscimento*. Milano, Udine: Mimesis.

Plessner, Helmuth (2019). *Levels of Organic Life and the Human. An Introduction to Philosophical Anthropology*. Translated by Millay Hyatt. New York: Fordham University Press.

Quadflieg, Dirk (2011). "Zur Dialektik von Verdinglichung und Freiheit. Von Lukács zu Honneth— und zurück zu Hegel." *Deutsche Zeitschrift für Philosophie* 59. No. 5, pp. 701–15.

Quante, Michael (2004). *Hegel's Concept of Action*. Translated by Dean Moyar. Cambridge: Cambridge University Press.

Quante, Michael (2010). "'The Pure Notion of Recognition': Reflections on the Grammar of the Relation of Recognition in Hegel's *Phenomenology of Spirit*." In: Hans-Christoph Schmidt am Busch and Christopher F. Zurn (Eds.): *The Philosophy of Recognition. Historical and Contemporary Perspectives*. Lanham: Lexington Books, pp. 89–106.

Renault, Emmanuel (2004). *L'expérience de l'injustice*. Paris: La Découverte.

Renault, Emmanuel (2010). "A Critical Theory of Social Suffering." In: *Critical Horizons* 11. No. 2, pp. 221–41.

Ricken, Norbert (2013). "Anerkennung als Adressierung. Über die Bedeutung von Anerkennung für Subjektivationsprozesse." In: Thomas Alkemeyer, Gunilla Budde, and Dagmar Freist (Eds.): *Selbst-Bildungen. Soziale und kulturelle Praktiken der Subjektivierung*. Bielefeld: transcript, pp. 69–99.

Ricoeur, Paul (2004). *Memory, History, Forgetting*. Translated by Kathleen Plamey and David Pellauer. Chicago, London: University of Chicago Press.

Ricoeur, Paul (2005). *The Course of Recognition*. Translated by David Pellauer. Cambridge, London: Harvard University Press.

Rössler, Beate (2013). "Kantian Autonomy and Its Social Preconditions. On Axel Honneth's *Das Recht der Freiheit*." In: *Krisis. Journal for Contemporary Philosophy* 1, pp. 14–17.

Rousseau, Jean-Jacques (1992). *Discourse on the Origin of Inequality*. Translated by Donald A. Cress. Indianapolis, Cambridge: Hackett Publishing Co.

Rundell, John (2001). "Imaginary Turns in Critical Theory: Imagining Subjects in Tension." In: *Critical Horizons* 2. No. 1, pp. 61–92.

Samonà, Leonardo (2016). "The Community of the Self." In: Italo Testa and Luigi Ruggiu (Eds.): *"I That Is We, We That Is I." Perspectives on Contemporary Hegel. Social Ontology, Recognition, Naturalism, and the Critique of Kantian Constructivism*. Leiden, Boston: Brill, pp. 286–98.

Sartre, Jean-Paul (1993). *Being and Nothingness*. Translated by Hazel E. Barnes. New York: Washington Square Press.

Schafer, David T. (2017). "Pathologies of Freedom: Axel Honneth's Unofficial Theory of Reification." In: *Constellations* 25. No. 3, pp. 421–31.

Schaub, Jörg (2015). "Misdevelopments, Pathologies, and Normative Revolutions: Normative Reconstruction as Method of Critical Theory." In: *Critical Horizons* 16. No. 2, pp. 107–30.

Scheuerman, William E. (2017). "Recent Frankfurt Critical Theory: Down on Law?" In: *Constellations* 24. No. 1, pp. 113–25.

Schmetkamp, Susanne (2012). *Respekt und Anerkennung*. Paderborn: Mentis.

Schürmann, Volker (2006). "Positionierte Exzentrizität." In: Hans-Peter Krüger, and Gesa Lindemann (Ed.): *Philosophische Anthropologie im 21. Jahrhundert*. Berlin: Akademie, pp. 83–102.

Schürmann, Volker (2010). "Der/die oder das Dritte?" In: Thomas Bedorf, Joachim Fischer, and Gesa Lindemann (Eds.): *Theorien des Dritten. Innovationen in Soziologie und Sozialphilosophie*. München: Wilhelm Fink, pp. 73–89.

Searle, John R. (1995). *The Construction of Social Reality*. New York: Free Press.

Seel, Martin (2004). "'Jede wirklich gesättifte Anschauung.' Das positive Zentrum der negative Philosophie Adornos." In: Martin Seel (Ed.): *Adornos Philosophie der Kontemplation*. Frankfurt am Main: Suhrkamp, pp. 9–19.
Shafer, Matthew T. C. (2008). "The Utopian Shadow of Normative Reconstruction." In: *Constellations* 25. No. 3, 406–20.
Siep, Ludwig, (1979). *Anerkennung als Prinzip der praktischen Philosophie. Untersuchungen zu Hegels Jenaer Philosophie des Geistes*. Freiburg, München: Alber.
Siep, Ludwig, (2010). "Recognition in Hegel's *Phenomenology of Spirit* and Contemporary Practical Philosophy." In: Hans-Christoph Schmidt am Busch, and Christopher F. Zurn (Eds.): *The Philosophy of Recognition. Historical and Contemporary Perspectives*. Lanham: Lexington Books, pp. 107–27.
Siep, Ludwig, (2011). "Mutual Recognition: Hegel and Beyond." In: Heikki Ikäheimo and Arto Laitinen (Eds.): *Recognition and Social Ontology*. Leiden, Boston: Brill, pp. 117–44.
Siep, Ludwig, (2014a). "The Contemporary Relevance of Hegel's Practical Philosophy." In: Katerina Delgiorgi (Ed.): *Hegel. New Directions*. London, New York: Routledge, pp. 143–57.
Siep, Ludwig, (2014b). *Hegel's* Phenomenology of Spirit. Translated by Daniel Smyth. Cambridge: Cambridge University Press.
Sinnerbrink, Robert (2004). "Recognitive Freedom: Hegel and the Problem of Recognition." In: John Rundell, Danielle Petherbridge, Jan Bryant, John Hewitt, and Jeremy Smith (Eds.): *Contemporary Perspectives in Critical and Social Philosophy*. Leiden, Boston: Brill, pp. 271–95.
Sinnerbrink, Robert (2007). *Understanding Hegelianism*. London, New York: Routledge.
Smith, Adam (2017). "The Turn to Acknowledgment in Recognition Theory." In: *Constellations* 24. No. 2, pp. 206–18.
Smith, Nicholas H. (2011). "Recognition, Culture and Economy: Honneth's Debate with Fraser." In: Danielle Petherbridge (Ed.): *Axel Honneth: Critical Essays. With a Reply by Axel Honneth*. Leiden, Boston: Brill, pp. 321–44.
Smith, Robert C., (2017). *Society and Social Pathology. A Framework for Progress*. Cham: Palgrave Macmillan.
Smulewicz-Zucker, Gregory R. (2019). "Losing Sight of Power: The Inadequacy of Axel Honneth's Theory of the Market and Democracy." In: Volker Schmitz (Ed.): *Axel Honneth and the Critical Theory of Recognition*. Basingstoke, New York: Palgrave Macmillan, pp. 125–44.
Sobottka, Emil A., and Giovani A. Saavedra (2009). "Die Debatte um den Begriff der Anerkennung." In: *Soziale Passagen* 1, pp. 193–207.
Sperotto, Tommaso (2017). "Il paradigma honnethiano del riconoscimento: interazione, antropogenesi e normatività." In: *Rivista internazionale di filosofia e psicologia* 8. No. 3, pp. 294–308.
Stahl, Titus (2011). "Verdinglichung als Pathologie zweiter Ordnung." *Deutsche zeitschrift für Philosophie* 59. No. 2, pp. 731–46.
Stahl, Titus (2017). "The Metaethics of Critical Theories." In: Michael J. Thompson (Ed.): *The Palgrave Handbook of Critical Theory*. New York: Palgrave Macmillan, pp. 505–22.
Strydom, Piet (2013). "Review Essay: Honneth's Sociological Turn." In: *European Journal of Social Theory* 16. No. 4, pp. 530–42.
Taylor, Charles, (1994). "The Politics of Recognition." In: A. Gutmann (Ed.): *Multiculturalism: Examining the Politics of Recognition*. Princeton: Princeton University Press, pp. 25–74.
Teixeira, Mariana (2017). "The Sociological Roots and Deficits of Axel Honneth's Theory of Recognition." In: Michael J. Thompson (Ed.): *The Palgrave Handbook of Critical Theory*. New York: Palgrave Macmillan, pp. 587–609.
Teixeira, Mariana (2019). "Can Honneth's Theory Account for a Critique of Instrumental Reason? Capitalism and the Pathologies of Negative Freedom." In: Volker Schmitz (Ed.): *Axel Honneth*

and the Critical Theory of Recognition. Basingstoke, New York: Palgrave Macmillan, pp. 173–205.

Testa, Italo (2005). "Naturalmente sociali. Per una teoria generale del riconoscimento." In: *Quaderni di teoria sociale* 5, pp. 165–217.

Testa, Italo (2010). *La natura del riconoscimento. Riconoscimento naturale e ontologia sociale in Hegel (1801–1806)*. Milano, Udine: Mimesis.

Testa, Italo (2012). "How Does Recognition Emerge from Nature? The Genesis of Consciousness in Hegel's Jena Writings." In: *Critical Horizons* 13. No. 2, pp. 176–96.

Testa, Italo (2015). "Ontology of the False State. On the Relation Between Critical Theory, Social Philosophy, and Social Ontology." In: *Journal of Social Ontology* 1. No. 2, pp. 271–300.

Testa, Italo (2016). "Recognition as Passive Power: Attractors of Recognition, Biopower, and Social Power." In: *Constellations* 24. No. 2, pp. 192–205.

Theunissen, Michael (1991). "The Repressed Intersubjectivity of Hegel's *Philosophy of Right*." In: Cornell Drucilla, Rosenfeld Michel, and Carlson David (Eds.): *Hegel and Legal Theory*. New York: Routledge, pp. 3–63.

Thompson, Michael J. (2011). "Ontology and Totality: Reconstructing Lukács' Concept of Critical Theory." In: Michael J. Thompson (Ed.): *Georg Lukács Reconsidered: Critical Essays in Politics, Philosophy and Aesthetics*. London, New York: Continuum, pp. 229–50.

Thompson, Michael J. (2014). "Axel Honneth and the Neo-Idealist Turn in Critical Theory." In: *Philosophy and Social Criticism* 40. No. 8, pp. 779–97.

Thompson, Michael J. (2015). "The Neo-Idealist Paradigm Shift in Contemporary Critical Theory." In: Harry F. Dahms (Ed.): *Globalization, Critique and Social Theory: Diagnoses and Challenges*. Bingley: Emerald Group, pp. 137–63.

Thompson, Michael J. (2017). "Collective Intentionality, Social Domination, and Reification." In: *Journal of Social Ontology* 3. No. 2, pp. 207–29.

Thompson, Michael J. (2018). "Axel Honneth and Critical Theory." In: Werner Bonefeld and Chris O'Kane (Eds.): *Sage Handbook of Frankfurt School Critical Theory*. Newcastle: Sage, pp. 564–80.

Thompson, Michael J. (2019a). "The Failure of the Recognition Paradigm in Critical Theory." In: Volker Schmitz (Ed.): *Axel Honneth and the Critical Theory of Recognition*. Basingstoke, New York: Palgrave Macmillan, pp. 243–72.

Thompson, Michael J. (2019b). "Hierarchy, Social Pathology and the Failure of Recognition Theory." In: *European Journal of Social Theory* 22. No. 1, pp. 10–26.

Thompson, Simon (2005). "Is Redistribution a Form of Recognition? Comments on the Fraser-Honneth Debate." In: *Critical Review of International Social and Political Philosophy* 8, pp. 85–102.

Thompson, Simon (2006). *The Political Theory of Recognition: A Critical Introduction*. Cambridge: Polity Press.

Thompson, Simon, and Paul Hoggett (2011). "Misrecognition and Ambivalence." In: Simon Thompson and Majid Yar (Eds.): *The Politics of Misrecognition*. London: Ashgate, pp. 32–60.

Tobias, Saul (2007). "Hegel and the Politics of Recognition." In: *The Owl of Minerva* 38. No. 1, pp. 101–26.

Tuomela, Raimo (2006). "Joint Intention, We-Mode and I-Mode" In: *Midwest Studies in Philosophy* 30, pp. 35–58.

Varga, Somogy (2010). "Critical Theory and the Two-Level Account of Recognition—Towards a New Foundation?" In: *Critical Horizons* 11. No. 1, pp. 19–33.

Varga, Somogy, and Shaun Gallagher (2012). "Critical Social Philosophy, Honneth and the Role of Primary Intersubjectivity." In: *European Journal of Social Theory* 15. No. 2, pp. 243–260.

Vetlesen, Arne Johan (2015). "Surplus of Indeterminacy. A Hegelian Critique of Neoliberalism." In: Odin Lysaker and Jonas Jakobsen (Eds.): *Recognition and Freedom. Axel Honneth's Political Thought*. Leiden, Boston: Brill, pp. 124–46.

Whitebook, Joel (2001). "Mutual Recognition and the Work of the Negative." In: William Rehg and James Bohman (Eds.): *Pluralism and the Pragmatic Turn. The Transformation of Critical Theory*. Cambridge: The MIT Press, pp. 257–91.

Whitebook, Joel (2008). "First Nature and Second Nature in Hegel and Psychoanalysis." In: *Constellations* 15. No. 3, pp. 382–89.

Wildt, Andreas (1982). *Autonomie und Anerkennung. Hegels Moralitätskritik im Lichte seiner Fichte-Rezeption*. Stuttgart: Klett-Cotta.

Wildt, Andreas (2010). "'Recognition' in Psychoanalysis." In: Hans-Christoph Schmidt am Busch and Christopher F. Zurn (Eds.): *The Philosophy of Recognition. Historical and Contemporary Perspectives*. Lanham: Lexington Books, pp. 189–209.

Williams, Robert R. (1992). *Recognition. Fichte and Hegel on the Other*. Albany: SUNY Press.

Williams, Robert R. (1997). *Hegel's Ethics of Recognition*. Berkley: University of California Press.

Winnicott, Donald Woods (1990). *The Maturational Processes and the Facilitating Environment. Studies in the Theory of Emotional Development*. London, New York: Karnac.

Wood, Allen W. (1990). *Hegel's Ethical Thought*. Cambridge: Cambridge University Press.

Worsdale, Rosie (2017). "Recognition, Ideology, and the Case of 'Invisible Suffering.'" In: *European Journal of Philosophy* 26. No. 1, pp. 614–29.

Young, Iris Marion (2007). "Recognition of Love's Labor: Considering Axel Honneth's Feminism." In: Bert van den Brink and David Owen (Eds.): *Recognition and Power. Axel Honneth and the Tradition of Critical Social Theory*. Cambridge: Cambridge University Press, pp. 189–212.

Zurn, Christopher F. (2000). "Anthropology and Normativity: A Critique of Axel Honneth's 'Formal Conception of Ethical Life.'" In: *Philosophy & Social Criticism* 26. No. 1, pp. 115–24.

Zurn, Christopher F. (2003a). "Arguing Over Participatory Parity: On Nancy Fraser's Conception of Social Justice." In: *Philosophy Today* 47, pp. 176–89.

Zurn, Christopher F. (2003b). "Identity or Status? Struggles over 'Recognition' in Fraser, Honneth, and Taylor." In: *Constellations* 10. No. 4, pp. 519–37.

Zurn, Christopher F. (2005). "Recognition, Redistribution, and Democracy: Dilemmas of Honneth's Critical Social Theory." In: *European Journal of Philosophy* 13. No. 1, pp. 89–126.

Zurn, Christopher F. (2011). "Social Pathologies and Second-Order Disorders." In: Danielle Petherbridge (Ed.): *Axel Honneth: Critical Essays. With a Reply by Axel Honneth*. Leiden, Boston: Brill, pp. 345–70.

Zurn, Christopher F. (2015). *Axel Honneth. A Critical Theory of the Social*. Cambridge: Polity Press.

Zurn, Christopher F. (2016). "The Ends of Economic History: Alternative Teleologies and the Ambiguities of Normative Reconstruction." In: Hans-Christoph Schmidt am Busch (Ed.): *Die Philosophie des Marktes—The Philosophy of the Market*. Hamburg: Felix Meiner, pp. 289–323.

Index of Subjects

Affirmation   11, 41–43, 49, 63, 72, 81, 83–85, 88, 93f., 111, 123, 133, 151, 183, 204, 208, 210, 218, 220f., 224, 239f., 249, 255, 259f., 268, 294
Agency   37, 50, 54, 80, 94, 128, 131, 242, 264–266, 269f., 289f., 292f., 296, 300, 304f.
– Authorship   12, 220, 234, 236, 238, 240, 244, 247, 260, 265, 270, 301
Anthropology   6, 10f., 13, 18–20, 27, 31, 37, 53, 61, 68, 76, 89, 91f., 105, 147, 154, 160, 199, 209, 211, 251
– Anthropological justification   36, 69, 75, 91, 105, 122, 140, 149, 154, 185, 205, 269
Attributive model   2–4, 11, 23, 89, 204, 206f., 210f., 225, 232, 235, 244, 257, 260, 262, 266, 269, 271, 273, 283, 295
Authorization   12, 204, 220, 235–237, 239, 241, 243, 245–247, 255, 260, 262, 269, 274–277

Commitment   81, 168, 191, 236–238
– Joint commitment   190, 201f., 247
Complementarity   11, 47, 80, 89, 170, 179f., 189, 201f., 204, 209, 233, 269, 277, 303f., 306
– Complementary role obligations   173f., 201, 236, 255, 288
– Need for complementarity   170, 185, 199, 201f., 247, 279
Conflict   1, 7, 9, 27, 29, 31f., 37f., 40, 43, 46–48, 50, 57–62, 64–71, 76, 86, 89, 91, 121f., 131, 138f., 142, 145, 151–154, 156f., 160, 175, 180, 182f., 193, 195f., 200, 212, 214, 217f., 233f., 237, 241, 245f., 249–251, 265, 269, 283f., 287, 292, 302, 304, 307f.
– Struggle   1, 8, 10–12, 27, 36–38, 40, 42–44, 48, 50, 52, 54, 57–70, 73, 76, 81, 87, 89–92, 94, 96, 105, 109–111, 116, 119, 121f., 124, 126, 131, 133, 135f., 139, 141f., 151–153, 156, 161, 172–176, 186f., 195f., 200, 204, 206, 209, 211–214, 217, 234, 239, 251–253, 255, 263, 266, 269, 278, 284, 286–288, 300, 302, 308

Determinacy   25, 127, 131, 135, 279, 283, 288, 292, 295, 298f., 301f.
– Finitude   266f., 287, 289, 294, 300, 305, 307
– Indeterminacy   14, 123, 127f., 130–132, 135, 161, 168, 170, 213, 249, 252, 279, 283, 301f.

Emancipation   28, 177, 210, 219
– Emancipatory interest   15, 22, 24, 27, 31, 67, 70, 74f., 158, 182–184, 197, 200, 218, 253, 285
Esteem   3, 8, 10, 36, 53, 72, 76, 81, 85–88, 91, 111–113, 126, 132, 135, 138, 141f., 152, 173, 181, 183, 189, 201, 206f., 210, 215f., 218, 244, 246, 255, 258
– Self-esteem   10, 14, 36, 53, 64, 68, 87f.
Ethical life   37, 40f., 43f., 46–49, 63, 69, 71, 75, 123–125, 129, 131f., 134f., 154f., 159, 161, 167f., 174, 184, 186, 188, 201, 204, 249, 252f., 288, 296
– Formal conception of ethical life   10, 14, 32f., 36, 49, 69f., 87, 89, 253
– Lifeworld   28f., 31f., 39, 41f., 102, 104–106, 130, 135f., 140, 143, 147, 166, 179f., 189, 199, 211–213, 232, 238–240, 249, 254, 277, 286, 292, 296, 300
– *Sittlichkeit*   41, 123, 125, 131, 133

Forgiveness   12, 256, 284–287, 289, 292, 296–298, 300, 304–308
Form of life   5, 12, 18, 29, 38, 44, 46, 71, 79, 86f., 96f., 103f., 138, 142, 169, 189, 235f., 248, 254, 256, 269f., 277, 284, 286, 291, 304
Freedom   3–5, 8f., 11–14, 25f., 42, 44, 57f., 61f., 71, 75f., 81, 86f., 90, 95f., 116f., 121–135, 138, 140, 146, 148f., 153–156, 158–178, 180f., 183, 185–187, 189–192, 194–202, 204, 206f., 213f., 216, 218, 223f., 230, 232–234, 236–238, 240, 242–245, 247f., 250, 252–255, 260, 262, 269, 274f., 288, 296, 298, 301f., 307f.
– Autonomy   1, 6, 8, 13, 32, 57, 64, 76, 91, 95f., 114, 118, 126–129, 135, 137, 143, 151, 158, 161, 163–165, 185, 187, 201, 206, 209, 211, 213, 219, 238, 285, 307

– Being with oneself in the other   57, 59, 128 f., 133, 135, 153, 169, 174, 177, 189, 204, 214, 247, 279
– Legal freedom   161, 163, 165 f., 168, 170, 201
– Moral freedom   166–170, 173, 184, 201
– Negative freedom   128, 130, 161 f., 165, 178 f., 185, 198
– Reflexive freedom   164 f.
– Social freedom   11, 102, 122 f., 127, 134, 153 f., 170 f., 173 f., 177–179, 181–187, 189–191, 193–196, 198 f., 201 f., 238, 247, 254 f., 279

Generativity   12, 15, 35, 39, 47, 75, 88 f., 175 f., 195, 208, 210, 224, 256, 282, 284, 299, 303, 307 f.

Identification   7, 9 f., 15, 18 f., 23, 27, 29, 37, 43, 45, 47, 50 f., 54, 60 f., 63, 65 f., 70, 92 f., 100 f., 103, 109, 111 f., 117–120, 123, 137, 153 f., 164, 174, 179 f., 190, 193 f., 198, 200, 211, 215, 217, 233, 235, 249, 251, 255, 268, 270 f., 273, 275, 281, 285, 294, 303, 307
Identity   1 f., 6, 9, 12, 28 f., 32–35, 37, 41–46, 49, 65, 68–71, 73, 76, 80, 86, 90, 97 f., 101, 107, 136, 140, 142, 149, 154, 165 f., 169 f., 189, 199, 201, 215, 222, 225, 231, 250, 256, 264–268, 270–272, 274, 278, 282 f., 290, 292 f., 300 f., 304, 306–308
– Identity politics   11, 15, 32, 35, 62, 65, 123, 142, 264, 267
– Practical identity   5, 8, 10, 36, 42, 50 f., 53 f., 58, 61, 68, 78, 87, 119, 136, 139, 141, 149, 151, 187, 212, 265, 269, 283
Ideology   100, 106, 116, 154, 215, 217, 220
– Ideological recognition   11, 93, 204, 214 f., 217–221, 235, 242–245, 280, 296, 301
Institution   3, 5–7, 9, 26, 31, 39–41, 44 f., 48–50, 58, 61, 68, 71, 74, 84, 89, 101, 113, 118, 121 f., 125 f., 128–132, 134 f., 141, 144–150, 152–154, 156–162, 165, 167, 171–173, 175, 177–182, 184–187, 189, 194, 196–200, 202, 206–208, 216–218, 225, 233, 236 f., 240–243, 246, 248, 250, 252–254, 261, 268 f., 283, 286, 297, 305 f., 308

– Institutional sphere   7, 26, 31, 37, 89, 121, 125, 130, 146, 156, 171, 198, 203, 216
Intersubjectivity   2 f., 5, 7, 9–11, 19 f., 28–31, 33 f., 36–38, 41, 43, 46–50, 53, 55, 62, 69, 71, 74–80, 88 f., 91–93, 96, 102 f., 105 f., 109–111, 113 f., 118–121, 123, 125 f., 129, 131, 133–135, 141, 143, 146 f., 153, 155, 158–160, 163, 166–173, 175–177, 202, 204, 206, 211, 214 f., 226, 228, 233, 235, 239, 243, 248, 250, 260 f., 268 f., 276, 280, 283 f., 298
– Interaction   3, 8, 14, 19 f., 22 f., 28 f., 39 f., 44, 47, 51–55, 60, 64, 80–82, 87, 90 f., 94, 99, 108–112, 114–116, 118, 120, 126, 133, 135, 137 f., 141, 145–147, 155 f., 158, 163 f., 166, 168, 170, 172, 175, 177, 179 f., 183, 187–189, 199, 202, 205, 210–212, 221, 227 f., 232 f., 239–241, 244, 248, 251, 254, 257, 260 f., 268, 275–277, 279 f., 286–288, 296, 299, 301, 303, 305–307
– Interpersonality   3, 5, 8, 12, 26, 32, 40, 44, 51, 77, 80, 84, 110 f., 118, 120, 138, 162, 207–211, 216, 224, 229–231, 237, 241, 244, 248, 254, 256 f., 260–263, 269 f., 272–274, 277, 299, 301–304
– Intersubjective relations   3, 40, 62, 68, 74, 97, 101, 108, 110, 115, 119, 126, 141, 145 f., 162, 167, 169, 172, 206, 262

Justice   5–9, 26 f., 29, 31 f., 34, 37, 61, 64, 67, 69, 87, 98, 104, 106, 112, 115, 117, 124 f., 127, 130 f., 135, 137–139, 142–145, 147–149, 158, 160, 162, 165, 172, 183–185, 188 f., 196–199, 220, 237, 246, 250 f., 266 f., 295, 301
– Injustice   7, 10, 15, 21, 27, 29, 31–35, 60 f., 63–65, 67, 137 f., 140–142, 154, 185, 207, 249 f.
– Theory of justice   11, 13, 121–123, 125 f., 129 f., 134 f., 140 f., 144 f., 149, 151, 155 f., 161, 165, 170 f., 176, 181, 188

Love   8, 10, 36, 40, 42, 48 f., 63, 68, 71 f., 76 f., 79–81, 83–85, 88, 91, 93, 110–113, 117, 125 f., 132, 135, 140–142, 148–152, 157, 173–175, 177 f., 201, 206 f., 210, 212, 217, 219, 224, 230, 233, 242 f., 246, 252, 255, 280, 306
– Self-confidence   10, 14, 36, 68, 70, 76 f., 79, 81, 88, 116, 187

326 — Index of Subjects

Misrecognition   10, 36 f., 57 f., 60, 62–68, 70–72, 78, 85 f., 89, 91–93, 99 f., 112 f., 137, 154, 160, 207, 210, 212, 215, 217 f., 223, 254, 269, 279
– Disrespect   28–30, 33, 42, 58, 60–62, 64–66, 68, 72, 86, 92, 99, 118
Monism   8, 13–15, 35, 95, 136 f., 144 f., 148, 153, 249–251, 253 f., 261
Mutuality   3 f., 6–8, 11 f., 26, 32, 39, 43 f., 49, 77–80, 84 f., 87 f., 99, 107, 120, 123, 131–133, 136 f., 143, 151, 163, 170, 173–178, 185, 189, 195, 198, 201, 204, 207, 211, 214 f., 219, 224, 229 f., 232–237, 239, 242–249, 254 f., 258–263, 268–270, 274 f., 277, 279, 281 f., 286 f., 294, 296, 299–301, 303, 305, 308
– Experience of mutuality   5, 261, 275 f., 281, 285, 296, 300, 308

Normativity   3, 5–9, 11–16, 20 f., 24 f., 27–37, 39 f., 42, 44, 46–49, 51–56, 58, 60 f., 63, 65–70, 73, 75–77, 81, 83, 87–93, 99–105, 107 f., 110, 113, 116–123, 127–129, 131, 136, 139 f., 142–161, 163–170, 173, 176, 178–185, 189, 192–194, 196 f., 199–214, 216 f., 220, 225–228, 233–250, 252–257, 259–263, 268–270, 272–279, 284–289, 291–294, 296, 299–301, 303–305, 308
– Normative integration   8, 123, 130 f., 145, 156, 158, 179 f., 183 f., 197, 250, 254, 301
– Normative principle   7, 50, 121–123, 131, 145, 148, 150 f., 153, 156, 196, 198, 250 f., 253
– Normative reconstruction   11, 123, 154–159, 161, 170 f., 173, 176, 179, 182 f., 185, 189, 191–196, 198–200, 218, 308
– Normative sphere   102

Participation   83, 85, 99, 137, 140, 187–189, 191, 194
– Participant   3–5, 7, 34, 51, 54, 86, 107–109, 131, 146 f., 149 f., 156 f., 164, 171, 173, 178 f., 181, 184 f., 192, 197, 199 f., 213, 224, 241–243, 245, 247 f., 254, 259–263, 267, 269, 273–277, 280, 282, 285, 287 f., 296, 298, 300 f., 303, 305 f., 308
– Participatory parity   34, 137, 140, 251

– Social partners   16, 40 f., 52–55, 62, 83 f., 109 f., 114 f., 140 f., 149, 166, 173–175, 188, 202, 206, 210, 232, 242 f., 258
Person   3–6, 24–26, 28, 30–33, 35, 38, 42–44, 46 f., 49, 52, 62 f., 68, 72 f., 75–77, 79 f., 82–86, 88 f., 93, 96, 101, 103, 106, 108 f., 111 f., 114, 120, 128, 152, 163, 166 f., 170, 174, 187, 189–191, 204, 206–211, 213 f., 216, 222 f., 226–232, 236, 238 f., 241 f., 247, 254, 257–259, 262, 264 f., 268, 271 f., 275–283, 288, 298, 301, 304 f., 307
– Personal integrity   14, 32, 61 f., 81, 83, 86 f., 91, 188, 258, 269
– Personhood   5, 14, 76, 89, 205–207, 209–211, 258, 283, 299
– Undamaged self-relation   71, 116, 209, 213, 247
Power   1, 3–6, 11, 13, 22, 25, 34, 37, 39, 42, 48, 54 f., 58, 74, 78 f., 91, 95, 101, 106, 114, 145 f., 154, 157, 172, 175, 184, 187, 192 f., 199, 204, 210, 219, 224, 231, 236 f., 246–248, 258, 260–264, 271, 280, 289, 299, 301 f.
– Domination   4, 13, 28, 42, 58, 66, 97, 139, 154, 176, 187, 190, 192 f., 210, 212, 215, 219, 221, 224 f., 236, 241–243, 248, 265, 271
– Subjection   4 f., 46, 62, 215–217, 241, 280, 285
Progress   10, 19, 28, 34–36, 45, 47 f., 58, 60, 66–68, 70, 73, 75, 83 f., 91, 109, 122, 141, 145, 149–153, 158, 160, 173, 194–196, 205, 212 f., 217 f., 220, 234, 251–254, 283, 302
– Intramundane transcendence   15, 28, 150, 157, 171, 184, 197

Receptive model   2 f., 6, 11, 100, 204, 210 f., 244, 246 f., 255, 258, 263, 266 f.
Reciprocity   3–6, 20, 27, 30, 43–45, 47, 66, 78 f., 88, 90, 94, 102, 108 f., 120, 151, 158, 162, 171, 173, 177, 180, 201 f., 206, 215, 219, 224, 230, 232, 236, 247 f., 255, 257–259, 261, 263, 266, 270, 273, 275 f., 280–283, 296, 299, 303–308
– Logic of reciprocity   261, 276, 282, 285, 296, 300, 308
Recognition   1–15, 19, 27, 29–63, 65–72, 74–79, 81–96, 98, 101–126, 129, 131–

139, 141–146, 148–158, 160 f., 163, 166 f., 169–177, 179 f., 182 f., 185–189, 194–196, 200–286, 288, 290, 293–296, 298–308
- Acknowledgment   54, 110, 114, 201, 225, 230, 265–267, 271, 273–278, 280, 282 f., 286, 292–296, 298–300, 305–308
- Anerkennung   2, 12, 39 f., 47, 91 f., 107, 120, 209, 223, 227, 233, 261, 263, 267 f., 271, 286
- Erkennen   2, 47, 91–93, 107, 120, 227, 262 f., 267, 272
- Mutual recognition   4, 12, 46, 111, 133, 140, 145, 154, 163, 165 f., 170 f., 173, 202, 215, 219, 224, 232, 239–241, 245, 249, 251–254, 256 f., 260 f., 263, 268 f., 274–284, 286–289, 292, 295–308
- Reciprocal recognition   4, 113, 132 f., 179, 248, 252, 270, 276, 284, 297
- Re-cognition   2, 12, 256, 271–273, 275, 277 f., 280, 282, 296, 299
- Recognitional act   14, 82, 88, 109, 148, 208–210, 212, 216, 226, 229, 246, 248, 262 f., 301, 303
- Recognition principles   141, 145, 148–151, 153, 181, 251
- Recognition relations   4, 7, 11, 41 f., 47, 53, 60, 67, 73, 80, 82, 122, 124, 143, 146 f., 152, 187 f., 201 f., 204, 207, 211 f., 234, 237, 244, 247 f., 250, 253 f., 257, 263, 274–276, 281, 303
- Spheres of recognition   8, 10, 36, 40, 45, 47, 49 f., 60 f., 68, 71–73, 82, 121–123, 132, 135, 141, 197, 200, 202, 246 f., 249, 253 f., 275, 286, 288
Reconciliation   12 f., 46, 142, 168, 283, 288, 297, 300 f., 304, 307 f.
Redistribution   11, 32, 34, 70, 86 f., 122, 131 f., 135 f., 141, 149, 154, 156–158, 179, 182, 196, 202, 212, 249, 251 f., 255, 266
Reification   10, 12, 16, 47, 53, 63, 90–93, 95–108, 112–120, 122, 124, 130, 141, 146, 154, 160, 164, 168 f., 182, 197, 205, 223 f., 226, 244, 252, 255, 262, 272, 277, 299
Respect   3 f., 8, 10, 12, 29 f., 36, 38, 43 f., 58, 61, 65 f., 68, 70, 76, 82–85, 88, 91, 93, 101, 106, 111–113, 115, 118, 122, 126, 135, 138, 142 f., 146, 148–151, 154, 156 f., 159, 163 f., 166 f., 171, 173, 176, 179, 181, 185 f., 189, 192 f., 200 f., 204, 206 f., 210, 212,

217, 224, 227, 229–231, 233 f., 236 f., 246, 251–255, 258, 260, 266–269, 271, 273 f., 277, 280, 283 f., 289–293, 295 f., 299 f., 304, 307 f.
- Self-respect   10, 14, 36, 64, 68, 70, 85, 88, 217
Right   1, 3, 6, 8, 11–13, 44 f., 61, 64, 68, 71 f., 79, 82–88, 121–127, 129–132, 134, 137 f., 140, 143, 149, 152–158, 160–163, 165, 167 f., 171–173, 176, 178, 180 f., 184–187, 189–191, 195–197, 199–202, 204, 206, 208, 213 f., 216 f., 233, 236–238, 240, 242 f., 247 f., 250–253, 255, 257, 261, 284 f., 289–292, 301 f., 306

Second nature   93 f., 100, 106, 121, 133 f., 150, 170, 172 f., 202, 205, 211–214, 216 f., 220 f., 233, 236–238, 240 f., 243, 246, 248, 250, 253 f., 261 f., 268, 277, 279, 286, 292, 302
Self-realization   17, 19–22, 25, 27, 30, 33 f., 42, 48, 57, 59, 64, 71, 73, 75 f., 86, 89, 92, 95 f., 100, 115, 119, 121, 123–125, 127, 132, 134 f., 140, 142, 146, 149, 154, 164 f., 207, 213, 218, 245, 249, 251–255, 269, 302
- Authenticity   92, 96, 115 f., 124, 163–165
Social critique   9, 14, 26, 29, 92, 118, 120, 139, 151, 160, 184, 205
- Immanent critique   18, 21 f., 196, 199, 219
Social ontology   8, 13, 26 f., 31, 34, 37, 87, 91, 103, 113, 116, 119, 123, 129–131, 143, 145–148, 157, 173, 197, 200, 206, 249, 284 f.
Social pathology   10, 15–17, 20–24, 26 f., 42 f., 46, 62, 66, 68, 75, 97, 99 f., 105, 129 f., 160 f., 168, 249
- Misdevelopment   9, 16 f., 21, 24, 27, 29, 100, 125, 154, 159–161, 171, 180, 182 f., 187, 193, 196, 198 f., 249, 251, 287
Status   1, 3 f., 14, 34, 64, 84, 137 f., 157, 163, 165–167, 169, 173, 196, 200–202, 208, 210, 212, 215, 217, 236–238, 242, 247, 255, 260, 263, 273 f., 295, 306
Surplus of validity   11, 122, 135, 150 f., 153, 156, 158, 197, 205, 212, 214, 218, 251, 253, 255, 269, 283, 288, 302
Symmetry   4, 6, 8, 36, 43, 49, 72, 78 f., 81, 84, 87 f., 177, 219, 257–260, 262 f., 270, 274, 281 f., 285, 299 f., 303

– Asymmetry   6, 36, 44f., 72, 78, 115, 257, 259, 262f., 269f., 280, 285, 297, 299, 303, 305
System   16, 18, 24, 28, 37, 40, 43, 46, 49, 66, 70, 74, 82–84, 86, 95f., 99, 101f., 104–107, 123, 137, 143–147, 157, 160, 162f., 165–168, 172, 176, 178, 180, 182f., 185, 187, 190, 194, 197, 199, 215, 224f., 230, 237, 239f., 242f., 245, 248, 250, 268, 287
– Systemic integration   143, 145, 179, 181

Vulnerability   5, 27, 30f., 61f., 76, 81, 88, 174–176, 178, 249, 264, 269, 276, 279, 297, 301
– Injury   27, 30, 32f., 44, 60f., 63, 65, 75f., 92, 100, 133, 149, 154, 181, 249, 279, 287
– Suffering   15f., 18, 22–24, 27, 29–33, 35, 37, 49, 58, 61f., 65f., 69, 73, 93, 96–98, 100, 113, 123, 125, 130, 139, 154, 160f., 183, 197, 215, 265f., 301

Index of Names

Aboulafia, Mitchell 58
Adloff, Frank 262
Adorno, Theodor W. 17, 35, 90f., 96–98, 100, 103f., 107, 110, 112, 114f., 190
Alexander, Jeffrey C. 67
Alford, C. Fred 308
Allen, Amy 5, 216, 219, 276, 280, 301
Allen, Jonathan 61, 75, 82
Althusser, Louis 4, 214–216, 218, 224, 231, 235, 240f., 243, 268, 283
Alznauer, Mark 216f., 289
Anderson, Joel 167
Arendt, Hannah 17, 165, 190, 266, 305
Arentshorst, Hans 159, 180, 183, 194
Aristotle 33, 38, 40, 117
Athens, Lonnie 58

Bankovsky, Miriam 87
Basaure, Mauro 57
Bedorf, Thomas 261, 264f., 267–272, 281, 301, 307
Bennett, Christopher 305
Berendzen, Joseph C. 279
Bernstein, Jay M. 31, 63, 276, 295–297, 306
Bertram, Georg W. 4, 245, 284, 287, 294, 296, 300, 302, 305, 308
Borman, David A. 159, 185, 197
Brandom, Robert 5, 235f., 287, 291, 293, 297
Brownlee, Timothy L. 231, 280
Buchwalter, Andrew 157f., 167, 199
Busen, Andreas 123, 151, 154, 158–160, 176, 183, 185
Butler, Judith 4f., 92, 99, 102, 108, 112, 114, 118f., 235, 241, 268, 272, 280, 301

Canivez, Patrice 278, 283, 301
Cavell, Stanley 91, 107, 110f., 118, 265f., 272
Chari, Anita 91, 102, 104–106, 118
Claassen, Rutger 154f., 157, 170, 198f.
Cobben, Paul 74
Cortella, Lucio 79, 261f., 287, 306
Crespi, Franco 94

Da Cunha De Souza, Luiz Gustavo 154
Dejours, Christophe 147
Deranty, Jean-Philippe 14–17, 19, 27, 37, 39, 44, 47–50, 55f., 58, 60, 62, 64, 73, 75f., 78–80, 83f., 86, 90, 101, 108, 110, 118, 120, 124, 126, 128, 130, 132, 143, 148, 256
Derrida, Jacques 289
Descombes, Vincent 306
Dewey, John 59, 91, 107f., 120, 147, 166, 187–192

Feenberg, Andrew 100, 103, 105, 107
Ferrara, Alessandro 91, 96, 101, 107, 111f., 114f., 119, 188
Fichte, Johann Gottlieb 2f., 12, 230–238, 247, 281
Foster, Roger 176, 184, 192
Foucault, Michel 14, 192, 215
Frank, Manfred 223
Fraser, Nancy 11, 33f., 66, 70, 76, 96, 122, 135–140, 142–144, 146, 148–150, 161, 207, 250f.
Freyenhagen, Fabian 18, 20, 154, 196

Gabriëls, René 196
Geuss, Raymond 118f., 272
Gilbert, Margaret 202
Giorgini, Giovanni 255
Greblo, Edoardo 138, 143

Habermas, Jürgen 10, 18f., 28, 30, 32, 35f., 39f., 44, 47f., 50–54, 56f., 90, 98, 101f., 115, 136, 160, 164, 166, 190, 192, 242, 247f., 284, 287
Hedrick, Todd 99–102, 106
Hegel, Georg Wilhelm Friedrich 2, 4f., 10–12, 17, 20, 36–41, 43–51, 53f., 60f., 69, 71–74, 82–84, 86, 101, 121–134, 148, 155–158, 161f., 167, 169–171, 178–181, 184, 186, 196, 199, 230f., 233–243, 245, 248, 256, 263, 275, 277–279, 281, 283–304, 306–308
Heidegger, Martin 91, 96, 107, 115, 120, 278
Heidegren, Carl-Göran 143, 205, 209, 253
Held, Jacob 140
Herzog, Benno 142
Herzog, Lisa 123, 151, 154, 158–160, 176, 183, 185
Hirvonen, Onni 23, 29
Hobbes, Thomas 38, 40, 161
Hoggett, Paul 63

Honneth, Axel 6–40, 42–202, 204–258, 260–266, 268–272, 274–280, 283–285, 287, 296, 301–303, 305f., 308f.
Horkheimer, Max 28, 91, 190
Horn, Anita 153, 172, 176, 178
Hume, David 226f., 237, 239f.

Ikäheimo, Heikki 5, 20, 205–212, 229, 232, 259, 268f., 271, 274, 277, 283, 286
Illetterati, Luca 278
Irrera, Elena 255

Jaeggi, Rahel 4, 104
Jakobsen, Jonas 58, 120–122, 154
Jansen, Yolande 191
Jütten, Timo 99–102, 105, 111, 184f.

Kant, Immanuel 12, 41, 74, 83, 128, 164, 212, 217, 226, 229–231, 234, 236
Kauppinen, Antti 124, 130, 137, 205
Kavoulakos, Konstantinos 98–100, 105f.
Koch, William 107, 119
Kompridis, Nikolas 67, 75, 136, 139f., 150
Krüger, Hans-Peter 239, 278

Lacan, Jacques 215, 224f.
Laitinen, Arto 79, 100, 157, 169f., 183, 205, 207–211, 259, 261, 263f., 271, 274, 277, 283, 304
Lara, Maria Pia 67
Lauer, Christopher 140, 152, 297
Lear, Jonathan 92, 99, 118f.
Lepold, Kristina 241, 264, 280, 301
Lindemann, Gesa 239
Loick, Daniel 101
Loose, Donald 130
Lovell, Terry 136
Lukács, György 16, 91, 97–103, 106f., 112, 114
Lysaker, Odin 58, 120–122, 154, 187

Markell, Patchen 56, 208, 264–267, 270f., 274, 281, 283, 290, 300f.
Martineau, Wendy 32
Marx, Karl 17, 20, 26, 179, 181, 197, 250
Mauss, Marcel 261
McCarthy, Thomas 136
McNay, Lois 34, 67, 136
McNeill, David N. 199
McPherson, Tristram 150

Mead, George Herbert 10, 36, 50–56, 58–61, 69, 71, 82f., 90, 109, 176, 205f., 213f., 239, 248
Meehan, Johanna 78, 94
Menegoni, Francesca 295

Neuhouser, Frederick 124, 131, 170, 279
Ng, Karen 154, 171, 197
Nozick, Robert 161f.
Nys, Thomas 154, 167

O'Connor, Brian 127
Owen, David 94, 105, 212

Pedersen, Jørgen 160, 178, 183
Pensky, Max 130
Petherbridge, Danielle 13, 37, 42f., 47f., 53f., 59, 75, 78, 81, 92, 110, 119, 192
Pippin, Robert 5, 123, 128, 131, 158, 235, 290, 300
Piromalli, Eleonora 13, 62, 72, 79, 116, 118, 134, 176, 181
Plessner, Helmuth 17, 238f.

Quadflieg, Dirk 100, 102f., 105f.
Quante, Michael 281f., 290

Rawls, John 252
Renault, Emmanuel 15, 29, 31f., 132, 148
Ricken, Norbert 264
Ricoeur, Paul 5, 62f., 72f., 93, 261, 270f., 276, 283, 285, 289, 300
Rössler, Beate 167
Rousseau, Jean-Jacques 4, 16f., 128, 164, 221–225, 228f., 231, 236, 240f., 257, 268
Rundell, John 58

Saavedra, Giovani A. 136, 255
Samonà, Leonardo 307
Sartre, Jean-Paul 91, 118, 161, 221–225, 235, 257, 268
Schafer, David T. 104f., 109, 115
Scheuerman, William E. 143
Schmetkamp, Susanne 136, 138
Schürmann, Volker 248, 278
Searle, John R. 2f., 157, 250
Seel, Martin 97
Shafer, Matthew T. C. 178, 196
Siep, Ludwig 5f., 10, 36, 39f., 43–45, 48–50, 56, 60f., 68, 72, 87–89, 121, 123,

126, 251f., 256, 268, 278, 280, 284–286, 301
Sinnerbrink, Robert   39, 287
Smith, Adam   179–181, 226–228, 231, 237, 239f., 264
Smith, Nicholas H.   136f., 143, 145
Smith, Robert C.   16
Smulewicz-Zucker, Gregory R.   185, 187, 193
Sobottka, Emil A.   136, 255
Sörensen, Paul   123, 151, 154, 159f., 176, 183, 185
Sperotto, Tommaso   109
Stahl, Titus   100, 106, 150

Taylor, Charles   1, 6, 32, 136, 182, 235, 265
Teixeira, Mariana   65, 121, 126, 143, 147, 154
Testa, Italo   13, 271, 277
Theunissen, Michael   284
Thompson, Michael J.   13, 34, 65, 70, 74, 106, 139, 143, 172, 176, 184, 192, 198, 250f.
Thompson, Simon   32, 62, 136f., 143, 150
Tobias, Saul   136, 286
Tuomela, Raimo   157, 304

van den Brink, Bert   75, 172, 176, 186, 212
van Leeuwen, Bart   107, 114
Varga, Somogy   97, 107–110, 118–120
Vetlesen, Arne Johan   127

Whitebook, Joel   47, 78, 152
Wildt, Andreas   5f., 10, 36, 39–43, 45, 48f., 59, 61, 68, 72, 81, 84, 266, 273, 278f., 282
Williams, Robert R.   124
Winnicott, Donald Woods   77–80, 90, 117, 239, 278
Wood, Allen W.   124
Worsdale, Rosie   33, 215

Young, Iris Marion   78

Zurn, Christopher F.   13, 19, 23, 32, 34, 64f., 72f., 75, 84f., 92f., 95f., 100, 116, 136, 138f., 145–147, 153, 173, 177, 188, 192, 197–200, 250

www.ingramcontent.com/pod-product-compliance
Lightning Source LLC
Chambersburg PA
CBHW080917170426
43201CB00016B/2173